PIMLICO

499

CHARACTERS OF FITZROVIA

Mike Pentelow moved to Fitzrovia in the early 1970s, from Essex where he was a trainee journalist on the *Thurrock Gazette*. He has worked as a sports reporter and industrial correspondent. Since 1983 he has been a reporter for the Transport and General Workers' Union magazine. He is a member of the Management Committee of the Fitzrovia Association, and Joint World President of the 'Stand By Me' club.

Marsha Rowe was a secretary in Fitzrovia, when she co-founded the feminist magazine *Spare Rib* in 1972. She was born in Australia, and worked her passage, on a ship, arriving in England in 1968, where she joined the magazines and newspapers of the underground counter-culture. She is a freelance editor and writer, and lives in London. Anthologies she has edited include *Spare Rib Reader* and *Infidelity*.

CHARACTERS OF
FITZROVIA

———

MIKE PENTELOW
&
MARSHA ROWE

A FELIX DENNIS BOOK

PIMLICO

Published by Pimlico 2002
in association with Felix Dennis
2 4 6 8 10 9 7 5 3 1

First published in Great Britain by Chatto & Windus 2001
Pimlico edition 2002

Pimlico
Random House, 20 Vauxhall Bridge Road,
London SW1V 2SA

Random House Australia (Pty) Limited
20 Alfred Street, Milsons Point, Sydney,
New South Wales 2061, Australia

Random House New Zealand Limited
18 Poland Road, Glenfield,
Auckland 10, New Zealand

Random House (Pty) Limited
Endulini, 5A Jubilee Road, Parktown 2193, South Africa

The Random House Group Limited Reg. No. 954009
www.randomhouse.co.uk

A CIP catalogue record for this book
is available from the British Library

ISBN 0-7126-8015-2

Editor Marsha Rowe
Design and art direction Richard Adams Associates
Chapter illustrations Clifford Harper
Picture research Juliet Brightmore
Cartography Mapworld, Henley-on-Thames
Based on the Ordnance Survey mapping with the permission of
The Controller of Her Majesty's
Stationery Office. © Crown copyright 43358U
Index John Barker

Printed and bound in Hong Kong by
C & C Offset

Contents

Dedicated by *Mike Pentelow* to his very dear friends John-Michael, Ann Goodburn and John Fisher, by *Marsha Rowe* to her daughter, Emily Rowe Rawlence, and by *Felix Dennis* to the memory of Hetty Clarke, flapper, seamstress, and long-time resident of 39 Goodge Street.

Foreword

My first real contact with Fitzrovia came about for the same reason, I suspect, as for many of the characters described in this book – the frustrating search for affordable accommodation in central London.

I had already acquired a clapped out, serviceable flat in west Soho (a minor miracle in itself) and was determined to be able to 'walk to work', so Notting Hill Gate, my first choice, was out of the running.

This was in the early 1970s, which were hard times for Britain. The Vietnam war had barely ended, OPEC was already planning to ratchet up the price of oil and the Three Day Week lurked just around the corner. Hardly the best economic climate in which to launch a new publishing company, whose total assets were two enthusiastic, long-haired hippy types, a shambolic collection of old office furniture, one electric typewriter and 50 quid in the bank.

Still, 'Hope springs eternal in the youthful breast', and, along with my partner, Dick Pountain, I began pounding pavements and scanning the small ads in *Time Out* and the *Evening Standard*. More than one prospective landlord took one look at us and literally slammed the door in our faces. No doubt a haircut would have opened a few more doors, but in those days it was virtually a traitorous offence to sport anything shorter than a shoulder-length coiffure.

Eventually our friend Lemmy from the underground band Motorhead suggested that we check out the top floor of 39 Goodge Street, over a paint shop. Here was our salvation. The entrance reeked of methylated spirits, the stairs were lethally twisted, and the rooms stank of straw and dogs' turds (the result of the previous tenants' failed attempt to raise cash by breeding Labrador puppies). None of which were insurmountable problems to the likes of us.

Better still, the landlord, Norman Small, was willing to accept us providing we 'kept a low profile', as he put it. Although the top floor was zoned as 'residential', we had no intention of living there, and Norman was worried that if Camden Council were to discover our activities, he would be obliged to chuck us out on the street without notice. He was finally persuaded when we promised to move in a sofa-bed and pay the rent regularly. Neither promise, I regret to say, was ever kept.

As soon as we moved in we began to realise just how lucky we were to have hit on Fitzrovia – both the local people and the surroundings suited our temperament, and our (often empty) pockets.

Our neighbour on the floor below was one Hetty Clarke, a retired seamstress, who had lived on the premises for nearly 40 years. A feisty, jovial old stick, Hetty loved the idea of a bunch of youngsters working into the night above her flat because, she said, 'it makes me feel more secure, like, knowing you're up there. Any roads, you're better than the last lot. This place was going to the dogs! Hah, hah!'

Hetty would regale us with stories of the area between the wars when she was a flapper, tearing about the West End and getting into all kinds of scrapes. After we persuaded Norman to install a new lavatory only half a flight down from her front door (there were no loos en suite in any of the flats), her gratitude knew no bounds. Fruitcake, scones and weak tea were produced at such regular intervals that Dick and I took to creeping up and down stairs to avoid premature corpulence.

The Fitzrovian pubs and small restaurants, too, were light years away in quality from those in Soho – as generations long before us had discovered. Waitresses and publicans remembered your name; they treated you as locals and didn't charge tourist prices. And the variety of shops was astounding for the West End: butchers, bakers, delicatessens, grocers, a fish stall, a paper shop, a cobbler, an art supplier, a hardware store, a jeweller (not much trade from us there!), and scores more of just the kind of place that makes a real community.

That's an over-used word, these days. But it's what Fitzrovia was then, and to a lesser extent (alas) still is. A community.

Surrounded on all sides by a roaring sea of commercialism (Oxford Street), strident academia (the University of London and the British Museum) and the 'embassy dead zone' of Portland Place, our new found base offered a kind of sanctuary in the heart of London. Even the traffic wardens and coppers seemed a mite more forgiving and a touch more 'involved'. Sure there were a couple of seedy clip joints and a few enclaves of obnoxious characters dossing about, but even they felt less threatening than their Soho counterparts.

Dennis Publishing, as our company came to be called, has always remained Fitzrovia-based. We've had offices in Rathbone Place, in Brewer Street, Mortimer Street, Bolsover Street, Cleveland Street, and a few more besides. We've grown larger, of course (with more than 500 people now, and outposts in New York and Los Angeles), and the temptation to relocate has more than once reared its cost-efficient head. But as owner and chairman, I have the luxury to insist that we stay put. The excuse, that I want to be able to 'walk to work', is nowadays threadbare, a hackneyed fiction – more often than not, I roll up in a chauffeured Rolls-Royce. (Well, age, vanity and success have their compensations.)

But in my heart I know why we stay put. As for so many of those whose names you'll find inside this book – rogues or heroines, artists or con-artists, misfits, mad inventors or revolutionaries – for better or worse, whether for most of their lives or as struggling transients, this tiny, square half-mile has meant acceptance.

For me, it was from the first moment that Anna, a no-nonsense Italian waitress, cajoled me into trying scaloppine in Bertorelli's. It was from the first time I helped Norman pump his 'meths' for the paint shop into plastic bottles from the huge metal drums he kept in the tiny back yard, my heart in my mouth and my cigarette firmly extinguished. It was from the first, numbing gulp of retsina in the Cypriana. It was from the first time I stepped foot in the One Tun or the Crown and Sceptre or the Ship.

It's the people. It's the feeling of belonging without being smothered. It fits. It's the Fitz. It's home.

Felix Dennis

Preface

The wide variety of characters who mixed informally and easily as equals is what most fascinated me about Fitzrovia when I first moved into the area in 1972, and why I have stayed in it ever since.

It was no surprise therefore to discover that two of my favourite quotes, 'Variety's the very spice of life, That gives it all its flavour' and 'We hold these truths to be self-evident, that all men are created equal', were coined by Fitzrovians (William Cowper and Thomas Jefferson respectively).

The attitude of celebrating cultural diversity has long been a reality in Fitzrovia, a cosmopolitan community where different classes live in close proximity.

Where else would Karl Marx and Prince Eddy (in direct line of accession to the throne) have gone to meetings about 20 yards apart? Or in the 1930s a cabinet minister and a road sweeper have attended the same wedding reception in the Fitzroy Tavern. Or, more recently, the Duke of Kent and a local homeless street-dweller have eaten in the same Charlotte Street restaurant?

This book has grown from articles I wrote for *Fitzrovia News* (and its predecessor *Tower*).

Mike Pentelow

Authors' Note

Names of streets and roads change with surprising frequency. To indicate a previous name of a road or street, where this information is relevant, we have italicised the old name and put it inside brackets following the present-day name. We have sometimes indicated previous numbers of an address or an old building name in the same way.

Oxford Street's numbering changed dramatically in 1882. Before that, beginning with 1 Oxford Street at the junction of Tottenham Court Road, the numbers ran consecutively along the north side of the street to Marble Arch, where they crossed and ran back down the south side, ending opposite Tottenham Court Road. New Oxford Street (Nos.441-552) was included as part of the same system. In 1882 the numbering switched to a dual method, still starting at Tottenham Court Road, but placing even numbers on the north and odd numbers on the south sides of the street, both leading sequentially up to Marble Arch.

We have maintained the imperial measurements used historically. There are not many distances or heights, and they are given in feet. One foot equals 30.48 centimetres. We also use the currency of the period. Before decimilization was completed in 1971 there were 20 shillings (20s.) to the pound and 12 pence (12d.) to a shilling. Today's one pence has the value of 2.4 old pennies.

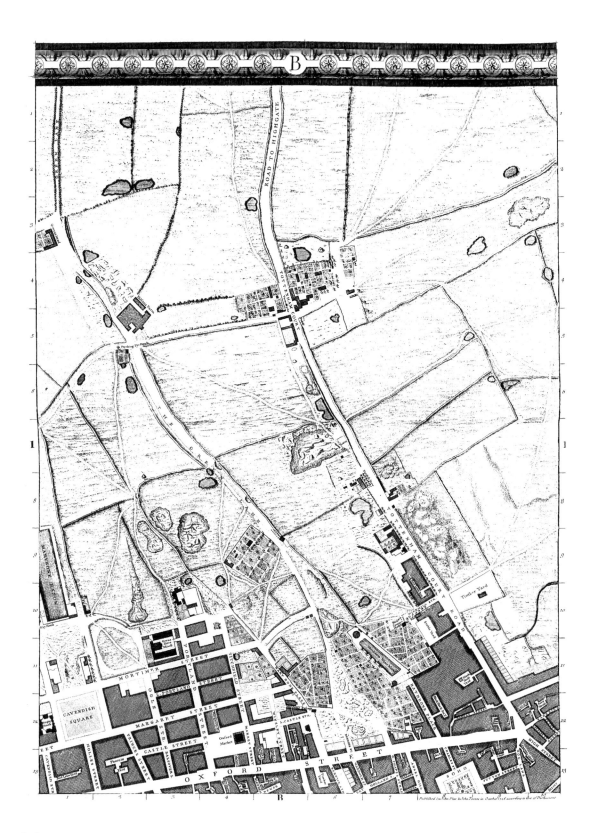

Introduction

Placing the People

All those souls, these assembled 'characters', show a Fitzrovia bustling with vigour and change, continuous in many ways with the urban topography that its 18th century occupants first put into place. Fitzrovia has a past characterised by its racy contrasts and raucous dissonance. Although history often obscures the lives of ordinary people as much as it reveals the lives of a few, here a bigger, more encompassing picture can be glimpsed. This presents a Fitzrovia that is as much a space of the imagination, swirling with the past glimpsed in the present, as it is a neighbourhood determined by those who live and work there today

Fitzrovia mixes the arts and sciences, has an outgoing street life and an inward, concealed one, combines commerce and domestic living, and sometimes its political bottom has been burnt. Fitzrovia has fired up, on occasion, and that, too, is part of its history.

Fitzrovia's parameters can be seen at a glance in the fold-out map at the back of this book: an area of central London roughly oblong in shape, with a cut-out snipped off the bottom right-hand corner and, inside, a jig-saw of buildings criss-crossed by streets. Arch, rather self-conscious and defensively ironic, the word 'Fitzrovia' was coined in the middle of the 20th century to apply to a longer, narrower map that pushed down into Soho as far as Shaftesbury Avenue. It described the bohemian *quartier* of London, in particular the eclectic, artistic ambience of some of its pubs, such as the Fitzroy Tavern and the Wheatsheaf, during the 1930s and 40s, and the environs of Charlotte Street, and Fitzroy Square. It was a name charged with aspiration and nostalgia and it came bearing witness. A name to keep. The present-day conservationist organisation, the Fitzrovia Trust, cuts the map off at Oxford Street, and squares it up, between Portland Street and Gower and Bloomsbury Streets¹. But for its current residents, Fitzrovia is bordered on the north by Euston Road, on the west by Portland Place, on the south by Oxford Street, and on the east by Tottenham Court Road and Gower Street.

Fitzrovia was never a village. It never had that homogeneous, all-in-the-round sense of place out of which the vast metropolis of London is stitched together, a patchwork of 150 ex-villages. Its residents never pretended to harmony. To the west Fitzrovia encompasses a section of the suburb of Marylebone, under the juridisction of the borough of the City of Westminster. To the east, it includes sections of St Pancras and Holborn and its administrative borough is Camden. Although Westminster Council has traditionally had a Conservative majority, and Camden Council a Labour majority, the creative tension that distinguishes what is culturally distinct about Fitzrovia cannot be reduced to a contest between right and left wing politics.

Before Fitzrovia

The footfalls of confident Roman troops once paced the Oxford Street bus route, between clearings occupied by Britons living in hamlets, and lime and

In Charlotte Street there was the sound of revelry by night...bookies and burglars, actresses and artisans, poets and prostitutes; and there was an entirely new caste brought into being by the war – deserters. These did not merely frequent the cafes. They couldn't leave.

Quentin Crisp

Map of the area by John Rocque 1746

In 1725 Daniel Defoe was astonished by the construction of fine buildings and squares north of Oxford Street, where there had been fields 25 years earlier. It seemed like a new town, 'the like of which no city, no town, nay, no place in the world can shew; nor is it possible to judge where or when, they will make an end or stop of building.'

oak woodland where wolves roamed. The Romans had constructed the road before they established Londinium, the first 'London', in AD43. The Anglo Saxons called it Lundenburgh, meaning fortified town, when they abandoned their previous riverside village, Lundenwic, further upriver, to retreat inside the safety of the old Roman walls in the face of the Danish onslaught. What does this have to do with modern Fitzrovia? It prefaces the way future Fitzrovia was to become divided. Edward the Confessor (1042-1066) chose an island in the open marshland where the river Tyburn flowed into the Thames, west and upriver from the thriving, prosperous City of London, for the building of his magnificent new church, Westminster, and next to it, his royal hall. This move separated the commercial centre of the city, in the east, from the seat of royalty, the court and its administrative powers, in the west, a geographical and social differentiation that articulated a pattern of influences that would later give Fitzrovia its own special topography.

In the 8th century Fitzrovia was a mix of fields and woods where the Anglo-Saxons, who loved hunting, were free to chase the wild game, the boar, stags and waterfowl that stuffed the forests. With the onset of feudalism it became part of the territory of the Middle Saxons – Middlesex. But after 1066, when the Normans introduced draconian restrictions, the right to hunt game on horseback became socially exclusive, the prerogative of the upper crust. However Henry I (1068-1135) famously agreed to a charter guaranteeing the citizens of London certain privileges in exchange for taxes, including his reassurance that they 'have chaces to hunt, as well and fully as their ancestors had, that is to say, in Chiltre and in Middlesex and Surrey.'[2] By then many of the peasants, who had begun to pay rents instead of the labour duties that chained them, as serfs, to the land, were moving to live in towns. Along with the development of the coin-based market economy and free trade, came an increasing distinction between the type of life in the countryside and that of the town.

The attraction of urban living was such that the monasteries that had grown rich throughout the land had been buying up property in town. The Abbess of Barking, for one, had bought no less than 28 houses in London, and she had had her rights to the Manor of Tyburn, which she let to a succession of owners, confirmed by William the Conqueror. This great feudal estate, the Manor of Tyburn, occupied the western half of what would become Fitzrovia – that is, it was the eastern aspect of the later metropolitan borough of St Marylebone, the origin of whose name now becomes apparent: *St Mary's*, the church that was built *by-the-bourne*, the Tyburn.

By the time that the spring feeding the Thames tributary, the Tyburn, bubbling up where the Bond Street underground station is today, was conduited in lead pipes towards the City in 1236, the population of London had doubled and the much travelled Tyburn Road (now Oxford Street) was becoming dangerous.

The manor on the eastern side of Fitzrovia was Tottenham Court. Its name probably originated from 'Tote', the ancient word for a look-out post (although it might have been the name of its Saxon owner), and 'halh', meaning a 'corner or nook of land'. It appears in the *Domesday Book* (1086) as Totenhall, later as Totehele or Tottenheale. 'Court' was simply the old word for 'manor'. Today's Tottenham Court Road thus began as a track leading from the manor to market – its name was not upgraded from 'Lane' to 'Road' until 1730. It passed the village of St Giles, which spread from today's Windmill Street into Holborn, and included what is now the corner of Tottenham Court Road and Oxford Street. The growing municipal authority and commercial vitality of the walled City of London meant that Tottenham Court Road was frequently travelled. While this made its crossroads at St Giles a primary exit to the north, and an entrance south-eastwards to the City, the route west along Tyburn Road was even more important

Still relatively wild and unguarded as late as the beginning of the 18th century, a 'deep hollow road, and full of sloughs...the lurking place of cut-throats'[3], the threat of Tyburn Road was also of legal kind. At various times up until 1417, temporary gallows were set up at the junction with Tottenham Court Road. A 'Cup of Charity' would be offered to the prisoners as they passed St Giles hospital on their way to execution. In 1388 the Tyburn gallows stood at today's Marble Arch. The first permanent London gallows were erected there in 1571, consisting of a tall, tri-polar structure on which up to nine people could be hanged from one beam, 'the deadly Nevergreen that bears the fruit all the year round'[4]. Crowds gathered for the eight hanging days, the annual Tyburn Fair, and watched as the carts carrying the prisoners rolled along Tyburn Road. Leaving Newgate at dawn, and stopping at taverns along the way, the journey took two hours and the prisoners would often be drunk by the time they reached Tyburn.

The deterrent effect of these occasions is hard to judge. As an act of defiance, prisoners might dress in white, or wear a cockade, or a buttonhole nosegay. An unpopular or disliked prisoner might have to dodge the missiles, dead cats, bricks, thrown as the cart passed along Tyburn Road. Sometimes people in the witnessing crowd around the gallows were crushed, or had bones broken, or teeth knocked out. By 1783 the authority's view of the reforming effect of the public spectacle of death by hanging had changed, and the Tyburn gallows were demolished. Thereafter executions took place at Newgate (the last public hanging in England was outside Newgate prison in 1868), and no more carts trundled along Oxford Street carrying prisoners facing east and sitting next to their coffins.

However, at the junction of Tottenham Court Road with St Giles, there was a whipping post, and a 30-foot-square lock-up, where petty thieves and prostitutes were herded nightly in the 18th century. And passers-by could gape, or throw dead vermin or stones, at prisoners fastened into the stocks, or see the charity boys of St Giles flogged at the boundary stone if they were caught out of bounds.

By 1620 there was a tavern on the north side of Tyburn Road (6 Oxford Street) opposite the old gallows site. Providing for travellers, such taverns offered the same facilities as the inns on the principal thoroughfares out of town. They had large courtyards reached by a narrower entrance, where horses could be stabled, or coaches repaired, and private rooms were available. Refreshments were taken in the taproom or bar, which were furnished with tables and benches and a fireplace. London had become a major international port, and the convivial and often comfortable surroundings of these taverns became a focus for social life, a favourite place to relax, meet friends, do business, drink wine, eat, gamble, play dominoes or chess. By 1690 there were inns named the Rose and the Hercules Pillars on Tottenham Court Road, which itself was still an unpaved highway, bordered either side by ditches, where a footpad might take advantage of the unwary. The corner by today's Great Russell Street became particularly infamous as no place to linger, where robbers skulked in the hedges.

In 1569 Tottenham manor was leased to Robert Dudley, on behalf of Queen Elizabeth I. Alexander Glover, an Exchequer Clerk, was given custody of the house and grounds, and the sheep and cattle of the royal household were pastured on the property. In 1649, the house was described as having a moat and a gatehouse, with a chamber and two closets over the gate, leading to a

Unlicensed beggars above 14 years of age are to be severely flogged and branded on the left ear unless some one will take them into service for two years; in case of a repetition of the offence, if they are over 18, they are to be executed, unless some one will take them into service for two years; but for the third offence they are to be executed without mercy as felons.

Elizabeth's Poor Law Act (1572), which lasted for some 200 years

courtyard, then the main hall. By 1749, the house itself seems to have been partially demolished.

The puritan zeal of the Commonwealth under Cromwell (1649-1660) brought sober reflection to bear on some public forms of entertainment, but the popular, bawdy Tottenham Court fair on the fields opposite the old Elizabethan manor continued annually from 1645 right up until 1807, when the fair was finally banned. Many of London's recreational activities, previously woven into a religious or civic ceremonial calendar of festivities, were being commercialised, and the subversive, festival spirit of the Tottenham fair is mentioned in the prologue to a lost play that has become one of the favourite quotes about early Fitzrovia:

Y'are welcome, Gentlemen to Tot'nam Court,
where you (perhaps) expect some lusty sport,
such as rude custom doth beget in hay,
when straggling numbers court that jovial day,
with early riot...[5]

Theatrical booths would be set up, but the outdoors amusements on the fields by Tottenham Court were not confined to fairtime. Much of Londoners' entertainment still had a violent mediaeval flavour. There were contests between animals – dog fights, cock fights, as well as bull and bear baiting, when the animals were tied to a stake and attacked by dogs. The tethered animal would try to toss the dog into the crowd. Occasionally it broke free, leading to violent scenes. There were sword fights. Gambling and drinking were pervasive. People would walk to Tottenham Court from the city, 'for cakes and cream', or for rambling, or the 17th century sports of archery, bowls, racing, wrestling, boxing. 'Anything that looks like fighting is delicious to an Englishman', said a French visitor to London in 1690[6].

During the civil war (1642-48), when parliament was expecting Charles I to attack the city with 15,000 royalist troops, it ordered 23 forts to be erected around London's perimeter. At the bottom of Tottenham Court Road a 'small fort' was built, and next to it, across Tyburn Road from Wardour Street up to present-day Berners Street, a 'large fort, with 4 half bulwarks.'[7] The forts were linked by 18 miles of nine-foot deep, earthen ramparts, but they were never tested. The royalist troops stopped at Turnham Green, Charles I withdrew and in a few short years all trace of them had been eroded.

An inn named the Red Cow (1678) at the corner of Tottenham Court Road and Tyburn Road typified the continual use of both these as the routes along which horses, pigs and cattle were driven to the huge Smithfield market. Stray animals found wandering between the scattered houses and fields would be penned in St Giles pound, erected at the bottom of Tottenham Court Road in 1656, and in use until 1765.

Bubonic plague had reached London from Asia in the early 14th century. Carried in the blood of rats, the plague virus is injected into humans through the bites of the rat flea. London's population rose in proportion to the rest of the country, but it did so only very gradually because of the high number of plague deaths. The final catastrophic outbreak of plague started in 1665 in the desperately overcrowded, dark, unsanitary, shantytown conditions of the unregulated buildings that had spread beyond the City walls to St Giles. These 'newly erected tenements'[8] had been allowed to stand partly because Charles I preferred to collect the fines liable for unregulated building such as these, than to insist on their demolition. The walls of these shacks and alleys at the lower end of Tottenham Court Road and through St Giles were described as thick with 'flies and ants'[9]. Scores of plague victims died. There were so many bodies that there was no room to bury them, and corpses were piled in a huge mound

Hide-bound student that...wencheth at Tottenham Court for stewed prunes and cheesecakes.

Thomas Nabbes,
The Bride (1638)

just off present-day Goodge Street, until a plague pit was dug at the bottom of Tottenham Court Road.

The great fire of London in 1666, which followed the year of the plague, destroyed whole swathes of the City, and accelerated the expansion of London outside the City walls. For a brief period, between the 1670s and 1680s, the most fashionable address in London was Soho (named when the area was still a pasture and 'so-ho' was the old hunting call), developed during the 1660s. Bloomsbury (*Southampton*) Square had also been laid out by its owner, the fourth Earl of Southampton. He significantly extended the terms of leasehold system (by which the building developers leased the land from the ground landlord, who remained in possession of the leasehold, receiving rent from the buyers of the property once it was built) from 42 to 99 years. Completed in the 1660s, and the first such development in London to be called a 'square', it was consolidated by the Earl's daughter, Rachel Wriothesley, who married Lord Russell, the Duke of Bedford. She oversaw its development into a smart, residential district, with the 'best air and finest prospect'[10], but it would be over a hundred years before the northern aspect of the Russells' Bedford estate would be urbanised, with the construction of Fitzrovia's Gower Street and Torrington Place.

18th century – Fitzrovia arrives.

The development of Fitzrovia was an 18th century phenomenon, along with its two other borders, Portland Place, the grandest street of the day, and Euston Road, the first ever London by-pass. The birth of Fitzrovia coincided with the age of enlightenment when London was at its apogee of aristocracy and privilege. However, at the start of the century all that lay north of the Fitzrovian length of Tyburn Road were some fields, some scattered buildings, a few ponds, a large timber yard (belonging to William Rathbone and Samuel Hindes), and a windmill (now Windmill Street). Ownership of the land had, of course, changed hands several times by then, and a couple of inns, as well as the Marylebone Manor House, could be seen across the meadows. The Marylebone estate had passed to the crown when Henry VIII claimed the monasteries to finance his wars against France and Scotland between 1543 and 1547. It was sold by James I and bought in 1708 by the Duke of Newcastle, whose heiress was his daughter Henrietta, wife to Edward Harley, the Earl of Oxford, and son of the First Minister of Queen Anne's last years. By this astute marriage, a start was made on the development of Fitzrovia-to-be, and in 1725 Tyburn Road was renamed Oxford Street.

The Earl and his Countess engaged John Prince (who liked to call himself the 'Prince of Builders') to lay out plans for the Cavendish-Harley estate, and the first house in Cavendish Square was built in 1720. Today this appears to be at a vast remove from the environs of Fitzrovia, but back then there was no Oxford Circus – nor any Regent Street. A sizeable chunk of what is now the south-western aspect of Fitzrovia was built at that time, contiguous and all of a piece with this impressive square to the west. Fields disappeared under houses. These were the building boom years following the treaty of Utrecht in 1713, when Daniel Defoe described Marylebone as having turned into a 'world full of bricklayers and labourers; who...like gardeners...dig a hole, put in a few bricks, and presently there goes up a house'[11]. When the Duke of Chandos moved into his new house in Cavendish Square he complained that the air was 'poisoned with the brick kilns and the other abominate smells which infect these parts'[12], the smoke from tileries, piles of garbage, ash, night soil.

This was also the age of the new colonies, the rich had money to spend, and London needed houses for the growing middle class, the throng of

> If you once have a vigorous pestilence raging furiously in St Giles's, no mortal list of Lady Patronesses can keep it out of Almack's.

Charles Dickens

Daniel Cropp, the sweeper of the crossing from Mortimer *(Charles)* Street to Rathbone Place (1816)

manufacturers, the tradesmen, shopkeepers. While a tiny proportion of the population, around three percent, were of the landed aristocracy, up to a quarter was composed of the new urban gentry, rich city merchants, those who made money in shrewd investments, banking, the maritime trade, and offices of the state. There were also new types of professionals, such as portrait painters, writers, those who worked in law; there were surgeons, apothecaries, and preachers

So while the Harley-Cavendish estate followed the same distinctive design of spacious square with its mansions, it too had to have the surrounding subsidiary terraces of smaller, cheaper housing for those who served their needs, such as the tradesmen, artisans, servants. There might be plasterers, painters, glaziers, tilers, plumbers, bakers, butchers, brewers, wine merchants, seamstresses, tailors. The estate extended to the north-east, Bolsover Street being laid out between the 1720s and 50s.

Oxford Market (on today's Market Place), a plain square building with a steep roof and a weather vane, designed by James Gibbs, was built in 1721 (demolished in 1880), to service and stimulate the Cavendish Square development. Under its arcades it would have been possible to buy apples, cherries, pears, cabbages, cauliflower, peas, parsnips, turnips, carrots, medicinal herbs, as well as milk, butter, eggs, poultry, bacon. Just as today the market traders could cast a jaundiced eye on the housewife scouring for a bargain. A pupil of the sculptor Joseph Nollekens remembered that when Mrs Nollekens trawled the market in the 1770s so that her dog could scoff a free meal, the affronted jibes of the butchers' stopped her in her miserly tracks, 'When she went to Oxford Market to beat the rounds, in order to discover the cheapest chops, she would walk round several times to give her dog Cerberus an opportunity of picking up scraps. However, of this mode of manoeuvring she was at last ashamed, by the rude remarks of the vulgar butchers…"Here comes Mrs Nollekens and her bull-bitch".'[13]

Building faltered in the 1730s but revived after the signing of the Peace of Paris, 1763, which ended Anglo-French rivalry in North America and established Britain as a major colonial power. The next Harley-Cavendish heiress, Margaret, married the second Duke of Portland, and together they picked up the reins of the development of the Harley-Cavendish-Portland estate. Margaret's cousin, Lord Foley, was determined that no other building should be allowed to obscure the north-facing view of his house, erected in 1767 (the site of today's Langham Hilton), and he succeeded in gaining the guarantee of the good tradesmen of the St Marylebone vestry to this effect. Because of his obduracy, Portland Place, which was laid out by the architect brothers from Scotland, Robert and James Adam, in 1778, was 125 feet wide, and is still today one of the broadest, more tranquil public thoroughfares of London.

Following the great fire, a series of acts had laid down measures for floor space and ceiling heights, curtailed the amount of exterior wood such as overhanging cornices, and set the scale for house ratings. These standards were summarised in the 1774 Building Act, and they regulated all new building. The houses on Portland Place, with their elegant designs, emblematic of the golden age of Georgian architecture, were of the highest rateable value. The exteriors were embellished with coade stone (the artificial stonework produced by Mrs Eleanor Coade at her factory in Lambeth, South London) and their interiors were designed for space and light.

The specialist craftsmen, George Jackson and Sons, who were the first to work the fibrous *carton-pierre* plaster into mouldings and ornaments for the Adam brothers' designs, set up their workshops on the other side of Fitzrovia, in Rathbone Place, in 1790. An interesting example of the social divisions and working inter-connections within Fitzrovia, and a prototype of its future. Building here was on a less grandiose scale. Taking advantage of the availability of long leases at low ground rents, new streets and houses were put up following the irregular, disjointed configuration of Crab Tree Field, Walnut Tree Field and Culver Meadow. Captain Thomas Rathbone, who was one of the few to have had a house north of Oxford Street as early as 1684, devoted the years between 1721 and 1725 to demolishing his old property and putting up Rathbone Place. In 1750 its highly fashionable tenants included the Bishop of Peterborough. Writers and artists, many of whom appear in the following chapters, moved into Rathbone Place, alongside the craftsmen on whose products they depended, such as Robert Keith, maker of musical instruments, whose Rathbone Place premises were opened in 1780, or the artists colourmen, George Rowney and Co, who moved there in 1815, to be followed by Winsor and Newton in 1832.

At the same time, William Berners, whose ancestor, Josias, had bought the wedge-shaped estate abutting Hanway Street back in 1654, did a deal with a gardener turned builder named Thomas Hubble, by which Berners took responsibility for constructing sewers and Hubble for erecting new buildings. With the completion of Berners Street between 1750 and 1763, together with Newman Street and Charlotte Street (after George III's queen) and Rathbone Place, this became London's first *Quartier Latin*.

The nephews of John Goodge, a carpenter, began developing Crab Tree fields in the late 1740s – Goodge Street, with its provision shops and pubs, was destined to become the village heart of Fitzrovia. By the 1790s, nearby Gower

GEORGE JACKSON & SONS established in Rathbone Place in 1790 and still operating in 1908.

The craftsmen at this workshop were the first in the country to apply carton-pierre, *used by Robert Adams for his ornamental mouldings.*

Street was completed. Of brick, unadorned but well-constructed, the street had an austere dignity that made it a favourite for lawyers and other members of the new urban professionals, such as teachers, clergymen, government officials and medical men. They would have passed on the street the artisans, servants, dancing masters, portraitists, hacks and tradesmen going about their business, especially during the London Season, which lasted from late October through to June. This was when the great landowning families arrived in London to see to legal matters, replenish their wardrobe, go to the theatre, meet each other, and attend parliament

Across the top of Fitzrovia was another story. By the middle of the 18th century, the Tottenhall ground landlords were the Fitzroys, the Dukes of Grafton, Earls of Euston. By then the new buildings of the Harley-Cavendish-Portland estate were pressing northwards, and traffic along the main thoroughfares into London, Oxford Street and Tottenham Court Road, was frequently blocked for up to three hours by flocks of animals being led to market

The modish new residents of Marylebone wanted a quicker route for their carriages and the second Duke of Grafton wanted a better route for his herds. Along with a group of gentlemen, tradesmen and other farmers, the Duke won a petition from parliament to build a new turnpike road that would lead from the village of Paddington across to Islington, although the Duke of Bedford protested, as did some tenant farmers. The formidable Capper sisters, who chased off anyone who strayed onto their fields beside Tottenham Court Road (above today's Capper Street), complained that the dust would ruin their hay, 'They wore riding habits and men's hats. One used to ride after boys flying kites with a large pair of shears to cut the strings. The other seized the clothes of those who trespassed to bathe.'[14]

Once approved, the road was built in record time. Named the New Road, it was 40 feet wide, and completed in 1756. The Fitzrovian sections would be re-named Marylebone Road and Euston Road in 1857.

But when Charles Fitzroy, Duke of Grafton, who had inherited Tottenhall and was created the Baron of Southampton in 1780, decided that he too, would develop his estate along the pattern of chequerboard squares and neat, neighbouring terraces, he had to re-possess the freehold of Home Field. As with the other London estates, the old mediaeval law stood – this held that existing tenants could act as if they themselves owned the land, and lease it to developers – but the manor of Tottenhall had been appropriated by parliament at the outbreak of the civil war. On the restoration of the Stuart king, Charles II, to the throne in 1660, it had reverted to the crown, and its freehold remained in the hands of the Canons of St Pauls. The Duke was lucky: his elder brother, Augustus Henry, the third duke of Grafton, was prime minister. The transaction to approve his freehold of the manor was agreed by an act of parliament in March 1768, and Charles Fitzroy then commissioned the estimable Adam brothers to design him a new square. The street names around Fitzroy Square – Grafton Way, Fitzroy Street – follow the extent of the estate, which stretched from the top of Tottenham Court Road to Cleveland Street.

In the space of a 100 years Fitzrovia had been transformed from open countryside into an integral suburb of the burgeoning capital city. Its denizens were the elite and the powerful; the middle class, especially those with an interest in the arts, favoured it, and their patronage supported its concert halls, theatres, the tea and pleasure gardens. Old Petty's Playhouse, which had opened in Hanway Street in 1736, also staged ballad operas, farces, pantomimes, contortionists, wire-walkers.

[I] saw at midnight twenty-three young women...looking for coal, beneath the root of a plantain, to put under their heads that night and they should dream who would be their husbands.

John Aubrey, on the meadow adjoining today's Gower Street (1694)

It was the era when the word 'characterisation' entered the language. The blending of a 'character' into a linear narrative was a recent phenomenon, more usually achieved in drama, than in the relatively new form of the novel. Writers, painters and sculptors were starting to represent the ordinary lives around them, to paint scenes that went beyond the portraits of their courtly and aristocratic patrons. William Hogarth saw the subjects of his paintings as characterising their positions in life. Their moral nature, the stresses and strains of their work, moulded them into recognizable types. Chairmen developed stout calves, and so were '*characters* as to figure'. Thames boatmen were top heavy, 'were I to paint the character of a charon, I would thus distinguish his make from that of a common man's...venture to give him a broad pair of shoulders, and spindle shanks.'[15]

'For heaven's sake, dear ladies, afford me some protection!' cried the spirited, young heroine of Fanny Burney's novel *Evelina* (1778), who has been startled by the explosive conclusion of the Orpheus and Eurydice firework display in 'Marybone Gardens'. Separated from her group, and lost in the crowd, she walked at a breathless pace to throw off the insolent young gallants who, with their facetious offers of protection, were trying to latch onto her, claiming to be her companion. She rushed towards two women, only to find herself arm-in-arm with two hoydens, who shouted with laughter at her every word. She saw an apparently good-natured young man and she beseeched him to rescue her, only to realise that he was too lily-livered – he went on to complain how hard the women pinched his arm.[16]

The lessees of Marylebone Manor had built a new mansion just to the west of Fitzrovia and they opened their grounds to the public in 1650. When Samuel Pepys visited on a May evening in 1668, he had found it charming, a 'pretty place...stayed till nine at night, and so home by moonlight.'[17] There the classes mixed and mingled. Marylebone Gardens were popular for strolling, flirting, dining alfresco. They offered concerts, supper-boxes and fireworks. In the early years there was animal baiting. Later there were pugilist displays. Families would go to the gardens for a day out, take the medicinal spring waters, appreciate the brilliant playing of the Westminster organist. There were tree-shaded walks, latticed alcoves set at discreet distances, offering plenty of chances for romantic dalliance and sexual assignation. Card sharps and gamblers played there. But at the zenith of their popularity, the gardens at night were also places of 'ill-repute', and in 1738 the proprietors began to charge an entrance fee, and to ban anyone wearing the livery of a servant. Nevertheless, as dusk turned to dark, and the orchestra played, the raffish, the ruffians and the rakes were still to be found, walking the balustraded pavilions, where visitors could sample the wine and Mr Trustler's famous tarts and plum cakes. On the day that 600 spectators marvelled at the human pyramid of war dancers, trained by Mrs Stewart, of Great Portland Street, there was also a highwayman in the audience, and three drunken shepherdesses, who were arrested for 'excesses'. In 1778 the owners, keen to end, 'riotous outbreaks and uncivil commotions', decided that land should be used for development and the gardens were closed.[18]

The vast and elegant Pantheon, designed by James Wyatt, with its richly decorated rotunda based on Santa Sophia, opened to a gathering of 1,500 invited guests at 173 (359) Oxford Street in 1772. It had assembly rooms, dimly lit basement supper rooms, and held magnificent balls and masquerades where the costumed guests concealed their identities behind masks and could play at dissembling – a footman flirt with a duchess, a prostitute with her client, or a ballroom bully pursue his quarry. The Pantheon ended its life as dramatically as it began when it was destroyed by a sensational fire in 1792.

[The duty of the portrait artist is] to raise the Characters; to divest the unbred person of his Rusticity, and give him something at least of a Gentleman.

Jonathan Richardson (1715)

The sex would certainly gain by shewing a little more of their legs, such things though apparently trifling, may have great influence over female character.

Alexander Jardine (1789)

London was noted for its relative freedom between the sexes; it was commented upon by overseas visitors, 'The Englishwomen have great freedom to go out of the house without menfolk...Many of these women serve in the shops...If a stranger enters a house and does not first of all kiss the mistress on the lips, they think him badly brought up.'[19] Nevertheless, streets of 18th century London were not particularly safe for women. Apart from the hazards of being unaccompanied, there was the mess. Although the western, Marylebone side of Fitzrovia was now well-lit with gas lamps, and new granite-slab pavements edged with gutters had replaced the central drains and separated pedestrians from the increasing traffic of vehicles, slops might still be thrown out of windows. Carts full of coal dust would careeer along, scattering ash. There were piles of animal manure. Straw. Human excrement. Dead animals. Live animals: horses, poultry, even cows, were kept in town houses. Cows were milked in the street, and wandering pigs were a hazard.

Cheek by jowl with the gentry, lived those who supplied their needs. A favoured area for the newly rich mercantile gentry, Marylebone seemed to combine the benefits of the country with easy access to central London; it was the place to be for those who were making their fortunes from the colonies. The West End, which included the Fitzrovian rich, generated a colossal demand for services.

Fitzrovia's population also included foreign emigrés and, from the 1790s, freed slaves from the colonies. For most of the 18th century the death rate of London exceeded the birth rate; nearly half of all children born there died before they reached the age of two, infectious diseases were rife, insanitary conditions were the norm, there were high bread prices at times of low wages, and London's growth relied on its immigrants. Young people came to the city from the country at a rate of about 9,000 a year.

As well as dressmakers and tailors, pastry cooks and confectioners, there were carpenters, carvers, piano makers, bed-makers, picture framers. A former Chippendale employee set up a workshop in Tottenham Court Road in 1752, as did a French specialist in ormulu and inlaid commodes, and another who made chairs and library steps. Quality furniture was made in Fitzrovia from the 1750s, and would be, for the next two hundred years. There were artists and engravers in Warren Street. Goodge Street traders included carpenters, oilmen, tallow chandlers, undertakers, tobacconists, grocers, wine merchants, and a silk dyer. Clothing, boot and shoemaking were a Fitzrovian mainstay.

From 1717 the Crab Tree Alehouse, on the Tottenham Court Road end of Percy Street, would have been frequented by artisans and workmen, breaking off at noon for a meal of bread and cheese, washed down with porter, the highly malted beer similar to stout that was produced by a number of London brewers from the 1720s.

Coffee houses opened early, at 6 a.m., for those on their way to work, and were used for exchanging all kinds of information, for posting letters, for business meetings, for fountains of masculine wit, if the patrons were not sunk in cards or sodden with wine. The more scholarly might peruse the latest periodical or weekly newspapers, workers might club together to buy a cheap farthing newspaper, or listen to someone else read a newspaper aloud; the merchants, the lawyers, would not miss the daily or thrice weekly newspapers. By the end of the 18th century, there were three well-known coffee houses in Rathbone Place, two in Great Portland Street, and another on Oxford Street. Many more were opened in the next decades.

Coffee houses were not places for women. They might work there – indeed many were run by women – but they did not sit around reading, smoking, discussing the affairs of the day in a coffee house. They went in only to buy coffee beans, or perhaps cocoa, or tea, for home. Most small purchases could be made at the local chandler's. For the poor, living in one room with a fireplace not designed for cooking, the most essential utensil was the kettle. If meat or a pie were to be cooked, it would have to be carried to the local baker's oven where, for a small fee, it would be roasted or baked. Bread and cheese were the staple, but possibly a busy working women would purchase ready-meals from a local cookshop. However, taverns were now places where respectable women could eat out. A family might go on Sunday to the Cock and Magpie (1740s) on Rathbone Place, for a fixed-price meal, the 'ordinary',

THE HUMOURS OF THE PANTHEON mezzotint engraving by Humphrey (1772)

The Pantheon on Oxford Street, regarded as 'the most elegant structure in Europe', held magnificent balls, masquerades and concerts. Despite attempts to keep out 'gay ladies', prostitutes openly promenaded its supper rooms and sought out clients. Here they flirt with bewigged visitors, drinking tea, while a child plays nearby.

They have learnt nothing and forgotten nothing.

Prince Talleyrand on exiled emigrés.

for which all the dishes for different courses were placed on the table at once. Otherwise there were snacks, such as the fresh oysters sold by the oyster girl outside by the tavern door.

Only a minority of women did not work. Over half of all women relied on paid work; up to a quarter worked as domestic servants; others worked as hawkers or street sellers or shopkeepers or washerwomen, or in the clothing industry; more middle class positions were as inkeepers, teachers, or in manufacturing. Others were brothel keepers, or found work as prostitutes. The social life of genteel women focused on the home. It might be enlivened by an occasional visit to the pleasure gardens or the tea rooms, such as the famous Adam and Eve beside Tottenham Court, with its rustic arbour in the garden, laid out with lawns, walks, ponds and statues.

Of the French style brothel or serraglio which had appeared in 1750, Marylebone had more than its fair share. Indeed, some have argued that it was neither the sugar nor the slavery of the West Indies that made the profits of Marylebone in the 18th century, but the sex industry: 'In Marylebone alone 1,700 houses are occupied by wealthy courtesans. Without these girls many thousands of houses in the West end would stand empty', wrote the author of a German travel guide published in 1789.[20]

Between building booms, the reforming philanthropists saw to the establishment of the St Pancras Female Charity School at 12 Windmill Street in 1776, where a few young girls were educated and trained for domestic service. One of the first four London hospitals, the Middlesex, was established in 1745, in two houses in Windmill Street. In 1756, sited near the open fields of outer London, famous for good snipe shooting, today's Middlesex was erected, a big symmetrical block designed by James Paine, with a paved forecourt and tall Palladian windows (later extended, and re-built in 1935). The Middlesex aimed to lessen the number of deaths of women in childbirth, 'make proper provision for the wives of poor tradesmen labouring under terror, pains and hazards of childbirth'.[21] When money was tight, medical students supplemented their allowances by poaching in the surrounding countryside, returning with sackfuls of rabbits which they sold to the landladies from whom they rented a room.

As well as dissenting chapels, a great number of new Anglican chapels were built for the growing middle class, where the church-goers provided the chaplain with an income by renting pews.

Hanway Street, then the main route into Oxford Street from the east, was lined with lace shops and milliners. Oxford Street, not yet in its heyday, was lit with lamps by the end of the century, and its row of small shops entranced Sophie von la Roche, a writer visiting from Germany in 1786, 'First one passes a watchmaker's, then a silk or fan store, now a silversmith's, a china or glass shop. The spirit booths are particularly tempting, for the English are in any case fond of strong drink. Here crystal flasks of every shape and form are exhibited: each one has a light behind it which makes all the different coloured spirits sparkle. Just as alluring are the confectioners and fruiterers, where, behind the handsome glass windows, pyramids of pineapples, figs, grapes, oranges and all manner of fruits are on show.' Breathlessly, she admired a display of dress cloth, 'a cunning device for showing women's materials. They hang down in folds behind the fine, high windows so that the effect of this or that material, as it would be in a woman's dress, can be studied', and she is struck by the range of women's shoes – one woman's daughter is even kept amused by 'searching amongst the dolls' shoes for some to fit the doll she had with her.'[22]

For the shoemakers who supplied the footwear, for the seamstresses who

The Coster-Girl, an engraving after a daguerrotype by Beard

'Apples! An 'aypenny a lot, Apples!'

stitched the dresses, there were to be profound changes in the century ahead. The journeyman tailors had already tried to organise, but their attempts to unionise had been stamped on hard by the government. Wages disputes had been bloody during the 1760s, and had included some of the two thirds of the working population of London, and half of the working men, who were unskilled or semi-skilled, such as the sawyers in the furniture industry in Fitzrovia. Their frustration at being undermined by cheaper, unskilled immigrants had led to violent protests. There had been riots against the rich. The economy was being transformed, not simply by inventions and technology but by global links; through trade and the wealth created by slavery. The British had established a presence in India; in 1788 the first convicts had been transported to the first penal settlement in Sydney, Australia.

Politically, these were turbulent years. Britain had signed the Treaty of Paris, recognizing American independence in 1783. In 1789 the storming of the Bastille had marked the start of the French revolution. Connections were being made by working men between their own wage levels and their potential strength in combination. They began to demand a political say. Amongst the skilled artisans and craftsmen, there was a growing political awareness of a separate class identity. Initially the idea of the French revolution also appealed to members of the upper classes and the 'the middling sort', as those in the professions and trade were called. They were inclined to favour constitutional monarchy or political rights. In 1792, Mary Wollstonecraft was to apply these notions of equality, rights, usefulness, to women in her *Vindication of the Rights of Women*, which challenged the dependence that forced women to rely on sexual allure.

19th century – rupture, style, new men and dining.

Fitzrovia was a microcosm of London; affluence existed alongside the deepest poverty, and was to prove a volatile combination. The demarcation between classes was to become more marked. While the middle class drew westwards, some inner and eastern areas of Fitzrovia attracted the political and artistic dissidents who were to give the area its specific character. As the town spread outwards, a new longing for the countryside, for an unsubdued 'nature', became evident, fostered by romanticism. John Nash's plan for Regent Street, which transformed Fitzrovia, employed 'nature' to separate the privileged from the potential disorder of the lower classes.

In 1811, when the farm leases of northern Marylebone reverted to the Crown, the Prince Regent accepted John Nash's designs for the old manor's redevelopment. Villas and terraces iced with stucco were to be set around what would become today's Regent's Park, to give the houses the impression of being in the country. Nash hoped that this would be the winning combination to persuade 'people of consequence' to buy the property, once built. He hoped that it would work even better with the addition of Regent Street, a triumphal way by which he wanted to create the illusion of bypassing the New Road, and link Regent's Park up with Portland Place. From there it would lead down to the house of his patron, the Prince Regent (the subsequently demolished Carlton House) and Westminster. The dusty, disruptive work of new construction was again undertaken on the western flank of Fitzrovia.

To enhance this Westminster/courtly connection, Regent Street was designed to have circles instead of crossroads to punctuate its junctions with Oxford Circus and Piccadilly – although Park Crescent, at the top of Portland Place, remained a semi-circle. Portland Place, of course, was already built. And Nash erected his small church, All Souls (1822-24), with its round Greek

When in the Lying-in Hospital he endeavour'd to improve Midwifery. He allowed women to deliver themselves, or at least give nature leave to exert her own powers.

Samuel Foart Simmons on Dr Hunter at Middlesex Hospital

I was the last to consent to the separation, but the separation having been made and having become inevitable, I have always said that I would be the first to meet the friendship of the United States as an independent power.

George III to John Adams, first ambassador from USA

peristyle and spire, to catch the eye at the curvy stretch of Langham Place, between Portland Place and the top of Regent Street.

Effectively completed by 1820, Nash was hoping that Regent Street's grandeur would encourage exclusive Bond Street retailers to open shops on the thoroughfare, but he also intended it to be a cordon sanitaire, to emphasise an already existing social division between the West End and the further reaches of Fitzrovia and Soho. 'It is highly essential', he wrote, 'and is the leading principle of the plan...that the whole communication...will be a boundary and complete separation between the streets and squares occupied by the nobility and gentry, and the narrow streets and meaner houses occupied by mechanics and the trading part of the community.'[23]

Fitzrovia's meaner streets were excommunicated. By the middle of the century Fitzrovia Square would no longer be such a fashionable or desirable address. A visiting Frenchman, flinching from the squalid streets, from where the middle classes had begun to depart, wrote, 'I recall the alleys which run into Oxford Street, stifling lanes, encrusted with human exhalations.'[24]

Many of the grand houses of Fitzrovia, meant for the rich, were split up and partitioned, so that they could accommodate separate lodgings, studios, workshops, with a maze of passage ways and halls.

The poorest took a single room. This might be the tenement cellar: dark, damp, unventilated, vulnerable to overflowing drains and cesspits. Sometimes whole families lived in one room, and shared a bed. The room might double up as the workplace, and be cluttered with materials, tools, or a barrow. The 1841 Census recorded that in Goodge Place, 485 squeezed into 27 houses – 64 were individuals, the rest were families. In just one house, there were 32 people.

The worst slums remained the St Giles rookery, which went from Great Russell Street south to Long Acre: tenements let in no light, cesspits stank, roofs leaked, and diseases such as typhus and cholera were endemic.

In the Victorian public mind, the overcrowded rookeries were synonymous with criminality, and their occupants had only themselves to blame for their grinding poverty, ill health, petty crime and worse. The powerful housing charities thought that the lives of slum dwellers would be improved by slum clearance and pushed through a new road. In 1846-47 New Oxford Street was bulldozed through St Giles rookery. No new housing was provided for the inhabitants, and it was the landlords who benefited (the Duke of Bedford was paid £114,000 for the freeholds). The dispossessed poor moved into the nearest available housing in Fitzrovia, in order to remain within walking distance of work, so intensifying the pressure and the overcrowding.

Tenement facilities for washing, privies, waste removal, were totally inadequate. For labouring women, washing was a two-days-a-week task. Soap was expensive. The family might share a sink with other families, or they washed in the yard. After 1831, when the householders of St Marylebone and St Pancras voted to replace the local oligarchies which administered the parishes by elected vestrymen, some improvements were made to the more neglected eastern half of Fitzrovia (although the St Pancras Paving Commission, set up in 1768, was empowered to levy rates for improving light, paving and street cleaning, it was notoriously inefficient). Water mains were installed in Tottenham Court Road in 1834. A municipal bath and wash-houses were provided. In St Pancras, one survey showed that each week between 1846 and 1848, 900 people paid one penny to use the laundry, and 3,000 people paid the same to use the public baths. The Metropolitan Board of Works completed their sewage plans for London in 1868.

Overcrowding increased as buildings were torn down to be replaced by railways, new offices, and public buildings. In 1884-85 a Royal Commission found overcrowding was worse than ever.

Only very well off artisans could afford a house. Most rented rooms in a house that was subdivided. Better-off families might have two, or even three, rooms. Other labouring people could only afford temporary rooms in a common lodging house, where their neighbours might be prostitutes or criminals.

At the start of the 19th century, the Adam and Eve Tea Gardens had become notorious as the haunt of local prostitutes and criminals and were shut down by the magistrates (they were re-opened as a tavern, in 1813). Between the northern end of Great Portland Street and Cleveland Street during those years every house was said to be a common lodging house, a brothel, or a tavern with 'access to the upper floors' – rooms with 'posture women' (striptease performers). Along the southern ends of these streets, brothels were more up-market, and operated free from the interference of any authority. Portland Place had a well-known brothel in the 1850s. Discreetly disguised to look like a respectable building, it was furnished with chairs and sofas covered in twill, chandeliers and handsome green curtains, the blinds were lowered before nightfall, and wine was served to the 'guests.' Some of the women working there were literally sex slaves; the story of an East End orphan who was kidnapped, tricked into drunkenly signing an agreement to hand over most of her earnings to the brothel owner, abused and kept against her will, was symptomatic. The age of consent was 12, and child prostitutes would be among the streetwalkers working Oxford Street. During the 1860s and 1870s, awareness of prostitution became a cause of concern. The Contagious Diseases Acts meant that women suspected of prostitution would be forcibly inspected for VD. Feminists were divided about the issue. The first woman doctor, Elizabeth Garrett Anderson, argued that it was necessary for public health. But Josephine Butler, supported by nonconformists and radicals, led a campaign to repeal the Acts.

When London's growth began to extend to the new outer suburbs, those whose work was in most demand during the London Season, and who could not afford to travel, were forced into whatever housing they could find. The famous 'poverty map' of London produced by Charles Booth in his *Life and Labour of the People of London* (1889-1900) pinpointed several areas in Fitzrovia where occasional employment was the norm. People lived in 'chronic want' and/or semi-criminality in Rathbone Street, Riding House (*Union*) Street, Charlotte Mews and Adam and Eve Court, off Oxford Street. There were streets of 'standard poverty', where people had intermittent work, and 'lacked comfort' – life was an unending struggle, but just above starvation. They wore only second-hand clothes that did not fit, making them appear 'disreputable' at best, and had 'deplorable' boots.[25]

Portland Place was lined with houses for the wealthy, rated the highest in London, £100, with three, if not more, servants. Alongside the border roads, Regent Street, and along Tottenham Court Road, Oxford Street, some portions of Euston Road, and also Great Portland Street, lived the 'lower middle class', the more well-to-do shopkeepers, clerks, other employers, and professionals. These families had at least one servant, and often two.

Fitzrovia was marked by the industrial transformation of the late 18th and early 19th centuries. For example, on Tottenham Court Road, where the Dominion Theatre stands today, the Horseshoe brewery (named from a nearby tavern) pioneered the mechanization of industrial mass production. By applying the use of thermometers, new technical aids, constructing huge vats,

Florence Nightingale undressed the woman, who was half tipsy but kept saying, "Would not think it ma'am, but a week ago I was in silk and satins; in silk and satins dancing at Woolwich. Yes! Ma'am, but for all I am so dirty I am draped in silks and satins sometimes. Real French silks and satins."

Elizabeth Gaskell on patient care during the cholera epidemic, Middlesex Hospital in 1854

Entering the kitchen we found it so full of smoke that the sun's rays, which shot slanting down through a broken tile in the roof, looked like a shaft of light cut through the fog...A number of the inmates were grouped around the fire, some kneeling, toasting herrings, of which the place smelt strangely.

Henry Mayhew on a common lodging house

Our local area was possibly even more Jewish than the East End of London – and it did have some strange notions, now that I think about it. People who lived on the north side of Oxford Street thought themselves a cut above those who lived on the south side.

Max Jaffa

and in 1790, steam engines, brewers were able to produce a better quality, stronger, cheaper brew. The enormous vat of the Horsehoe Brewery, which was built in 1810 for Henry Meux, burst its hoops in 1814, and ten thousand gallons of beer flooded onto the road, demolishing three adjoining houses and causing the death of eight people. Others in the vicinity eagerly found ways to cup the running liquor, and drank themselves stupid. Two years later the brewery became a focus of rage and resentment when it was attacked by anti-Tory rioters. These were years when claims for political reform were once again being taken up by both the middle and working classes. Reform societies were formed by men and by women.

London had long been a city of migrants. By 1800 the city had a Jewish population of 20,000 and a large Irish community, many of whom had come to St Giles. More were to arrive from Ireland during the famine years of 1845-58. Protestant Huguenots fleeing France had also settled in Soho in the 18th century, and moved up into Fitzrovia. Ruined aristocrats escaping from the terror in France were to be followed by European left-wing exiles during 1848, when uprisings shook the establishment and boosted the forces of liberalism and nationalism. German Jews fleeing archaic religious repression also arrived in the 1840s, while more were to flee from central and Eastern Europe in the 1880s. The defeat of the Paris Commune brought another wave of idealistic rebels.

An extraordinary number of these immigrants, many of them radicals and socialists, chose Fitzrovia. Its spacious housing, now degraded, divided up into multiple tenancies, offered central, relatively cheap accommodation. There were lively, intense social areas, pub rooms and halls which seethed with talk. After the turn of the century, there were 29 coffee houses in Fitzrovia and by 1850 the number of pubs had reached around 150. They may not all have had skittle or bowling alleys outside, but they had upstairs rooms, available for clubs and meetings. In the coffee shops, the radical weeklies, which were priced at a penny, in defiance of the government's fourpenny stamp duty, sold like hot cakes, and workers could read the latest developments and disagree about whether political or economic reform was important. Foreign radicals intermingled with Chartists, trade unionists, secularists, utopian socialists, and advocates of women's rights.

When the 1832 Reform Act gave the vote to the middle class male ratepayers, who owned or rented property of not less than £10 value, it meant that St Marylebone won the right to be represented by two elected members of parliament – rather than be subsumed under the mantle of Middlesex – it was not until 1885 that St Pancras would gain a similar right (when the metropolitan constituency was extended to 73 members).

Fitzrovia also enabled the immigrants to find work, in craft, manufacturing and clothing workshops, and catering. Many Jewish immigrants were employed in the area as casual workers in the clothing trade; others set up business as garment manufacturing employers. London depended on the availability of a pool of casual labour. This included all those whose work was most in demand during the London Season. Labourers looking for casual work gathered at the old animal pound, at the bottom of Tottenham Court Road. At the beginning of the century, a bricklayer's labourer was paid 2s. 9d. for carrying a hod of bricks up five sets of ladders, at least 120 times in the working day. Paviers, wielding rammers that weighed over half a hundredweight, 2,000 times a day, earned a similar amount. On the fringes of Fitzrovia, there were dust carters, rag-pickers, horse-dealers, washerwomen. In premises and mews off Tottenham Court, were knife grinders, hackney cab drivers, hawkers of fruit and vegetables, rag and bone collectors and dustmen.

The general diffusion of manufactures throughout a country generates a new character in its inhabitants...an essential change in the general character of the mass of the people.

Robert Owen on the psychology of industrialisation

Cartoon by JOHN LEECH,
Punch (1848)

'*My Mistress says she hopes
you won't call a meeting of
her creditors; but if you will
leave your bill in the usual
way, it shall be properly
attended to.*'

Local market workers lived near the premises; as well as Oxford Street market, there was a general market on the upper, east side of Tottenham Court Road.

In the second half of the 19th century, conditions of work were changing in many local trades.

The invention of the sewing machine in 1846 and a method for multiple pattern cutting in 1858 encouraged the piecework system, lowered prices and decreased wages. Tailors paid by the piece worked more than 80 hours a week. Often the work was taken over by cheap female or child labour. Near Oxford Circus, women seamstresses, shirtmakers, staymakers, embroiderers, bonnet-makers, dressmakers and milliners, a high proportion of whom were under 20 years old, worked for up to 17 hours a day for 6*s.* a week, and by the age of 30 looked ten years older than domestic workers of the same age. During the slack summer months, in between the start and end of the London Season, when work was scarce, there was nothing but 'air pie' to live on; they often supplemented their low wages by begging, prostitution and the pawn shop.

Casual and unskilled workers were without financial resources, isolated, easily replaced, and unable to unionise. Public pressure over the exploitation in the sweated trades finally resulted in legislative attempts to regulate these, from the late 19th century. The Liberal government in 1901 was to establish a system of minimum rates in low paid industries. But law would do little to stem market forces. By this time Fitzrovia's shoemaking workshops were

BEDROOM·FURNISHERS·ESTABLISHED·1818. HEAL & SON Nos·195·196·197·198 TOTTENHAM·COURT·Rd

"THE NEWLYN" A SET of PLAIN OAK FURNITURE with DULL STEEL HINGES & HANDLES. SOUND CONSTRUCTION : INEXPENSIVE

C.H.B. Quennell
woodcut (1898)

*One of the earliest sets of
bedroom furniture designed
by Ambrose Heal Jnr. After
he served an apprenticeship
as a cabinet maker, he went
on to produce simple, well-
proportioned Arts and Crafts
furniture, which gained a
wide following.*

losing out to mechanisation. Machines for sewing, cutting and riveting, meant factory production was increasingly to take over and most of the trade moved out of London.

Up until the 1840s, furniture makers in Fitzrovia had sold direct to the customer from the workshop. However, after the success of the Great Exhibition, held in the Crystal Palace built in Hyde Park in 1851, which celebrated the 'Industry of All Nations', furniture workshops were increasingly subcontracted by a retailer, who marketed their products. By the 1870s and 80s, the large furniture stores were replacing workshop point-of-sale, and the link between producer and customer was broken. Although the demand for their products increased (in the 30 years from 1861, London's furniture workforce went up by 16%), wages declined.

Fitzrovia was an important furniture making area. In the 1861 census, over 3,000 were employed in making furniture in St Pancras. At the start of the 20th century, cabinet makers, chair makers, furniture makers, French polishers, turners, carvers, and sawmills were still to be found in Fitzrovia. Even in the 1940s 2,205 furniture makers continued to work in the area.

It also became an established area for the retailing of furniture. For example, Shoolbred (now defunct), which started in Bloomsbury in 1820, moved to 155 Tottenham Court Road, and expanded. Maples opened as a large furniture emporium in 1851; by the end of the century it was selling furniture to everyone from the lower middle classes to royalty. Clients included Queen Victoria, Indian princes and the Tsar of Russia. Heal's moved to Tottenham Court Road in 1840, and established a reputation for producing high-quality furniture, which continues to this day. In 1916 the premises were re-built, with recessed shop windows and an arcade.

The later 19th century saw a new enthusiasm for the 'simplification of life', which merged with interest in the exotic 'East'. Boldly the Arts and Crafts movement swept away the fussy extras of interiors, such as tablecloths, or those brass doorknobs that required so much polishing. Eclectic, slightly mysterious, the look of the aesthetic interior reached its popular apotheosis during the 1880s. Household manuals published advice on how 'art' furniture should be arranged: occasional tables in the style and lightweight chairs, in the centre of the room; heavier pieces such as a display cabinet of ebonised mahogany or deal, at the edges – all available from the Tottenham Court Road stores. Stained floorboards were scattered with oriental rugs, walls were painted sage green or peacock blue to harmonise with a William Morris wallpaper – patterns such as pomegranate or willow were the most popular, and the final touch was a Japanese inspired overmantel on which to display the current mania for blue and white chinaware.

Ironically, the passion for the 'house beautiful' could turn into an obsessive preoccupation with life-style; wittily underscored by the ultimate aesthete, Oscar Wilde, who said, 'I find it harder and harder everyday to live up to my blue china.'[26]

None of this had been the original intention of the Art and Crafts pioneer, William Morris. A profoundly practical man, he wanted 'arts and crafts' to be accompanied by change in society. He criticized those who focused only on art, for their 'absurd ignorance of the very elements of economics', and for their attitude to the working class as merely 'instruments to be played on'.[27] Morris's furnishings were bought by the wealthy, but he took a full-time part in the socialist movement which emerged during the 1880s and addressed open-air meetings in Regent's Park and Marylebone on the right to public speaking on the streets.

After the 1867 Reform Act, which gave upper working class men the vote, political activism in Fitzrovia intensified. There were campaigns to extend the franchise to workers and to women. Demands for free education, support for Italian nationalism, republicanism and secularism, were followed by the formation of new socialist groups: the Social Democratic Federation (1882), the Fabian Society (1884), and the Socialist League (1884). All these groupings held meetings in Fitzrovia, along with those rebellious outsiders, the anarchists. There were German anarchists around the Middlesex hospital area, French anarchists in Charlotte Street, a Scandinavian Anarchist club in Rathbone Place, a Jewish Anarchist Club in Berners Street, and Windmill Street's Autonomie Club. Disputes tore the clubs apart, and ambitious conspiracies against foreign tyrants were hatched in smoke-filled rooms.

Fitzrovia was a place for fun as well as ferment. Pubs offered music and communal singing and some took the chance of turning into licensed theatres, where customers could sit around tables with their drinks, smoking, talking, wandering about, while being entertained by a variety of short sketches on a small stage. The galleried inn on the Tottenham Court Road corner, the Boar and Castle, was re-opened in 1861 by Charles Morton and expanded into the Oxford Music Hall. There, boisterous audiences shouted direct, crude responses, while waiters weaved amongst them serving pies and ale, and smoke plumed through the air. It was a phenomenal success; Victorian prudery was always accompanied by the bawdy, sexual innuendo of the music hall. Expanded and reconstructed twice more, the music hall remained open until 1926, when cinema wooed the audience away to the flickering screen.

The area had already become an entertainment centre in the early 19th century. The highly fashionable and profitable Prince of Wales (later the Scala) in Tottenham Street, in 1865, had been the King's Concert Rooms, and a circus, before re-opening as a theatre. Its popularity was matched by the Princess Theatre on Oxford Street from 1836, where concerts, opera and burlesque were performed. During the 1850s Charles Keane's famous

The aim should be to combine clearness of form and firmness of structure with the mystery which comes from abundance and richness of detail.

William Morris on his principles of good design

In 1810 John Harris Heal set up his feather-dressing firm in Rathbone Place. In 1840 the firm moved to a stables at 196 Tottenham Court Road, where the family lived in an old farmhouse behind the shop. The business expanded, and Heal's became known for its adventurousness in mounting fully-furnished room displays of quality furniture.

PAGANI'S, 42 Great Portland
Street. *Founded in 1871, it
became known as the best
Italian restaurant in London.
After supper, theatrical and
literary London scribbled
their autographs on the lino-
panelled walls of its special
artists' room, where
admission was jealously
guarded by Signor Pagani.
Signatures included those of
George Gershwin, Sarah
Bernhardt, Tchaikovsky,
Lillie Langtry, Henry
Irving, Maurice Chevalier
and Oscar Wilde.*

productions of Shakespeare and melodrama made the theatre's reputation and
drew the middle class audiences in large numbers. By the 1860s a new realism
had appeared in drama as well as in fiction, and audiences flocked to plays
highlighting the moral and social issues of the day.

The success of the theatres came at a time when access into London was
speeded up by the opening of the first underground trains across the city.
London's population increased from just over one million at the start of the
19th century to over six million by its end, offering entrepeneurial
opportunities to which Fitzrovia, poised by the West end, near the first of the
big metropolitan inter-city railway stations, Euston (1837), and the first of the
underground lines, the Metropolitan (1863), was quick to respond. The
Langham Hotel was built in 1864, on part of the site of the old Foley house
(which had been replaced by Langham House, designed by John Nash). It was
the second of the grand hotels for the new railway age (the first being at

Euston) and looked like a Florentine palace. Combining English comfort with French elegance, it aimed for a modern 'American' standard of efficiency, and introduced catering on a mass scale, and for a different public. The popularity of the Great Exhibition in 1851 had shown the dearth of eating places for families. Unlike traditional inns, whose coffee rooms were only open to men, the Langham dining rooms opened to both sexes.

Then, as now, immigrants could most easily find service jobs in catering; French, Swiss and Italians worked as washers-up, became waiters, cooks, *chocalatiers*, confectioners, and they opened restaurants.

By the 1870s the best Italian food in town was at Pagani's, the restaurant founded by the Swiss-Italian, Mario Pagani, on Great Portland Street. Upstairs, above the potted palms and round tables of the ground floor, where customers could drink chianti, and feast on dishes of jugged hare followed by peach melba, was the gorgeous Art Nouveau first floor, where a special room,

Life engenders life. Energy creates energy. It is by spending oneself that one becomes rich!

Sarah Bernhardt

Well, if these are your
haristocrats, give me the
roughs, for I've only took
fourpence.

Orange seller outside
Marie Wilton's theatre
on its first night

eight feet square, with walls of lino, was reserved for artists. By the 1890s over
5,000 actors, writers and musicians had autographed the walls. To celebrate the
opening of the Omega Workshop, one of its co-directors, the painter Vanessa
Bell, sent a note off to its founder, Roger Fry, suggesting they all celebrate with
a special dinner at Pagani's, 'We should get all your disreputable and some of
your aristocratic friends to come – and after dinner we should repair to Fitzroy
Sq. where would be decorated furniture, painted walls etc. Then we should all
get drunk and dance and kiss. Orders would flow in and the aristocrats would
feel sure they were really in the thick of things.' She and Duncan Grant
devised a special menu, starting with 'Potage Alpha', and ending with 'Ruisses
Glaces a l'Omega Dessert.'[28]

By the 1880s it had become acceptable for a respectable woman of the
middle class to be seen eating out in public with a man at one of the new café-
restaurants, serving anglicised versions of the haute cuisine introduced into
London by immigrant French chefs, of whom Alexis Soyer was the star.
Shocked by the hardship of the poor, he first involved himself in the
establishing of soup kitchens in February 1847, advising on ingredients: for the
soup, vegetable peelings (which have the most nutrients) were essential, 'it is
a well known fact, that the exterior of every vegetable, roots in particular,
contains more flavour than the interior of it.'[29] The first soup kitchen was set
up in 1846 at 295 Euston Road by Isaac Negus Jackin. On a cold day, it served
140 gallons of soup which were consumed by up to 550 people, and it was still
operating in 1901.

Food for the mind which, according to Victorian values, should be morally
uplifting, should enlighten, inspire, as well as educate – invigorative, earnest
inquiry was the spirit of the age – was close by. The British Museum,
established in 1759, finally opened its doors to the wider public, and 30,000
visited on January 2, 1843. A 'truly equalizing place' declared Charles Kingsley,
'where rich and poor may meet together.'[30] The title of his first novel *Yeast*,
published in 1848, signified the social, economic and spiritual ferment of the
decade.

A woman looked up to our
box, and seeing us staring
aghast, with, I suppose, an
expression of horror upon
my face, first off 'took a
sight' at us, and then
shouted, 'Now then you
three stuck-up ones, come
out o' that, or I'll send this
'ere orange at your 'eds.'

Marie Wilton, on visiting
the local 'dusthole' in
Tottenham Street, which
she re-launched, creating
the first of the West End
theatres as we know
them today.

Not only relationships between classes, but between men and women were
being altered in the middle of the 19th century. Among the middle classes, it
was assumed that women were destined for a sharply defined domestic sphere,
separate from production. The pre-Raphaelite painters, Holman Hunt,
Rossetti and Millais, who went to the art school just off Fitzrovia, run by
Henry Sass (1788-1884), in nearby 32 Bloomsbury (6 *Charlotte*) Street, painted a
different ideal of woman as a symbol of transcendence, elevated above the
pervasive cash nexus. The luminous, flat planes of the pre-Raphaelite style
rendered their subjects, with their loose tresses, long necks and languorous,
melancholy beauty, with a church-glass untouchable glow.

In the real world, women were expressing aspirations for a life beyond the
constraints of Victorian convention. Women's need to support themselves
stimulated efforts to improve schools and gain entry into higher education.
The University of London on Gower Street awarded the first degrees to
women students during the 1880s. By the early 1890s, 45% of the students at
the university were women.

20th century – world war, new women, music and media.

The city was transforming, quickening; the twopenny tube ride on the Central
Line (1900) made access to Oxford Street easier.[31] Along the pavement sped
stenographers, typists, telephonists, clerical assistants, teachers, nurses, shop
assistants on break. Women workers were joining the men in the new offices
and shops. From 1905 motorbuses were replacing the ubiquitous horse drawn

omnibus. The Princess's Theatre closed in 1902, and its ground floor was converted into a shopping bazaar.

Oxford Street had been transformed in the latter half of the 19th century. Its 150 small shops formerly specialising in silks and satin, Indian muslin, wool, buttons, fancy trimmings, disappeared as successful drapers had turned themselves into department stores, with steel-framed buildings, lit by electric light (1880s), and plate glass display windows. Peter Robinson (Top Shop), which had opened in 1833 as a linen drapers at 103 Oxford Street, had taken over five adjacent shops. In 1923 its corner facade was re-built as part of the re-design of Oxford Circus by Sir Henry Tanner.

Women coming in from the suburbs or up from the country for a day's shopping entered London's department stores almost as foreigners and found familiarity. In their welcoming spaces, glittering with goods, in the perfumed air, there were enticing possibilities of buying into dreams of new worlds. The broken horizons of shopping promised an urban essence with every purchase. Glamorous, tawdry, essential, frivolous, it hardly mattered. Shopping was the perfect excuse for wandering, for reverie, when a woman could be anonymous. On Oxford Street women had the right to dawdle, to window shop, without expecting to be accosted.

These same windows, resplendent with all that London, city of conspicuous consumption, had to offer, were smashed by suffragettes in 1912, when it became clear that the Liberal Party, returned to power in January 1911, would continue to oppose votes for women. The Queen's Hall (1893-1941) in Langham Place was regularly used for suffragette gatherings. These women had no doubt about their claim to public spaces, and commercial London was responding. Not only did department stores open restrooms, grill rooms and restaurants for their customers, but large scale caterers were providing further places for inexpensive meals in pleasant surroundings. The first Oxford Street Lyons Corner House, with its gilt and marble interior, opened on the site of the old Oxford Theatre in 1926.

NORTH WEST PUBLIC SOUP KITCHEN ON EUSTON ROAD
The Illustrated Times (1858)

Charitable members of the public bought tickets for a free meal at the soup kitchen, and distributed them to the poor. At the North West Public Soup Kitchens, a ticket cost 2½d., and paid for a quart of beef soup made from oxhead, or pea soup, or two pounds of rice milk with a roll of bread.

A Life Class at the Slade
etching by R. Brown (1881)

*The Slade Faculty of Fine
Arts at the University of
London was modeled after
French schools, where male
and female students studied
the semi-nude models together.*

In 1901 Frederick Schmidt, an immigrant butcher from Wurtemburg, who married a May Queen from Bethnal Green, opened a delicatessen at 37 Charlotte Street. One day a customer asked for half-a-dozen frankfurters. The assistant asked, 'How do you want them, a string of six or three pairs?' The customer dithered, not knowing the difference.

'Make up your mind, I can't spend all day serving you.'

The customer settled for three pairs and while they were being wrapped, asked in German, 'Why are you so rude?'

'I could understand you being so stupid if you were English, but a German...'[32]

At the turn of the century Fitzrovia was the German quarter of London, and the famous Fitzroy Tavern across the road was called The Hundred Marks. All this changed with the first world war, when the Germans were interned. After the war many Germans were repatriated, but not Frederick Schmidt who, a naturalized citizen, had been drafted into the British army as a cook. Despite the Kaiser-bashing mobs who attacked his shop, he was inspired to open a restaurant, and Schmidt's, with its rude waiters and splendid cheap food, 'the advertisement is on the plate', entered Fitzrovian folklore.[33]

Cultural difference gave Fitzrovia its fascination and draw; a kind of integration that was not a greying-down into smudgy sameness under London's opal sky. Galvanic Charlotte Street also had L'Etoile, with its

romantic dark interior, founded in 1906, and Bertorelli's, with its crisp tablecloths and large dining room, started by four Italian brothers in 1912 and still managed by the son of one of them up to 1982. Now expanded to include a brasserie and a wine bar, in the 1930s and 1940s it was well known as a place to go for the basic plate of spaghetti. In the 1950s it was the venue for the Wednesday Club, founded by art historian Ben Nicolson and Philip Toynbee, the reviewer and novelist. It attracted numerous writers, including John Berger, Christopher Isherwood, the historian Hugh Thomas, the philosopher A.J. Ayer, the poets Stephen Spender and T.S. Eliot. In the late 1950s, after his novel *Lucky Jim* was published, Kingsley Amis began to lunch there once a week with Anthony Powell.

In the early years of the 20th century, the streets of Fitzrovia were thick with artists. Those who were alive to the zeitgeist delighted in the slant of modernism, the sliding of the fixed conditions of perspective on which the human character had been centred since the Renaissance. The shift in perception had been presaged in the paintings of Cezanne, as Roger Fry, who arranged the first Post-Impressionist exhibition in London in 1910, recognised. The new awareness in art coincided with Einstein's relativity theory, which revolutionized science. Ideas buzzed along with gossip among the painters and poets and political radicals who sought out these cosmopolitan, continental restaurants, as congenial, cheap places to eat and converse, and

Great heavens, no, madam. Why, it took *me* a fortnight to learn it.

A (male) hairdresser to Louise Smith (Langham Place Circle), on whether women might learn to be hairdressers.

even make love. Young, upper class women gleefully threw off the shackles of propriety, dressed as outrageously as the most pretentious or precious of 'egoist' male painters. Of all the restaurant proprietors in Fitzrovia, it was perhaps the romantic, portly, Austrian chef Rudolph Stulik, who presided over La Tour Eiffel in 1 Percy Street, who was the most expansive in cultivating the bohemian avant-garde. Nancy Cunard called the restaurant their 'carnal-spiritual home'[34], and Stulik commissioned Wyndham Lewis to decorate one of the private dining rooms. He charged astronomical prices for the fashionable society who flocked there to savour the adventurous atmosphere, but there was always a *plat du jour* at a modest price that his regulars could afford. Renamed the White Tower in 1943, when the restaurant went under Greek ownership, its subsequent evolution demonstrates the leading and innovative role Fitzrovian immigrants have played in expanding the gastronomic repertoire of English dining. By the end of the 20th century, 1 Percy Street had turned into Bam Bou, with a Parisian trained chef serving exquisite Vietnamese food. London's food had gone global.

One way or another the bohemianism and a mix of cultures persisted into the second half of the 20th century. By the end of the 1960s, informality was the key, and again Fitzrovia set the scene for a further loosening up of the boundaries between indoor and outdoor, private and public, when the Venus Kebab House in Charlotte Street set tables for its customers to eat outside, the first London restaurant to do so. Cleverly combining the Greek penchant for making eating a casual, sociable affair, with the English enthusiasm for a picnic, whatever the weather.

In the 1930s Anglo-Italian gangsters had moved into gambling and prostitution. Favouring knives over guns, their operations in Soho spilled over into Fitzrovia. Internment and repatriation reduced the Italian presence in Fitzrovia during the second world war, but perfectly legitimate trattoria, cafés, delicatessens continued to give Fitzrovia an Italian bite and flavour. One of the best-stocked, Fratelli Camisa, closed the doors of its Fitzrovia address in 1999, keeping them open on-line, informing its customers of a new web-site order address.

Warren Street, the uppermost cross street, on the back border of the Euston Road, had been taken over by used-car dealers, 'lovely '33 Packard brought over by the Cousins, 20s Bentley for nothing in the rationing'[35], jamming the pavements and taking over ground floors, leaving upper ones to rot. By the 1960s it was a street of Indian restaurants. Another infusion of immigrant culture into Fitzrovia, this time initiated by the break-up of the British empire and the re-shaping of colonial alliances.

Colonial powers were weakened across the world by the second world war. India won its independence from Britain in 1947 and from then on, almost the entire fabric of colonisation crumbled. South African exiles were to find refuge in Fitzrovia. Immigrants from the Indian sub-continent, Bengali and the Punjab, the ex-British colonies most affected by the Indian and Pakistan partition in 1947, arrived in Britain at the beginning of the 1960s, following a relaxation of emigration laws in their own country, and before the 1962 Immigration Act in Britain restricted entry. Settling into cheap accommodation offered by Fitzrovia's dilapidated Georgian tenements, the Bengali Asian community, like the Greek-Cypriot, the Spanish, and the Chinese, who predominated during that time, at first had few English-speaking residents. The old Scala, which had shown the earliest colour films in the country in 1911-14, took on a new lease of life as an Indian cinema before it was demolished in 1971.

West End Fitzrovia remained smart. In the 1920s the London Season was

just fluttering, hardly alive; no longer needed as a marriage market for high society boys and girls, who were now increasingly seeking independence and income through work. Aristocratic landowners were selling property in their estates of St Marylebone, Euston and Camden. Lord Howard de Walden sold 40 acres around Great Portland Street at the end of the 1920s. Rich American heiresses walked into the limelight in Portland Place in the 1930s, glitzy, madcap and attention-seeking, adding their bit to the Americanisation of the London scene. The old court-based commercial rhythm of the Season gave way to the seasonal fashion changes of couture and modern retail. In the 1960s Doris Lessing could see the remnants of the garment industry still operating in the area, 'badly paid girls running up dresses and blouses on their machines'.[36] Many of the old workrooms were replaced by wholesale showrooms. Today visitors to Great Portland Street are still more likely to be fashion buyers, not shoppers.

In the wake of the centrifugal flow of manufacturing away from central London, came the westward expansion of the London office economy. Small businesses, some of which would grow into big businesses, were edging into Fitzrovia, as 20th century corporations grew and based their central offices in London.

On or about 1910 human character changed...And when human relations change there is at the same time a change in religion, conduct, politics, and literature.

Virginia Woolf

After the arrival of the Belgians, Charlotte Street became very gay. There were Bal Musettes all up the street. A big Belgian played an accordian and everyone danced and a hat was taken round after for halfpennies, as they do in France and Belgium in work people's dances.

Nina Hamnett

The Georgian town house had an intrinsic appeal for small business. Its layered interior was easily appropriated into ground floor shop, two floors of offices or workshop, while the servants quarters at the top made an ideal flat. The larger, once grand houses such as those of Fitzroy Square made good small hotels, schools, clubs, offices, as well as excellent studios, with their high ceilings and tall sash windows and elegant proportions. Dirt cheap when Fitzroy Square was at its seedy, down-at-heel, turn-of-the-century worst, and the writers and artists who make their appearance as characters in this book found them delightfully unstuffy, and suitable on all counts. In the 1880s, half of Fitzroy Square was still residential. Between 1940 and 1970 the number of business-occupied premises in the Square rose from 40 to 70, and only a couple of houses were left in private hands.

The structure of 18th century Fitzrovia was, paradoxically, both its weakness and its strength. It was the malleable nature of the lime mortar used for cement, the soft wood of its timberwork and joists, that gave the terraces a flexibility that endured the ground-shaking bombardments of the blitz on London during the second world war. It was the changing fortunes of its landownership that produced its quixotic 20th century character, a mosaic hybrid that has already metamorphosised into a different blend at the start of the 21st century. The very conditions that made Fitzrovia affordable to immigrants struggling to make a living in a foreign environment, made them vulnerable, especially if they did not speak English.

Two women enjoy their newspapers in a Lyons Teashop (1953).

In 1974 England converted to natural gas but by November the following year, the appliances used by Bengali and Chinese tenants in overcrowded houses on Goodge Place remained unconnected. The local firm sub-contracted by the North Thames Gas Board had failed in its object. Racism was one factor, profiteering another. The sub-contracting workmen were deliberately negligent, entering the houses, then walking right out again. Inter-ethnic hostilities were revealed. It was estimated that the St Pancras side of Fitzrovia at the time had a population that was 60% immigrant, and the subcontractors were Indian. It was a combustible situation – natural gas was shooting two feet into the air from the cooking stoves, threatening to explode any minute. One tenant was even still using gas lighting. The people who alerted the Gas Board were from the Fitzrovian newspaper, the *Tower*, set up a year earlier by local community activists. Since re-named *Fitzrovia News*, it was part of a surge of new organisations, including the Fitzrovia Neighbourhood Association and the annual Fitzrovia festival, that came into being during 1974-75 when local residents, energised, politicised and idealistic, were determined to conserve the best of Fitzrovia for its residents and save its buildings from developers.

The wartime blitz had left strange ruins. In the middle of the Schmidt's premises, a burned-out house had not been re-built as late as the 1970s. And by then Fitzrovia property was being sought out, often brutally, by developers keen to buy up the kaleidoscope streets of old terraces and replace them with office skyscrapers. Judith Thomas, a resident during the 1960s and 70s, whose flat was the *Tower* newspaper's office for several years, remembers eastern Fitzrovia when it was like a 'war zone' under continual threat from developers, 'you went round with your eyes peeled. Six buildings that were listed in Whitfield Street were knocked down overnight'. In the days before the heritage industry, it was largely due to the efforts of such community-minded activists that many areas of London were preserved. The air was always full of building dust, and huge cranes. For the people who lived there it was like a return to the 19th century. Landlords who wanted to sell did not maintain the properties, and residential Fitzrovia was substantially reduced. 'Sweet little terraces with apple trees at the back, small warehouses, a dairy, and the old silver-smiths in Tudor Place' all went[37]. The Fitzrovian residents group lost a four-year campaign to prevent developers from the giant musical and electrical group, EMI, from building the massive grey edifice that now spans a block on the middle of west-side Tottenham Court Road. A second planning inquiry, at which they had argued for the need for housing for local people, was overturned by the Labour Government Environment Secretary, Anthony Crosland, in July, 1975 – and EMI never moved into the building.

But there were other voices that were to make a powerful impact in the cultural life of the country. They were in Fitzrovia, they were musical and often black. In the 1930s Charlotte Street had a sufficient black presence for one author, extolling the cosmopolitan spirit of London in 1935, to write 'negroes seem to make Charlotte Street their own'.[38] It was not until after the second world war, during which 8,000 West Indians had served in the RAF, and the passing of the British Nationality Act in 1948, that migrants from the West Indies began to arrive in large numbers, seeking work, and, often, having to accept a real drop in status. For those without relatives or family, housing was hard to come by. Landlords discriminated, 'No coloureds' was a frequent response. But in Fitzrovia some found rooms, or entertainment. Some of the Fitrovia basement music dives became the jazz clubs of the 1950s, and their sounds were a black-white mix, as much European-influenced as American, and not perceived to be a singular musical language.

Sensationalist press reports focused on the packets of hemp and knives found discarded on the floor of the Paramount Dance Hall, on Tottenham Road, when it was raided by the police in 1950. 'The coloured instrumentalists in the bands in these places are often under the influence of the drug which keeps them going and stimulates them in their fantastic jive sessions', wrote Arthur Tietjen, fanning perceptions of the Black British as extraordinary and exotic, sexualised and different, dressed in flamboyant suits, and peddling reefers to white girls 'craving excitement'.[39]

Bertorelli's menu of 1938 reproduced to celebrate its 60th anniversary.

My first job was marking up with long loops of thread and then cutting out very carefully; we all wore white arm-cuffs so as not to mark the material.

Elena Salvoni on working at Dorville Models, Mortimer Street

A myriad of other voices whispered, shouted, until they were hoarse, sang, recited, cried, through the smoky bars of the Fitzrovia pubs during the convulsions of the second world war. In blitz-torn London, spirits and wine were hard to buy, and the pubs were a world of their own. Foreign uniforms, French, Polish, Dutch, Belgian, deserters, conscientious objectors, con-men, students, mixed with literary editors, poets, writers bewailing their war-induced sense of intellectual futility, introspective and incestuous to a degree in the artificially compressed environs of those years. Women writers seem to have been few on the ground. There were faded women artists, and prostitutes, and ordinary women, who lived or worked there, whose voices have not been recorded. It was where homosexuals could meet, a sub-culture that continued, despite police prosecution, until homosexuality was decriminalised two decades later.

Fitzrovia might have developed a unique and distinct character, but it has also had a wider national impact. Just as influential as its famous, pioneering hospitals, polytechnic and university, has been its media presence. Such as the establishment of the BBC's Broadcasting House, established on its western artery – 2-8 Portland Place and 1-7 Langham Street. Between 1922, when BBC radio broadcasts were first transmitted, and 1931, when the organisation first moved into the Portland stone-clad purpose-built building, the clipped BBC accents reported on startling events: a Labour government in 1924, voting 'flappers', the nine-day General Strike of 1926, the onset of the depression.

Throughout the 1930s depression, the mood in Fitzrovia's night-spots, the night clubs, the dance halls, continued to swing. Out-of-hours drink clubs, jazz dives, bohemian pubs like the Fitzroy Tavern with its honky tonk piano, the Wheatsheaf with its Younger's Scotch Ale (which was to appear in the novels of Anthony Powell), and the George, where aspirant writers hoped to strike up a conversation with BBC editors and producers. Then the standardised BBC vowels seemed to represent the voice of the people.

During the previous three centuries the inhabitants of Fitzrovia achieved, broadly speaking, three categories of rights: the civil rights of the 18th century, the political rights of the 19th century and the social rights of the 20th century. Class hierarchies that once shaped character to patterns of deference and deferral, authority and arrogance, have today been much eroded. Humour, failings, absurd collisions between character and incident, have also forged the character of Fitzrovia so far. 'What is character but the determination of incident? What is incident but the illustration of character?' wrote Henry James[40]. Over the last century the artists of Fitzrovia unhinged 'character' from some of its exterior underpinnings. The inner qualities, of consciousness, of the unconscious, and of emotion, feeling, play out.

After post-war rationing came the reconstruction years. During the hyper-conformism, everyone-in-their-place 1950s, Fitzrovia again became the cultural power-point for a new age. The beat generation brought up with the benefits of the welfare state, in a boom economy, frustrated with the old establishment hierarchies, began to mingle through music. Jazz, folk and skiffle transmuted into rock in its basement clubs and cafés. Again Fitzrovia was to be ideally placed; it was near the welter of new media industries, which spanned advertising, fashion, photography, magazine publishing, film production companies, and the book publishers who were still located in Bloomsbury. Briefly, London was in the spotlight, and when it dimmed in the 1970s, and the exuberance and the gloss of the 1960s faded, the clubs that honeycombed through the Fitzrovian length of Oxford Street took on the punk style-reaction. Fitzrovia was to turn into a stamping ground for a different Britain. Margaret Thatcher's government took the fetters off market forces. Alongside

this neo-liberal disestablishment, a new, less culturally homogeneous Britain was already becoming more visible, more audible.

Fitzrovia's media have contributed to the democratisation of the culture over the last half century. In 1970 the Independent Television News studios started broadcasting from 48 Wells Street, and Thames Television from 306 Euston Road. In 1982, they were joined by Channel Four on Fitzrovia's main drag, at 60 Charlotte Street, with its remit to represent outsider Britain, and to enfold the marginal – a multicultural rainbow cake. (In 1990 ITN moved out, to Grays Inn Road, and Channel Four moved to Horseferry Road in 1994.)

Just as television, at its best, brought people together and mediated their differences, so has the Fitzrovia community. For example, qualities of loyalty and commitment characterise the Fitzrovia Neighbourhood Centre, opened at 39 Tottenham Street in 1975. Canadian born Dave Ferris has worked there since 1976, Bangladeshi Samina Dewan has been there since 1989 (the first Nepali people settled in Whitfield Street in 1965), and Nichola Charalambou, who has Greek Cypriot ancestry, has worked there since 1999 (the first Cypriots settled in the area in the 1930s).

Layers of complexity have been added to Fitzrovia's communications infrastructure. In 1954 the increase in long distance telephone calls siphoned through the focal point for London's trunk call system, the Museum Telephone Exchange in Howland Street, plus the addition of new commercial television to the existing channels, pointed up the need for future network expansion. Located on land owned by the Post Office behind the telephone exchange, work was started on the British Telecom Tower in 1961. It was designed by the Chief Architect's Division of the Ministry of Public Buildings and Works, to meet the requirements specified by the Post Office (now Consignia), and the main contractors were Peter Lind and Co Ltd. During its design, news arrived of other international towers, which had not only restaurants but revolving restaurants. The structural engineers and architects were not to be outdone, and, to the consternation of the planning authorities and the fire brigade, a restaurant with a revolving floor was added to its

LANDSCAPE WITH FIGURES – III by Osbert Lancaster

Fitzrovia in wartime. Outside the Marquis of Gransby a fiddle player busks on the corner, and a sailor chats up two good-time girls. Military men are everywhere. A pair of sharp-suited spivs cross the street, an American GI gets directions from a helmeted policeman, and a woman with her shopping basket passes the time of a day with a local patron. A literary couple (glasses, bicycle) are about to enter the Café Suisse.

George Orwell...sometimes appeared in the Wheatsheaf or the Fitzroy Tavern to down a silent half.

Anthony Burgess

For 75 years the family firm of Schmidt's made the best wurst in town. The shop on Charlotte Street stayed open 365 days a year, its windows festooned with 33 varieties of Continental sausage which were made fresh daily, allowed to cool overnight, and hung on the hook behind the counter the next morning.

You won't be able to feel it yourself, or even hear the wind through the triple glazing, but if you are lunching up there in strong gale conditions, you may notice, as we have, that your soup is gently swaying in its bowl.

Structural engineer, British Telecom Tower

original observation galley. In 1966 the glittering sheath of steel and glass, with its necklace of microwave signalling dishes, soaring 650 feet up from the blue clay subsoil (189 metres from ground level), was opened to the public. A giant minaret, a tower of Babel, it is the nerve centre of the city's telecommunications system, beaming out to relay stations at 30 mile intervals, throughout the British Isles, including satellite transmission and services for cellular radio and cable television. A bomb explosion on the night of October 31, 1971, shattered its viewing galleries, which have since been closed to the public (no individual or group has ever been finally identified as responsible for the bombing).

Wildness, with its vibrant energy, its capacity for destruction as well as its fertility, has always been part of the Fitzrovian human landscape, and it has not lost is capacity to surprise. The character of Fitzrovia today has attitude. It's never been 'NIMBY', said a recent FNA Annual Report[41]. Fitzrovia shows a continuing tolerance, and a willingness to take on the new.

But when the Cleveland Street Needle Exchange for drug addicts was set up without consultation by the Health Authority in 1987 in a residential block, the tolerance of Fitzrovians was stretched beyond its limits. The consequences of discarded needles that were a danger to local children, the fact that Fitzrovia was turned into the nationally known druggies' capital, with its concomitant dangers and abuses, meant there had to be damage limitation. Measures undertaken by the Fitzrovia Neighbourhood Association have included a campaign to limit the hours of the opening of the needle exchange, demanding that at least 80% of old needles should be returned, and the extension of the service to include local pharmacies, such as Boots.

'Whose Street? Our Street' shouted some of the 3,000 protestors on Oxford Circus, in the afternoon of May Day 2001[42]. They were demonstrating against global corporate capitalism, for cancelling third world debt and to save the environment. Along with bystanders and tourists, they were penned in by twice their number of police, some dressed in riot gear, stationed at 25 yard intervals along Oxford Street, where one in five department stores windows had been protectively boarded up, temporarily and surreally emptying the surrounding streets of traffic for nine hours. A pagan celebration and worker's celebratory holiday, turned into an effectively squashed buzz, with its sting taken out.

But the new theme restaurants and fast-food outlets are also stirring up fresh concerns for residents. Local residents say that the 22 planning applications for air-conditioning plants registered in the year 2000 will contribute to the already over-heating mini-climate of central London, and add further percussive hum to the background noise. Proposed changes to licensed opening hours threaten more, not less, noise for local residents from drinkers and clubbers, based on the experience of Westminster, where public disorder incidents now peak at 3 a.m. Nude lap-dancing at the Embassy Rooms, on the top end of Tottenham Court road, and the licensing of a One-on-One 'Adult Centre' sex shop are making the striptease clubs such as Capricorn at 32 Goodge Street, or Jacks at 38 Goodge Street, seem quaintly old-fashioned. Plans for cycle routes, for making parts of Fitzrovia a traffic-clear zone, and the building of a massive new hospital which will stretch along Euston Road replacing local hospitals including the Middlesex and University College Hospital, will alter the Fitzrovian map considerably.

Old traditions are being continued in new ways. The discontinuities of consciousness expressed in the art and culture that sprung from Fitzrovia spectacularly over the last century are mirrored in its urban geography. These contradictory architectural and historical signatures are making for a post-modern Fitzrovia. The west of Fitzrovia with its classicism, its embassies, and treasure houses of traditional expertise and authority, such as the Royal Institute of British Architecture, is never bland. There is an elegantly re-furbished café in RIBA's 1930s HQ. Eastwards, alongside the new foodie institutions, such as Villandry, and the sand-blasted glass fronts of the new cafés, there is the cobbled lane of Goodge Place, or the wrought iron curlicues on the Foley Street underground (closed) loo, or the tiled frontage of the Langham Place nurses home, or the chequered brick (more expensive than stone) and the multi-coloured marble and muralled interior of the Gothic revival All Saints ('free from all signs of timidity or incapacity', said John Ruskin[43]). The words *TJ Boulting, stove manufactory, established 1808*, glimpsed in *Karaoke*, partially filmed in Fitzrovia, have not faded from the flats of 59 Riding House Street[44]. Nowadays, the modern designer of a lamp, or a sofa, would be happy to be selected by Purves & Purves, for display in its store opposite Habitat. In theatre spaces such as the Drill Hall, drama still pushes at the boundary of what is respectable or safe.

Today the art students are still there, in Fitzrovia, bicycling into the Slade, as are the doctors and nurses of the Middlesex, the medical students of University College, the neuroscientists, the would-be intelligentsia from Gower Street. Amidst the advertising agencies, art galleries, small publishers, the cyber-café, the new technology on sale in the precinct of lower Tottenham Court Road, again Fitzrovia is renewing itself commercially. It has retained several hard-won, proudly begotten institutions of a democratic culture. It remains an exceptional combination, both a city space and a domestic space, with a children's playground, neighbourhood associations, and multi-ethnic-English identity, interesected and intertwined with urban commerce, service industries, tourism, big stores, finance. Some of the characters making their mark on contemporary Fitzrovia appear in these pages; but this book is for all those, unnamed, and yet to come, who will sustain and change Fitzrovia in the future. Their lives too will mark the area and give it a new existence, and another character.

Marsha Rowe

Larry Lynch cuts in the doorway at 79 Oxford Street...there is a vast black room heaving with music...a lot of boys and girls in this kinetic trance, dancing by themselves...The point is simply immersing yourself for one hour in The Life, every lunch hour.

Tom Wolfe

Last night there were riots in Central London – just like 1981. All the anarchist scum, class-war, random drop-outs and trouble-seekers had infiltrated the march and started beating up the police. But it is bad. Civil Disorder. Could cut either way, but I fear it will scare people into wanting a compromise ...In the corridors and the tea room people are now talking openly of ditching the Lady to save their skins.

Alan Clark, when anti-poll tax demonstrators churned into Oxford Street (1990)

CHAPTER I

Rabble-rousers, Radicals and Revolutionaries

The mutton pies and the skittle alley at Farthing Pye House, now called the Green Man (opposite today's Great Portland Street tube station), were popular with the artists and writers during the 1760s and 1770s, when the tavern was run by a 'very facetious man' called Price, and one of the regulars was the cheerful rabble-rouser JOHN WILKES (1727-97). Wilkes washed down his pies with large quantities of claret or port, when he canvassed there for votes among the 'forty-shilling freeholders' – small merchants, manufacturers, tradesmen and craftsmen – some of whom were making the radical demands for constitutional reform that re-surfaced with the Chartists in the next century.

The cry of 'Wilkes and Liberty' was first heard on the streets of London in 1763, after Wilkes was arrested for publishing his criticism of the Terms of Peace with France (Issue No.45 of the *North Briton*). He launched his challenge to the government's power to arrest unnamed writers and publishers, and was imprisoned for a week on the charge of seditious libel. Parliament ordered that the hangman should publicly burn all copies of the offending Issue No.45, and an angry crowd intervened, pelting the hangman with rubbish, and shouting 'Wilkes and Liberty'.

Port was again Wilkes' favourite tipple when he went to the Hell Fire Club in Wickham, where a group of men from the aristocracy indulged in esoteric and erotic rituals. Wilkes played a prank on the Club members by releasing a baboon dressed in a black robe and devil horns into a darkened room. The animal's alarmed shrieks sounded like the gibberings of the devil to the Club members and when the baboon jumped onto the back of the Earl of Sandwich, Lord of the Admirality, the man was terrified and begged for mercy. Subsequently the Earl held a grudge against Wilkes and plotted his downfall. Following Wilkes' arrest for publishing his obscene poem, *An Essay on Women*, Sandwich read out extensive passages from the pornographic *Essay* to parliament. He later declared that Wilkes would die, either of the pox or on the gallows. Wilkes' celebrated riposte was, 'That depends, my lord, on whether I embrace your principles or your mistress.'

Wilkes finally took his parliamentary seat for Middlesex in 1774, was twice appointed Lord Mayor of London, and was the first MP to propose elections by adult male suffrage.

London's largest and most disruptive disorder, the Gordon Riots (June 1780), was precipitated by the young LORD GEORGE GORDON (1751-93), who lived just outside of Fitzrovia, at 64 Welbeck Street. Gordon mobilised traditional anti-Popery and assembled 60,000 supporters to march on parliament with a petition of protest against the Catholic Relief Act. As they gathered outside and intimidated MPs leaving the chambers, Gordon found himself accosted by JAMES HOLYROYD (later first Earl of Sheffield) of Portland Place. Holyroyd seized Gordon by the throat and pronounced, 'My Lord George, do you intend to bring your rascally adherents into the House of Commons? If you do, the first man of them that enters, I will plunge my sword, not into *him*, but into *your* body.' The marchers subsequently went on

> The meanest mechanic, the poorest peasant and day labourer has important rights respecting his personal liberty, that of his wife and children, his property however inconsiderable, his wages...Some share therefore in the power of making those laws which deeply interest them...should be reserved even to this inferior but most useful set of men.
>
> John Wilkes

JOE DEAKIN

Joe Deakin was arrested carrying explosives on his way to the Autonomie Club. After the police staged bogus 'confessions' of his comrades in the next cell, he was persuaded to 'confess' and was jailed for five years.

JOHN WILKES engraving
by William Hogarth (1763)

*The popular hero of
metropolitan radicalism,
John Wilkes, worked the
crowd. He also distrusted the
volatile, emerging political
consciousness of the crowd.
Watching his cheering,
electoral supporters at the
hustings, he commented
cynically to his opponent,
'Do you suppose that there
are more fools or rogues in
that assembly?'*

**Mr Wilkes held a candle
to show a fine print of a
beautiful female figure
which hung in the room,
and pointed out the
elegant contour of the
bosom with the finger of
an arch connoisseur.**

James Boswell on
John Wilkes

the rampage, many mustering on Tottenham Court Road. Attacking Catholic chapels, shops and taverns, they controlled London for five days. After the Bank of England was threatened, the authorities brought in 10,000 troops; 200 rioters were killed, 450 were arrested, 25 were to be hanged. One of the protestors, a public hangman named Edward Dennis, was granted a pardon 'in order that he may hang his brother rioters'.

Gordon, acquitted of treason, was lampooned by Fitzrovian writer DR JOHN WOLCOTT (39 Howland Street) for 'burning poor papists for the love of God'. Seven years later, two years before the French revolution, Gordon was imprisoned for libelling Queen Marie Antoinette. He died in Newgate prison from jail fever, singing a song of the French revolution, and was buried in St James churchyard just north of the present-day Warren Street tube station.

Next to cause a storm was THOMAS PAINE (1737-1809) whose *Rights of Man* was published in 1792. Arguing that government's authority derived from a conquest of the governed and that Britain should become a republic, Paine was threatened with seditious libel, a charge that carried the death penalty. He went into hiding at 154 New Cavendish (7 *Upper Marylebone*) Street, the home of his friend, the radical poet THOMAS RICKMAN (pseudonym Clio, 1761-1834), who had a shop selling stationery. Paine had been sentenced to death in France the year before when he opposed the beheading of the king during the Revolution, a fate he himself escaped only because the jailer failed to notice the execution mark chalked inside his cell door.

Rickman described Paine's sojourn at New Cavendish Street as 'a quiet round of philosophical leisure and enjoyment…occupied in writing, in a small epistolary correspondence, in walking about with me to visit friends, occasionally lounging at coffee houses and public places, or being visited by a select few.' Paine took a nap after dinner, played games such as chess, dominos and draughts with the Rickman family, and sang and conversed with them in the evenings. Among his visitors were the radical John Horne Tooke, the writer Mary Wollstonecraft, the artist George Romney (for whom he sat at nearby 32 Cavendish Square), and the French and American ambassadors.

Another of Thomas Paine's visitors, the visionary poet William Blake, persuaded him to flee from imminent arrest, and Paine returned to France in September 1792. Thomas Rickman soon joined him to escape persecution while his wife continued to run their shop in New Cavendish Street and his sister-in-law ran the inn next door – probably the Wheatsheaf, at 166 New Cavendish (*4 Upper Marylebone*) Street.

The British government prosecuted Thomas Paine in his absence and suppressed publication of *Rights of Man*. Paine had been responding to *Reflections on the Revolution in France* by his former friend EDMUND BURKE (1729-1797), who denounced popular sovereignty and referred to the people as 'the swinish multitude'. Burke lived at 18 Charlotte Street, where his house was attacked by rioters, and at Queen Anne Street (on the site of present-day Broadcasting House).

Paine left Britain for America in 1774 where, because of his fiercely pro-independence reputation (it was Paine who coined the appellation 'United States of America'), he was outlawed by certain stage-coach companies, who feared that his presence would bring divine retribution, 'God's thunderbolts', on their coaches. An anti-independence official refused Paine the right to vote and he died in penury on an American farm, his *Rights of Man* banned in Britain until 1817.

THOMAS HARDY (1752-1832), a shoemaker and a good friend of Paine's, founded the London Corresponding Society (LCS), which kept its subscription at a penny a week, so that its membership – artisans, mechanics and tradesmen – could afford to pay. It was a period of rising prices in England and revolutionary events in Paris and, with aims such as universal suffrage, a demand that was deemed to be one of high treason, the LCS was seen as a threat by the government. The LCS president, MAURICE MARGAROT, a member of the branch which met in the Black Dog pub, in Market Place, at the bottom of Great Titchfield Street (*Market Row*), was arrested by armed police in November 1793 and brought to trial for sedition in March 1794. Hardy described Margarot as brave and defiant, 'a man of a strong philosophical understanding, ready wit, undaunted courage, and incorruptible integrity'. He was sentenced and transported to Australia for 14 years, after which he returned to England where he died in 1815.

A further trial of the LCS on charges of high treason in September 1794 brought Fitzrovians of opposing political views face to face. Sir John Scott, later Lord Eldon, the Attorney General, who lived at 42 Gower Street, was prosecuting. Those in the dock were the reformer Thomas Holcroft, of Clipstone Street, Thomas Hardy himself, John Horne Tooke (a friend of Paine who lived at Richmond Buildings, Dean Street), and John Thelwall. Although they were all acquitted, the government continued to harass the LCS. Habeas

The sublime and the ridiculous are often so nearly related that it is difficult to class them separately. One step above the sublime makes the ridiculous; and one step above the ridiculous makes the sublime again.

Thomas Paine

Thomas Paine by Auguste Millière, after engraving of 1793 by William Sharp, after George Romney (*c.*1880)

By arguing for the abolition of the monarchy in Rights of Man, *Thomas Paine broke century-old taboos, The book's outstanding success fired discussions on democracy and reform, before the prime minister, William Pitt, began his systematic repression to destroy any revolutionary tendencies in Britain.*

corpus was suspended and LCS members were interned for long periods without charge, during which collections were made for their families by a second-hand furniture dealer, JOHN POWELL, who lived at 8 Goodge Street. Later it emerged that Powell was a government spy.

Other prominent members of the LCS were ARTHUR SEALE, a printer who lived at 11 Goodge Place (*Cumberland Street*), producing cheap editions of revolutionary works and leaflets at his print shop at 160 Tottenham Court Road, and auctioneer ROBERT THOMPSON, who wrote and published popular songs about liberty. Both were members of the branch that met at the Marquis of Granby public house, 33 Eastcastle Street (*Castle Street East*).

Perhaps the member of the London Corresponding Society who achieved the most eminence was OLAUDAH EQUIANO (1745-97). A former slave, he had been kidnapped from a part of Africa that is now south-east Nigeria when he was aged about 11, and he worked in captivity for decades in the West Indies, in Virginia and the British Royal Navy, before gaining his freedom in 1766. For four months in 1776, Equiano worked again for his former employer, Dr Charles Irving, as an overseer, setting up a plantation in Central America. This involved purchasing some slaves on the doctor's behalf in Jamaica, 'and I chose them all of my own countrymen'. He was disgusted at how they were treated and returned to London.

LONDON CORRESPONDING SOCIETY MEDALLION

Radical artisans and self-educated working men who joined the London Corresponding Society debated for five nights in succession the question, 'Have we, who are Tradesmen, Shopkeepers and Mechanics, any right to obtain a Parliamentary Reform.' Two years later members of the society were arrested on charges of high treason.

In 1788 Equiano (baptised Gustavus Vassa in 1759) moved to 13 Tottenham Street and, a year later, moved to what is now 73 Riding House Street (*10 Union Street*) where he wrote his autobiography (as recorded on a green plaque erected on the site in 2000). Published in 1789, its first 300 subscribers included artists, opponents of the slave trade, politicians, members of the aristocracy, of the royal family, and fellow Black Britons. In vivid prose, Equiano described the cruelty and brutality of his slave experience, 'Torture, murder, and every imaginable barbarity and iniquity, are practised upon the poor slaves with impunity. I hope the slave trade will be abolished.'

Equiano organised Black Poor, which was based in Warren Street. Among atrocities exposed by Black Poor was the throwing overboard of 130 sick slaves from a ship at sea, as insurance company policy was to pay out for drowned slaves, but not for any who had died on board. Equiano married an English woman, Susan Cullen, in 1792 and they had two daughters.

The last series of big meetings of the LCS were held at the Store Street dancing rooms (1794), at Marylebone Fields just west of Cleveland Street (December 1795), and at St Pancras (1797). At the latter, mounted soldiers dispersed the members and arrested the leaders. The LCS was suppressed by an Act of Parliament in 1799, but many of its members became involved in the Chartist movement, which had similar aims and was strong in the area.

The Latin American revolutionary FRANCISCO DE MIRANDA (1750-1816) lived at 58 Grafton Way (*Grafton Street*) between 1797 and 1810*, where he was visited by SIMON BOLIVAR (1783-1830), a comrade who later turned against him, and BERNARDO O'HIGGINS (1778-1842), the future liberator of Chile, to whom he gave lessons in mathematics.

Miranda was born in Venezuela, then under Spanish rule. He had an affair with Catherine the Great in Russia in 1787, and in 1792 he fought as a general in the French army, in support of the 1789 French revolution. Arriving in London he formed a circle with other Latin Americans dedicated to independence. While at Grafton Way, Miranda had a relationship with an English woman called Sarah Andrews. They had two sons – Francisco, who was to become a soldier fighting for Bolivar, and who was executed in 1831 on unspecified charges, and Leandro, who went on to found Venezuela's first bank after the country had achieved independence.

* There is some dispute about when Miranda first moved to Grafton Way. In *Liberators* Robert Harvey writes that it was the year *1798*, and he gives the address as *27* Grafton Way (possibly the original of No.*58*). An English Heritage blue plaque at the site gives the year as *1802* while, next to it, a British Council memorial stone cites *1803*.

In 1806 Miranda attempted to seize power in Venezuela. He failed, but a successful revolution followed, and in 1811 Miranda was declared leader of the new independent republic. A royalist counter-revolution ousted Miranda from power a year later. He was arrested by Bolívar and spent the rest of his life imprisoned in Spain.

Simón Bolívar, later known as the 'Washington of South America', threw all his energy into the independence movement following the death of his wife from yellow-fever, soon after they were married in 1802. He succeeded in driving the Spanish out of Venezuela (where he was appointed the first

Olaudah Equiano,
or
GUSTAVUS VASSA,
the African?

When you make men slaves, you deprive them of half their virtue, you set them, in your own conduct, an example of fraud, rapine, and cruelty, and compel them to live with you in a state of war; and yet you complain that they are not honest and faithful!

Olaudah Equiano

Engraving of OLAUDAH EQUIANO from the frontispiece of *The Interesting Narrative of the Life of Olaudah Equiano*, or *Gustavus Vassa, The African.*

In 1766 Olaudah Equiano chose to buy his freedom from slavery (a process called 'redemption') rather than escape. He arrived back in London in 1786, and took a leading role in the movement to abolish the African slave trade.

president), out of Colombia and Peru (where he was declared leader), and also
out of Ecuador and northern Peru (Bolivia, established 1825). He contracted
tuberculosis and, upon realising that one of its symptoms, itching genitals,
could be eased by sex, he risked capture by the Spanish army while he waited
for his lover to arrive before giving his soldiers the order to march. He was
later exiled from Venezuela and he died in poverty in Colombia.

ROBERT OWEN (1771-1858), the philanthropic, industrialist reformer who was
to inspire many in the socialist and co-operative movement, lived at 3
Devonshire Street, on the corner of Hallam Street (49 Charlotte Street), in 1817.
He set up the National Equitable Labour Exchange at 4 Charlotte Street in
1833, where he tried to put into practice his idea that services could be
exchanged, using a credit system of labour notes. When this failed he opened
a school at the same address in 1834, for which half the fees had to be paid in
labour notes. Others in the Owenite movement set up the Scientific and
Literary Institute at 36 Whitfield Street in 1840.

THOMAS SPENCE (1750-1814) founded a radical debating club that met at the
Cock tavern in Grafton Way and he published and sold tracts from 9 Oxford
Street. His followers, the Spenceans, believed that land should be shared
equally, 'the land is the people's farm'. Spence was, in the words of E.P.
Thompson, 'one of the only Jacobin propagandists to address his writing to
working women themselves', and he championed the rights of the common
people to divorce. When Spence died, his followers carried his coffin up
Tottenham Court Road to be buried in St James's, Hampstead Road, just
north of Warren Street station.

Among the Spenceans who continued to meet at the Cock was the poet
P.B. Shelley, who wrote *The Mask of Anarchy* after the Peterloo Massacre (when
11 out of over 60,000 demonstrators for constitutional reform were killed and
hundreds injured in a field outside Manchester in 1819).

Another Spencean, JOHN THOMAS BRUNT (1782-1820), expressed his anger at

FRANCISCO DE MIRANDA,
the precursor of Latin
American independence,
in prison.

*After successfully
overthrowing the Spanish in
Venezuela, de Miranda was
arrested in 1810 and
imprisoned in Cadiz, where
he died five years later.*

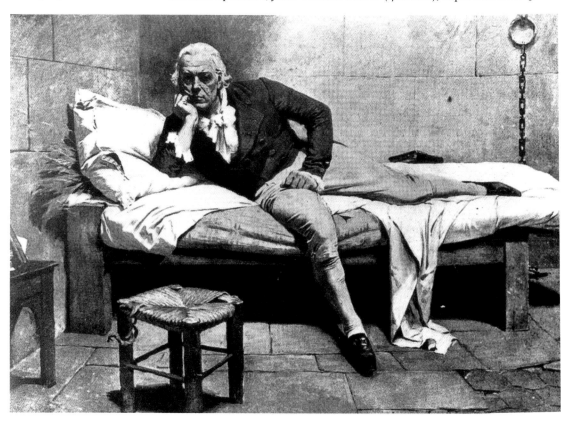

the sheer horror of the events by declaring that 'nothing was too severe for men who had not only caused, but even applauded, the dreadful scenes which occurred there'. Brunt, a bootmaker, had been born, raised and, aged 14, apprenticed, in Riding House (*Union*) Street. In 1820, during the economic dislocation and unemployment following the Napoleonic wars, Brunt's earnings were reduced from £4 to 10s. a week – not enough to support his family. Brunt and some other Spenceans, were convinced that just one, initial revolutionary coup would set off a movement to rescue the country from repression. They were persuaded into a plot, actively encouraged by a government *agent provocateur*, George Edwards, who provided them not only with false information but also with blunderbusses, cutlasses, pistols and pikes. On February 22 they set off along Oxford Street, making for a stable loft in Cato Street, where they planned to prepare to assassinate members of the Cabinet who were dining at Grosvenor Square. The loft was hired by a cowman, John Firth, who had regularly attended Spencean meetings at the Cock.

JAMES INGS, Cato Street conspirator

Ings wrote to his wife, Celia, from prison, 'Now, my dear, I hope you will bear in mind that the cause of my being consigned to the scaffold was a pure motive. I thought I should have rendered my starving fellow-men, women, and children, a service.'

The dinner was a ploy, the Spenceans were ambushed and arrested, and the government used the subsequent trial as a pretext for repressive measures against the growing talk of reform and the perceived threat of insurrection around the country.

Brunt, second in command, was found guilty and sentenced to death. He defended himself by saying he had acted for the public good against the enemies of the people and would continue to fight for liberty 'with the last nerve of his body', even if it meant death. In his Newgate cell on April 30, 1820, he wrote:

Tho' in a cell I'm close confined,
No fears alarm the noble mind;
Tho' death itself appears in view,
Daunts not the soul sincerely true!
Let Sidmouth and his base colleagues
Cajole and plot their dark intrigues;
Still each Briton's last words shall be,
Oh! Give me death or liberty!

As the rope was placed around his neck, he nodded derisively at the coffin in front of the scaffold, spurned the offered blindfold, took a pinch of snuff and declaimed, 'It is better to die free than to live like slaves'.

Executed alongside Brunt were Arthur Thistlwood (who lived just north of Fitzroy Street at 40 Stanhope Street), William Davidson (Jamaican born cabinet-maker, a 'man of colour'), James Ings (unemployed butcher), and Richard Tidd (shoemaker).

The masked executioner who displayed the victims' heads was nearly castrated by the angry spectators.

Brunt's widow, Mary Welch, along with the other widows, had petitioned the king for access so that they may 'shed a silent tear over their mutilated remains 'ere they are consigned to the tomb'. Their request was dismissed and the coffins were filled with quicklime and buried in an underground passage near the cells.

THOMAS BRUNT, Cato Street conspirator

Brunt was executed on May 1, 1820. This drawing was published the following day.

Another five Spenceans who had regularly visited the Cock, John Harrison (baker), James Wilson and John Strange (tailors), Michael Bradburn (carpenter), and Charles Cooper (shoemaker), were transported for life.

Nevertheless, reformist agitation for manhood suffrage continued, reaching a wide audience through the radical 'unstamped' press. A demonstration by the National Union of Working Classes (a forerunner of the Chartist London Working Men's Association, 1836) was violently attacked by police in 1833 and during the armed battle that ensued a police constable was fatally stabbed. One of those arrested, a carpenter called JAMES HUTCHINSON, lived at 1 Tudor Place between 19 and 20 Tottenham Court Road (now built over). Anti-police feeling was so high, however, that all charges against him were dropped. The inquest returned a verdict of justifiable homicide and those accused of the stabbing were acquitted.

One of the most famous nationalists of his generation, DANIEL O'CONNELL (1775-1847), MP for Kilkenny, Ireland, moved to Langham Place in 1836. Hailed as 'the liberator' for his instrumental role in the passing of the Catholic Emancipation Bill, he was elected in 1828, then denied his seat because he was a Catholic, which triggered off a public clamour for change.

Whilst O'Connell lived in Fitzrovia, he was challenged to a duel by the future prime minister, Benjamin Disraeli, whom he had insulted as 'an abominable, foul and atrocious miscreant'. However O'Connell had killed an opponent in a previous duel and vowed never to fight another. Frustrated, Disraeli caused a commotion outside O'Connell's house, where he was arrested by Marylebone police and bound over to keep the peace.

O'Connell was hostile to trade unionism, to minimum rates of pay, and in favour of child labour. He helped to vote through the Reform Bill in 1832, but then opposed social reforms. In Ireland he campaigned for repeal of the union with England. A skilled orator, he drew huge crowds. After a rally at Tara in 1843 attracted a million people, an even bigger rally was planned for Dublin but banned by the nervous English government. When O'Connell agreed to this he lost much public support from the Irish, yet the English government still charged him with making seditious speeches and 'attempting to alter the constitution by force', and sentenced him to a year in prison.

FEARGUS O'CONNOR (1794-1855), a leading charismatic Chartist orator, stayed at the Boar and Castle Inn at 14 (6) Oxford Street by the corner of Tottenham Court Road in 1822. An Irish MP from 1832 to 1835, he was unseated after losing his property qualifications. In 1835 he formed the Great Radical Association at Marylebone, which eventually merged with the Chartists. He edited the official Chartist organ, *Northern Star*, and was jailed for 18 months for seditious libel in 1840.

In May 1842 he was involved in the Oxford Street march attempting to block the movement of troops up Tottenham Court Road on their way north, where they were to be deployed against Chartists. In August, he took part in another march protesting against the arrest of a number of Marylebone Chartists (including a shoemaker and a tailor).

On April 10, 1848, a year of Europe-wide popular revolts, O'Connor gave an impassioned speech to a large crowd outside 36 Whitfield Street (home of the Albert Room dancing academy and the Owenite Scientific and Literary Institute) before it joined the big Chartist rally at Kennington Common. In May there was another large Chartist march along Oxford Street and in July a large detachment of police, armed with cutlasses, was sent to Tottenham Court Road to keep order. That Christmas a shop in Windmill Street, just below Goodge Street, sold 'Chartist pork' – cuts of meat from pigs reared on Chartist experimental co-operative farms.

CHARLES MURRAY, a shoemaker who lived in Riding House (49 *Union*) Street, directly opposite No.73, was elected secretary of the Soho Chartists (which included Fitzrovia) in 1852. Venues used by the Chartists for their meetings were Chesney's Rooms in Foley Street, the Bay Malton pub in Clipstone Street, the King & Queen pub at 1 Foley Street (where the Washington Brigade of the Chartists also met), and 11 Tottenham Court Road (home of a boot and shoe co-operative).

THE CATO STREET
CONSPIRATORS by George
Cruikshank (1820)

*Such visual satire reached a
wide audience. This shows
Smithers, foremost of the Bow
Street officers, stabbed with a
sword by Thistlewood.*

Murray and his brother James became members of the first International Working Men's Association, which met in Rathbone Place. Charles Murray also organised the Social and Political Education League that developed out of the Artisans Club (Newman Street, 1862) and met at 29 Eastcastle (*Castle*) Street, by Oxford Circus. He organised hundreds of lectures, inviting speakers such as the anarchist Peter Kropotkin and the socialist Sidney Webb. A keen internationalist Murray went to Kansas in 1872 to view an experiment in land-sharing, and he gave lectures about it on his return to London. Like many others, he thought that land nationalisation was a key element of any strategy to end inequality and exploitation. He organised revolutionary meetings in pubs such as the Spread Eagle, 8 Mortimer (*6 Charles*) Street in 1877, and one in Tottenham Street (probably the Lord Masons Arms which used to be at No.56) in 1881. By 1882 he was on the committee of the Marylebone Central Democratic Association which met in Ye Olde Surgeon Inn (*New Inn*) at 183 Tottenham Court Road. One of his fellow committee members was ADAM WEILER, a local cabinet-maker who had spent several months in jail for picketing in 1875.

Christian Socialists were among those who believed that co-operatives could eradicate the wretched conditions of sweated labour. The Working Tailors' Association flourished when it set up a co-operative at 34 Great Castle Street in February 1850. It was soon able to double its workforce to 24 and increase average pay by 12½% a week. It had its own library and weekly lectures. The Central Co-operative at 76 Charlotte Street was formed in the same year. The Boot & Shoe Co-operative was opened at 11 Tottenham Court Road in 1846 by the National Association of United Trades (devoted to 'Labour's Emancipation from Capitalist Tyranny') which had headquarters at 259 Tottenham Court Road.

Among the supporters of the Christian Socialist movement in the 1850s was the author CHARLES KINGSLEY (1819-75), who wrote *The Water Babies*, and THOMAS HUGHES (1822-96), author of *Tom Brown's Schooldays*.

Kingsley attended Chartist demonstrations and preached at St John the Evangelist church, 74 Charlotte Street, until the Bishop of London, who

The men died like heroes.
Ings, perhaps, was too
obstreperous in singing
'Death or Liberty', and
Thistlewood said, 'Be quiet,
Ings; we can die without all
this noise.'

John Cam Hobhouse, on
the executions of the Cato
Street conspirators

WILLIAM GODWIN and
THOMAS HOLCROFT at the
1794 Treason Trials,
sketched by Sir Thomas
Lawrence

*Two years earlier Thomas
Holcroft wrote to William
Godwin enthusing over
Paine's linking of political
and economic demands, 'Huy
for the New Jerusalem! The
millennium! And peace and
eternal beatitude be unto the
soul of Thomas Paine.'*

considered Kingsley's sermons too subversive, banned him from the pulpit. Kingsley's amusements including drawing erotic pictures for his devoted wife Fanny. He examined the links between sweated labour and chartism in his novel *Alton Locke, Tailor and Poet*, which described the lives of tailors, 'poor wretches who sit stifled in reeking garrets and workrooms, drinking in disease with every breath, bound in their prison-house of brick and iron, with their own funeral pall hanging over them, in that canopy of fog and poisonous smoke from their cradle to their grave.'

Kingsley visited his dying friend, the chemist Charles Mansfield (1819-55), in Middlesex Hospital, 2-4 Mortimer Street, after Mansfield was burned in an accident while producing benzol. Eventually Kingsley became a Liberal MP.

In 1840 Thomas Hughes intervened in a scuffle in Regent Street between the police and a gang of labourers who were trying to rescue a ragpicker from arrest. Hughes flung himself into the fray, holding the labourers at bay until police reinforcements arrived. However, when the labourers were dispersed and the police started to punch the rather sickly looking ragpicker, Hughes promised to testify on the ragpicker's behalf in court.

Hughes attended meetings of the First City of London Regiment (Royal Fusiliers) at St John's Institute in Cleveland Street, which moved to 33 Fitzroy Square in 1871. He left for the United States and set up a model community in Tennessee.

Many exiled revolutionaries took refuge in Fitzrovia. The Italian GUISEPPE MAZZINI (1805-72), a nationalist committed to the liberation of his country from Austrian rule and its unification into a republic, fled to London in 1837, after being sentenced to death on conspiracy charges. He lodged in a six-room flat in Goodge Street where the bed bugs appalled him, as did the dirt in the streets and the drunkenness of the local population. He preferred light ale to the local water, which he described as being full of worms and insects. For a while he sold sausages for a living. He attended weekly literary gatherings in Berners Street. Before long he moved to nearby 187 North Gower (*183 Gower*) Street, where he lived until 1840. Although he was an opponent of communism and atheism, Mazzini was seen as a threat, and imprisoned by the English authorities. While exiled in London he helped organise several Italian uprisings (one plan was to invade the Papal States in balloons) for which he was again sentenced to death in his absence. In 1848 he returned to Italy to form a Republic, which was soon overthrown. After a spell back in London he returned to Italy again in 1868, and was imprisoned briefly for conspiracy.

One of Mazzini's followers, the Italian terrorist FELINE ORSINI (1819-58), who accused the French emperor NAPOLEON III (1808-73) of betraying a promise to free Italy from Austrian rule, had escaped from an Austrian prison under sentence of death for high treason in 1856, and fled to London. While he was walking in Fitzroy Square one foggy day he was pelted with half-frozen balls of horse dung by young mudlarks. And it was at Fitzroy Square that he manufactured the bomb, which he took to Paris and threw at Napoleon III in an attempted assassination. The emperor received only a grazed nose, but eight bystanders were killed and 156 were injured. Before Orsini was guillotined in front of a huge crowd, he chanted 'Viva l'Italia! Viva la Francia!'

Orsini's desire was fulfilled four years later when Napoleon was persuaded by the alluring charms of a 19-year-old Sardinian noblewoman, the Countess di Castiglione, into waging war to liberate Italy – or so it was rumoured. When he made love to her his moustache is supposed to have drooped because the wax holding it up melted.

The exiled emperor Napoleon III had previously fled to London, where he stayed at the Langham Hotel, 1 Portland Place. He lived with Elizabeth Howard (on whom he later bestowed the title of Countess) from 1846 to 1848 in Holles Street, Cavendish Square (and was imprisoned for a short while for breaking the lease).

Another exile, the Hungarian revolutionary LAJOS KOSSUTH (1802-94), lived at 129 Gower Street from 1858 to 1859 following his release from a Turkish prison for planning an unsuccessful uprising in Hungary. Earlier he had spent three years in jail for publishing a revolutionary journal and, while living at Gower Street, he tried to incite further nationalist revolts without success. A qualified lawyer, he believed that 'Despotism and oppression never yet were beaten except by heroic resistance'. He published three volumes of his autobiography *Memories of My Exile*. The sign that hangs over a pub named after him, *The Independent*, 65 Bingfield Street, off Caledonian Road in north London, carries his image.

The First International met in Rathbone Place in the 1860s. One of the principal participants, KARL MARX (1818-83), knew the place well. During the 1850s Marx practised fencing with EMANUEL BARTHELEMY at Barthelemy's salon in Rathbone Place, where, according to Wilhelm Liebknecht, Marx 'lustily gave battle to the Frenchman...what Marx lacked in science he tried to make up in aggressiveness...unless you were cool he could really startle you'. Barthelemy had fought to the last barricade to defend the Paris uprising in

Education is the bread of the soul.

Guiseppe Mazzini

1848. A fervent revolutionary, he later fell out with Marx who, he said, 'would not conspire and disturb the peace'.

In the 1850s Marx, who had a prodigious capacity for drink, went on a pub-crawl with a German friend, Edgar Bauer. They called at all of Tottenham Court Road's pubs: Blue Posts at 6 (demolished 1998), Black Horse at 19, Rising Sun (which is still there) at 46, Rose & Crown at 62, Talbot at 64, Kings Arms at 82, Bulls Head at 101, Roebuck (now the Court) at 108, Northumberland Arms (also still there) at 119, Southampton Arms at 141, Plasterers' Arms at 157, Mortimer Arms (still exists at 174), New Inn (since renamed Ye Olde Surgeon) at 183-6, Apollo at 191, White Hart at 199, Italian (now Jack Horner) at 236, Fox & Hounds at 264, and Horseshoe (demolished 1983) at 267.

Marx and Bauer were well oiled by the last pub, where they encountered a group of 'Odd Fellows' out on a celebration. Everything went smoothly until politics, and in particular patriotism, cropped up in the conversation. At first the groups exchanged 'fluent' arguments, then Marx and Bauer began proclaiming the value of all things German and insulting English culture. A fight broke out, and the two Germans, outnumbered, beat 'a dignified retreat'. Stumbling over paving stones at 2 a.m., remembering their days of 'mad student pranks', they smashed four or five gas lamps before a policeman arrived, and they hared away through alleys and back yards, until they arrived at Marx's lodgings in nearby Dean Street.

The funeral of Marx's nine-year-old son, Henry Edgar (known affectionately as Mouche), who died of consumption and an inherited intestinal disorder, was held in Whitefield Tabernacle at 79 Tottenham Court Road in 1855. Marx was so distressed that he had to be restrained from hurling himself on the grave. A Prussian government spy was appalled by the wretched conditions in which the Marx family lived at nearby Dean Street (Nos.64 and 28, 1850-56), reporting that their rooms were like some foggy cave, filled with broken furniture and covered in dirt and dust.

> The philosophers have only *interpreted* the world, in various ways; the point is to *change* it.
>
> Karl Marx

When Marx arrived to address a meeting celebrating the first anniversary of the 1871 Paris Commune at St Georges Hall in Langham Place, the manager threw everyone out, and the meeting continued at Cercle d'Etudes, an inn in Torrington Place (*Francis Street*) off Tottenham Court Road.

Marx went to meetings of the Communist Club at the Blue Posts, 81 Newman Street, from 1874 to 1877, and in the basement of 49 Tottenham Street, where the Club moved in 1882. FREDERICK ENGELS (1820-1895) also frequented the Communist Club.

Marx dined frequently with H.M. HYNDMAN (1842-1921), leader of the Social Democratic Federation (who lived at nearby 10 Devonshire Street). Hyndman addressed a meeting commemorating the Paris Commune in Store Street in 1888, and was a regular at the Tottenham Street Communist Club, along with Bernard Shaw, Keir Hardie, Johann Most and others.

When the communists and anarchists split in 1882, the Communists took over the Tottenham Street club. As well as a choir, the club provided billiards and cheap meals for its members. A co-operative kitchen for communist refugees was also being run in Newman Passage around that time.

The anarchists set up the International Club in Stephen Mews (off Gresse Street, Rathbone Place) in 1883. Two years later the club was raided by the police, with the assistance of a group of civilians who were suspected of being plain-clothes police. They were all armed or carried staffs, and wounded many of those present. The police confiscated jars of beer among other items.

Two other anarchist clubs were started in the 1880s. One was in Whitfield Street. The other was the Autonomie Club, 32 Charlotte Street (1886), which later moved to 6 Windmill Street. By 1894, in addition to the number of

DANIEL O'CONNELL, Irish
Nationalist leader

*By his own admission,
O'Connell's climb-down in
Ireland enabled the English
government to concentrate its
attention on suppressing the
growing Chartist movement
at home.*

English anarchists who lived in the area – mainly tailors, shoemakers and
cabinet-makers – the *Evening News* claimed that there were 1,000 German
anarchists living near Middlesex Hospital and 400 French anarchists living in
Charlotte Street.

Among those to attend meetings of the First International at Rathbone
Place was WILLIAM TOWNSHEND. He was a 'tall, gaunt, kindly old shoemaker',
wrote the socialist author Max Beer, 'like Thomas Hardy's Jude'. Townshend
lived at 49 Tottenham Street (above the Communist Club) in 1895. He was an
avid collector of books, which he sold and lent from his house in Tottenham
Street, and lectured around Fitzrovian clubs until 1889. Later he died in
poverty.

The son of a domestic servant, FRANK KITZ, was a garment dyer, tramping
printer and prominent anarchist, whose favourite retort to other socialists was
that he 'needed no lectures upon surplus value'. He founded the Social
Democratic Club in 1871. The club met in the Spread Eagle, 8 Mortimer Street
(now Middlesex Hospital), and was dedicated to 'social enjoyment and
propagating the principles of social and political reform'.

An anarchist joiner called JOHANN NEVE was a member. Between 1877 and
1878 the club met at the Grafton Arms, 72 Grafton Way. In 1881, when Kitz
organised a meeting at a pub in Tottenham Street (probably the Lord Masons
Arms at No.56) against internment of Irish republicans, the landlord described
those present as 'some of the most red hot Fenians and dynamiters in
England'. During that same year Kitz went to a revolutionary conference at
Cleveland Hall, 54 Cleveland Street, and was among those raided at the
International Club in 1885.

**Anarchism, as a theory,
negatives society, and puts
man outside it. Now, man is
unthinkable outside
society. Man cannot live or
move outside it.**

William Morris

KARL MARX

Karl Marx settled in nearby Dean Street with his family in 1849, and researched Capital *in the library at the British Museum.*

Many languages were to be heard in Fitzrovia as nationalists and socialists arrived from Italy, Hungary, Poland, the Balkans, France and Germany. London offered a freedom of expression and opportunities to talk, meet and organise, for exiles fleeing Europe after the year of revolutions, 1848.

Another prominent anarchist and leading member of the International Club in Stephen Mews, JOHANN MOST (1846-1906), a bookbinder, spent 18 months in prison for incitement to murder heads of state. He wrote an article applauding the assassination of the Russian Tsar Alexander II and published instructions on the manufacture of dynamite and bombs, *Revolutionary Warfare*, after he had worked at a munitions factory in America just long enough to gain the necessary experience. He was also a member of the Whitfield Street anarchist club, where he helped to print the *Commonweal*. (This became the journal of the Socialist League and subsequent editors included William Morris, Charles Mowbray and David Nicoll).

A breakaway group, who were expelled from the Whitfield Street club because they opposed the collectivism of Most and supported the German anarchist JOSEF PEUKERT, formed the Autonomie Club at 32 Charlotte Street, then 6 Windmill Street. It hosted a revolutionary conference in 1890, attended by an Italian anarchist, ERRICO MALATESTA (1853-1932). He worked as an electrician and lived in nearby New Oxford Street having twice escaped from prison and survived being shot at by an American 'comrade'. (The Malatesta Anarchist Club, set up at 23 Percy Street in the 1950s, was named in his honour.)

The Autonomie Club made the headlines in 1892, when some of its members were given ten-year sentences for manufacturing a bomb. JOE DEAKIN, who was arrested in Tottenham Court Road on his way to the club, protested sincerely that he thought the explosives he was carrying were for use in Russia. He said that the scheme had been organised by AUGUSTE COULON, who lived at 19 Fitzroy Square. Suspected of being a police spy (he had been in the pay of the police for two years), Coulon was expelled from the Autonomie Club between the arrests and the trial, and barred from writing for *Commonweal* after 'celebrating the blowing up of a cow in Belgium as a great and good revolutionary act'.

Coulon's neighbour at 18 Fitzroy Square, the Italian anarchist JEAN BATTOLA, was working in a Soho shoemaking co-operative at the time of his arrest and was described as an exile 'burning with hatred against the tyranny that had driven him from his native land'. He took a defiant stance at the trial, turning the charges around and accusing his accusers (or the class they represented) of 'all the crimes of the age, of all the murders prompted by want, and all the suicides'. How many generals had been imprisoned for using weapons of death, he asked, declaring that society was based on sham, hypocrisy, and theft, 'Long live anarchy! It is anarchy that is the future of humanity and concord'. He was one of those who accused Coulon of supplying the bombs and of being in league with the police.

After the trial two editors of *Commonweal* were arrested. Battola served eight years of his ten-year term. DAVID NICOLL was sentenced to 18 months' hard labour for an article questioning whether the judge in the case, Justice 'Hanging' Hawkins, was 'fit to live'.

CHARLES MOWBRAY, a self-educated tailor, had declared at the Windmill Street conference that London's slums should be burned, and their inhabitants moved into West End mansions. He had argued in favour of the use of explosives ('propaganda by deed') and said at one meeting 'We have heard much of the doctrine of brotherhood and love tonight, but the doctrine of hate and vengeance is just as necessary and right'. He too was arrested, and taken into custody just hours after his wife, aged 35, died of consumption. Annie Besant, who organised the London matchgirls, looked after his children. William Morris put up bail so that Mowbray could attend his wife's funeral. Mowbray was charged with incitement to murder, but acquitted. A

ELEANOR MARX, *aged about 18, youngest daughter of Karl Marx*

Forced to abandon her acting career on the death of her father, she began to teach, and was soon active in the socialist movement, translating, writing, and helping to organise unskilled workers.

How I wish people didn't live in houses and didn't cook, and bake, and wash and clean! I fear I shall never, despite all efforts, develop into a decent Hausfrau.

Eleanor Marx

that she had committed suicide while 'labouring under mental derangement'.

Aveling's failure to collect Eleanor's ashes added to his unpopularity in certain circles. Four months later he died from kidney disease.

FREDERICK LESSNER (1825-1910) received Eleanor's ashes. A tailor by trade, and an old friend of the family, Lessner had been imprisoned in Germany for his revolutionary politics and (with Marx) launched *The Workman's Advocate*, the official journal of the International Working Men's Association. Later he witnessed the will of Engels; the other witness being Ludwig Freyberger (1865-1934) of 11 Gower Street, a liberal who sponged off Engels.

In 1902 the Russian leader V.I. LENIN (1870-1924) attended the grand re-opening of the Communist Club, when it moved from 49 Tottenham Street to new premises at 107 Charlotte Street, during his year of exile in London. His presence was pointed out to the young Frank Jackson, who later became the librarian at Marx Memorial Library on Clerkenwell Green. Later that year, in August (July in the Russian calandar) Lenin was at the Anglers Club (otherwise known as the English Club), in Charlotte Street, for the second congress of the Russian Social Democratic Party, which had been re-convened

after having been hounded out of Brussels by the police. At this historic congress the Mensheviks and the Bolsheviks parted company, an event of profound political significance that Lenin was to analyse in a pamphlet, *One Step Forward Two Steps Back*, published the following year. In February 1903, Lenin wrote to his mother describing a concert at Queen's Hall, Langham Place, where he and his wife 'were very pleased – especially by Tchaikovsky's last symphony (Symphonie Pathetique).'

JOSEF STALIN (1879-1953), who succeeded Lenin as head of the Soviet Union, is believed to have visited the Communist Club in Charlotte Street around 1910, when he was involved in Bolshevik activities in London. He was frequently seen in the Continental Café in Little Newport Street, Soho, as remembered by James Burley, 'The café was popular because it was only a short walk from the Communist Club in Charlotte Street. Josef Stalin used the Continental Café a lot. Josef Georgi he called himself. He was a bombastic little man, not very big. But there was always an air of mystery about him.'

While Stalin was in Charlotte Street in 1910, Alois, half-brother of the future Nazi second world war foe ADOLF HITLER (1889-1945), was living at 4

He was quite a pleasant fellow who would have gone to the stake for Socialism or Atheism, but with absolutely no conscience in his private life. He seduced every woman he met, and borrowed from every man.

George Bernard Shaw on Edward Aveling

Better to enjoy and suffer
than sit around with folded
arms. You know the only
true prayer? Please God,
lead me into temptation.

Jennie Lee

Percy Street with his wife Bridget. After Alois had left home at the age of 14, only young Adolf remained to take the full brunt of their father's bad temper. Bridget, whose maiden name was Dowling, married Alois at Marylebone registry office on June 3, 1910. Their son, William Hitler, later worked for an engineering firm in nearby Wigmore Street in 1929, and was the first to reveal, in 1939, that Hitler may have had a Jewish grandfather. According to Bridget, Adolf visited them in 1912, at the time when Charlotte Street was the main German area of London. So it is possible that Hitler and Stalin missed meeting each other in Charlotte Street by just two years.

The police finally raided and closed down the Communist Club in Charlotte Street in 1918. At the time REUBEN FALBER, future assistant general secretary of the Communist Party of Great Britain, was a four-year-old living at 35 Tottenham Street, where he was born. At the age of seven he had a nasty fall in the street, which left him with a permanently scarred face. He joined the Party in the 1930s, regarding it as the main bulwark against fascism. When he was acting general secretary of the Party in 1968, he issued a statement criticising the 'intervention' of Soviet and Warsaw Pact troops into Czechoslovakia, and calling for their removal. In 1991 it was revealed that he had laundered up to £100,000 a year between 1957 and 1979 from the Soviet embassy to fund illegal communist parties around the world.

At the start of the Spanish civil war in 1936, many British people joined the International Brigade to fight on behalf of the democratically elected republican government. Among them was WOGAN PHILLIPS (1902-93), later Lord Milford, the first Communist peer in parliament. He left the artist's studio at 8 Fitzroy Street, where he had lived for a year, and joined up with the republicans. He was wounded while driving an ambulance. On his return he visited Fitzroy Street to let the painter, Vanessa Bell, whose studio was on the floor below, know that her son, Julian, also an ambulance driver in Spain, was as yet safe and unharmed.

The introduction of the National Health Service, one of the greatest social reforms of the century, was masterminded by the firebrand Labour minister ANEURIN 'NYE' BEVAN (1897-1960), who, during the last years of his life, stayed in a poky flat at 35 Gosfield Street. With him was his wife, JENNIE LEE (1904-98), who took the pioneering step of creating the Open University when she was Minister for the Arts. She described the two-roomed flat as cheerless, appallingly furnished, and without a bath. They had used it simply as 'a camp where we could sleep' after late parliamentary sessions. The future Labour Party leader MICHAEL FOOT (b.1913), then editor of *Tribune*, used to visit the flat to collect articles that Nye had written. During the 1930s and 1940s Bevan and Foot were regulars in the Fitzroy Tavern at 16 Charlotte Street. When Bevan was at Gosfield Street, they preferred the Crown & Sceptre pub at 86 Great Titchfield Street.

Men of power have no
time to read; yet the men
who do not read are unfit
for power.

Michael Foot

During the 1950s, when many African countries were negotiating for their independence, Fitzrovia became a centre for students and exiled politicians from South Africa, as well as for Ghanians, Kenyans, and Tanzanians. South African exiles worked for the struggle against apartheid during the 1960s and 1970s at the offices of the African National Congress (ANC), 49-51 Rathbone Street. THABO MBEKI (b.1942) worked there from 1967 to 1970.

Expelled from school for his political activities when he was 17 years old, Thabo had been exiled to London in 1964 when his father, Govan, was sentenced to life imprisonment for sabotage and conspiracy against apartheid. Thabo was a member of the ANC choir, which practised in Fitzrovia. He was elected president of South Africa in 1999, to succeed Nelson Mandela.

Some ANC meetings were held at the home of sympathisers, Martin and

Fiona Green, 28 Tottenham Street. Mbeki and the others dined regularly at the Glory restaurant, 57 Goodge Street, not far from the office of the *African Communist* journal, over Morgan's Paints, 39 Goodge Street. The Anti-Apartheid Movement moved its office to 89 Charlotte Street in 1964 (its first office, in the basement of David Pitt's surgery, 200 Gower Street, having been burned down by right-wing extremists in 1961, when South Africa was forced out of the Commonwealth). Pubs used by the exiles included the Marlborough Arms at 36 Torrington Place, the Duke of York at 47 Rathbone Street, and the One Tun at 58 Goodge Street.

Among those to visit the ANC office in Rathbone Street was DULCIE SEPTEMBER (1953-88). Born in Western Cape, she became a teacher, but was forced out of the profession for her stand against the Bantu Education Act. She was jailed for five years for her political opposition to apartheid, after which she was banned from the country.

Dulcie worked as membership secretary on a voluntary basis for Anti-Apartheid in Charlotte Street. 'She also organised events for children of ANC members in exile, to help them keep a sense of community', recalled Christabel Gurney, who worked for Anti-Apartheid. 'Dulcie organised parties for them and taught them gumboot dancing, which was a very energetic dance popular among South African miners. She was a person of tremendous vitality and friendliness.' Dulcie was assassinated by agents of the South African secret police (BOSS), who shot her in the street, in Paris, where she was attending a meeting.

In London her flatmate was George Johannes (now working in International Labour Relations at the South Africa High Commission). 'When she was studying here full-time in the 1970s, she often visited the ANC office in Rathbone Street', he recalled. 'We also went to the South African Communist Party office round the corner, at 39 Goodge Street, over a paint

ANEURIN BEVAN and JENNIE LEE, British Labour politicians, disembarking from an aeroplane (1957)

Theirs was a famous political partnership and a remarkable marriage. When the uncompromising and charismatic Bevan was making one of his controversial speeches in parliament, Jennie Lee would be there, 'half looking forward to it, half apprehensive.' But when it was her turn to address the house, she said he 'hated to be present...Because he was nervous for me and protective.' Of this misplaced 'nannying', she commented, 'our rational selves and emotional selves don't always move along parallel lines.'

As I was saying before I was so rudely interrupted.

Joe Slovo on his return to South Africa after 27 years' exile

shop, where we would sometimes see Dudu Pukwana.' DUDU PUKWANA (1941-90) was a black South African township jazz musician with an international reputation, who played at the 100 Club in Oxford Street on Friday nights through the late 1970s and early 1980s. 'Another of our friends was Herbie Pillay, who had a place in Torrington Place, which was burgled a few times by BOSS', George added. 'Just over the road was the Marlborough pub, where we regularly met for a drink.'

JOE SLOVO (1926-95), a lawyer who had acted for the defence in many political trials in South Africa, was charged with treason himself in 1961. He managed to escape in 1963, and fled to London where he worked under cover for the South African Communist Party in Goodge Street, and the ANC in

DULCIE SEPTEMBER (front row, far left) *picketing South Africa House, Trafalgar Square, London, in the 1980s demanding the release of Nelson Mandela. Also on the picket line were mineworkers' union leader Mick McGahey (front row, second from right),* and *actor Joanna Lumley (front row, far right).*

Rathbone Street, as well as addressing many public meetings for the Anti-Apartheid Movement in Charlotte Street.

After the ANC opened its membership to white people he became chief of staff of its military wing (1985), and the following year became the first white member of its national executive. He was general secretary of the SACP from 1987 to 1991 and then its chairman.

In 1990, after the CP had been legalised, he returned to South Africa, and was a major figure in the negotiations to end apartheid. He became minister of housing in 1994, just before his death from cancer, and was accorded a state funeral.

Another key figure in the underground, anti-imperialist circles, DR YUSUF DADOO (1909-83), chairman of the South African Communist Party, also worked at 39 Goodge Street.

The Marlborough was also used by SAM NUJOMA (b.1929), elected president of Namibia in 1990. A strong opponent of the illegal invasion of his country by South Africa, he was arrested in 1959 and exiled the following year, when he became co-founder and president of the South West Africa People's Organisation (SWAPO). He turned to armed struggle, 'an important strategic shift from reliance on the politics of protests and petitioning', as he put it, in 1966, 'to counter-act the reactionary violence by the colonial regime of our country', after the International Court of Justice rejected SWAPO's complaints against South Africa. But he continued to act as an international negotiator and the United Nations finally recognised Namibia's independence in 1989. The following year Nujoma was awarded the Indira Gandhi Peace Prize; he received the Lenin Peace Prize in 1973 and the Ho Chi Minh Peace Award in 1988.

No stranger to clashes with authority, JOHNNY MORTEN (1912-98) was born in Holborn, and lived at 9 Chenies Street from 1947 until he died. In 1946 he made the front page of the *Evening News* as well as cinema newsreels when he was arrested and frogmarched to Tottenham Court Road police station for taking a leading role in a squat set up by homeless people at a luxury hotel in nearby Great Russell Street. He was charged with 'mutiny', and as a result lost his job as a baker. He joined the Communist Party a year later.

Two of his comrades still live within a stone's throw of his Chenies Street flat. The first, BRUCE DUNNET (b.1923), a singer and songwriter, befriended and became the agent of the famous radical folk singer EWAN MACCOLL (1915-89), who frequently visited Dunnet at his flat in Torrington Place, after the two had met in the East End in 1958. Dunnet has considered himself a communist since his stepfather took him, aged eight, to a meeting in Fife against the Japanese invasion of Manchuria. He joined the Party formally when he was 20, after reading Engels' *Socialism, Utopian and Scientfic* given to him by the doctor who was treating him for the tuberculosis that confined him to bed for two years. From his office at 118 Tottenham Court Road Dunnet has promoted many performers who later became famous.

The second of Morten's comrades, KARL DALLAS (b.1931), who resides at Huntley Street, and has achieved distinction as a musical journalist, collected milk for the republicans in the Spanish civil war when he was seven years old. He formed the Original Riverside Skiffle Group in the 1950s and published *One Hundred Songs of Toil, 450 years of workers' songs*. Now a Christian communist, he writes chiefly about liberation theology. Karl's guiding philosophy was summed up by the Young Communist League tutor, whom he heard reply to a student's accusation that he had expressed 'a very dangerous line of thought' with the words, 'You're quite right, let's pursue it!'

I am an African. I owe my being to the hills and the valleys, the mountains and the glades, the rivers, the deserts, the trees, the flowers, the seas and the ever-changing seasons that define the face of our native-land.... At times, and in fear, I have wondered whether I should concede equal citizenship of our country to the leopard and the lion, the elephant and the springbok, the hyena, the black mamba and the pestilential mosquito. ...South Africa belongs to all who live in it, black and white... Today it feels good to be an African.

Thabo Mbeki on the adoption of the Republic of South Africa Constitution (1996)

CHAPTER 2

Royalty and Gentry

QUEEN MATILDA (1080-1118) was released from her nun's vows so that she could marry Henry I, on condition that she established a leper hospital. Built on eight-acres stretching between present-day Windmill Street and Holborn, the hospital was provided with a servant, a chaplain and a clerk, and dedicated to St Giles, patron saint of outcasts.

KING JOHN (1167-1216) hunted in the vast forests of Middlesex, and may have used a hunting lodge (*King John's Palace*) to the west of the top end of today's Tottenham Court Road. By signing the Magna Carta in 1215, he endorsed London's ancient liberties and acknowledged the strategic importance of the embryonic capital. An inn known as King John's Palace (next to the Tottenham Court manor) survived on the site until 1808.

EDWARD IV of York (1441-83) was crowned in 1461, then deposed in 1470, but returned to power when his forces recaptured the city in 1471, after which he stayed at King John's Palace with Jane Shore. He had an underground passage constructed as an escape route, which led to old St Pancras church. After Charles I was executed in 1649 during the Civil War, OLIVER CROMWELL (1599-1658) was said also to have occupied King John's Palace.

KING HENRY III (1207-72) held a banquet for seven hundred nobles at Tottenham Court (on the north side of Grafton Way), at which King Alexander of Scotland and his queen were among the guests who tucked into the 'rich and abundant feast' under silk tents.

At the the dissolution of the monasteries, KING HENRY VIII (1491-1547) appropriated the Manor of Tyburn (incorporating the western half of today's Fitzrovia), and set aside 554 acres of the northern half in 1539 for his royal hunting park. It was protected by a ditch and a rampart and later surmounted by a fence, to keep the deer in and poachers out. While hunting in the park Henry was capable of tiring out four or more horses a day, until he was prevented from riding by syphilitic leg ulcers. Edward VI (1537-53) entertained the French ambassador in the park, and Henry's daughter, Elizabeth I (1533-1603), hunted there with the Duke of Anjou in 1582. Elizabeth I would have stayed at the nearby manor house (later Marylebone Manor, next to today's Devonshire Street, west of Portland Place) which the king had converted into his hunting quarters in 1544. His other daughter, Mary Queen of Scots (1542-87), also utilized the manor. In February 1600 it was the scene of a hunting party given by the crown for some ambassadors from the tsar of Russia.

HENRY FITZROY (1663-90) was born shortly after the Restoration, one of the many illegitimate children of King Charles II (who used to 'flatulate gleefully') and Barbara Villiers, the Duchess of Cleveland – the name Fitzroy means 'illegitimate king's son'. A reminder of the origin of Fitzrovia's title appeared as late as the 1820s, when an alehouse in Clipstone Street was called the Bastard Arms. At the age of nine Henry was married to five-year-old Isabella Bennet, 'a swete child if ever there was any', the only daughter of Lord Arlington, who owned the manor of Tottenham Court and the estate of Euston. By this marriage, Henry Fitzroy not only gained possession of Tottenham Court, he was created Earl of Euston and, later, the Duke of Grafton.

We are, by the sufferance of God, King of England; and the Kings of England in times past never had any superior but God. Wherefore know you that we will maintain the rights of the Crown...as any of our progenitors.

Henry VIII on refusing to allow a dispute over an ecclesiastic to be referred to Rome

ROBERT ADAM

Robert Adam's designs for Portland Place and Fitzroy Square set the tone of early Fitzrovia. His town houses were intended to be glamorous backdrops for socialising and discussion, the new 'art of living', as he put it, 'The parade, the convenience, and social pleasure of life, being better understood, are more strictly attended to in the arrangement and disposition of apartments.

Better than a play.

Charles II on the House
of Lords debate on the
Divorce Bill

Henry Fitzroy lived dangerously and packed a lot into his 27 years. In 1686 he survived two duels within 17 days, killing both of his opponents: during the first, his belt buckle stopped the thrust of Jack Talbot's sword, and in the second, he defeated a Mr Stanley, brother of the Earl of Derby.

Henry conspired with his own brother, George, Duke of Northumberland, to kidnap George's wife, Catherine Lucy. They deposited Catherine in a convent in Ghent, Flanders, but she escaped and took out criminal proceedings against them. He often took on members of his own family: he helped to overthrow his half-brother, the Duke of Monmouth, when the duke laid claim to the throne (the Monmouth rebellion, after which the duke was executed) and again, in 1688, his uncle, James II. He mixed easily with all classes, and when he fought in the navy, joined in with the rough sports of his seafaring colleagues – wrestling, drinking, dancing, singing, and 'a bout or two of rude lovemaking'. He died in battle.

His exuberance might be recognised in his mother, BARBARA VILLIERS (1641-1709) Duchess of Cleveland. She was aged 19 when she became the lover of Charles II (1630-85). Described as 'the fairest and lewdest of the royal concubines', she bore the king six children. An uninhibited and forceful woman, after the king's death her scandalous acts continued. In a divine gesture of irreverence, she was said by Lord Coleraine to have bitten the penis off a recently exhumed bishop. She had an affair with a highwayman, Cardonell 'Scum' Goodman, who was thrown into jail for conspiring to poison her sons, the Dukes of Grafton and Northumberland. At the age of 64, she married a reprobate called Robert 'Bean' Fielding, who already had a wife. He was sentenced to have his hand burned for bigamy. In later years dropsy swelled the Duchess into a 'monstrous bulk'. Descendants of this formidable character include the late Lady Diana, Princess of Wales, and Sarah Ferguson, the present Duchess of York.

Many gentry who incurred the wrath of monarchy and church were linked with Fitzrovia, even if it is solely because it was the place of their execution. SIR JOHN OLDCASTLE (1377-1417), later Lord Cobham, led the Lollards, a group of religious dissidents who asserted that it was unChristian for the established Church to own huge amounts of land and demand tithes from starving peasants. This anti-clerical, evangelical movement was declared illegal in 1401, but Sir John was arrested in 1414 for attending secret meetings of the Lollards in St Giles. He was brought before the bishops, condemned to death as 'an obstinate heretic', and handed over to the civil authorities. On the eve of his execution he escaped from the Tower of London and fled to Wales, where he hid for nearly four years, until he was discovered by an old woman. She threw a stool at him and broke his legs, and Oldcastle was recaptured and condemned to death. His bravery – he 'endured the pain and agony of a most excruciating death rather than forfeit liberty of faith and freedom of opinion' – as he was led in chains to the gallows set up at the lower end of Tottenham Court Road, was impressive. He was burned for heresy, and buried nearby. Shakespeare used Oldcastle as a model for Falstaff.

ANTHONY BABINGTON (1561-86) was hanged and quartered on a gibbet at the same site for organising a Catholic conspiracy to murder Elizabeth I and restore her deposed sister Mary. The conspiracy was plotted in St Giles fields and involved KATHERINE BELLAMY, then resident at Tottenham Court, and her sons, Jerome and Robert. Robert killed himself while in prison, Jerome was executed, and Katherine died in the Tower of London. Four others were also executed on Tottenham Court Road for the crime, including the Catholic priest JOHN BALLARD, who was tortured on the rack beforehand.

Three rebel lords lived in Rathbone Place. The first, SIMON FRASER (1667-

1747), the 12th Baron Lovat, was beheaded for treason after helping the French to invade Scotland (he had been outlawed for marrying Dowager Lady Lovat for her wealth, then locking her up and marrying two other women). The second, JOHN ELPHINSTONE (1623-1704), Lord Balmerino, was fined £6,000 for co-operating with the Roundheads during the civil war. The third rebel, WILLIAM BOYD (1704-46), fourth Earl of Kilmarnock, was executed at Tower Hill after being captured at Culloden Hill supporting the Young Pretender.

HENRY FITZROY, the first Duke of Grafton. Drawing after Sir Peter Lely (c.1678)

Henry Fitzroy, soldier, sailor and adventurer, whose descendants developed Fitzrovia.

Barbara Villiers, Duchess of Cleveland after Sir Peter Lely (*c.*1666)

The Duchess of Cleveland was mistress to Charles II, whose court was arguably the most frivolous in British history.

From 1773, a direct descendant of William the Conqueror, ADMIRAL THOMAS PYE (1713-85), lived with his married lover, Mrs Anna Bennett, at 5 Nassau (*New Suffolk*) Street (opposite No.22, and now part of Middlesex Hospital). This open cohabitation was a public scandal for which Pye was much pilloried in the press. At the age of 14 Pye had joined the navy, but he was suspended for three years in 1755, for fraud and neglect of duty. Acquitted of the more serious charges at the court martial, his pay was docked by half.

Pye, who was known for making unwanted advances to women, was hoisted by his own petard while serving in Antigua, when a woman he planned to seduce agreed he could visit when her husband was out. She cleverly arranged that Pye would be pulled discreetly up to her window in a basket. But on the fateful evening, she instructed her servant to stop tugging the rope when the basket was halfway. Pye was left stranded, 'prey to the mosquittos and other noxious insects' all night. In the morning he was exposed to 'the derision of the multitude, who flocked from all parts to behold the exaltation of the lascivious commander in chief'.

In 1773 Pye was knighted at Spithead even though he was 'almost too drunk to accept the accolade'. Anna, his lover, became a popular novelist after his death. She bore him two children at Nassau Street: Harriett, who became a popular actress, and Thomas who joined the navy.

The flair and style of Fitzroy Square (a circle within a square), is the distinctive work of the innovative Scottish architect, ROBERT ADAM (1728-92) who, with his brother James, designed town houses to rival the grandeur of the country estates. Stairwells were top-lit and daylight flowed through tall sash windows. Reception rooms segued into one another, their graceful proportions set off by surprising oval recesses, glass-domed rotundas, and delicate plasterwork decoration.

Both the east and the south of Fitzroy Square (built from 1792 to 1794) were the designs of Robert Adam. He lived at 7 Conway Street, which leads off to the south, but he was to die before the square was completed.

The Adam brothers were so persuaded by the development of Fitzroy Square that James and the third brother, William, took out leases for houses on the east and the south sides. The north and west sides of Fitzroy Square, delayed by the Napoleonic wars, were added later. Nos.33 to 37 Fitzroy Square on the south side and 2, 9 and 10 on the north side were built from 1827 to 1828; the west side was built from 1832 to 1835. (The present south side is a pastiche, rebuilt after the blitz of the second world war.)

From 1809 to 1995, the pub opposite Robert Adam's address in Conway Street, now part of the O'Neills Irish Bar chain, was called the Adam's Arms. A plaque at 36 Fitzroy Square commemorates his contribution.

In 1781 LADY ELEANOR STRATHMORE was shopping on the corner of Tottenham Court Road and Oxford Street, when she was carried off screaming into a coach, and driven to Durham, where she was thrown into a pigsty. The kidnap had been planned by her husband, Captain Andrew Stoney, 'a romantic adventurer with a streak of villainy', who kept a lover. He had rapidly gone through his wife's fortune, and was trying to prevent her divorcing him. But Lady Eleanor (from whom the present Queen Mother is directly descended) escaped and Captain Stoney was jailed for three years.

LADY EMMA HAMILTON (1763-1813), famous for being Nelson's lover, was a 17-year-old, living at 14 Oxford Street, when the writer Henry Angelo observed her walking in Rathbone Place looking, as he noted, better dressed than when he had seen her two years earlier, practically starving in Soho. By the time she was 20 Emma was working as a dancer for a quack doctor, James Graham, who guaranteed conception to any couple using the 'grand celestial bed' of his Temple of Health. Among the attractions of the bed meant to encourage fertility were dancing girls, music, and magnetic lodestones. Emma danced naked, immersed herself in mud, and 'demonstrated' the bed in the pose of the Goddess of Health, where she attracted the attention of artists including Thomas Gainsborough and Joshua Reynolds, who hired her as a model. George Romney became obsessed with Emma and painted many portraits of her in his studio at 32 Cavendish Square.

Charles Greville, MP, who escorted Emma to the circus and to the Pantheon, 173 Oxford Street, introduced her to his uncle, Sir William Hamilton, the illegitimate half-brother of George III. Hamilton was ambassador in Naples (where he paid young boys to swim naked, gleefully encouraging his pet monkey to pinch their private parts). Emma married Sir William at Marylebone Church in 1791.

> [We] have adopted a beautiful variety of light mouldings, gracefully formed, delicately enriched and arranged with propriety and skill. We have introduced a great diversity of ceilings, freezes, and decorated pilasters, and have added grace and beauty to the whole, by a mixture of grotesque stucco, and painted ornaments together with the flowing rainceau, with its fanciful figures and winding foliage.

Robert Adam on harmonising all aspects of interior decoration

> Thence the King walked to the Duchess of Cleveland, another Lady of Pleasure and curse of our nation.

John Evelyn

Emma met ADMIRAL HORATIO NELSON (1758-1805) while she was visiting Naples, and the admiral was returning from his triumph at the Battle of the Nile. In Naples Nelson ordered the unilateral breaking of the truce negotiated between the royal family and the republicans, and a mass slaughter ensued, during which the decapitated heads of republican men, women and children were kicked around like footballs. Emma and Nelson became lovers.

A daughter was born to Emma and Nelson, in England, in 1801. They baptised her Horatia, in St Marylebone Church (where Emma had been married). Pretending that she was their godchild, they took Horatia to be reared by Mrs Gibson, a widow, who lived in reduced circumstances with her disabled daughter, Mary, at 9 Little Titchfield Street (off Great Titchfield Street). Emma and Nelson visited Horatia frequently. Nelson adored his infant daughter. Playing on the carpet with her during one of his visits, he said, 'A finer child never was produced by any two persons. It was in truth a love-begotten child.'

Nelson officially adopted Horatia in 1803, wrote her letters in which he addressed her as 'my dearest angel', and, finally acknowledging that she was his daughter, amended his will in her favour. But two years later he was killed at Trafalgar. Although one of his last acts was to pray that Horatia led a happy life, his deathbed plea to king and country, that ample provision be made for Emma and the daughter, fell on deaf ears. Emma was deprived of the pensions left to her by both her husband and Nelson. Ill with dropsy, inertia affected her efforts to push her claim and she died in debtors' prison. Horatia married a clergyman, Reverend Philip Ward, in 1822 and lived to the age of 81.

PRINCE CHARLES-MAURICE DE TALLEYRAND (1754-1838), the dissolute French statesman and diplomat, who was made president of France in 1790, excommunicated and exiled in 1792, came to London, where he lived at 51 Portland Place. A rake and a cynical wit, he had an iron leg and rolled his tongue in a disgusting manner, a combination of qualities that apparently made him irresistible to French females. He returned to France in 1796 and was appointed minister of foreign affairs and, for a short time, prime minister.

The royal couple KING GEORGE IV (1762-1830) and CAROLINE OF BRUNSWICK (1768-1821) were frequent visitors to Fitzrovia. When George proposed to Caroline he was under pressure to produce an heir, as it was on this basis parliament had agreed to pay the enormous debts he had accrued from his gambling and other vices. But George had secretly married Mrs Marie Fitzherbert in 1785, and he told Caroline bluntly that he was committed to another, 'As soon as you shall have given an heir to the throne I will abandon you, never to meet you more in public.'

The royal wedding in 1795 was farcical. George, drunk on brandy, eyed up his latest mistress, Lady Jersey, and smiled coldly at Caroline, his bride, 'like a mechanical toy'. Afterwards he collapsed at the reception and either never made it to the bridal chamber or, according to another account, slumped in the fireplace all night. Nine months later, however, Caroline gave birth to their only child, Charlotte. Two days after Charlotte was born, George made a will in which he bequeathed one shilling to Caroline and the rest of his property to Marie Fitzherbert.

Caroline often visited Portland Place to see her friend Lady Sheffield.

George visited a brothel run by a Mrs Collett in Portland Place, where he liked to be whipped.

Caroline and George often went to concerts at the King's Concert Rooms at 21-25 Tottenham Street. George took part in an amateur production of a play there in 1802. When he attended concerts there with his father, KING GEORGE III (1738-1820), the king had been 'often accustomed to tell the conductor to

And take care of my dear Lady Hamilton, Hardy, take care of poor Lady Hamilton. Kiss me, Hardy.

Admiral Horatio Nelson, dying, to Surgeon Beatty

take his cue from the royal box, where the royal hand might have been seen giving the time of the composition performed, as the king wished it to be taken.'

Caroline was said to have smelled from infrequent washing. She had a penchant for topless dancing at balls, and her favourite toy was a Chinese clockwork figure, which performed unusual sexual movements. Two of her brothers suffered porphyria. All of which did not make her popular with her mother-in-law, Queen Charlotte, who did her utmost to discredit Caroline in order to provide grounds for divorce.

QUEEN CHARLOTTE (1744-1818) may have visited the novelist who had been the Keeper of Her Robes, FANNY BURNEY, at 23 Chenies Street. She visited the artist, MARY MOSER, who married Hugh Lloyd and lived in northern Huntley (*21 Upper Thornhaugh*) Street.

LADY EMMA HAMILTON by George Romney (*c.*1785)

Emma Lyon, later Lady Hamilton, was George Romney's favourite model.

His work captured her beauty and set a new fashion for naturalness in portrait painting.

elsewhere at that time, Virginia changed her evidence and said that he had seduced her in the morning. She was then asked to draw a plan of the Warren Street bedroom, which she did with an assurance that impressed the court, although nobody bothered to check it for accuracy (a committee after the case found it wrong in almost every detail). The jury ruled that the adultery had not been sufficiently disproved to prevent the divorce.

Although Dilke had not legally been found guilty of adultery, or even been put on trial, the publicity ruined his chances of becoming leader of the Liberal Party. He resigned as MP and was made the butt of music hall jokes and songs. A staunch republican he later returned to parliament and he helped to establish the first Wages Councils in 1910, which set minimum pay rates in four industries. He often visited the artist Ford Madox Brown near Warren Street at 37 Fitzroy Square.

As for Virginia, she lived in Marylebone Road, and was a Labour councillor for 14 years before her death in 1948. It was suggested that she had named Dilke to distract attention from another affair, on the assumption that her husband would not petition so prominent a person.

In 1889 another sex scandal broke. The police raided a male brothel at 19 Cleveland Street where gay members of the gentry had been paying for the sexual services of local telegram boys since it opened in 1885. Lord Arthur Somerset (1851-1926), superintendent of the royal stables and a close friend of the Prince of Wales, had been a regular customer. He fled the country to avoid prosecution. Others said to be clients were GEORGE CAVENDISH BENTINCK and HENRY JAMES FITZROY (Lord Euston 1848-1912), descendant of the Henry Fitzroy, first Duke of Grafton, who had come into ownership of Tottenham Court two centuries earlier. Fitzroy later said that he had visited in the mistaken belief he would see striptease by women (*poses plastiques*). Public interest was fanned by the rumour that the brothel had been patronised by PRINCE ALBERT 'EDDY' VICTOR (1864-92), the Duke of Clarence and Avondale. As the eldest son of the Prince of Wales, he was in direct line of succession. Police files referred to someone with his initials, PAV, who was found at the brothel and Eddy was named openly in American newspapers. Under the assumed name of 'Victoria', Eddy was already listed as a member of a transvestite club in Portland Place. This was The Hundred Guineas Club, run by a Mr Inslip, where there was dancing and discussion until 2 a.m., after which the lights were turned down and various forms of sexual contact allowed, before the club closed at 6 a.m.

The *North London Press* commented that there had been an unusually long delay between the police's discovery of the Cleveland Street brothel and the subsequent raid, and suggested that this had been deliberate, allowing the aristocratic clients to flee before the police arrived. The brothel keeper, Charles Hammond (who had previously operated from 35 Newman Street) was even able to remove the furniture under the watchful eye of police undercover agents. In the view of the *North London Press*, the 'victims' were punished – two male prostitutes were prosecuted: an 18-year-old lad, Henry Newlove and an older post office employee, 40-year-old George Veck (who lived at 2 Howland Street) – while the clients ('instigators') went free because of their powerful social connections.

Lord Euston then sued Ernest Parke, editor of the *North London Press*, for criminal libel. During the trial several inhabitants of Cleveland Street and Tottenham Street gave evidence that they had seen Lord Euston entering the premises. One of the prostitutes, John Saul (who also worked in the Hundred Guineas Club in Portland Place under the name of 'Evelyn' and in another brothel at 13 Nassau Street, now part of Middlesex Hospital), said he had

A good sensible wife with some considerable character is what he needs most, but where is she to be found?

The Prince of Wales, despairing of his son, Prince Eddy.

masturbated Euston. The jury accepted his lordship's version and Parke was jailed for one year with hard labour.

Prince Eddy died of pneumonia and influenza in 1892. However, as his peers considered the prince to be too unstable for the throne, it was rumoured that he had been poisoned (and his hands and feet had turned black), and also that his death had been faked, and that he was kept hidden until his actual death, in 1933. Lord Euston died of dropsy in 1912.

Lady Ottoline Morrell (1873-1938), the grand and generous literary hostess, held her at-homes at 44 Bedford Square and then at 10 Gower Street, which she described affectionately as 'the dearest little doll's house', although one of her guests, the historian Lytton Strachey, derided its 'wretched pokiness'.

Descended from the Hapsburgs, she was born Ottoline Violet Anne Cavendish-Bentinck, niece of the fifth Duke of Portland. She married the Liberal MP Philip Morrell, and gave birth to twins in 1906. She had many lovers, including Fitzrovian artists, Augustus John and Henry Lamb, but was always discreet to avoid embarrassing her husband.

Sir Charles Wentworth Dilke

'Hullo Maskelyne and Cook are performing one of my tricks!'

Leading radical politician Sir Charles Dilke was wrongly cited as co-respondent in a divorce petition, and Fanny, a servant also named, did not appear.

LADY OTTOLINE MORRELL
by Augustus John (1919)

*Lady Ottoline Morrell's
affair with Augustus John,
'one doesn't meet Ottolines
every day', led to this
striking portrait.*

Many fledgling writers were helped and encouraged by Ottoline's gatherings, including T.S. Eliot and Aldous Huxley. WALTER DE LA MARE (1873-1956) was a frequent visitor. The Russian dancer VASLAV NIJINKSY (1890-1950) admired her at one of her lunches, 'Lady Morrell is so tall, so beautiful, like a giraffe'. Tactfully he added that the giraffe was graceful, not gangling. Ottoline, who was six feet tall, accepted the compliment.

Ottoline liked to dress in exaggerated fashions, to wear feathers, flamboyant make-up, and huge hats over her copper-coloured hair. Frank and outspoken in her views, she had a robust sense of fun and revelled in vulgarity and music hall comedy. But the philosopher BERTRAND RUSSELL (the third Earl Russell, 1872-1970) was attracted by her air of calm and serenity. He felt drawn to her in 1910, when he was a guest at one of her parties in Gower Street, at which he danced the hornpipe.

In March 1911, Bertrand Russell asked if he could spend the night with Ottoline when her husband was away. Ottoline invited a friend, Ethel Sands, the painter (who lived at 40 Portland Place) to stay as chaperone. Ottoline went on to complain of Bertrand's bad breath and to insist that he shave off his large moustache and 'cremate it in the fireplace', while he complained of her 'excessive use of scent and powder' and said her long, thin face was 'something like a horse'. They became lovers, and spent two nights together at 130 Tottenham Court Road. Between March 1913 and January 1914, at the height of their involvement, Bertrand wrote Ottoline over a thousand letters, and after their affair they remained lifelong friends. He appreciated her criticisms of his *The Problems of Philosophy* and she enjoyed the intellectual challenge offered by the relationship. In conversation with Bertrand, as she put it, any idea she put forward would be 'driven on to the end of a subject, through tangled bushes, and swamps, till it reached open ground. I often wriggled and rebelled, and wanted to hide under shady, sentimental willow trees, but this was never allowed. Bertie would take me metaphorically by the hand and pull me up and urge me on...tearing down old dusty growths in my mind, and opening dark windows that had been blocked up in the lower depths of my being.'

Another regular guest at Lady Ottoline's literary gatherings was D.H. Lawrence, who lived at 73 Gower Street. Lawrence caricatured Ottoline as Hermione Roddice in *Women in Love* (1921). He probably used Ottoline as a model for Lady Chatterley in his novel *Lady Chatterley's Lover* (1928, and banned for over 30 years). Aldous Huxley portrayed Ottoline as Priscilla Wimbush (a malicious portrait, in Ottoline's view) in his novel *Crome Yellow* (1921).

After Ottoline's jaw was badly disfigured by an operation in 1927, she wore a scarf to hide the scars, and was given regular injections of a powerful antibiotic, Prontosil, which had severe side effects. Dr Cameron, who administered the drug, committed suicide while under investigation, and Ottoline died shortly afterwards while she was being injected by one of his assistants.

When Bertrand Russell was imprisoned in 1918 for his militant pacifism he wrote *Introduction to Mathematical Philosophy* (1919) and began work on the *Analysis of Mind* (1921). After meeting Lenin, Trotsky and Gorky (who cooled his early enthusiasm for communism) he wrote about Bolshevism, but was disillusioned by the results of the Russian revolution, and he dropped his pacifist stance in order to counteract fascism in the second world war. As the guiding star of the Campaign for Nuclear Disarmament, and Chairman of the Committee of 100, he was participating in a sit-down demonstration in 1961, in Whitehall, when a policeman accosted him with blows from a truncheon. The policeman was unimpressed when an onlooker told him that Russell was a great philosopher and mathematician. However, on hearing that he was an earl, the policeman hastened to dust the protestor down and made sure he was comfortable, before carting him off to the clink.

I like mathematics because it is *not* human and has nothing particular to do with this planet or with the whole accidental universe – because, like Spinoza's God, it won't love us in return.

Bertrand Russell in a letter to Ottoline Morrell

I would not mind if you and he had an ordinary love-affair – what I hate is this "soul-mush".

Frieda Lawrence on her husband's relationship with Ottoline Morrell

Murderers and Manslaughterers

The first of the famous murderers who stalked the streets of Fitzrovia was CATHERINE HAYES, who was executed at the age of 34 for killing her husband, John Hayes. He had a chandlery and coal business, with premises on Tottenham Court Road and on Oxford Street (*Tyburn Road*), in 1725. She met her future husband when she was working for his father, a farmer, as a servant.

On her husband's death, Catherine expected to receive £1,500. She promised to share the legacy with BILLINGS, her son by a previous partner, and THOMAS WOOD, the lodger, if they agreed to help her to kill her husband. Together they planned to make John Hayes drunk, and then bet him that he could not down six bottles of mountain wine and remain standing. Hayes drank the six bottles and was still on his feet, dancing around the room 'like a man distracted', but at the seventh, he fell to the floor, senseless. Billings hit Hayes with a hatchet, but the victim stamped his legs against the floor in agony, and the noise woke a neighbour. Wood then took hold of the hatchet and, with two more blows, fractured Hayes' skull. While Wood severed Hayes' head with a knife, Catherine collected the blood in a bucket. She proposed that they boil the flesh off the head so that it would be unrecognisable, but this was too much for the men. They dumped the head in the Thames and dropped the dismembered body in a pond in Marylebone Fields.

The head was washed up on the shore of the river. The authorities arranged for it to be displayed on a pole, with its hair combed, in the hope that someone would recognise it. Two people, to each of whom Catherine Hayes had given different explanations for her husband's absence, recognised it as the head of John Hayes, and Catherine was arrested. Later that day the rest of the body was found. Wood was captured and confessed. Billings later confirmed the facts of the murder. Catherine Hayes denied them.

All three were found guilty. Thomas Wood died in prison. On May 9, 1726, Catherine, who had attempted to poison herself in prison, and her son Billings, were drawn by sledge to Tyburn. Billings was hanged and his corpse suspended by the pond where he had disposed of the body of John Hayes. Catherine Hayes was chained and burned at the stake. Women who suffered this punishment were usually strangled before the flames reached them, but the flames spread fast and the executioner had to scramble to safety before performing his task. As she burned Catherine's screams could be heard for a considerable time, and it took three hours for her body to be reduced to ashes.

On New Year's Day, 1828, a pot-boy named Gardner, employed by the Gower Arms (corner of Gower and Store Streets), delivered the regular pint of beer to a customer named Elizabeth Jeffe at her house nearby, and was the last person to see the 75-year-old woman alive. The next day she was found with her throat cut. Gardner informed the police that he had seen Elizabeth Jeffe talking to a young man. This was WILLIAM JONES, aged 25, a sailor, who had fled his lodgings. His razor fitted the case found by the body, and he had a cut thumb. Jones was found not guilty but, after being transported to Australia (*Van Diemen's Land*) for stealing a coat, and before he was executed as a bushranger, he confessed to Elizabeth Jeffe's murder.

In the session papers of the Old Bailey there are strong facts. Housebreaking is a strong fact; robbery is a strong fact; and the murder is a mighty strong fact: but is great praise due to the historians of these strong facts? No, Sir.

James Boswell

ARMED ROBBERY AT JAY'S

Three armed men who robbed Jay's jewellery store on Charlotte Street in 1947, shot and killed a man as he tried to stop their getaway. They were tracked down by the famous Superintendent Robert Fabian, who inspired a television series.

Hayes Murder, engraving by Valois (1725)

Catherine Hayes hacked off the head of her husband, John Hayes, with the aid of her son, Thomas Billings, and her lover, Thomas Wood. She was caught, and sentenced to be strangled and burned at the stake.

The hangman failed to strangle her because his hands were burned by the flames, and he dropped the rope.

The 'Red Barn' murderer, WILLIAM CORDER (1804-28), was strung-up in 1828 for killing his lover and burying her in a barn, to avoid marriage after she gave birth to their son. Following his death he had an even more ignominous end: 'a piece of the skin of the wretched malefactor, which had been tanned, was exhibited for a long time afterwards at the shop of a leather seller in Oxford Street.'

On Christmas Day, 1836, 46-year-old Hannah Brown, a washerwoman, left the basement of the shoemaker's shop in 48 Riding House Street (*45 Union Street*, now part of Middlesex Hospital), where she lived, saying she was to be married the next day and that she would return for her belongings. Later that day, Hannah visited Mrs Glass, a plasterer's wife, in Windmill Street. She arranged to stay the night, but was never seen again.

Hannah had met her husband-to-be, JAMES GREENACRE (1785-1837), when she took her mangle for mending to John Ward, 48 Goodge Street. Greenacre was visiting the shop to commission a prototype of a washing machine he had invented.

On the day after Boxing Day, Greenacre visited a friend of Hannah's, Mrs Blanchard, who ran a second-hand furniture business at 10 Goodge Street, where he announced that the wedding had been called off, saying that Hannah had run into debt. William Gay, Hannah's brother, who worked in the shop, overheard the conversation and introduced himself. Greenacre fled.

Over the next few days Hannah's dismembered torso was discovered in Edgware Road, her head was found blocking the passage of a barge through Regent's Canal, and her legs were picked up from a ditch near Greenacre's home in south London. A month after the murder Greenacre advertised for investors in his washing machine, giving his address as Bishops, 1 Tudor Place (between 19 and 20 Tottenham Court Road).

William Gay tracked Greenacre down and informed the police. Incriminating evidence included a remnant of Hannah's dress and a bag identified as the one Greenacre had stolen from John Ward's shop a week before the murder, and which Greenacre had used to wrap the body.

At the trial a surgeon testified that Hannah's death was caused by decapitation, and Greenacre was found guilty of murdering 'and mangling' his victim. He divulged that he had killed Hannah because she did not own the property that he thought she did.

RICHARD DADD (1817-1886) trained at Henry Sass's art school, 32 Bloomsbury (6 *Charlotte*) Street, off the bottom of Gower Street. He lived and had a studio at 70 and 74 Charlotte Street between 1838 and 1841, before moving to Newman Street, where he lived on a diet of eggs and ale, and his landlady grew afraid of him. On his return from nine months' travel in Egypt, where he felt the heat and camel-riding were affecting his mind, his friends noticed that Dadd was showing signs of insanity. One day he was found streaming with blood and said he had cut out a satanic birthmark.

On August 28, 1843, Dadd asked to see his father to 'disburden his mind'. They dined on boiled ham and a glass of porter, before Dadd killed his father, whom he believed to be the devil, with a knife and razor. On his arrest Dadd said that he was an envoy of God, sent to exterminate men possessed by demons. His rooms at 71 Newman Street (where he had moved in 1842) were searched and some disturbing drawings were found of many of his friends, all with their throats cut.

The picture *The Fairy-Feller's Master Stroke* (now in the Tate Gallery), which Dadd painted while incarcerated in Broadmoor, depicts his father, who was a chemist, with a pestle and mortar. Charles Dickens based his novel *Martin Chuzzlewit* (serialised 1843-44) on the case.

Two soldiers were tried for murder following a duel in 1843: Lieutenant ALEXANDER MUNRO, aged 39, a frequent visitor to the Great Portland Street barracks, and Lieutenant DUNCAN GRANT, who was quartered there. Munro had quarrelled with his brother-in-law, Lieutenant David Fawcett (awarded the OBE for heroism in China during the opium war) over the treatment of a tenant. He challenged Fawcett to a duel, and asked Grant to be his second. Fawcett shot in the air to satisfy his honour, but Munro took advantage and shot Fawcett in the chest. Munro and Grant fled the country. A year later Grant gave himself up. Four years later Munro was finally tried, and sentenced to death for murder – later commuted to one year's imprisonment. Grant was found not guilty. The army refused Fawcett's widow a pension on the grounds that this denial would deter others from duelling.

In 1845 a 22-year-old violin teacher, THOMAS HOCKER, killed his companion and piano teacher, James de la Rue, who lived off Drummond Street. Hocker had two lovers nearby, one whose address was in Grafton Way (*Grafton Street*) and the other in Osnaburgh Street. Straight after the murder, Hocker rushed round to one of the women. When she asked Hocker why his sleeve was torn, he brazened it out, saying that it was because of a frenzied 'sex romp' with his other lover. However, the dead man's watch was found in his possession, and Hocker was arrested. He claimed that he had deliberately stained his clothes with blood so as to divert suspicion from another, but his motive for the murder was considered to be financial, after money was found to be missing from the much wealthier de la Rue. His other lover was promptly sacked when, during the trial, it was revealed that she had been having sex with Hocker on the employer's premises.

Karl Marx's fencing companion, the French revolutionary EMANUEL BARTHELEMY (1821-1855), had killed a police sergeant at the age of 17 during the political revolt of 1838. He was saved from the guillotine by an amnesty, after he was arrested for fighting on the barricades in the Paris uprising of 1848. He was branded on the shoulder as a galley convict and transported for life, but escaped to London where he was a frequent visitor at Marx's house – Jenny Marx (Karl's wife) said she found Barthelemy's piercing eyes repulsive.

One fateful day in December 1854, Barthelemy, a skilled mechanic, left his fencing saloon in Rathbone Place. He was carrying some deer shot steeped in sulphur with which he intended to assassinate Napoleon III in France. On his way he called at 73 Warren Street to see George Moore, a soda manufacturer, who owed him wages. Moore was dismissive and Barthelemy turned violent. He shot and killed Moore. As Barthelemy made his escape he was confronted by Mr Collard, an ex-policeman and greengrocer, of 74 Warren Street. Barthelemy shot and killed Collard. As he tried to flee he was cornered by the crowd which had gathered, and marched off to the local police station.

At the trial Barthelemy pleaded self-defence. He was found guilty and hanged in January 1855. His death mask, showing an expression of iron determination and the mark of the hangman's rope round his neck, was put on public display at Newgate.

CATHERINE WILSON'S execution in 1862 attracted a crowd of 20,000. She had been a resident nurse for a Mr Dixon in Huntley (*Alfred*) Street, parallel to and east of Tottenham Court Road, who then died in 1855, leaving his money to his landlady, Mrs Soames, of Bedford Square. Catherine Wilson then worked for Mrs Soames, who subsequently died. Several others nursed by Wilson died and large sums of their money disappeared. Wilson was then charged with poisoning a Mrs Connell of Marylebone, with oil of vitriol. She was acquitted of murder, but a Dr Taylor recognised the symptoms described in the publicity about the case, as being the same as those suffered by two of his ex-patients, Mr Dixon and Mrs Soames. He went to the police and Wilson was re-arrested. She was found guilty of murdering Dixon and Soames by putting colchicum seeds in their wine, brandy and tea.

DR GEORGE HENRY LAMSON (1850-82) inherited £8,000 on the death of his brother-in-law, who had died in suspicous circumstances. His money, which had been left to his sister, Kate, automatically belonged to her husband. Dr Lamson, a morphine addict, soon went through his wife's inheritance. On October 24, 1881, he moved into Nelson's Hotel, 99 Great Portland Street. He began to pawn his surgical instruments to pay for his habit, and plotted to kill his other brother-in-law, 16-year-old Percy John. Percy was paralysed with curvature of the spine, and if Percy died before the age of 21, his inheritance would also pass to Kate. In November Lamson tried to buy aconite from the chemist Bell and Co, 225 (*338*) Oxford Street and was refused. He went to another chemist who, after insisting that Lamson supply his name and address, sold him enough of the poison to kill 30 people.

On December 1, 1881 Lamson wrote a letter from the hotel to the young

JAMES GREENACRE, drawn at his trial for the murder of Hannah Brown (1837)

Greenacre proposed to Hannah Brown before he killed her. He had three previous wives: one died of a 'putrid sore throat', another of brain fever, and the third of cholera.

Percy. Two days later he visited, taking sweets and cakes for Percy 'to help him take his medicines'. Percy swallowed capsules, ate the sweets and cake, and died that night. At the murder trial an analyst explained that a mouse injected with an extract of Percy's vomit died, proving that the cake contained aconite. Just before he was hanged, Lamson confessed to the prison chaplain.

Among the conjectures about the unsolved JACK THE RIPPER murders of 1888 is the theory that the victims died because they knew of a secret child fathered by the heir presumptive to the throne, Prince Eddy, and born to Annie Crook, a young Catholic woman. Annie worked in a tobacconist at 22 Cleveland Street and lived in a basement at 6 Cleveland Street from 1883.

Annie also worked as an artist's model for Walter Sickert, in his studio at 15 Cleveland Street (demolished 1887 to make space for Middlesex Hospital Trainee Nurses Institute). Sickert said that Prince Eddy visited him at the studio, where he introduced the prince to Annie. (This presents the fascinating possiblity that Prince Eddy could have passed Karl Marx on Cleveland Street, when Marx was on his way to the Communist Club opposite, during the last year of his life.)

Sickert's son, Joseph, reported that his father had told him that Annie and the prince were married at St Saviour's. This could have been St Saviour's Church on the corner of Maple Street and Whitfield Street, or the chapel in St Saviour's Infirmary, 10-12 Osnaburgh Street, near the top of Cleveland Street (the infirmary was later moved to Kent, and no records from the period survive).

Annie gave birth to a daughter, Alice, at Marylebone Workhouse, in April 1885. The birth was registered on April 18 – the name of the father was left blank. Mary Kelly (last of the ripper victims), who worked with Annie at the tobacconist, acted as midwife. She was also nanny to Alice and claimed to have witnessed the marriage of Annie and the prince. It was a time of civil unrest, and the establishment feared that news of an infant, born to the prince and Annie Crook, might topple the royal family. The Conservative prime minister, Lord Salisbury (who had earlier lived at 21 Fitzroy Square) supposedly intervened and advised that the relationship should end. Cleveland Street was raided in 1888, and Annie was dragged off, certified insane by the royal physician, Sir William Gull, and confined to a series of institutions.

However Mary Kelly took the child, along with the couple's marriage certificate, and escaped to Whitechapel. Sickert then helped her to place Alice with relatives. Mary Kelly, her tongue loosened by gin, blurted out the story to her friends Annie Chapman, Elizabeth Stride and Mary Nichols. These women were all killed and all had connections with Fitzrovia: Stride lived at 67 Gower Street, Nichols stayed at St Giles workhouse in nearby Endell Street, and Chapman lived at 32 Upper Albany Street, Regent's Park.

According to the theory, Mary and these three friends were murdered because they attempted to use the information to blackmail the royal family. A fifth victim, Catherine Eddowes, sometimes went by the name of Mary Kelly, so the murderer may have mistaken her identity.

The Ripper was, so the story goes, none other than the royal physician, Sir William Gull, with accomplices, John Netley, a coachman, and a further man. It is purported that they lured their victims into the coach and fed them poisoned grapes. The women fell unconscious, and the physician carved up their bodies, which the coachman then dumped in the streets. This account would explain each victim's extensive wounds, why there were no signs of struggle, why there was so little blood on the streets, and why the deaths occurred in the few minutes between police patrols in the area.

Sickert, of course, never allowed anyone to rub out. He claimed that the first impression, depicted by the first outline, was of great value and had a personal quality.

Art student on
Walter Sickert

RICHARD DADD painting at
Bethlem Hospital (*c.1856*)

The picture Contradiction.
Oberon and Titania
illustrates a scene from
A Midsummer Night's
Dream.

Other extravagant versions of the Ripper crimes involve Prince Eddy
himself in the murders, aided by a man who was Annie Crook's second cousin
and tutor to the Prince, James Stephen; or Walter Sicket and Lord Randolph
Churchill; or freemasons helped by the Earl of Euston and Lord Arthur
Somerset. They also suggest that the body, mutilated beyond recognition, but
thought to be Mary Kelly and found in her lodging, was in fact that of her
visiting friend Winifred Collis, a parlourmaid, who worked at 27 Cleveland
Street. Inspector Abberline, who was in charge of the inquiry, reported that
Winifred was never heard of again. He also said that a witness saw Mary Kelly
hours after it was thought that she had been murdered, and that he had seen
a postcard that Mary sent later, from Canada, addressed to her aunt.

Annie Crook returned to Fitzrovia as an inmate at Cleveland Street
Infirmary from 1907 to 1913. In 1916 she was reunited with her daughter at the
home of her mother, Sarah Dryden, at 5 Capper (*Pancras*) Street. Sarah lived
and worked in a bakery at 12 Nassau Street (now Middlesex Hospital) where
she had met her husband, William Crook (Annie's father), a cabinet and piano
maker in Rathbone Street, who later moved to 9 Capper Street and lived there
until his death in 1891.

In 1891 a gang of Whitechapel pickpockets, known as the Blind Beggar
gang, taunted Fred Klein and his wife with anti-Semitic insults on a train and
followed them when they got off the tube at Euston Square (*Gower Street*)

station in Gower Street. Nineteen-year-old PAUL 'ELLIS' VAUGHAN then stabbed Fred with an umbrella. Klein died from the injuries and Vaughan was found guilty of manslaughter.

The following year DR THOMAS NEILL CREAM (1850-92) ventured out onto the streets from Edwards Hotel, 14-15 Euston Square, to give strychnine to prostitutes, telling them that the pills were a remedy for venereal disease, and leaving them to die in agony. In October 1891, after he had killed four women this way, he met Louisa 'Lou Harvey' Harris in Regent Street, and spent the night with her at the Green Man, 57 Berwick Street, a few yards from the bottom of Wells Street. The following evening Cream gave her two pills to 'improve her complexion'. Lou, who did not like the look of them, only pretended to put them in her mouth. She hid them in her hand and threw them away when he was not looking. Cream then gave her 5s. to go to the Oxford music hall (corner of Tottenham Court Road and Oxford Street) where he promised to meet her later. She waited until 11.30 p.m. Cream never showed up – presumably he thought she was dead.

Cream then, perversely, gave himself away. He visited Scotland Yard to complain that the police were following him in connection with the murders. He was not a suspect and the police were puzzled, especially when he mentioned Lou Harvey, who had not died. Lou saw her name included in press reports and realised Cream had intended her to be his next victim. One of her friends testified that she saw Cream give Lou the capsules.

Cream was found guilty after the body of one of the other victims was exhumed and found to contain strychnine. When he was hanged at Newgate in November, 1892, 5,000 'drink sodden men and repulsive females' gathered outside, the largest crowd for a hanging since the ending of public executions in 1868.

MARIE HERMANN was a destitute 43-year-old Austrian who worked as a prostitute to support her three children, one of whom was blind, on the first floor of 51 Grafton Way in 1894. She described herself as a music teacher and in her younger days was known as 'the Duchess'. A 70-year-old retired cab driver, Henry Stephens, drunk and weighing 16 stone, refused to pay Marie for her services after meeting her late one night in Euston Road and going to her flat. A struggle followed during which Stephens seized Marie by the throat and threatened her with a poker. Marie, a small, emaciated woman, wrested the poker from Stephens and hit him on the head.

Living upstairs was a young woman, Louise Hutchins, who heard a man moan out 'murder'. She disregarded it and went out to a dance. Marie tried to revive Stephens with some brandy. She bandaged the wound to his head, but he died at 7 a.m. She managed to heave his body into a trunk. The next day she arranged for two removal men to take the trunk and her furniture to new lodgings at 115 New Cavendish (56 *Upper Marylebone*) Street. Louise's mother, Mrs Hutchins, was suspicious. She too had heard sounds of a scuffle the previous night, and when she found blood on the communal sink, she followed Marie to the new address and then went to the police

The newspapers made much of the case and prejudged it as 'the most terrible murder of the age'. Her defending barrister, Marshall Hall, whose address at Welbeck Street was relatively close geographically but worlds apart socially, took on the case, one of the first by which he was to earn a reputation as an outstanding, if melodramatic, advocate. He argued passionately for the plea of self-defence, reminding the jury that a total of 12 bruises were found on Marie's neck when she was taken into custody. The jury returned a verdict of not guilty of murder, but guilty of manslaughter, and Marie was jailed for six years.

He wore Gold rimmed Glasses and had very Peculiar eyes. As far as I can remember he had [a] dress suit on, and [a] long mackintosh on his arm. He spoke with a foreign Twang. He asked me if I had ever been in America. I said no. He had an Old Fashioned Gold Watch, with an Hair or silk fob Chain and seal. Said he had been in the army. I noticed he was a very hairy man. He said he had never been married.

Louisa Harris on serial killer Dr Thomas Neil Cream

Of the three local doctors hanged for poisoning, the most famous was the American, Dr Hawley Harvey Crippen (1860-1910). He arrived in London in 1897 and took rooms in South Crescent, off Store Street, where he was joined by his wife, the singer Kunigunde 'Belle Elmore' Mackamatotzki, as soon as she arrived from America. Immediately, according to Crippen, their troubles began. His wife let him know that on board ship there had been men who 'made a fuss of her'. Some of her admirers visited her at South Crescent.

The Crippens moved to 34 and then 37 Store Street. In 1905 they moved out of the area, to 39 Hilldrop Crescent, Camden, but Crippen continued to commute to work at Munyon's Homeopathic Remedies in Albion House, 59-61 New Oxford Street, where he was also a partner in Yale Tooth Specialists. Crippen was by then in love with a typist at his office, Ethel le Neve, and when Belle told Crippen that she wanted to leave him for another man, and that she intended to withdraw money from their joint bank account, Crippen planned her murder. On January 15, 1910 he ordered poison from Lewis and Burrows at 108 New Oxford Street, just 100 yards from Tottenham Court Road corner. It was an unusual order and Crippen had to wait four days before he could collect it. He administered the poison on January 31.

Two days later, Belle was dead. Crippen went to Messrs Attenborough, 142 Oxford Street, on the corner of Adam and Eve Court, to pawn some of her jewellery, and received £80 for it. A week later he returned with more of her jewellery, which he pawned for £115 – but not before Ethel had worn the jewellery to the Vanbrugh Theatre in Malet Street, where it had been recognised by Belle's friends.

Chief Inspector Walter Dew of Scotland Yard questioned Crippen at his New Oxford Street office, where Ethel was present, wearing the jewellery. Crippen claimed that Belle had left him for another man. Dew believed him, and there the case may have rested, had not Crippen panicked and left the country. The Chief Inspector called at Crippen's house to verify a date, and found the place abandoned. The police searched the building and discovered the corpse of Crippen's wife, filleted, and buried in lime under the brick floor of the cellar.

Crippen was on a ship sailing to America, and remarked on the radio aerial to the ship's captain, 'What a wonderful invention it is.' The captain recognised the description of Crippen broadcast on the radio and Crippen became the first murderer to be apprehended with its aid. He was hanged in 1910.

The following year Stinie Morrison (1881-1921) was arrested for the murder of Leon Beron, a receiver of stolen goods, whose body was found in the early hours of New Year's Day on Clapham Common. Morrison, a burglar, regularly visited 18 Charlotte Street, a Greek grocery store run by Barnett Rotto, a pimp, as a front for stolen goods and prostitution. It was here that Morrison met Jane Brodsky. He slept with her on her 16th birthday and they became lovers.

When he was arrested for the murder of Beron, Jane provided a false alibi, saying that he had been with her at a music hall. Morrison may have been on another burglary at the time but, with his previous convictions for burglary, this would have meant an extended prison sentence and Morrison hated prison so much that he said he would rather hang.

Although he was convicted, his sentence was commuted because of doubts about his case. Morrison petitioned four times, asking to be hanged instead of locked-up. When these failed he went on hunger strike and died.

George Joseph Smith (1872-1915) was the 'Brides in the Bath' murderer. In 1900 he nearly charmed a local 'buxom young lady' to an early drowning by

THE JUST END OF A MONSTER OF INIQUITY.

THE CONDEMNED MAN. NEILL. MENTALLY REVIEWS HIS AWFUL PAST

bath. He stopped and talked to her as she was gazing at a hat in an Oxford Street shop window, and told her that he wanted to pay tribute to two works of art: herself and the hat. She was seduced by his charm until Smith was arrested for theft and frogmarched down Regent Street and past Hanover Square (where he had been bigamously married in St George's church), to the police station.

Smith returned to the area in 1908 and, using the alias of George Love, obtained work in a club. Between 1912 and 1914 he insured three wives, each for a large amount of money (Smith was himself the son of an insurance agent), before subsequently drowning the women in guest-house baths. He had married his last victim, Margaret Lofty of Holloway, in the town of Bath. When a nurse dressed in a swimsuit demonstrated the drowning procedure in court, she passed out, and had to be revived. Smith was executed in August 1915.

In September 1912 a demented Armenian-Turkish tailor, STEPHEN TITUS, who was staying in Room 13 at the Horseshoe Hotel, 267 Tottenham Court Road, and keeping company with local anarchists, ran amok in the hotel's Bohemian Bar. Brandishing a revolver, he shot the manageress point-blank, killing her instantly, and wounded a barmaid.

Titus fled out into the street. A newspaper vendor, John Starchfield, whose pitch was on the corner of Tottenham Court Road and Oxford Street, rugby-tackled him. Titus shot Starchfield twice in the stomach. Writhing in agony, Starchfield managed to grab hold of the gunman. A passer-by, Thomas Johns, pinned Titus down, taking a gunshot wound from which he later died. The murderer was concussed during the struggle and arrested.

At his trial Titus refused to plead. The court interpreted his 'malignant silence' as 'mute by malice', and found Titus guilty but insane. He was sent to Broadmoor.

Starchfield, the newspaper seller, was awarded £1 a week from the Carnegie Hero Fund. His five-year-old son Willie was subsequently found dead on a train in January 1914. At the inquest, a witness pointed at Starchfield and said that she had seen him with a boy who looked like Willie, but other witnesses testified that Starchfield was in a Drury Lane common lodging house at the time of his son's death. The judge directed the jury to acquit Starchfield. He himself thought that friends of Stephen Titus had murdered his son in

Le Petit Journal

ADMINISTRATION
61, RUE LAFAYETTE, 61

Les manuscrits ne sont pas rendus

On s'abonne sans frais
dans tous les bureaux de poste

5 CENT. SUPPLÉMENT ILLUSTRÉ **5** CENT.

21 me Année
Numéro 1.030

DIMANCHE 14 AOUT 1910

ABONNEMENTS

	SIX MOIS	UN AN
SEINE et SEINE-ET-OISE..	2 fr.	3 fr. 50
DÉPARTEMENTS...........	2 fr.	4 fr. »
ÉTRANGER	2 50	5 fr. »

ARRESTATION DU DOCTEUR CRIPPEN ET DE MISS LE NEVE
SUR LE PONT DU « MONTROSE »

revenge. In August 1916, Starchfield died as a result of complications from his gunshot wound.

During a wartime zeppelin raid on October 31, 1917, Mrs Emilienne Gerard, a 32-year-old Belgian, went to take shelter at Great Portland Street station (near where she lived at 50 Munster Square), then changed her mind, deciding it would be safer in her lover's basement. She arrived at 101 Charlotte Street, only to discover that her lover, LOUIS VOISIN (1875-1917) was there with another woman, BERTHE ROCHE.

Roche and Voisin repeatedly struck Emillienne about the head. They strangled her with a towel, and Voisin used his butcher's skills to carve up the body. He drove off with parts of Emilienne's corpse in a horse and trap. He deposited her torso and arms in Regent Square, and her legs in a nearby garden, together with a scrap of paper on which he had scrawled 'blodie Belgium' to make it appear to have been a xenophobic killing.

The police traced Emilienne's address through a laundry mark on the body's clothing. At her house they found a note signed by Voisin which led them to his address. There they discovered Emilienne's head and hands in the coal cellar. There were bloodstains up to the ceiling, and one of Emilienne's earrings was found. Voisin claimed he had visited Emilienne to feed her cat while she was away. He pretended to have found the head and hands of her body there, and taken them to hide in his cellar, because he feared he would be accused of her murder. 'The rest of the body was not there', he shrugged, 'it is unfortunate.'

When asked to write 'bloody Belgium' Voisin's misspelling, 'blodie Belgium', gave him away. The death sentence was read out to him in French and he was hanged. Roche, his accomplice, was sentenced to seven years in jail. She was diagnosed insane a few months later, and died within two years.

Ted Farrell, a turner at Hewson Manufacturing Company (which produced electric signs and aeroplane components), 9 Newman Yard, Newman Street, recognised a newspaper photograph of a military badge found at the scene of the murder and rape of 16-year-old Nellie True in 1918. It was the same as the badge belonging to another turner at Hewson's, 21-year-old DAVID GREENWOOD, an ex-soldier from the first world war.

Greenwood told Farrell that he had sold his badge to a man he met on a tram. Farrell suggested that they should clear up the matter, and took Greenwood to Tottenham Court Road police station. There a policeman noticed that the buttons on Greenwood's overcoat matched the button found by Nellie True's body, and that one of his buttons was missing. The wire thread on the button at the scene of the crime also matched thread used at the Hewson workshop.

Greenwood was found guilty of the murder. However, it was argued that shellshock had made Greenwood act out of character: aged 17 he had been buried alive by earth from an exploding shell in Ypres. On the eve of his execution, he was granted a reprieve and thousands signed petitions, but he spent 15 years in prison and was not released until 1933, when he was 36 years old.

In the early hours of September 27, 1927, a car dealer for Pytchely Auto Car Company, 216 Great Portland Street, FREDERICK GUY BROWNE (1891-1928), shot and killed a police constable named George Gutteridge, who had stopped him when he was driving a stolen car. The police found several guns – including a first-world-war army rifle that required an obsolete type of ammunition – in a garage owned by Browne in south London. Browne asserted that he had bought the rifle for self-protection, after being robbed twice on remote roads delivering cars for his employer.

DR HAWLEY HARVEY CRIPPEN and his lover, LE NEVE, made a bid for freedom on a ship bound for Quebec (1910).

Although Crippen was without his spectacles, the captain of the Montrose noticed the telltale red marks on either side of his nose. A radio message went out to the ship-owners, who forwarded it to Scotland Yard. The subsequent sea chase took 11 days, and was reported by the British press at every stage.

Go on, let her work. She'll do the strike a lot more good by going on and singing than by stopping out! You go and work Belle!

Marie Lloyd to Crippen's wife, Belle Elmore, who sang during the performers' strike at the Euston Palace music hall.

On hearing Belle, the audience streamed out from the hall, and stopped to listen to Marie Lloyd as she sang on the picket line.

Browne and an accomplice, William Kennedy, were arrested for murder. In the words of a prison officer, Browne was 'a complex sort of character, and would respond to human treatment. A pleasant word was sufficient to move him, but at the very whisper of a command, his prickles would go up like a hedgehog's.' Truculent in court, Browne took issue with the wording of the oath, and antagonised the judge. Ballistics evidence, used for the first time in the court trial, proved that a bullet fired by one of the guns found in Browne's garage had killed the officer. Browne and his accomplice William Kennedy, who both denied the murder, were found guilty and hanged.

ALFRED ARTHUR ROUSE (1894-1931), a travelling salesman who was strapped for cash and paying maintenance for his many illegitimate children, found that his latest lover, Ivy 'Paddy' Jenkins, a probationary nurse at University College Hospital, Gower Street, was pregnant. He decided to stage his own death to avoid paying any more maintenance for his previous children. He took a road near Northampton and picked up a hitchhiker. He stopped the car, pretending he needed to urinate, and walked into a field, secretly pouring a trail of petrol, which he then ignited, anticipating that the charred body of the dead hitchhiker would be mistaken for his. Two passers-by chanced to see Rouse climb out of the ditch near the blaze.

After his arrest young Ivy sent him violets and messages of affection until he started to boast publicly about his 'harem'. Ivy bitterly threw his wedding ring into the fire, and became ill. Her baby was stillborn. Rouse denied guilt, pleading that he had merely refilled the petrol tank, and that the hitchhiker had started the blaze by lighting a cigarette. Just before he was hanged on March 10, 1931, Rouse admitted the crime.

Sylvia Gough, society heiress, ex-dancer and local eccentric who frequented the Fitzroy Tavern, 16 Charlotte Street, in the 1930s, went to live with Douglas Bose, a black-magic devotee and writer, who was half her age, above Schmidt's restaurant, 33-37 Charlotte Street. Bose was said to exert 'hypnotic powers' over Sylvia. One day in 1936 Sylvia (then aged 42) turned up at the Tavern with a black eye, and DOUGLAS BURTON, a 30-year-old book reviewer, invited her to take shelter at his place for a few days. When Burton saw Bose (aged 21) at a party, he lost his head, picked up a sculptor's hammer and battered Bose to death.

Burton was found guilty and declared insane. He was said to have lusted over the 'pantherine' artists' model Betty 'Tiger Woman' May in the Fitzroy Tavern, and to have gone mad after she rejected his advances.

RAF airman, GORDON CUMMINS (1914-42), was dubbed the 'Blackout Ripper' because he killed four women in four days during the London blitz in the second world war. His most gruesome killing was that of a 43-year-old prostitute, Florence 'Pearl' Margaret Lowe. Pearl's daughter, who had been evacuated to Southend, returned to their flat, No.4, 9-10 Gosfield Street on Friday, February 13, 1942, to celebrate her 14th birthday the next day, only to find the body of her mother strangled with a silk stocking. Pearl's pelvis had also been horribly mutilated with a razor blade and knife.

Detective Chief Inspector Edward Greeno and Detective Inspector Higgins, of Tottenham Court Road police station, summoned the pathologist Sir Bernard Spilsbury, from Gower Street. Despite being hardened by dozens of sickening cases Spilsbury was moved to describe the injuries on Pearl's body as 'quite dreadful'. Apart from a single bed, Pearl's room was almost bare. Fingerprints, later identified as Cummins', were found on a candlestick and on a half-bottle of stout in the kitchen.

Pearl's neighbour recalled that, despite the police protection – 'There were police on all corners' – local people became doubly nervous at night, 'if ever

there was an air raid during the blackout people were scared to use the surface air raid shelter in Middleton Buildings by the Yorkshire Grey in Langham Place because the first woman [Evelyn Hamilton, a Marylebone teacher] was killed in one.'

Cummins was unmasked, literally, by a woman who tore off his gas mask when he attacked her – the police were able to identify Cummins from the mask's service number, 525987. They then searched and found Pearl's cigarette case in his Regent's Park billet. On June 25, 1942, Cummins, who was diagnozed schizophrenic, was hanged during an air raid.

It was also during an air raid that HAROLD LOUGHANS (1896-1963) bunked down as usual in the underground shelter at Warren Street tube-station on November 28, 1943. Just after midnight he crept out, stole a jeep, and drove down to Portsmouth, where he burgled the John Barleycorn pub. When disturbed by the pub's landlady, Rose Robinson, a 63-year-old widow, he strangled her. Afterwards he drove back to London. By 5 a.m., he had bunked down again in the Warren Street shelter.

At Loughans' trial the bruises on the victim's larynx – a deep thumb print and three lighter prints lacking fingernail impressions – were identified as belonging to Loughans, who had lost the ends of the fingers of his right hand

Louis Voison's kitchen in Charlotte Street, where he and Berthe Roche brutally butchered Emilienne Gerard.

The room was stained and splashed with blood. Body parts were hidden in a low, barrel-vaulted coal-cellar. In order to prove that the murder took place in the kitchen, the bloodstained door was produced in court, and the jury were taken to see the room.

in a brickyard when he was 15 years old. The pathologist, Bernard Spilsbury, contended that, with this disability, Loughans could not have strangled anyone.

Loughans, having been arrested for selling stolen goods, gave testimony that he had committed the murder, 'I was sorry for it the moment I done it. I haven't slept since, it preyed on my mind; she must have had a weak heart, the poor old girl.' However he later retracted, saying that he had slept in the Warren Street shelter all night. A rail-worker and five others in the shelter testified that they had seen Loughans at various times during the night. The jury failed to agree. There was a retrial and Loughans was acquitted. Sixteen years later, just before he died of cancer, Loughans admitted to the murder. A photograph in the *People* showed Loughan signing his confession with his deadly, deformed digits.

While Jack Tratsart (1918-47), a toolmaker, was celebrating his 27th birthday on April 20, 1945 with his family in the Lyons Corner House Tea Rooms, 10-16 Oxford Street, he took out a revolver. He tried to shoot but the safety catch was still on. His aunt asked him what he was doing, and he told her it was a water pistol. She laughed. He aimed again and fired six shots: two at his 28-year-old epileptic sister, Claire, who died on the way to hospital, two at his 57-year-old father, John, who died almost immediately, and two at his young brother, Hugh, who had palsy, and who was seriously injured. Tratsart then pointed the revolver at his own head and attempted suicide. He failed because he had used up all six bullets. With remarkable dexterity, he threw the gun into a hanging lightbowl, and the police took some time to find it.

Tratsart was marched to Tottenham Court Road police station, where he made a statement highlighting the difficulties experienced by his disabled brother and sister and by his father's lack of sympathy, 'They've never stood a chance and my father didn't help them in their deficiences. He is miserably, terribly bigoted, and the worst person to have as a father.'

Tratstart, a manic-depressive who was suffering from insomnia, was sent to Broadmoor, where he learned to play tennis and the piano to a high standard.

Immediately after the second world war RONNIE MAURIE, of 66 Cleveland Street, was hanged for strangling his common law wife, Vera Guest, on July 11, 1945, when she threatened to inform on him to the police over the robbery of a large consignment of cigarettes. Maurie, a keen boxer, had been a pupil at a school on the corner of Cleveland Street and New Cavendish (56 *Upper Marylebone*) Street. He drifted into crime and by the age of 27 had spent three years in Dartmoor. On the run after strangling his wife he was shot and wounded in a river by police during his capture.

The post-war television series *Fabian of the Yard* was based on the real-life SUPERINTENDENT ROBERT FABIAN of Scotland Yard. Fabian investigated a murder one afternoon in April 1947, at Jay's the Jewellers, 73-75 Charlotte Street. The victim was a passing motorcyclist, Alex de Antiquis, father of six, who had been shot as he tried to prevent an armed robbery, and who died shortly afterwards at Middlesex Hospital.

The three robbers, HARRY JENKINS (aged 23), CHRISTOPHER GERAGHTY (aged 21) and TERENCE ROLT (aged 17), escaped in a black saloon car that Jenkins had stolen from nearby Whitfield Street. The car stalled and they made a run for it, hiding in a disused office in Brook House, 191 Tottenham Court Road. Geraghty worked in John Line's paint shop, 213-216 Tottenham Court Road, directly opposite the police station from where the superintendent and his detectives conducted their inquiries.

Fabian searched Brook House and found his first clue, a raincoat with a ticket that he traced to Jenkins, but 27 witnesses of the robbery failed to recognise Jenkins in an identity parade. Jenkins was released and Fabian followed him to a pub, where he arrested Jenkins, Geraghty and Rolt altogether. Rolt revealed that the trio had travelled on the underground to Goodge Street tube station to seek a likely target for robbery. They picked Jay's jewellery shop, estimating that its window display was worth £5,000. As it was lunchtime, and the shop was crowded, they waited in a nearby café.

Geraghty and Jenkins were hanged. By coincidence, their executioner, Albert Pierrepoint, had been walking away from the Fitzroy Tavern where he and Superintendent Fabian were regular customers, and had seen Alex de Antiquis as he lay wounded in the street. Rolt, who was too young for execution, spent nine years in prison.

This was to be the last murder case of hard-working pathologist BERNARD SPILSBURY (1877-1947). During his examination of de Antiquis's body, Spilsbury failed to notice when the bullet fell out. Superintendent Fabian handed the bullet to Spilsbury with diplomatic words of congratulation but Spilsbury realised that his powers were beginning to wane. A few weeks later he gassed himself at his Gower Street laboratory, close to where he had been a pupil at University College School in 1888. At the time of his death he was a leading member of the Medico Legal Society in Portland Place. He had been depressed since the death of his son, Peter, in the second world war blitz on London.

Double-murderer DONALD HUME (b.1919) met his first victim, Stanley Setty, in the shady world of Warren Street second-hand car dealers. As a teenager, Hume had been a communist and street fighter, and he had designed an electric toaster. Setty ran a garage in nearby Cambridge Terrace Mews, had premises at 144 Great Portland Street, but conducted most of his business on the pavement outside the Goat and Compasses pub, 60 Fitzroy Street.

There were a lot of them in the area at that time, but I never guessed she was one. She was always very smartly dressed and seemed so ladylike and refined.

A moralistic neighbour gives her opinion of the dead prostitute 'Pearl', whose appearance had belied her poverty.

It's a relief to get it off my mind. I had to stop her screaming. I didn't mean to kill the old girl, but you know what it is when a woman screams.

Harold Loughans

Hume and Setty met in a café on Warren Street during December 1947, and started to trade black-market nylon stockings (still rationed) in exchange for forged petrol coupons in pubs such as the Feathers. Hume moved on to stealing cars, which Setty then sold, until Setty made the mistake of treating Hume's wife Cynthia too nicely and his dog Tony too badly: he made love to the former and kicked the latter, for scratching his car.

On October 4, 1949 Setty dropped off a friend at Fitzroy Square at 5 p.m. He was seen by his sister in nearby Osnaburgh Street at 5.30 p.m., and by his cousin in Great Portland Street at 5.50 p.m. At 7.30 p.m., when Hume arrived home, he found Setty in the flat in a compromising situation with Cynthia. Hume stabbed Setty with a German SS dagger, taking grim satisfaction from the fact that the dagger was stamped with Setty's initials.

Hume cut Setty's body up with a hacksaw. He put the head in a carton of baked beans and the rest in two packages. He hired a plane from the appropriately named Dagger Lane in Elstree. Accompanied by Tony the dog (to witness this form of rough justice) Hume flew across the channel and dropped Setty's remains off the French coast, then landed at Southend airport. Three weeks later the tide washed parts of the body back to the marshes near Southend. Police traced the finger prints on the arms of the torso, and traced the £5 note that Hume had paid for a taxi fare from there back to London. Setty was arrested and interrogated at Albany Street police station, where he pretended to have disposed of the body on behalf of a gang of three men, whose descriptions he modelled on his three interrogating officers. The jury found Hume not guilty of murder but sentenced him to 12 years as accessory. He served eight years.

Following his release he confessed to the killing in a newspaper article and fled to Switzerland, where he was re-arrested, after he had killed a taxi driver as he tried to escape from another bank robbery. On hearing that he was sentenced to life imprisonment, Hume had to be restrained with tear gas. He was released in 1976 and deported to Britain, where he was declared insane and sent to Broadmoor.

RUTH ELLIS (1927-55) was the last woman to be hanged in Britain. On Easter Day 1955, she shot her ex-lover, David Blaikely, while she was living with Desmond Cussen at nearby 20 Goodwood Court, 54-57 Devonshire Street (close to the corner of Great Portland Street). Blakely had persistently visited her there and caused trouble. During one visit he punched her. On her way to be treated at Middlesex Hospital for a black eye and a twisted ankle, she stopped at the Great Portland Street Café for a coffee. After Blaikely eventually persuaded Ruth to leave Cusson, he deserted her for another woman, and Ruth shot him in revenge outside a Hampstead pub. In the public mind it was a crime of passion, but a plea for reprieve failed. Her hangman was Albert Pierrepoint, a regular at the Fitzroy Tavern. Public disquiet over the killing of Ruth Ellis strengthened the pressure against capital punishment, and it was abolished a decade later.

JAMES HANRATTY (1936-62) was hanged for the A6 murder, protesting his innocence to the end. On October 6, 1961, Hanratty had telephoned to supply his alibi to Superintendent Bob Acott, who was investigating the murder of a man named Michael Gregston, in a car at Deadman's Hill, off the A6 road, on August 22, 1961. Gregston's lover, Valerie Storie, had also been shot and left for dead. Hanratty told the Superintendent that he had been with three men when the murder took place, but that they did not want to substantiate his alibi because they were 'fences'.

On the same day Hanratty saw the film *South Pacific*, at the Dominion Theatre in Tottenham Court Road, and stole a Jaguar in Portland Place, using

HARRY JENKINS leaving
Tottenham Court Road
police station on his way
to the court.

*Jenkins insisted he was
innocent. First, he claimed
that he had lent his coat with
its recriminating ticket to
another criminal. Then, that
his sister had given the coat to
Geraghty. Finally, that he had
been working at a model
manufacturer's, packing
statuettes, when the crime was
committed.*

his favourite method of noting the car key number on the ignition, then purchasing the appropriate key from a nearby garage.

Evidence given to the police that Hanratty was in Rhyl on the night of the murder was not made available to the defence, or to the jury, who found him guilty. Hanratty was hanged amid great controversy, and a campaign for a posthumous pardon continues to this day. An earlier suspect, Peter Alphon, confessed to the murder after the hanging, then retracted.

GRAHAM YOUNG (1948-90) was a serial poisoner. In November 1961, Young's sister, Winifred, felt peculiar as she was travelling to work on the tube, between Oxford Circus and Tottenham Court station. 'Everything was sort of coming and going', she said, 'and when I got out of the train I remember bumping into people and walking into walls and things like that. Somebody, I dimly remember, helped me up the stairs at Tottenham Court Road station and escorted me to the office.' Her boss put her in a taxi to Middlesex Hospital where her enlarged pupils were diagnosed as symptoms of belladonna poisoning. 'The only thing it could be is my young brother, Graham', Winifred told the doctor. 'He's terribly interested in chemistry and he may have mixed something up in a cup by mistake.' He had in fact laced her breakfast cup of tea with the drug.

Within a year Graham had poisoned his stepmother. At her funeral he offered his uncle a poisoned sandwich, but the uncle vomited and lived. When the 14-year-old Young confessed to these deeds, he added that he had also given poison to his father.

He was sent to Broadmoor where, with a startling disregard for his penchant for poisoning, he was given a job in the kitchen. At Broadmoor he added toilet-cleaning fluid to the nurses' coffee, and when another inmate died of cyanide poisoning, Young told the authorities – who did not believe him – that he had done it by extracting poison from laurel bushes.

Although his recommended sentence was a minimum of 15 years, he was released after eight, and he managed to find work that gave him access to chemicals. On April 24, 1971 he took some sheets of headed notepaper from London University* and walked through Fitzrovia to John Bell & Croyden at 52a Wigmore Street where, using the letterhead as authority, he bought some thallium, which he used to kill two of his workmates.

* University College, London (UCL) is sometimes confused with the University of London (London University). UCL was founded in 1826 at 43 Gower Street. In 1836 the University of London was formed as a federal structure (a government-chartered examining body, to award degrees and determine syllabus), covering both UCL and King's College (founded 1892). Since then the University of London has grown, and today it incorporates 37 separate institutions – colleges, schools, and institutes. Among these is Birbeck College (formed 1885), which became part of the university in 1920, and which has spread into Fitzrovia as far as Gresse Street, where its library is situated. University College Hospital Medical School and Bedford College are also part of the University of London, and Senate House in Malet Street (one street outside of Fitzrovia), built between 1933 and 1938, houses the university's administrative offices.

BERNARD SPILSBURY on his way to give evidence at the Old Bailey in the Antiquis murder trial (1947)

The first medical detective, Spilsbury's career as a hospital pathologist spanned nearly half a century. A generous man, unhurried in his work, methodical and always concise, he wrote summaries of all his post-mortems on case cards, noting his medical findings and a brief history of each case.

It is impossible to dictate to one's secretary while bodies are being sawn.

The pathologist at the trial of Donald Hume, replying to a question on the volume of noise made by sawing up the bones of a victim.

Before Young died in Parkhurst prison, he was discovered growing a deadly fungus and mixing it with his own excrement to produce poison.

The famous boxer and television personality, FREDDIE MILLS, was taken to the Middlesex Hospital after being shot dead in Goslett Yard, a few yards south of Tottenham Court Road, in the early hours of July 25, 1965. Although the official verdict was suicide, it was strongly rumoured that Mills was killed because he had refused to pay protection money for his club to one of the gangs operating in the area.

The most notorious of these gangs was led by the twins REG KRAY (1933-2000) and RON KRAY (1933-1995) who worked from a club off Tottenham Court Road, and who regularly wined and dined in Olivelli's restaurant, 35 Store Street. In the mid-1960s Reg learned to dance in Tottenham Court Road (most likely No 31, the Blarney dance club), in the hope that it would improve his 'social graces'. His tutors, Steve and Jimmy Clark, were partners in the club, which was run by Charlie Kray, older brother of Ron and Reg.

From 1962 to 1968 Ron and Reg ran a fronting business, the Carston Group of Companies, at 143 Great Portland Street, assisted by their financial adviser, Leslie 'Laurel' Payne, and an accountant, Freddie 'Hardy' Gore. Payne also acted as the middleman between the firm and the American Mafia. The Kray twins were arrested in 1968 and sentenced in 1969 to 30 years' imprisonment each, for two separate murders. The middlemen, Laurel and Hardy, both received prison sentences.

HARRY ROBERTS (b.1936) had spent four years in jail for robbery in 1966 when three policemen, who were on their way to Marylebone magistrates court, spotted him and two other men who had previous convictions, driving a car with false number plates and pulled them up. Desperate not to be locked up again, Roberts shot the two detectives. One of his accomplices shot the uniformed constable, making it a triple murder. The three men split up and went on the run. Roberts spent the night in the Russell Hotel, Russell Square. The next day he bought camping equipment in Tottenham Court Road, not far from the Euston council estate where he had grown up, and where his mother still lived. Roberts had learned jungle survival as a soldier in Malaya, and he spent the following three and a half months as a fugitive in Epping Forest before being captured and condemned to life imprisonment.

In 1975 PETER SUTCLIFFE (b.1946), the Yorkshire Ripper, asked to meet Joseph Sickert, son of the artist Walter Sickert, to question him about the Jack the Ripper murders. They talked in a café in Cleveland Street. That year Sutcliffe killed the first of his 13 victims.

Sutcliffe asked to meet Sickert again the following year. He arrived sweating and very agitated, saying that the Yorkshire Ripper should be shot, 'He kept going on about the differences between reality and fantasy and how they could be confused. I could tell he was a bit odd', Sickert commented later. Five years were to go by before Sutcliffe was arrested and sentenced to life imprisonment in 1981.

Mass killer DENNIS NILSEN (b.1945) was working at the Job Centre, 1 Denmark Street, just south of Tottenham Court Road station, when he carried out the first 13 of his 15 murders, in 1978. He boiled the flesh off the heads of three of these victims in the same pot that was used to cook food at the Job Centre's Christmas Party. At one time he also kept goldfish in the pot. He said that he killed all his victims after they had had sex, to stop them leaving him. He then cut up the bodies using the butchering skills he had learned as a soldier in the Army Catering Corps. In 1980 he lit a huge bonfire in the garden outside his flat to dispose of the remaining flesh and bones of his victims (including that of a homeless, undernourished man he had met in a doorway in Oxford Street near Tottenham Court Road). He then took the tube back to Tottenham Court Road to pick up another young man. On January 26, 1983, he bought his last victim, Stephen Sinclair, a hamburger in McDonalds, 8-10 Oxford Street, before they went for a drink in the Royal George, Goslett Yard. They then travelled by tube to Tottenham Court Road station to go to Nilsen's flat.

Shortly afterwards Nilsen attempted to flush the remains of his previous victims down the toilet, which blocked the drains. Nilsen was arrested and a sample of the blockage taken to University College Hospital for analysis, where it was identified by forensic expert David Bowen as human neck and hand. (Local student Paul Nobbs, whom Nilsen tried to strangle, had been treated at the same hospital). Nilsen's dog, Bleep, died in Battersea Dogs' Home after her master was imprisoned for life.

I vowed I would wait and get revenge. Fourteen years later, I was at a drinking party with him. He had had a few, so I deliberately set out to provoke him in a heated conversation. He fell for the trap, and had a go at me verbally, whereupon I hit him on the chin with a right hook which knocked him out and broke his jaw. To this day, that particular villain doesn't know I waited 14 years for my moment.

Reg Kray

He sniffed twice, looked around the room, and said, 'You mustn't smoke, please, Johnson. I can't smell the smells I want to smell.' He then bent down over the corpse and sniffed away as if it was a rose-garden.

H. Howgrave-Graham on his first post-mortem, which was conducted by Sir Bernard Spilsbury.

CHAPTER 4
A Variety of Villains

Swashbuckling highwayman and housebreaker, JACK SHEPPARD (1702-24), became a folk hero in his own lifetime for his escapes from prison. He rescued Elizabeth 'Edgeworth Bess' Lion, his lover and partner in crime, from St Giles Round-house, a small lock-up at the corner of Tottenham Court Road and Oxford Street, by knocking down the beadle on guard duty and breaking open the cell door. Later, he was imprisoned there himself, and he broke through the roof and went off into the night. By making his way through six doors, and descending a 75-foot wall before scaling another wall, 20-foot high, he escaped from Newgate prison twice. The second time he took refuge in a cowhouse in fields near Tottenham Court Road, with his legs still in fetters. From there he hobbled to a chandler's in Tottenham Court Road for food and beer, and then to a local shoemaker's for a hammer and punch to smash his chains. He stayed in a few local alehouses and inns and raided a local pawnbroker, but on recklessly returning to a pub near Newgate he was recaptured. A crowd of 200,000 flocked to watch him taken to the gallows.

Legendary highwayman DICK TURPIN (1709-39) often operated in the fields of Marylebone. He visited prostitutes in Marylebone Gardens, where he is reputed to have stolen a kiss from Mrs Fountayne, a schoolmaster's wife, telling her that now she could boast of having been kissed by the famous Dick Turpin. In 1735 he and five others raided Mr Francis, a Marylebone farmer. They tied up the farmer, beat the members of the family, and robbed them of their gold and silver. Two of the gang were caught and hanged, and a reward of £100 was put on Turpin's head. He fled north, where he was arrested and taken into custody for shooting a cock. His identity was discovered, and he was charged with horse stealing, for which he was hanged on April 10, 1739. His body was to be passed to a surgeon for dissection (a practice introduced in 1540), but a protesting crowd intervened and restored Turpin's corpse to its coffin.

MOTHER JANE 'THE EMPRESS' DOUGLAS (1700-61) was the most illustrious madam of her day. She ran the lavishly decorated bordello at the King's Head tavern (282 Euston Road, on the northern junction with Tottenham Court Road, demolished 1906), where her 'liveried lackeys' provided customers with aphrodisiac pills and an early type of condom (at inflated prices) wrapped in silk and tied with ribbons. She was frequently fined and imprisoned, but continued to attract blue-blooded customers such as Prince William, Duke of Cumberland, and Lord Fitzwilliam and Admiral Charles Homes – it was debatable which of the latter two fathered her daughter, Elizabeth.

Just before Mother Jane Douglas died, she was visited by the playwright Charles Johnson, who described her as 'much bloated by drink and debauch...her legs swelled out of shape...a nice cheerful old woman although suffering great discomfort.' She was the model for Mother Cole in *Fanny Hill* (1748) by John Cleland.

Two women, MARY HENDSOR and MARGARET PRENDERGASS, were found guilty of kidnapping a Miss Morris and holding her captive in Mother Jane's bordello, a crime for which they were hanged in 1726.

I had nothing but an old razor in my pocket, and was confin'd in the upper part of the place, being two stories from the ground; with my razor I cut out the stretcher of a chair, and began to make a breach in the roof...It being about nine at night, people were passing and repassing in the street...there was no time to be lost.

Jack Sheppard on his escape from St Giles's Round-house

JACK SHEPPARD

Jack Sheppard, highwayman, whose humour and daring made him a hero. For a few heady weeks in 1724, he was the most famous man in London. Girls dressed in white threw flowers at Sheppard on his way to be hanged at Tyburn.

THE MARCH TO FINCHLEY
by William Hogarth (1750)

Mother Douglas and her 'Cattery' at the King's Head, Tottenham Court Road turnpike, cheering the troops marching north to defeat Bonnie Prince Charlie. Hands clasped to the heavens, Mother Douglas stands at the bottom window on the right, praying for their safe return.

Caricature of HENRY
FAUNTLEROY, the bank
forger, by Richard
Dighton (1824)

*Fauntleroy's hanging was
a gruesome affair. On
November 30, a day of icy
rain and a raw wind, the
trapdoor was released and
Fauntleroy dangled over the
short drop of 18 inches, his
knees level with the floor of
the scaffold. The executioner's
assistants tugged Fauntleroy's
legs, and while he struggled
convulsively, the crowd of
100,000 took off their hats
to allow those behind a
better view.*

**I am now a spectacle
to men, and shall soon be
a spectacle to angels...
Many have been
overpowered by
temptation, who are
now among the penitent
in heaven.**

Dr William Dodd,
convicted of forgery,
before he was hanged

The plight of fresh country girls lured into prostitution became the subject of contemporary literature. Their sexual skills were marketed in a series of guides to London prostitutes with an annual print run of 8,000, launched by Jack Harris in the 1740s. In one copy issued in 1788, a Miss Johnson of 17 Goodge Street was written up gymnastically, 'She has such elasticity in her loins she can cast her lover to a pleasing height, and receive him again with the utmost dexterity.' Another entry represents Miss Corbett of 16 Goodge Street, who 'always measures a gentleman's *may-pole* by a standard of *nine inches*, and expects a guinea for every inch it is short of full measure.'

CHARLOTTE LORAINE ran a brothel in Goodge Street after moving there as an actress in 1764, following a brief marriage to a Mr Hazelwood. Under her married name she published a popular, scandalous memoir, *The Secret History of the Green Room*, about the bedroom antics between actresses and the nobility. The demi-rep SALLY HUDSON, known as 'Mother Hudson', set up a brothel in Margaret Street in the 1770s.

On a wintry day in 1726 Henrietta Perreau, who lived at the Cleveland Street end of New Cavendish (*Upper Marylebone*) Street, witnessed the hanging of her husband, ROBERT PERREAU, and his brother, DANIEL, at Tyburn in 1776, for forging bonds. Their first forgery, valued at £5,000, was carried out in the name of James Adair, a linen merchant of Soho Square. The brothers held hands as they awaited execution. The snow fell around them, and the mob japed and gawped, 'with the most inhuman indecency, laughing and shouting, and throwing snowballs at each other.' Two housebreakers were hanged at the same time, but at a respectable distance away because they were Jews, outcasts even in death.

The REVEREND WILLIAM DODD (1729-1777) who was sardonically tagged the 'divine dissolute' by Polly Kennedy, a prostitute, and taunted as 'the Macaroni Preacher' on account of his foppish manner and dress, tried to bribe the Lord Chancellor to appoint him to St George's in Hanover Square. Not only a dandy but a randy chaplain, his name was spotted in the rate book of a brothel, and he was dismissed by the king. He fell into debt while living in Argyll Street, Oxford Circus. Convicted of fraud for forging a bond worth £4,200, he was sentenced to be hanged. With just two weeks to live, Dodd feverishly set about writing his autobiography in verse, *Thoughts in Prison*. Published after his death it became a best-seller, inspiring his friend, Samuel Johnson, to comment that 'When a man knows he is to be hanged in a fortnight it concentrates his mind wonderfully.'

The crowds thronged along Oxford Street in 1777 to watch Dodd carried to the Tyburn gallows, and were 'moved to pity by the ghastly face at the coach window.' Dodd's friends bribed the hangman to cut him down before he was formally pronounced dead. They rushed his body onto a coach and hurtled through a rainstorm to an undertaker named Mr Davies in Goodge Street. There the eminent surgeon, John Hunter (1728-93), who was known to have saved patients from death by drowning, tried to resuscitate Dodd in a hot bath, without success.

HENRY FAUNTLEROY (1785-1824) was 22 years old when he became manager of the bank at 6 Berners Street (founded 1792, on the site now occupied by the Berners Hotel), following the death of his father, William, in 1807. He later embarked on what was to become the biggest banking scandal of the century. During the recession following the Napoleonic wars one of the bank's customers, a building speculator, went bust owing £60,000 and, after the Bank of England refused financial assistance, Fauntleroy turned to fraud to try to save the bank from collapse. By forging customers' signatures he was able to sell stocks and shares held by the bank on their behalf. Whenever dividends were due or a customer wanted to sell some shares, Fauntleroy simply resorted to more fraudulent sales to pay for them.

When Fauntleroy's debts spun out of control he increasingly sought solace by spending lavishly on women and drink, an extravagant, dissolute life requiring ever more expensive forgeries. His day of reckoning was January 23, 1824, when a rich customer who owned £40,000 worth of shares died, and the executors of his will discovered that Fauntleroy had been embezzling. He was arrested and all the bank's transactions were immediately suspended, leaving many local tradespeople, who had invested all their savings with the bank, in ruin. They were more than furious (some received just half of the money owed to them, and not until 26 years later) and the police had to be called to prevent a riot.

Fauntleroy's steamy double-life was a press sensation. Tickets for gallery seats in his Old Bailey trial sold for a guinea each. Joseph Parkins, a customer cheated out of £4,000, took a seat at the front intending to gloat over Fauntleroy's ordeal, but a court official, 'realising the motive of the vindictive nabob', ordered Parkins to the back of the court. His humiliation amused the court reporters, 'who were delighted to chronicle his discomfiture'.

Fauntleroy's mother, Elizabeth, continued to live at 7 Berners Street (where Henry had lived from 1806) for the remaining 16 months of her life. His brother John, a solicitor, who lived at 14 Great Portland Street, committed suicide in 1850.

A young butler, ROBERT WEBSTER (1803-27), stole £2 of silver from his employer, Reverend Jones, hid it in an orchard, then staged a commotion to make it sound as if there had been a burglary. He took the silverware to Mr Styles, a silversmith, 28 Tottenham Court Road, claiming it was an inheritance from his uncle. He sold some of it and exchanged the rest for gold watches. On his arrest he swore that a note left by the burglars led him to the silver. He was condemned to the gallows (six years later the death sentence for burglary would be lifted). Waiting for the rope, he admitted committing the robbery and prayed fervently on the scaffold for 25 minutes.

THERESA BERKLEY ran a brothel specializing in flagellation at 84-94 Hallam (*28 Charlotte*) Street* from 1828 to 1836. Clients were offered a choice of whips: thongs, cat-o-nine-tails, straps fastened with tin-tacks, wielded by 'assistant governesses'. Services listed were: birching, whipping, fustigating (cudgelling), scourging, needle pricking, phlebotomising (cutting veins), nettle stinging, holly brushing and firse-mising (gorse-scratching). There was also Theresa's own invention, the Berkley Horse, of which there were two types: a birch-flogging wheel that went at various speeds and a padded ladder to which the customer was tied to be whipped.

While Theresa would personally oblige some clients 'to a certain extent', if they wanted a stronger hand, 'if they were gluttons at it', her assistants, including one called One-Eyed Peg, did the beating. Any customer who needed to be revived after a session was treated with the stinging nettles that were displayed around the place in elegant china vases.

Ironically, Marylebone Parish records show that 6s. 8d., a portion of the annual rate bill paid by Theresa, was assigned to the building of new churches and chapels. She died in 1836 leaving most of her £10,000 fortune to her brother, a missionary in Australia. After he understood how his sister had made her money he renounced any claim to it. The Crown took over as executor of her estate and suppressed Theresa's autobiography in which she had named many royal and aristocratic clients.

Nineteenth century prostitutes in Fitzrovia, described as having 'a quick and intuitive method of observing the various aberrations of the human mind,

THE BERKLEY HORSE, devised by Theresa Berkley, for the flagellation of her clients

By the 1780s flagellation was so popular that foreigners referred to it as the English perversion. It was thought to be good for the health, promoting the circulation of bodily fluids.

* The address of Theresa Berkley's brothel is wrongly given by some authors as having been either present-day 28 or 64 Charlotte Street. This is because Hallam Street used to be called Charlotte Street and, when today's Charlotte Street was re-numbered in 1868, No.64 was changed to No.28. The Marylebone rate book of 1835 (Ward A, p.16) confirms that Sarah Theresa Berkley lived at 28 Charlotte Street, by Portland Place, which is today's 84-94 Hallam Street. (M.P.)

The Cleveland Street *maison de passé*, picturing clients, telegraph boys, a waiting cabby and an oblivious policeman.

The desire to make male and female prostitutes equal under the law, led to the Labouchere Amendment (1885), which helped to crystallise the concept of homosexuality. But puritan Victorians were horrified by the raid on the gay brothel on Cleveland Street, employing telegraph messenger boys. This was a crime that was not meant to exist.

and ready and willing to humour them', included 'EMMA LEE' RICHARDSON, 50 Margaret Street, and MRS JONES, of the northern end of Whitfield (*Hertford*) Street, and also of Maple (*London*) Street. Clients in Fitzrovia in 1875 who liked to be birched included Algernon Charles Swinburne (novelist and art critic) who regularly visited prostitutes in Portland Place, and Simeon Solomon (artist).

In 1880 a policeman's wife pretended to be pregnant so that her husband could trap a young chemist, THOMAS TITLEY, 44 Charlotte Street, into supplying her with an abortifacient drug. The police were charged with having incited a criminal act, but were let off on a technicality. Although there was a public outcry and thousands signed a petition in support of Titley, the chemist was sentenced to 18 months' hard labour, and had to complete the full term.

CHARLES WELLS, who lived at 162 Great Portland Street in 1885, was a swindler who duped people into investing thousands of pounds in his hare-brained inventions, which included a musical skipping rope. He used the money to decorate his apartment and to buy a sizeable yacht, large enough to hold a ballroom and a church organ. He sailed to Monte Carlo, where he made a spectacular win of £16,000 at the casino in 1892. The headlines, 'The man who broke the bank', brought him instant fame, which alerted his investors to his whereabouts, and he was sentenced to eight years' hard labour for obtaining £29,000 through false pretences. On his release he invented a lifebelt, which was demonstrated by a defrocked clergyman, but before long he was again cheating gullible investors, and he was sent back behind bars.

In 1894, during a police raid on a club at 46 Fitzroy Street, a music hall artiste, ARTHUR MARLING, was arrested for being dressed as a woman and charged with being 'an idle and disorderly person'. He appeared in court wearing female clothes and the defence argued that he was hired by the club to be an 'entertainer'. He was bound over for three months. The following year both the Fitzroy Street club and Marling were cited during the trial of Oscar Wilde. Two years later, Marling was charged with having attempted to blackmail Oscar Wilde and sentenced to five years' penal servitude. There was also a homosexual 'introduction house' in Fitzroy Street during this period.

Religious racketeers FRANK 'THEO HOROS' JACKSON and EDITH 'SWAMI' JACKSON dressed up as Chinese mandarins in order to debauch gullible young women in 1901. They persuaded the women to visit them in a room dimly lit with a few 'exotic lamps' at 99 Gower Street, where the women were duped into believing that they would conceive 'divine children'. Asked by one young woman why 'Christ' would need so many wives, Frank Jackson replied that Solomon had had 600 women as well as 300 wives. But after one of the women had agreed to offer her jewellery to God on a sacrificial altar, she had second thoughts, and went to the police. Her jewellery was traced to a pawnbroker and the Jacksons were arrested. Frank was sentenced to 15 years' imprisonment and Edith to seven years.

MAY 'QUEEN OF THE UNDERWORLD' CHURCHILL (1876-1929), also known as 'CHICAGO MAY', was an Irish emigré brought up in Chicago who picked men up in hotel bars as part of a blackmail scam operating from 107 Gower Street in 1907. She would slip a Mickey Finn into a man's drink, then lead him, half-stupefied, to her bed, whereupon there would be a loud knock on the door. May's lover and accomplice, Eddie Guerin, would burst in and announce that May's husband knew that the man was in her bed, and that only the payment of a certain sum of money would persuade him not to name the victim in a legal action. Several men with public reputations to protect fell for the scam. After Guerin was jailed for taking part in a £60,000 robbery, May found a new accomplice, Charles Smith. Unexpectedly, Geurin was released from prison, and he headed for Gower Street, bent on revenge. He was about to throw vitriol at May when Smith shot him in the foot. Guerin was sentenced to life imprisonment for attempted murder, and May was given 15 years.

Drug dealing increased in London during the first world war. FREDERICK FREEMULLER, a 19-year-old butcher, who lived in Wells Street, and MARK COHEN, a 46-year-old Russian, who lived in Tottenham Street, supplied cocaine to soldiers in 1916. They were each caught, jailed for three months and deported.

The Falstaff Club in Oxford Street was the first of many illegal nightclubs that were all the rage in Fitzrovia during the 1920s. Opened by Con Collins and his personal assistant, gangster MARK BENNEY, in defiance of the Defence of the Realm Act, which restricted licensed drinking hours, the Falstaff was a barn-like hall with an 'air of frenetic excitement' that 'induced bolder members of the upper classes to rub shoulders with its mainly underworld clientele'. When an Italian gang, called the 'Raddies' after Italian radicals, Mazzini and Garibaldi, staged pitched battles with rival racetrack protection racketeers, the police clamped down and closed the club.

KATE MEYRICK, who boasted that she was the first woman in Ireland to have ridden a bicycle, became London's 'Night Club Queen'. Her string of clubs included the Folies Bergère in Newman Street and her eclectic mix of customers included Russian Bolsheviks, European aristocrats, American gangsters, film stars, and the local artist Augustus John. Kate was arrested in 1924 and 1928, and given a six-month sentence each time.

It was then discovered that she had been bribing a police sergeant, Goddard of the vice squad, who could not justify having £18,000 in his bank account, a large house and a luxury car, on his weekly wage of £6. 15s. To the court he declared that he made his money from music publishing, selling rock, currency speculation, and horse racing, but the jury was not convinced and he was sentenced to 18 months' hard labour. This time Kate Meyrick was given 15 months in prison, during which her health suffered, and, after a further two six-month stretches, she decided it was time to quit. She died in 1932, leaving eight children and just £58 in her will, although she had earned enough during her life to send her two sons to Harrow and her four daughters to Roedean. Her daughters worked as hostesses, 'dance instructors', in her nightclubs and two of them later married peers.

FREDA KEMPTON worked for Kate Meyrick as a 'dancing instructress' and took cocaine to keep awake while she worked into the early hours. One night in 1922, after finishing at 3 a.m., she went with a friend, Rose Heinberg, to the New Court Club off Tottenham Court Road, where the two women met BRILLIANT 'BILLY' CHANG, a Chinese man in his mid-30s. Freda obtained a bottle of cocaine from Chang, and asked him if anyone had died from sniffing it. 'No,' Chang replied, 'the only way you can kill yourself is by putting cocaine in water.' The next day Freda had an excruciating headache. She dashed her head in agony against the wall, went into convulsions, foaming at the mouth, and died in her landlady's arms. The pathologist, Bernard Spilsbury, confirmed that Freda had died from an overdose of cocaine.

Chang was tried and jailed in an atmosphere of prejudice fanned by the press. The *Empire News* published a lurid and unsubstantiated story that two girls had disappeared from Tottenham Court Road for four days and, when they were found their clothes had been almost torn from their backs in a 'wild frenzy produced by Chang's opium pipe'. *John Bull* magazine painted a racist picture of the 'black peril' lurking between Tottenham Court Road and Great Portland Street. Self-appointed vigilante groups began to hound the dancing

It's my only fortune, Sir. But it really provides for all I want.

John Saul, professional 'Mary-Anne', boasting about his priapus

Saul lived with Charles Hammond at Cleveland Street. Later he was less sanguine about working as a prostitute, 'I have lost my character and cannot get on otherwise. I occasionally do odd jobs for gay people [female prostitutes].'

I had a strange sense of shadows closing protectively about me, of the rhythms of my being sinking into the silence of small night noises till I became as it were the focal point of a vast brooding darkness.

Mark Benney on burgling

GORDON ARNOLD
LONSDALE, sentenced by
Lord Parker in 1961 to 25
years for espionage.

Superintendent Herbert Sparks of Tottenham Court Road police station, who headed the investigation, declared that Hinds had made a verbal confession, which Hinds denied. Hinds said that the dust on his clothes, supposed to have come from blowing the safe, was from the mahogany in his garage, and that strands supposedly from the fuse were probably from the police blanket in his cell. Eleven days later the police destroyed the blanket and the dust samples. At the trial James Gridley, the Maples night-superintendent, was identified as the brains behind the robbery. He implicated Hinds, and was rewarded with a light one-year sentence, while Hinds was given 12 years.

In his youth Hinds had escaped from Borstal, from a remand home, and, later, the army, and he staged two dramatic escapes, one from prison and one from court, to call attention to his case and demand a retrial. Eleven years later he was in his cell listening to the radio when he heard Sparks (subsequently appointed head of the flying squad) advertising his memoirs in a commercial for a Sunday newspaper. Sparks mentioned the Maple's robbery and Hinds decided to sue Sparks for libel. Not technically a retrial, the case nevertheless involved a re-examination of the evidence. This showed that although the fuses at the robbery were burned the fragments on Hinds' clothes were merely heated, and that the police witness had used the phrase 'exactly similar' when he meant merely 'no difference' for the threads that could, after all, have come from the police blanket. Under cross-examination, Gridley admitted that he had made a false statement about Hinds' involvement and superintendent Sparks admitted he had no proof that Hinds had been the ringleader. The verdict went in Hinds' favour, and he was awarded £1,300 damages. On his release he moved to Jersey where, with his IQ of 150, he became secretary of the Channel Islands branch of MENSA.

Russian spy GORDON LONSDALE (1922-70) ran the 'Portland Spy Ring' from Flat 634 in the White House, opposite Great Portland Street station, apparently a good location for wireless reception and for transmission to Russia. In 1961 he was caught and sentenced to 25 years' imprisonment. His real name was Knonan Trofimovich Moloday. Raised in America he had returned to the Soviet Union to enlist in the Red Army during the war. After serving three years of his sentence, he was exchanged with the Russians for the British spy, Greville Wynne. In Moscow he worked as a KGB lecturer, and he died after a prolonged drinking bout.

Another spy who did not complete his sentence, GEORGE BLAKE (b.1922), was convicted in 1961 under the Official Secrets Act and sentenced to 42 years in prison – he had previously been in prison in Germany and Spain (second world war), and North Korea (1951). Six years earlier he had been living at 5 All Souls' Place, beside Broadcasting House, when he received orders from MI6 to become a double-agent, a job he did too well: he pretended to act for the Russians while actually doing so. Five years after the start of his sentence he escaped from Wormwood Scrubs and fled to Moscow, where he was awarded the Order of Lenin for his work in North Korea. Asked if he would like to return to Korea, he replied he would rather go back to Wormwood Scrubs.

In the 1940s Charlie Kray used to take his brothers, the KRAY TWINS, who were then 16 years old, boxing at Bill Kline's gymnasium, which Reg Kray recalled as being in Great Portland Street (others remember it as Fitzroy Square). There they boxed against Ben Valentine, middleweight champion of the Fiji Islands. Reg also fought at Clark Brothers' gymnasium in Tottenham Court Road, against Freddy Mack (whom he called the coloured heavyweight).

When they were 20 years old, Ron and Reg got into a fight with 'an African' (Reg's words), in a drinking club in Tottenham Court Road. Reg hit the man over the head four times with a truncheon, which broke in half, but the man remained standing. Ron then stabbed the man in the side and the twins ran off. In an identification parade, their victim picked out Ron, but not Reg, and as a result both the twins were released.

CHARLIE RICHARDSON and his brother EDDIE used the basement of 27 Windmill Street, which backed onto Tottenham Court Road police station, to store their illegal fruit machines, 'one-arm bandits', and rough up anyone who displeased them. Eddie and another gangster, 'MAD' FRANK FRASER (who later served 19 years for torturing victims for Richardson), bundled ERIC MASON, an associate of the Krays, into a car and took him to the Windmill Street basement. They sliced Mason's forehead, chopped his left knee and nearly cut through his left arm, before they dumped him unconscious on some waste

> If I thought that Guy was a brave man, I should imagine that he had gone to joint the Communists. As I know him to be a coward, I suppose that he was suspected of passing things on to the Bolshies, and realizing his guilt, did a bunk.
>
> Harold Nicholson on Guy Burgess

THE KRAY TWINS (1952)
Ron (*left*) and Reg Kray,
lightweight boxers,
photographed training
at Kline's Gym, before
beginning their National
Service.

*East End gangsters who
conquered London's East and
West End with their 'firm', the
Kray twins began their careers
in the boxing ring. Ron fought
at Kline's Gym against Rolly
Blyce, featherweight champion
of Trinidad. Ron was so
ferocious that he had to be
pulled off by his trainer, Harry
'Kid' Berry. Reg fought there
against Ron Barton, light
heavyweight champion
of Great Britain.*

ground. Found and taken to hospital, Mason needed 300 stitches for 30
injuries, including three skull fractures.

Mason had knocked out the Empire featherweight champion in a brawl at
the Paramount Dance Hall, 161 Tottenham Court Road, and in the 1940s he
had boxed with the Krays at Fred Kline's gym. On his release from hospital he
went straight to the Krays, thinking they would retaliate on his behalf, but the
Krays fobbed him off with £40.

It was only a short walk for Charles Richardson from the basement in
Windmill Street to the offices of the Anti-Apartheid Movement, 89 Charlotte

Ronnie was a fighter, the hardest boy I've ever seen. To stop him you'd have had to kill him. Reggie was different. It was as if he had all the experience of an old boxer before he started. Just once in a lifetime you find a boy with everything to be a champion. Reggie had it.

Boxing trainer describing the Kray twins in their early years

Street. During March 1966, just before the offices closed for the day, Richardson went there to steal the list of members' names and addresses for the South African secret police (BOSS). In exchange, BOSS had promised to turn a blind eye to Richardson's illegal mining and diamond smuggling in South Africa. He entered the building, hid himself in the toilet on the landing, and emerged after the doors were locked to steal the documents.

Later that year he was caught and charged with violence and extortion. He served 22 years of a 25-year sentence. On his release he ran a club in Charlotte Street.

CHAPTER 5
The Entertainers

Exhibitions of sword fighting and displays of boxing were popular along Oxford Street and Tottenham Court Road in the 18th century. JAMES FIGG, a promoter, staged numerous sword and boxing contests at the Boarded House, which stood on the junction of today's Wells Street and Eastcastle (*62 Castle*) Street, from 1723, and appeared in many of them himself. The sword-fighters used broadswords that were especially sharpened and light towards the point, so producing the maximum amount of blood from the slightest contact, 'the blood gushes out and the people shout applause'. In 1725 Figg opened his own arena behind his house, next to the riding school of Captain St Armour, on the corner of Wells and Oxford Streets, where he had been teaching swordmanship, 'Figgs School of Arms', since 1722. Samuel Pepys watched Figg fight a bruising bout with Sutton, of Gravesend, 'Took coach to Figg's ampitheatre, where Mr Leycester paid half a crown for me. Figg and Sutton fought. Figg had a wound which bled very much. Sutton had a blow with a quarter staff on the knee, so they gave over. There was a gentleman fainted away.' At another fight Pepys saw Sutton punch his opponent's nose 'clean off'. Figgs died in 1734 and was buried in Marylebone Church.

JOHN BROUGHTON, a former Thames waterman and skilled prizefighter, who dominated boxing for many years, took over the Boarded House in 1743. In 1745 he opened 'Broughton's Ampitheatre' for boxing at the top of Tottenham Court Road. It prospered, and two years later he opened a boxing academy in Haymarket, where he introduced gloves, 'mufflers', to prevent 'black eyes, broken jaws and bloody noses'. Broughton's last fight was for his patron, the Duke of Cumberland, who thought he had been cheated when Broughton lost. Broughton retired with a fortune of £7,000, and the Duke had the boxing ampitheatre closed down in 1751.

DANIEL FRENCH ran a boxing booth behind the Adam and Eve tea gardens, at the top of Tottenham Court Road from 1748, as did George Taylor, who was considered a highly-skilled boxer, but one who lacked 'bottom', although he defeated John Slack, the butcher, who had beaten Broughton. Taylor's Booth advertised both women's boxing and cudgel fighting. Another celebrated boxer of the day, 'THE IRISH LAD' RANDALL, was born and lived in Cock Court, an alley off the lower end of Tottenham Court Road.

The brilliant actor DAVID GARRICK (1717-79) was a frequent visitor to Fitzrovia. He arrived in London in 1737 after travelling down from Lichfield in Staffordshire, along with the young Samuel Johnson, hoping to find work. They had one horse between them, which they took turns to ride. Johnson lodged in Eastcastle Street, where Garrick would have called on him. Garrick regularly attended George Whitefield's Chapel on Tottenham Court Road, where he was impressed by the preacher's flamboyant oratory style. Garrick's acting of Shakespeare astounded audiences with its naturalism and conviction. He stripped away the social persona to reveal the 'true character' of the role. He married the Viennese dancer Eva Maria Veigel in 1749 at a chapel in nearby Great Russell Street. To ease his piles he used a remedy made of six grains of opium and 40 grains of white lead mixed with fresh butter, spread onto a piece

Sometimes the champions are naked to the waist, giving each other horrible blows, and throw their adversaries with violence to the earth, when their seconds raise them up, wipe off the sweat, encourage them like dogs to renew the combat and sometimes they strangle and suffocate each other.

Baron Beilfeld on the displays at the Tottenham Court boxing booth

JIMI HENDRIX

Hendrix's frenzied arrangement of 'Killing Floor' stunned the audience at Regent Street Polytechnic soon after he arrived in London in 1966. Four months later he played so loudly for Radio One in a 'sound-proof' basement studio at Broadcasting House that he was heard in the background on Radio Three, for which a string quartet was performing two floors above.

The interior of
BROUGHTON'S AMPITHEATRE,
where JOHN BROUGHTON,
the champion, was enticed
out of retirement to fight
SLACK, the Norwich
butcher, for a £600 prize.

*Slack punched Broughton in
the eyes until he could no
longer see. Seated on the left
is the Duke of Cumberland,
who lost a heavy wager on
the outcome.*

of linen and applied cold. He died from a combination of gout, herpes, and kidney disease.

An unpleasant death was narrowly avoided by the Italian soprano LUCREZIA AGUJARI (1743-83), who had a permanent limp as a result of being gnawed by a hog when she was an infant. Agujari sang to capacity audiences for three years at the magnificent Pantheon Theatre, 173 (359) Oxford Street, during the mid-1770s. Her death at an early age was rumoured to have been caused by slow poisoning, administered by jealous rivals. Officially she died of tuberculosis.

THOMAS HOLCROFT (1745-1809) moved to London in 1778 as a young actor and lived in Clipstone Street. He worked as a stable boy, shoemaker, and tutor before achieving fame as an actor, playwright, and poet. A political radical, friend to both Thomas Paine and William Godwin, his arrest in 1794 on the charge of treason, cost him his career. Although acquitted he was reduced to poverty and for a while had to leave the country. His own son, William, robbed him of £40 and then shot himself. A block of flats in Clipstone Street, Holcroft Court, is named in his honour.

CHARLES DIBDIN (1745-1814), a popular opera singer at Covent Garden and self-taught composer of operas and sea chanties, as well as novelist and performer, lived at 30 Charlotte Street. Despite success he fell into debt and fled to France in 1776, where he stayed for two years to escape his creditors.

CARL MARIA VON WEBER (1786-1826), the pioneering German composer of romantic opera, who wrote his first opera when he was 13 years old, lived at 91 Great Portland Street. He had been expelled from Stuttgard after being imprisoned for his involvement in a draft-dodging scheme, and came to London, where he became a successful pianist, composer and conductor. When Weber fell ill with consumption, the organist and conductor, SIR GEORGE SMART (1776-1867), who shared the premises, found him in bed 'with tubercles the size of breakfast eggs choking his ravaged lungs.' Fellow composer RICHARD WAGNER (1813-83) visited Great Portland Street in 1839 to pay homage to Weber, and insisted that his remains should be reburied in Dresden. George Smart persuaded the Philharmonic Society to send £100 to the destitute Beethoven after he had visited the composer in Bonn.

At the height of her fame as an actress SARAH SIDDONS (1755-1831) moved to 14 Gower Street where she stayed from 1784 to 1789. 'Perhaps in the next world women will be more valued than they are in this', she told her friend, the poet Samuel Rogers. Among her regular visitors were the wit Sydney Smith, who lived close by, and Lord Sidmouth when he was prime minister. She also lived at 8 Grafton Way (Street), Devonshire Street, 54 Great Marlborough Street, and at 228 Baker Street, said to be haunted by her ghost.

Her brother, leading Shakespearean and comic actor CHARLES KEMBLE (1775-1854), lived in Newman Street, where his daughter FANNY KEMBLE (1809-93) was born. Charles had achieved much critical acclaim in his own right, but only achieved financial success when he teamed up with Fanny for a tour of America. Fanny's early acting appearances were at the Princess's Theatre, 152 (73) Oxford Street, on the corner of Winsley Street.

Another acclaimed actor, WILLIAM CHARLES MACREADY (1793-1873), was born at the eastern end of Mortimer (Charles) Street. He managed the Theatre Royal, Drury Lane, 1841-43, and regularly performed at the Princess's Theatre. He was hailed as a star for his portrayals of King Lear and Richard III. Macready was expelled from America in 1848 after a quarrel with an American actor provoked a riot.

Another entertainer of the era, JACK BANNISTER (1760-1836), the 'master of comic drollery', spent his last few years at 65 Gower Street.

The Italian soprano ANGELICA CATALANI (1779-1849) lived at 37 and 82 Charlotte Street, and frequently performed at the Scala (King's Concert Rooms), 21-25 Tottenham Street, as well as at La Scala in Milan. She was the highest paid opera singer of the day, and when ticket prices were increased at Covent Garden to cover her salary there were riots by protesting members of the public.

The commercial success of the West End theatres in the years between 1880 and 1914 owed much to the great actor-managers, of whom HENRY IRVING (1838-1905) was renowned. He made his first London appearance at the Princess's Theatre in Oxford Street on September 24, 1859. He regularly dined at Pagani's restaurant, 54 (later 40-48) Great Portland Street, where he signed his autograph on the wall of one of the private dining rooms. The celebrated French actress SARAH BERNHARDT (1844-1923) ate frequently in the same restaurant during 1879. A wag quipped that Sarah, who had only one leg, 'has all Paris at her foot'.

One of Irving's greatest successes was his performance of Romeo to the role of Juliet played by ELLEN TERRY (1847-1928)*. Ellen Terry was born into a family of roving players and made her debut at the Princess's Theatre when she was eight years old, as a child in The Winter's Tale. She performed frequently at the Prince of Wales in Tottenham Street. Terry was also a theatre manager and her partnership with Irving lasted 25 years, until 1902. Later she performed in plays supporting women's suffrage.

The incorrigible LILLIE LANGTRY (1853-1929) both ran and acted in the Princess's Theatre for two years from 1890. Known for her earthy sense of humour, she was tickled when a newspaper gossip columnist wrote, 'Mrs Langtry has lost her parrot...That the lady possessed such a bird we were unaware, but we knew she had a cockatoo', alluding to one of her lovers, the Prince of Wales (later Edward VII). When the prince complained that he had

The awful consciousness that one is the sole subject of attention to that immense space, lined as it were with human intellect from top to bottom, and on all side round, may perhaps be imagined but can not be described.

Sarah Siddons on her first night.

The play was Isabella, and the praise for Siddons' performance was rapturous.

* Ellen Terry's date of birth was always given as February 27, 1848, until the publication of Roger Manvell's biography Ellen Terry (Heinemann, 1968). Following his discovery that her birth was registered on February 27, 1847 (St John's and St Michael's District of Coventry), he has suggested that Ellen's father made the claim that his daughter was younger by a year in order to prolong her childhood stage roles.

Lose the middle notes, and you lose-all. The very high and the very low notes are the ornaments.

Adelina Patti on the importance for any singer of cultivating middle tones

spent enough on her to buy a battleship, she retorted, 'And you've spent enough in me to float one!'

Another highly paid opera singer, ADELINA PATTI (1843-1919), lived at 29 Fitzroy Square. She refused to attend rehearsals, and was sometimes paid £1,000 for performing just one song.

The incomparable MARIE LLOYD (1870-1922) was only 15 years old when she made her West End debut as a comic singer at the Oxford Music Hall on the corner of Tottenham Court Road and Oxford Street. She had a wonderful talent for music hall and delivered songs full of innuendo with an accompaniment of mischievous nods, winks and saucy gestures that had her audience in stitches.

The Oxford Music Hall nearly lost its licence when Marie, dressed as a schoolgirl, sang 'What's that for Eh?', alluding to a range of phallic symbols. When she was asked to modify a double entendre about a young lady in a vegetable garden who sits 'among the cauliflowers and peas' for a Royal Command Performance, Marie had the last laugh by singing she 'sits among the cauliflowers and leeks'.

Marie teased one of the other peformers, VICTORIA MONKS, about some tripe she had bought, which led to a backstage squabble. MARQUERITE BROADFOOTE, another artiste, tried to sort it out by throwing the tripe at the quarrelling pair, but she missed and the tripe went flying through the window. The three women were still laughing when the barman from the Blue Posts, on the corner of Hanway Street, knocked, 'Which lady here slung that tripe? It came in through the open window and hit a lady customer of mine on the mouth, and she ain't half annoyed about it. Says it ruined her bonnet.' They paid 10s. to the woman to compensate her for shock and her damaged hat.

As a star, Marie had nothing to gain from the 1907 music hall strike, but she characteristically sang on the picket line. As a result she was excluded from the next Royal Command performance, but she hired the Palladium and put on a rival show the same night.

When she died, three days after singing 'A Bit of a Ruin that Cromwell Knocked about a Bit' on stage at the age of 52, the news was announced on a billboard outside her beloved Oxford Music Hall, and Tottenham Court Road was brought to a standstill, 'lost its hubbub.' Amongst those who paid tribute to her was the poet T.S. Eliot, who commented on her unique 'capacity for expressing the soul of the people.'

A drinking club at 17 Little Portland Street was called the Marie Lloyd until it was renamed the Blue Angel in 1995.

The Oxford Music Hall was also where GEORGE 'THE PRIME MINISTER OF MIRTH' ROBEY (1869-1954) made his first West End appearance. He was such a success that he was given a one-year contract and billed as 'The Coming Man'. At his entrance there would be roars of laughter from the audience before he said a word. With mock affrontery, he would ask them to 'desist', saying he had not come to be laughed at. He purveyed 'honest vulgarity' as the 'perfect antidote to hypocrisy'. He had been studying science at Cambridge when a family financial crisis forced him to leave and he found work on the construction of Birmingham's tramway, before he turned to comedy. One of his favourite restaurants was Pagani's in Great Portland Street, and he made one of his early radio broadcasts from St George's Hall, 18-20 Langham Place.

Another future star who made her premier appearance at the Oxford Music Hall was MARIA 'KILKENNY KATE' LOFTUS (1857-1940). She appeared in 1877, went on to international fame and became known as 'the Sarah Bernhardt of the Halls'. Another was the comedian HARRY TATE (1872-1940) who premiered at the Oxford in 1895.

Honest vulgarity is neither filth nor purity. It lies somewhere between the two.

George Robey

The German composer FELIX MENDELSSOHN (1809-47), stayed at 103 Great Portland Street during his ten visits to London. The Nazis banned all performances of his music in the 1930s – even, presumably, the ubiquitous bridal tune, *Wedding March*. He died suffering from migraines and chills at the age of 38.

Austrian composer GUSTAV MAHLER (1860-1911) lived at 22 Alfred Place and nearby 69 Torrington Square during his prolonged visit of 1892 to conduct at Covent Garden. His most ambitious piece, *Symphony of a Thousand*, required that number of performers. He had a morbid nature and once appealed to the Devil to take possession of his soul as 'madness seizes me, annihilates me.'

HENRY WOOD (1869-1944), the great conductor and promoter of classical music, started the popular annual Promenade Concerts (now held at the Albert Hall) at Queen's Hall, 4 Langham Place.

Wood was born and raised at 59 (*413*A) Oxford Street, at the bottom of Rathbone Place, where his father ran a jewellery and optician's business, when he was not playing the cello or making model engines. Before taking up music, Wood was an art student at the Slade, Gower Street. In 1886, he studied at the Royal Academy of Music in Marylebone Road. Aged 25 he moved to 1 Langham Place, next to the newly-built Queen's Hall, where he played the organ on the opening night, December 2, 1893.

In 1895 he was appointed Musical Director of the Queen's Hall and he lost no time in putting on the first of the proms the same year, planning an eclectic programme on the table cloth at Pagani's where he dined regularly. With the intention of breaking down the class barriers, he had the seating of the hall redesigned, taking out the central seats to make room for a cheap standing area for which tickets were sold at a shilling each, and having a 'Smoking permitted' sign erected to encourage a popular audience.

Interior of the Regency Theatre, Tottenham Street, Tottenham Court Road (1819)

Opened by Francis Pasquali in 1772.

During the halycon days of orchestral music, when Handel was resident in London, the city attracted the most glittering composers of Europe. The prevailing craze of the 1720s and 1730s was for Italian opera.

By 1776 these were the Kings Concert Rooms (later they became the Regency Theatre, then the Scala), under the direction of the fashionable Directors of Concerts of Ancient Music, and fast becoming one of London's favourite concert venues.

He also created the Queen's Hall Orchestra, which was to become the first orchestra to employ women as professional musicians. The musicians used a nearby pub, the George, 55 Great Portland Street, as an unofficial employment exchange and a watering hole during concert intervals. Sometimes the 'intervals' grew too long for Wood's liking and he called the pub 'the Gluepot' because the musicians got 'stuck' there. Eventually he arranged for a man with a handbell to summon them back to the hall.

During zeppelin raids in 1915, Wood (nicknamed 'Timber') continued conducting in Queen's Hall as plaster fell from the ceiling and the soloist sang, 'We won't go home 'til morning'. His response to the second world war blitz on London was similarly phlegmatic. On the night of August 20, 1940, performers and audience alike ignored the air raid sirens, and stayed, enjoying a picnic and a singsong, until 2 a.m., when the all clear sounded, and the concert was resumed. (One woman in the audience enjoyed the improvised participation more than the scheduled concert and afterwards only bought a ticket if an air raid warning had sounded.) On the night of May 10, 1941, however, the hall received a direct hit. Firewatchers had almost hosed down the flames when the water mains dried up and the fire flickered back to life, leaving the hall gutted. The next morning Wood wept over the ruins of the building that had seen so much mould-breaking musical history. He wanted a replica built on the same site. Instead the site was used for the new BBC office. It was named Henry Wood House and a bust of Wood stands in the reception hall.

Among the great composers who conducted their own works at Queen's Hall were SERGEI RACHMANINOV (1873-1943), EDWARD ELGAR (1857-1934) who lived at 58 New Cavendish Street, and JEAN SIBELIUS (1865-1957), who revolted customers at Pagani's by eating everything on the menu. Also CHARLES DEBUSSY (1862-1918), EDWARD GRIEG (1843-1907), GUSTAV HOLST (1874-1934) who, in addition, played trombone in the orchestra, RICHARD STRAUSS (1864-1949), who entrusted Wood to buy some knickers for his wife in a nearby shop, and RALPH VAUGHAN WILLIAMS (1872-1958). Programme notes often referred to compositions by Paul Klenovsky, and even included a biography – Klenovsky was the pseudonym Wood used for his own compositions.

Prolific composer of light music ERIC COATES (1886-1957) started his career as a member of the orchestra at Queen's Hall, Langham Place, in 1910. He was promoted to principal viola in 1912, but lost his place in the orchestra in 1919 after developing neuritis in his left hand. Thereafter he concentrated on composing, and wrote a string of signature tunes for radio programmes, such as 'By The Sleepy Lagoon' for *Desert Island Discs*, 'Knightsbridge March' for *In Town Tonight*, and 'Calling All Workers' for *Music While You Work*. Among his other compositions were 'Oxford Street' and 'Langham Place', written in 1936.

Many of the world's most celebrated conductors also performed at the Queen's Hall. Among them were HANS RICHTER (1843-1916), ARTURO TOSCANINI (1867-1957), THOMAS BEECHAM (1879-1961), ADRIAN BOULT (1889-1983), MALCOLM SARGENT (1895-1967), and JOHN BARBIROLLI (1899-1970), who was born nearby and made his first appearance in the Hall as a cellist at the age of 12.

Legendary pianists to play there included FERRUCHIO BUSONI (1866-1924) who went out and got drunk with Sibelius, MYRA HESS (1890-1966), and BENNO MOISEIWITSCH (1890-1963). PABLO CASELS (1876-1973) played the cello and hissed the orchestra for accompanying him too loudly. The tenor RICHARD TAUBER (1892-1948) sang there. The great Hungarian violinist JOSEPH SZIGETI (1892-1973) was often in the audience from 1906 to 1913; he described the hall as 'a classroom for me.'

SARAH SIDDONS rehearsing in the green room with her father, Roger Kemble, by Thomas Rowlandson

Sarah Siddons, the great tragic actress, used her 'brilliant piercing' eyes and spectacular gestures to create a dramatic language for the principal passions of anger, revenge, grief and joy.

You know whatta you do when you shit? Singing, it's the same thing, only up!

Enrico Caruso, Italian tenor

Luna Park was sheer magic
to me with the bearded
lady, coconut shies, helter-
skelters, the rifle range
and exotic side-shows.
At every turn there was
some new amazement, a
promise of excitement or
a demonstration of dare
devil skills.

Max Jaffa

Whenever the great ENRICO CARUSO (1873-1921) sang in London he went to dine at Pagani's restaurant in Great Portland Street – where he once swallowed a large peach whole. He was the 18th child of a Naples mechanic (all 17 of his elder brothers and sisters had died in infancy). He sang by ear and lost his first job for not following the orchestra, but his fees rose over his lifetime from $2 to $15,000 a performance. He was a connoisseur of fine food (a type of macaroni was named after him) and befriended fellow Italian GUISEPPE BERTORELLI (1893-1994) who opened the famous Bertorelli restaurant at 19 Charlotte Street in 1913.

The main attraction at Luna Park fairground, which stood at the bottom of Tottenham Court Road in the 1920s (on the site of the closed brewery, before the Dominion was built in 1929), was a woman called the HUMAN SEAL. In a bright spangled costume and a Neptune helmet, she climbed above the merry-go-round, the shooting galleries and coconut shies, to a diving board high above the heads of the crowd. There she wrapped herself in cotton wool, and set herself alight. As the audience drew a collective breath, she dived like flaming comet into a water tank far below. This 'beautiful if terrifying sight' drew large crowds. Another of her tricks was to stay under water for a long time.

In 1905 the magician JOHN MASKELYNE (1839-1917) performed plate dancing and the floating lady and other famous tricks at St George's Hall, which had opened in 1867 as a concert hall for the New Philharmonic Society, with entrances at 18-20 Langham Place and Mortimer Street. His shows continued until his death, and were carried on by his sons and grandsons, for another 16 years.

The charismatic conductor LEOPOLD STOKOWSKI (1882-1977) was born at 146 New Cavendish (*13 Upper Marylebone*) Street by the corner of Cleveland Street, of a Polish father and Irish mother. He found fame in America where he conducted the music for Walt Disney's cartoon classic *Fantasia*. He dispensed with the baton, preferring to conduct with his hands alone. He returned to London for the last four years of his life.

A regular at the Fitzroy Tavern, the composer CONSTANT LAMBERT (1905-51) lived at 15 Percy Street in the 1930s. He could whistle the national anthem through his punctured eardrum, and liked to feed coins into the pub's electric piano, claiming that its tunes inspired his writing.

In the 1940s he moved to 4 All Souls' Place where he started an affair with ballet dancer Margot Fonteyn, which lasted for eight years. He also held seances with another composer, CECIL GRAY. Lambert drank heavily at the George and afterwards practised his piano, to the discomfort of everyone else in the house. He would go without food for long periods when he was working and often spat blood (he was posthumously diagnosed as a diabetic). His son, Kit Lambert, was manager of the pop group, the Who, in the 1960s.

Comedian 'WEE' GEORGIE WOOD (1895-1979), who was four feet nine inches tall and known as 'the pocket sized Noel Coward', stopped calling himself 'The Boy Phenomenon' after it was misprinted on a theatre poster as 'The Boy Euphonium'. When he accosted an actor who had joked about Georgie being carried in a shopping basket, the actor asked Georgie who had let on. 'Nobody' Georgie snapped, 'I heard you from the shopping basket.'

At the age of ten, Georgie was in the same juvenile troupe as the comedian Stan Laurel, and he made his first appearance in London three years later. He was one of the first entertainers on television, and took part in early experimental broadcasts from 16 Portland Place and the Dominion Theatre in Tottenham Court Road. In one of the many anecdotes about Georgie's missionary zeal for converting others to Roman Catholicism, George gained

Great artists are people
who find the way to be
themselves in their art.
Any sort of pretension
induces mediocrity in art
and life alike.

Margot Fonteyn

an audience with the pope. He went into the room and stayed so long that a cardinal put his ear to the door, from where he heard the pope say, 'But Mr Wood, I *am* a Catholic.' He lived the last years of his life in Gordon Mansions, between Torrington Place and Huntley Street.

**Comedians on the stage
are invariably suicidal
when they get home.**

Elsa Lanchester

CHARLES LAUGHTON (1899-1962), stage and film actor, lived at 15 Percy Street from 1928 to 1931, while he was acting in West End theatres. During this time he married the actress and cabaret artist, ELSA LANCHESTER (1902-86) who ran the Cave of Harmony Club, 107 Charlotte Street, from 1924 to 1925. Undaunted when it was closed down after complaints that the noise went on until 2 a.m. she re-opened the club in Gower Street, where she served after-hours whiskey poured from a teapot, as 'Russian tea'. When Laughton told Elsa that he was homosexual, she went into shock and was struck deaf for a week. They continued to live together, staying close companions, and came to an arrangement that allowed each of them to have other partners.

Among the members of Elsa's club were actors MILES MALLESON (1888-1969) and HERMIONE BADDELEY (1906-86) as well as writers ARNOLD BENNETT, H.G. WELLS, ALDOUS HUXLEY, A.P. HERBERT and JOHN GALSWORTHY.

SIR ALEC GUINNESS (1914-2000) unveiled a blue plaque in honour of Laughton at the Percy Street address in 1992.

Aged eight, LAURENCE OLIVIER (1907-89) was sent as a boarder to All Saints church choir school, 7 Margaret Street, where he was a pupil for five years. There he was mocked for his lack of ability at sport and he decided to succeed as an actor. When he played Brutus in a school production, in which he had to murder his brother, Dickie, as Caesar, Ellen Terry was in the audience as was the young SYBIL THORNDIKE (1882-1976), both of whom recognised that Olivier was a born actor.

He gained a reputation as a show-off. A pupil who wanted to take him down a peg or two shut him in a room and jumped on him. Olivier recalled that his protests only increased the boy's ardour, 'His "excercises" were getting more powerful when to my relief he thought he heard someone coming up the stairs.' More unwelcome attention came from one of the school priests, who had been wounded and shell-shocked in the first world war. He punished Olivier with a strap until the boy's screams could be heard across the courtyard. Soon afterwards the priest was dismissed.

World-famous soprano
Adelina Patti (*c*.1888)

Adelina Patti electrified audiences with her voice and her presence. She commanded such high fees that opera buffs used to calculate the precise amount she earned per note. For the role of Violetta in Traviata *at Covent Garden, she had 4,000 of her own diamonds mounted onto the bodice of her dress. She retired to a castle in Wales where she had a private theatre built for her own performances.*

When Olivier was 19 years old and desperately seeking work as an actor, he returned to All Saints for the Sunday services. The vicar, noticing that he looked weak and undernourished, wrote to Olivier's father and suggested that he pay his son £1 a week, 'This made the difference between life and death for a while.'

Four years later, he married the actress JILL ESMONDE at All Saints. 'I found the ceremony very moving', he recorded. 'All Saints had given us the full choir as a present, a distinction not usually enjoyed except by the high, mighty, or rich.' Aged 75, he revisited the school for a television profile, and found himself weeping (which he could never do for a performance) at his memories of carrying the incense in church as a boy.

Graphic artist and television entertainer TONY HART (b.1925) also has love-hate memories of All Saints, where he was a pupil and chorister from 1934 to 1939. Pupils were made to run round the block each morning after a cold bath, and yet, when rehearsing the school plays, they were given advice by the likes of Laurence Olivier, Sybil Thorndike, and LILIAN BAYLIS (1874-1937), manager of the Old Vic and Sadler's Wells. He is drawn back by his memories, 'Whenever I am in the West End my feet drag me, almost reluctantly, back to Butterfield's sooty spire of All Saints.' A controversial appointment has also stuck in his mind, 'I remember police horses in Margaret Street ready to quell possible riots over the induction of Dom Bernard Clements, a Benedictine monk, as vicar of All Saints!'

The catchphrase 'She knows y'know' was popularised by comedian and actor, HYLDA BAKER (1908-86), who would mouth it in an exaggerated manner as part of her stage act with the tall, silent stooge 'Cynthia' – just as she had when working in a noisy Lancashire mill, where the girls communicated by lip-reading. Both Matthew Kelly and Derek Nimmo played Cynthia – the part was always taken by a man – who would dwarf the four-foot ten inches tall Hylda. She created the act after she saw two women, one tall and the other short, on a night out, and noticed that the short one did all the talking.

Hylda was presumed to be have been stillborn and it was only by chance that someone observed that the baby was moving and she was revived. She had also worked in a chip shop, before embarking on her stage career for which she wrote her own material. She was married briefly to Ted Martin, who was billed as the cowboy who 'undresses girls with bullets'. If his timing was wrong, his assistant's bra dropped before he fired a shot.

Hylda wanted children but after two miscarriages, she had to rely on her pet monkeys for company. She lived at 97 Ridgmount Gardens, Torrington Place, off Tottenham Court Road, from 1957 to 1980, and often had a tipple at the Marlborough Arms, 36 Torrington Place. Her condition deteriorated after she was attacked and robbed by a lodger, and she died in a mental hospital. On her death her ashes were scattered, at her request, on the escalator at Euston station.

From 1934 to 1937 the opera singer PETER PEARS (1910-86) shared a maisonette at 105 Charlotte Street with two musicians who worked at the BBC. He was visited there often by composer BENJAMIN BRITTEN (1913-76). From 1938 to 1942 Pears lived with Britten at 67 Hallam Street, and they remained together for the rest of Britten's life, although when they first met, at Queen's Hall and at Broadcasting House, they did not hit it off (Britten described Pears as snobbish and superficial). They warmed to each other following the funeral of a mutual friend in 1937, when Britten accepted a lift on Pears' motorcycle, which left him with a 'pretty sore behind'.

They were pacifists in the second world war and performed at concerts for the War Resisters' League, as a result of which the United States put visa

LAURENCE OLIVIER, actor, aged eight (1915)

Laurence Olivier was a boarder at All Saints, where he sang in the choir. Revisiting the church in later life his memories soared as his voice once had. It had 'most wonderful accoustics in London – you aimed for the West Wall – there – and up it went into the ceiling.'

The Oxford Theatre opened under the aegis of the 'father of the music halls' Charles Morton in 1861. It was rebuilt in 1892, and Marie Lloyd topped the bill on the first night.

When a well-known member of the French government waited at the stage door to tell Marie Lloyd that her 'Twiggy Vous' was all the rage in Paris, the doorman tried to eject the 'troublesome foreigner'. Marie invited him into her dressing room, where he produced champagne, and she rewarded him with a bawdy song about a young lady climbing to the top of a bus in a gale.

Every day, it became more and more alive, and responsive and glorious...the really great fiddles have a very straight grain in the wood, but my Guarnerius has a notch in the straight grain and it curves round. I've never ever regretted buying it and it has never let me down.

Max Jaffa on his Peter Guanerius violin made in 1704

restrictions on them for 30 years. After the war, they visited the composer Mstislav Rostropovich at his home in Armenia, and Pears drank so much slivovitz that he keeled over into some bushes when they were posing for a photograph. It was some time before anyone in the group noticed that he was absent and they found him by tracing the sound of his snores.

Violinist MAX JAFFA (1911-91) was one of five children, born in a house without a bath in Langham Street, close to where his maternal grandparents (the Makoffs) lived in Middleton Place (*Buildings*). His father, Israel, arrived as a Jewish refugee from Latvia at the age of 14, and became a tailor's presser in Great Titchfield Street (before setting up a business at 7 Middleton Buildings). Max remembered seeing the zeppelins when he was hustled along as a toddler during the first world war to the air raid shelter in the basement of the polytechnic, 309 Regent Street. He wrote in his autobiography that the first cows he saw were in the local dairy at Clipstone Street and he was sent on errands to buy dried mushrooms for his grandmother at the grocer's shop on the corner of Riding House Street and Great Titchfield Street. On the way home from school (All Souls, Foley Street) he liked to linger, fascinated by the market in Great Titchfield Street, 'The whole street was filled with stalls selling everything you could imagine. Everyone's favourite was the ice cream man, an Italian, who seemed foreign and exotic.'

His father chastised him for eating ice cream from a glass at the stall, and for playing football in Regent's Park on a Saturday. He forbad him from going on the dodgems or the roller coaster at Luna Park, in case he damaged his valuable fingers (although young Max was allowed to visit its exotic sideshows). He encouraged him in his music, giving him a violin for his sixth birthday, and sending him to Emanuel Kempinski for music lessons in Charlotte Street. After two years Max lost interest. But then he heard the violinist Joscha Heifetz at the Queen's Hall and was inspired. He took further lessons from Wilhelm Sachse over Gustave Meinal's violin shop in Hallam Street, and practised for hours at home in front of the open coal fire.

He remembered that when a fruit-barrow owner made some anti-Semitic remark as the family was strolling along Oxford Street one day, his father tipped over the barrow's owner and walloped him. The family left the area in 1930, and Max went on to form a successful music trio that played palm court music on television and on the long-lived radio programme *Grand Hotel*.

The first purpose-built home of national radio, Broadcasting House, was constructed between 1928 and 1931 on the sites of 2-8 Portland Place and 1-7 Langham Street, with studios themed to reflect the programme's subject – music studios were round like records, talk studios were oak-pannelled like libraries, and religious studios were designed to resemble a church. It was not until 1936, however, that the BBC was granted the freehold – after promising that the premises would not be used as a brothel, for selling tripe, or as a railway parcel booking office. In 1997 some studios were dismantled and revamped for BBC executive offices, and journalists and producers were moved out to offices in West London. But the Radio Theatre is still based there for live and recorded broadcasts, and some studios remain.

One of the earliest popular programmes was the talk show *In Town Tonight*, which was broadcast from 1933. Journalist J.C. CANNELL ferreted out the guests, whom he described as a 'mixed lot, picked as though from a lucky dip'. This mingling was behind its success. At the microphone there might be, 'the steeplejack, the public house musician, the man of science and of literature, the street beggar and the debutante'.

Another early success was the radio comedy *Band Wagon*, which was started in 1938, starring 'big hearted' ARTHUR ASKEY (1900-82) and RICHARD

'Stinker' Murdoch (1907-90). Set in a fictional flat on top of Broadcasting House with a splendid view over Langham Place, sackfuls of fan mail would arrive addressed simply to 'The Flat on top of Broadcasting House'. And when a fictional goat, Lewis, was scripted in, to supply milk during war rationing, visiting children began to ask if they could see the animal on the roof.

During the second world war, a 500 pound bomb landed on Broadcasting House – it was October 15, 1940, the very day that the painting of its exterior camouflage was finally completed. Bruce Belfrage was reading the Nine O'Clock News at the time. Despite being covered in fallen plaster and soot, he continued to read the news as if nothing had happened. Seven members of staff were killed and it took three years to restore the studios. The unflappable Belfrage was a regular at the Fitzroy Tavern. The previous year, after a couple of beers in the Fitzroy, he made a famous malapropism, when he read out the news of the pocket battleship in the battle of River Plate, as 'packet bottleship'.

Commentaries on bombing raids on London were broadcast live from a roof in Oxford Street by Wynford Vaughan Thomas, Stewart Macpherson, Raymond Glendinnning and Michael Standing. They also had a programme called *The Radio Allotment* in 1942, in which they discussed the cultivation of the small garden in Park Crescent at the top of Portland Place, and reported on its progress, giving tips to listeners on how to grow food at home or on allotments.

The American Edward R. Murrow (1908-65) riveted his American audience with his broadcasts from Studio B4 at Broadcasting House, for CBS radio. He risked life and limb to visit areas under bombardment, and he was knocked down by blasts several times. His programmes, which helped to turn the tide of American public opinion in favour of entering the war, reflected his view that class-ridden England was undergoing a moral revolution under the pressures of war. The programmes finished at 3.45 a.m. British time, after which he would retire to his flat at Weymouth House, 84 Hallam Street, where he liked to play poker, drink Scotch, eat sandwiches, drink coffee, and talk with his friends for the rest of the night. His guests included film star Clark Gable (1901-60), then a private in the US air force, and Eleanor Roosevelt (1884-1962), wife of the American president, Franklin D. Roosevelt. They often sang 'Joe Hill' (which Murrow had learned while a lumberjack), accompanied by Murrow's wife, Janet, who played the piano. Chronically fatigued, Murrow's habit of grinding his teeth woke up other sleepers when he was in the bomb shelter below Broadcasting House.

In the early years of the 20th century, the advent of American ragtime, swing and jazz introduced a new informality to London's dance halls. During the second world war, when London was 'dance mad', the Paramount on 161 Tottenham Court Road held swing contests and jitterbug marathons. Musician and broadcaster, Steve Race (b.1921), who was playing piano with Ivor Kirchin's band at the Paramount, remembers the hall during those years as a 'social sink', attracting a mixture of people, and that life on the ballroom floor seemed 'raw and utterly basic'. Although the hall's closing time was 11 p.m., when the air raids sounded the 500 dancers stayed – strictly segregated – the men bedding down on one side of the hall, the women on the other, while the band made the most of the fact that the bandstand, 'neutral territory', was not subject to the same rule.

A dancer at the hall recalled one of those nights. The musicians were indefatigable and the mood defiant, 'When a heavy blast shook the building the lights went out for a while and we danced by candlelight. It was all very romantic.' However he started to feel hungry. Borrowing a key from a friend of his, who lived in a flat above the ballroom, he went upstairs to fetch some food. 'By now the building was shaking with the shock of almost incessant gunfire and exploding bombs, and I went up to the roof to see what was happening. As I looked down Tottenham Court Road fires seemed to be blazing everywhere and debris was strewn across the roadway. The peculiar pulsating sound of enemy aircraft engines could be heard despite the gunfire.' He bolted downstairs with food wrapped in a teacloth and feasted with his friends, 'Dawn was breaking by the time the all clear sounded, and only then did the band stand down.'

ANNA WING (b.1915), who acted the role of Lou Beale in the BBC television soap *Eastenders*, moved to 89 Charlotte Street in 1936 (later to Newman and Great Titchfield Streets). During the war she trained as a Red Cross worker at the Middlesex Hospital, Mortimer Street, and remembers people buying Augustus John paintings for 10s. each in local pubs. She lives in the area, and has opened the Fitzrovia festival more than once.

BRIAN JOHNSTON (1912-94) won the Military Cross for digging out tanks under fire during the second world war. He made his first broadcast in 1946 and was so good interviewing people outside the Monseigneur News Theatre, Oxford Street, asking what they thought of butter rationing, that he was told he could stay on 'until the others came back from the forces'. He remained in radio for the next 47 years, mainly as a cricket commentator, his most celebrated double entendre being 'the bowler's Holding, the batsman's Willey.'

JOHN ARLOTT (1914-91), that most erudite of cricket commentators, lodged at 4 All Souls' Place (with ballet dancer MARGOT FONTEYN and her lover, the composer CONSTANT LAMBERT) in 1945. He started in radio as overseas literary producer, at 200 Oxford Street. Earlier in his career, when he worked as a policeman, he had to deal with a bizarre incident involving a pub customer whose penis had become stuck in a landlady's wedding ring, and he agreed, off-duty, to be the emergency 12th man for Hampshire in a cricket match against Worcester. By 1948, when he was commentating on England's cricket in South Africa just after the introduction of apartheid, he provoked an immigration official who asked him his race, by answering 'human'.

DAVID JACOBS (b.1926) befriended Arlott when working as a newsreader for the overseas service at 200 Oxford Street after the war – a job he lost for laughing too much on air. On one occasion it was because fellow broadcaster JACK DE MANIO was pouring water over his head. Later Jacobs became a disc jockey.

The comic, scriptwriter and game show host, BOB MONKHOUSE (b.1928) had his big break while doing his national service as an RAF corporal at the Central Medical Establishment, Kelvin House, 32 Cleveland Street, from 1947 to 1949 (where he also met his future ex-wife). One of his jobs was to prepare correspondence for a senior psychiatrist, group captain Thomkins. In March 1948, he slipped in a letter supporting his application for an audition at the BBC, which Thomkins signed without noticing. Monkhouse took Stan Tracey (jazz musician and composer) and Garry Miller (singer) along to the audition. Luckily for them the regular, hard-to-please auditioner was ill, and they were auditioned and accepted by Dennis Main Wilson. Dennis Goodwin and Monkhouse formed their scripwriting partnership at a greasy spoon café, next to Goodge Street tube station. Monkhouse presented popular radio shows such as *Variety Bandbox*. On one show he recalled, 'When I was a schoolboy they asked me what I was going to be when I grew up and I replied I was going to be a comedian. They laughed at the time, but they're not laughing now...unfortunately.'

In 1948 the ebullient GEORGE MELLY (b.1926), jazz singer, author, art critic

> **You must do the thing you think you cannot do.**
>
> Eleanor Roosevelt

> **It must be difficult for anyone who did not experience it to appreciate the quality, the intense, romantic feeling, of the English cricket season of 1946.**
>
> John Arlott on the first cricket season after the end of the second world war

and cartoon scriptwriter, arrived in London, and was immediately drawn to the basement jazz club at 100 Oxford Street. Now known as the 100 Club, it was then called the Swing Club, and was run by Humphrey Lyttleton who rented the basement from a Mrs Phillips, who was half-Indian and half-Welsh. The band was soon calling Melly 'bunny bum' because of his idiosyncratic dancing. Other regulars inspired equally graphic names, 'trick cyclist, rubber legs, the pointer', and one was called the 'rogue elephant' because of his habit of rampaging through the tables until he was practically up the wall. Melly liked to drink at the Blue Posts, behind the club, and to eat afterwards at a café, 'where they served up stodge, the kind of food you needed when you were young, a plate of spaghetti served with bread and butter and chips. It wasn't a very hygenic place – they kept tins of peeled potatoes next to the lavatory.' He has since sung at the 100 Club many times.

The drummer RAY ELLINGTON (1915-85) lived in Ridgmount Gardens, between Chenies Street and Torrington Place. He had an American father and a Russian mother, and had earlier been a wrestler, 'the body beautiful of British show business'. He backed stars such as Fats Waller before forming his own quartet in 1948, which made its debut at the London Palladium. In the 1950s the group played in the seminal, anarchic radio comedy programme, the *Goon Show*, in which Ray sometimes joined in the sketches. Although his popularity came mainly from his radio comedy and live performances, he recorded over 70 numbers, and was one of the first to record rock'n'roll, significantly bridging the gap between 1950s radio comedy and pop music.

KENNETH WILLIAMS (1926-88) also made his name in the 1950s, with radio comedies such as *Hancock's Half Hour*, and Kenneth Horne's *Round the Horne* and *Beyond Our Ken*. The characters he played included J. Peasemold Gruntfuttock, Arthur Fallowfield, Rambling Sid Rumpo (a folk singer who sang ditties such as 'The Runcorn Splod Cobbler's Song'), and, with Hugh Paddick, the camp couple, Julian and Sandy.

Williams spent his early years at nearby 57 Marchmont Street, where his parents ran a barber's shop. In 1952 he disliked having to wear ribbons in his hair when he played one of the lost boys in a Christmas production of *Peter Pan* at the Scala theatre. In 1972 he moved to 8 Marlborough House, Osnaburgh Street, opposite Great Portland Street station. When recording *Just A Minute*, at Broadcasting House, he would often say, in mock indignation, 'I didn't come all the way from Great Portland Street to be treated like this.'

He often went to the Fitzroy Tavern, which was popular with other comedians, including Kenneth Horne (1907-69), Richard Murdoch and TOMMY COOPER (1922-84). After a Royal Command performance, Cooper asked the queen if she was interested in football and when she said no, he replied, 'In that case, can I have your cup final ticket this year?'

When Williams was starring in the unashamedly corny *Carry On* films, he visited co-star Andrew Ray, who was a patient in Middlesex Hospital psychiatric ward, bringing along with him the showbiz celebrities GORDON JACKSON (1923-90) and DIANA DORS (1931-84), who had been a student at the Royal Academy of Dramatic Art (RADA) and often dined at Olivelli's restaurant, Store Street. Altogether they made such a rumpus that Ray was finally asked to leave because of his noisy visitors. Andrew's father, the comedian, TED RAY (1906-77), was visited when a patient in the same hospital by fellow comic MAX BYGRAVES (b.1922). Ted joked that when he was using the bedpan he feared EAMONN ANDREWS (1922-87) might appear with the *This Is Your Life* crew. Eamonn, who lived at nearby Bedford Square, previously hosted radio's *Sports Report*, after being introduced to its producer in the Cock Tavern, 27 Great Portland Street. PETER SELLARS (1925-80) actor and *Goon Show*

SIR HENRY WOOD rehearsing a Promenade concert in Queen's Hall, to celebrate his 50th year as a conductor. Rachmaninov was the guest soloist.

With his long white baton, 'cutting, thrusting, parrying and dissecting', Wood took the musicians into the daring realms of modern music. He believed there was also a place for light music, and was especially proud of the audience reaction to the Elgar marches, 'The people simply rose & yelled. I had to play it again – with the same result.'

A very lively *Loose Ends* in contrast to last week's pudding...We finished with George Melly who was in rumbustious form. Everyone came to the George afterwards – my first round came to £50, the highest yet. George in compulsive joke-telling mood. 'Have you heard about the new male morning-after contraceptive? It changes your blood group.'

Ned Sherrin

star, died in Middlesex Hospital after being treated unsuccessfully for a heart attack.

TERRY MANCINI (b.1942), the Arsenal and Irish international footballer, was born just north of Fitzrovia in a prefab in Munster Square, 'My playgrounds up to the age of 12 were the stations in the area which were as safe as houses in those days.' His family patronised the George & Dragon, 151 Cleveland Street, which became known as 'Mancini's pub'.

From 1948 to 1968, band leader BILLY COTTON (1899-69) shattered the silence of British Sunday lunchtimes by opening his weekly radio show with a bawled, 'Wakee waaaaaaa-KAY!', which was followed by his band's raucous rendition of 'Somebody Stole My Gal'. Previously he had been a motor racing driver and a professional footballer (playing for Brentford in the top division). In those days the pubs closed at 2 p.m. on Sunday afternoons and as soon the programme was over Cotton and his band rushed out of Broadcasting House to quench their thirst at the Yorkshire Grey, on the corner of Langham Street and Middleton Place. A singer with the band, ALAN BREEZE, was afflicted with a serious stammer which he only lost when he was singing, and which once so slowed down proceedings when he was in court for a traffic offence that he was given permission to sing his evidence.

The next wave of popular music, skiffle and rock'n'roll, centred on the Breadbasket coffee bar, 65 Cleveland Street, thanks to ALEXIS KORNER (1928-84), who opened up the basement as a music venue in 1953. He played guitar and mandolin for the Chris Barber and Ken Colyer bands and then formed his own group. Before they formed the Rolling Stones, Mick Jagger and Charlie Watts both played in his group.

Others who played at the Breadbasket early in their careers were England's first rock star, TOMMY STEELE (b.1936) and LIONEL BART (1930-99), both with the Cavemen, and EMILE FORD (who married the waitress, Monique), JIMMY JUSTICE (whose day job was working as sweeper in Tottenham Court Road's Woolworths), CHAS McDEVITT, JIM DALE, GLEN DALE (Tommy Steele's dresser who went on to join the Fortunes), as well as the ALLISONS and DIZ DISLEY.

The resident group was the VIPERS (from a song about cannabis) led by WALLY WHYTON (1929-97). He was born in Euston, attended the polytechnic at 309 Regent Street, and bought his first guitar when he played piano in the Perseverance pub, near Warren Street. LONNIE DONEGAN (b.1931) started the craze for skiffle, 'a potpourri of styles and sources' with improvisation, when he played it in the breaks between the jazz sessions at the 100 Club during 1953. In the Breadbasket he heard the band play Whyton's 'Don't You Rock Me Daddy O', which he went on to record in 1957, the same year that the band produced their own recording of the song. Donegan's version went to number four in the charts and the group's reached number ten. It did not help the rivalry between them when the Vipers' monkey defecated on Donegan at a party.

KEN AMES, now a professional musician, first heard skiffle at the Breadbasket, when he was a student at the London Foot Hospital, 33 Fitzroy Square from 1957 to 1961. He formed the skiffle group, MARK VII MANIACS, which played regularly at the Green Man.

A group of students from the Regent Street Polytechnic, who formed LES HOBEAUX SKIFFLE GROUP in 1957, went rapidly from busking to the top of the bill, a recording contract with HMV, and an appearance in Terry Dene's film *The Golden Disc*. The band leader, 17-year-old LES 'FAGS' BENNETTS, went on to play for Donegan, and later he became a boxer, a coal miner, a tractor driver, the manager of film star Diana Dors, and an egg salesman, before he died of cancer in 1995, aged 45.

Bill would creep along and put drawing pins on some of our seats. So when we dashed back and sat down, and then stood to take a bow, you can imagine us trying to hide our sudden stab of pain. Lots of gags like this used to happen, no harm and nothing vicious in them. We were an all-male band in those days.

Alan Breeze on joining Billy Cotton's band

In 1958 the first British-composed-and-performed single to top the charts, selling two-thirds of a million copies, was 'Hoots Man' by Lord Rockingham's XI, with BENNY GREEN (1927-98) on saxophone (for which Benny was paid just his session fee of £6). Benny Green, saxophonist, journalist and broadcaster, lived in the basement flat, Howard House, 171 Cleveland Street, for the first 34 years of his life – a blue plaque was erected there in 1999. Lost in the dense London smog of 1952 (which resulted in 1,600 deaths and lead to the new Clean Air Act of 1956) he made his way home using his nose, 'by following the smell of stale beer floating out of the local pubs along the way.' As a boy he spent a lot of time at his grandfather's, on the corner of Greenwell Street and Bolsover Street. He remembered riding with his father on the outside staircase of one of the omnibuses that used to travel along Euston Road. In turn, his father recalled the way the steam from the pre-electric underground trains swirled through the open roof of Great Portland Street station – the route of London's first underground railway (the Metropolitan line) built by the Victorians on the 'cut and cover' principle, under the wide Marylebone and Euston Road. His uncle Henry, an illegal street bookmaker, a 'disparate character', ran his betting business at that part of Hanson Street which was demolished to build Holcroft Court. Young Benny was once attacked by a boy twice his size in Hanson Street. He started to defend himself, thinking that his uncle, whose pitch was only 20 yards away, would come to the rescue. Henry arrived, but instead of breaking up the fight, he offered the crowd odds of seven to four against his nephew.

Between the ages of three and eleven Benny went to the Clipstone Junior Mixed elementary school, 115 New Cavendish (56 *Upper Marylebone*) Street, which was bombed during the war (since demolished, the site is now occupied by the University of Westminster). Other pupils there included MACKY McKAY (Prince Monolulu's son), Raymond Jackson who became JAK, the cartoonist, and Max Savelsky who became the actor, MAXWELL SHAW. Benny recalled many hilarious antics with his fellow pupils, 'a polyglot assortment' of Russians, Irish, Belgians, Italians, Greek and Spanish. One of them managed to swallow a marble during a school trip to the British Museum, and ended up in Middlesex Hospital where, to his great relief, the marble was saved. In his teenage years he went to the youth club, 39 Fitzroy Square.

During the swinging 1960s, when London became the capital of the pop music world, Fitzrovia provided the venues. The ROLLING STONES played their first gig at the Marquee, at 165 Oxford Street (underneath the Academy cinema, where it had started as a jazz club in 1958, before moving on to Wardour Street). It was July 12, 1962, and they were filling in for the Marquee house band, Alexis Korner's Blues Incorporated (who were doing a gig for the BBC). The club's jazz purists gave them a cool reception, and a little later in the evening there was trouble, when some Mods, in their well-tailored Italian style suits, were determined to make their presence felt, 'The immaculately attired scooter riders contemptuously eyed the goatee bearded jazzers up and down', and elbowed their way closer to the fledging Rolling Stones, 'Then they barged their way to the front of the stage where, after admiring Brian and Keith's Muddy Waters and Chuck Berry guitar riffs, they gleefully attacked the audience. Violent chaos ensued.'

The response of the club's owner, Henry Pendleton, was instant dislike for the Stones. His continual sniping got too much for Keith Richard. In September, later that year, Richard 'walked over to the sniggering club owner and promptly smashed him over the head with his guitar.' At which, Pendleton banned the Stones from the club – and immediately boosted the band's reputation.

They couldn't believe we had borrowed American folk music, added something to it, and turned it into a commercial proposition.

Nancy Whiskey, who fronted Chas McDevitt's Skiffle Group, on their recording of 'Freight Train' which sold 250,000 copies.

Elsa Lanchester, actress
and cabaret artiste

*Known for her comic,
eccentric roles, Elsa Lanchester
ran two nightclubs in
Fitzrovia during the 1920s.*

In March 1963, the Stones made their first recording (five unreleased tracks) at the IBC Studio, 35 Portland Place. Later that year they signed with Decca (recording their first album and two released singles, including 'Not Fade Away', produced by Phil Spector and Gene Pitney, at Regent Sound Studio, 4 Denmark Street, just south of Tottenham Court Road station). The following year they played at the 100 Club. Nearly three decades later they were to return to record a single in the Hit Factory, 31-37 Whitfield Street, in 1991.

Just after the Mods rioted at the Stones gigs in the Marquee, a young American folk singer, Bob Dylan (b.1941), provoked trouble at the King & Queen folk club run by Martin Carthy (who later joined Steeleye Span) at 1 Foley Street. When Dylan first sang at the King & Queen in December 1962, Nigel Denver sniped that Dylan 'couldn't sing his way out of a paper bag'. On New Year's Day, 1963, Dylan returned to the club and barracked Denver's singing. A slanging match ensued, until the audience ran out of patience and rebuked Dylan.

The Duke of York, 47 Rathbone Street, run by the eccentric Alf 'Major' Klein, attracted bohemian regulars such as Donovan and Ian Dury (1942-2000) who both became popular singer/songwriters. Donovan's self-penned song 'Sunny Goodge Street' (1965) was studded with images of hash smokers, chocolate machines, coloured lights, music boxes, plus a magician in satin and velvet.

In 1964 crowds of teenagers screamed at the Beatles, who were performing at the Scala theatre, 21-25 Tottenham Street, for their film, *A Hard Day's Night*.

A few months later Roger Waters (guitar), Nick Mason (drums) and Rich Wright (rhythm guitar), the first three members of what would become Pink Floyd, formed a group and played at the polytechnic, 309 Regent Street, where they were students and their band was headlined in the student newspaper as the Architectural Abdabs. Roger remembered haggling for money with the bank, 'When we all started spending all our grants on equipment I can remember threatening the bank manager at Great Portland Street or Great Titchfield Street that I was going to be immensely rich when I was trying to borrow a tenner.' At the end of 1965 his school friend, Syd Barrett, joined the group and they renamed themselves Pink Floyd. By March 1966 they were playing at the Marquee (which had moved to 90 Wardour Street), but it was between October 1966 and July 1967 when they were the resident band at the UFO Club, at 31 Tottenham Court Road, that they made their name.

I ran into some people in England who really knew those [traditional English] songs. Martin Carthy's incredible. I learned a lot of stuff from Martin. 'Girl from the North Country' is based on a song I heard him sing.

Bob Dylan

The UFO promoted mixed media events, where everyone was free to participate, and the conventional divisions between audience and performer were blurred. There the Pink Floyd had the chance to experiment with musical improvisation, psychedelic light shows and hallucinatory drugs, 'UFO was the one area where people were interested in what we were doing and it kept us alive in a way, and kept us carrying on', said Nick Mason. 'At UFO we played whatever we wanted and were very experimental…a mixture of bands, poets, juggling and all sorts of acts.'

Their first big hit 'See Emily Play', which was written by Syd Barrett after he woke from a sleep in a wood to see a girl dancing through the trees, was released on June 17, 1967. On the same day they were playing at Tiles, a club at 79 Oxford Street, run by Alexis Korner. But at the UFO later in the month, the drugs were taking their toll and Syd stood immobilised on the stage, his guitar hanging from his neck and his arms limp.

The Floyd also played at another famous Fitzrovian venue, the Speakeasy, 50 Margaret Street, where Jimi Hendrix (1942-70) liked to jam through the night. Hendrix's first gig in this country was at the Regent Street polytechnic on October 1, 1966. He was invited on stage by Eric Clapton, with the Cream.

Benjamin Britten, the composer, having a discussion with the tenor Peter Pears, in the garden at Aldeburgh.

Britten's opera masterpiece, Peter Grimes, was written with his partner, Pears, in mind. 'When I write it, & if it is put on here, I hope he'll do the principal part in Peter Grimes. The ideas are going well, but I haven't had time to start it yet', he told a friend in 1943.

Hendrix launched into a performance of a Howling Wolf number, 'Killing Floor'. Hearing just ten bars was enough to send Clapton lurching off the stage, saying 'Is he that fucking good?' At the end of the gig Clapton, put his arm around Hendrix, and later visited him whenever possible. Hendrix rented a flat in the White House by Great Portland Street station (his Cherokee ancestors had visited Marylebone 200 years earlier in an unsuccessful pursuit of a land claim). He mingled with other musicians in the UFO audience, such as JOHN LENNON (1940-80).

As the affluent youth culture of the sixties waned, the 1970s saw the musical mood turn cynical, and the 100 Club and, later the Speakeasy, became a focus for the punk movement. While many clubs banned punks (put off by their aggressive mode, their spitting and the safety-pins through their noses), they were welcomed at the 100 Club, where the SEX PISTOLS became the regular Thursday night band in March 1976. One night Johnny Rotten (so-called because of his decaying teeth) was playing, and Sid Vicious jumped up and down in the audience to get a better view, so, it is said, inventing the pogo-dance. Also in the audience was American singer, CHRISSIE HYNDE, who taught Johnny Rotten to play the guitar.

Both Johnny Rotten and Sid Vicious were supporting themselves by working at the first Fitzrovian branch of the Cranks health food restaurant, on the top floor of the furniture store, Heals, 196 Tottenham Court Road (later the restaurant opened at 9 Tottenham Street).

Sid Vicious later joined the Sex Pistols but as he watched them from the audience at the 100 Club, he was arrested for throwing a glass. He was also fined £125 at Wells Street Magistrates Court on August 2, 1977, for possessing a knife.

Sid Vicious played drums for SIOUXIE AND THE BANSHEES at the 100 Club, when it hosted the punk festival on September 20 and 21, 1976. Other bands came from all over the country to play at this historic event, which launched punk rock into the wider world, including the BUZZCOCKS, the VIBRATORS, the DAMNED, the CLASH, and the Sex Pistols.

During the Queen's silver jubilee celebrations in 1977 the Sex Pistols released a provocatively irreverent single, 'God Save the Queen'. Banned by all broadcasting authorities it shot to number two in the charts.

The endless punk graffiti, theft and damages eventually became too much for the 100 Club manager, Roger Horton, who barred punks from the premises, from April 1978.

Other local venues which hosted punks were the Speakeasy (where Sid Vicous attacked disc jockey Bob Harris with a glass, and Johnny Rotten gave one of Harris's friends a head wound that needed 14 stitches), the Green Man (383 Euston Road), the Other Cinema (Tottenham Street), and the Polytechnic of Central London at 32-38 Wells and 115 New Cavendish Streets.

Ex-manager of the Sex Pistols, MALCOLM MCLAREN (b.1946), currently lives in Scala Street.

Disc jockeys such as KENNY EVERETT (1944-95) and DAVE CASH (b.1942) from Capital Radio (which broadcast from Euston Tower opposite Warren Street station 1973-98) frequented the pubs, The Smugglers Tavern, 28 Warren Street and O'Neills (formerly Carpenters Arms) at 4 Conway Street. Cash lived at Fitzroy Mews before moving to a flat at 168 New Cavendish Street. Kenny delighted his audience with his crude spoonerisms in his successful, camp television show in the 1970s. He frequently offended authority and was sacked by the BBC and by Radio London (for mocking one of its sponsors, the evangelist Garner Ted Armstrong). Everett died of AIDS.

By 1979 squatters occupied several houses in the area around Warren Street. When BOY GEORGE (b.1961) visited the Middlesex Hospital to have a finger stitched after a fight in an Oxford Street club, he met up with some student squatters, and the following year he moved into a Great Titchfield Street squat. Although he found it filthy, he enjoyed its communal spirit, 'like a wartime community with everyone popping in and out, borrowing eyeliner and sugar.' Conspicuous because of his gender-bender garb and make-up, he was out one night painted yellow 'like a cosmic squaw', when he broke one of his feet drunkenly kicking a door, and was taken to Gower Street's University College Hospital for treatment. A Norwegian-Thai woman friend of his who was squatting in Warren Street died in bed from drink and drugs.

The punk singer KIRK BRANDON, of Theatre of Hate, made friends with George and spent several nights with him in Great Titchfield Street. George held a leaving party at Great Titchfield Street that was so rowdy that the police cordoned off the street, and then arrested George outside the Scala cinema.

I thought they were pretty good. Well, not good, really, but they could be.

Mick Jagger on hearing the Sex Pistols at the 100 Club

Marilyn and I spent our days doing loads of nothing, we often wandered down Oxford Street and cadged free make-up and perfume samples.

Boy George

George moved to 21 Carburton Street, where there was an outside toilet that lacked a door and a roof.

When the squat spread into Carburton Street, a beatnik, CHRISTINE BINNIE, opened a café in the same street, the Coffee Spoon, where friends projected their films over her naked body and read poetry. MALLAM 'SAM' IDRISSU, born in Ghana, who ran the Rambler Café, 145 Cleveland Street, often provided squatters with free meals and gave money to George and transvestite singer Marilyn (who lived in Carburton Street) to buy make-up.

In 1980 George moved into a bedsit at 37 Goodge Street, in a flat he shared with 'a big fat blonde woman who avoided eye contact and had squealing sex sessions with black men at odd hours.' Sometimes he joined the early morning queues outside the Job Centre at 33 Mortimer Street, to find work for a day, washing up in restaurants. He ate cheap meals at Gigs chippie, 12 Tottenham Street, and was sometimes provided with tea by the bohemian Burke family living at 31 Goodge Street, whom he visited by clambering over the roof. He liked the solitude of the roof, 'It was dangerous and peaceful up there, especially at night, when I was watching the city, thinking about my life.'

JON MOSS, drummer with the Damned, moved into George's Goodge Street room. There he and George wrote songs and formed the Culture Club, with Roy Hay (guitar and keyboards). George and Jon moved out in 1981. In May 1982 they visited friends, Jik and Jem, in their Fitzroy Square flat, where George wrote their first chart topper 'Do You Really Want to Hurt Me?'

For over 20 years (1970-91), the bulletins of Independent Television News were broadcast from the studio at 48 Wells Street. Newscaster REGINALD BOSANQUET (1932-84) enjoyed a tipple at the Kings Arms opposite and some regulars claimed to have seen him snatching a snifter in the advertisement breaks during News at Ten. TREVOR MCDONALD (b.1939) preferred a leisurely glass or two of wine with a meal after the broadcast was over, often at the

IN TOWN TO-NIGHT, cartoon by Leo Dowd

The democratic mix of people assembled for the BBC show was a celebration of the city. On any one evening, there might be a 'marquess, the chimney sweep, the hawker, the sewer man, the fruit seller, the film star and the famous author.'

Glory kebab restaurant, 57 Goodge Street, where he was happy to repeat the news for other diners who had missed it on television.

BBC broadcasters wet their whistles in the George at 55 Great Portland Street, where NED SHERRIN (b.1931) has been going after his Saturday morning radio show *Loose Ends* since 1985. One of his regular guests, the cockney comedian Arthur Smith, is very partial to their pork pies.

Until it closed in 1998 conjuror KYPROS PELEKANOS (1944-99), of Holcroft Court, entertained diners at the Anemos restaurant, 32 Charlotte Street, sometimes producing doves and bras from women customers' blouses, 'It was the kind of place where all kinds of people came to mix together like a family.' Customers, who ranged from the Duke of Kent to a homeless man called Richard, were encouraged to dance on the tables, and the restaurant was better known for its revelry and party atmosphere than its food.

DAVID JASON (b.1940), best known for his role as the street trader Del Boy in the television series *Only Fools and Horses*, chose the Duke of York as his watering hole when he lived at 29-35 Rathbone Street during the 1980s.

Television actress and author, BARBARA EWING, lives in Candover Street. Born in New Zealand, she studied at RADA and has starred in several films and the television serial *Brass*. She has written three novels and a play about Alexandra Kollontai, the only woman minister in the revolutionary Russian government in 1917.

IAN COLLIER created a roof garden above his flat in Great Titchfield Street. He acted in the television holiday comedy *Hi de Hi!*, and he played a racist policeman so convincingly in a fringe theatre production that Black members of the audience raised the roof; he himself was living with a Black partner at the time.

PROFESSOR RAY LEES (b.1931) was a professional wrestler, actor, and psychiatric nurse before becoming an academic. While teaching at the Polytechnic of Central London, based at 76-78 Mortimer Street during the 1970s and 1980s, he published three books on politics and social welfare, and wrote the couplet,

Divorced, unemployed, and pissed
I aimed low in life – and missed.

I am a West Indian peasant who has drifted into this business and who has survived. If I knew the secret, I would bottle it and sell it.

Trevor McDonald

CHAPTER 6
The Artistic Community

Of the many artists attracted to Fitzrovia, one of the earliest was WILLIAM HOGARTH (1697-1762), who painted and drew the sprawling, brawling chaos of London's street life and the debauchery of the 18th century city. When at his barber's, Joseph Watkins, 121 Tottenham Court Road, Hogarth once saw a lad drop his pie and gravy in the street outside, and he leaped from his chair 'with the lather still adhering to his face' to sketch the lad's discomfort and dismay. He used this for the boy in *Noon*, one of four paintings in which he re-worked the classical theme of the 'Times of Day'. It shows Apollo as a black servant, Venus as a maid, and her son, Cupid, as a squalling boy. The servant is squeezing the maid's breasts while she gazes over her shoulder, dreamily distracted, letting the pie dish that she's holding tilt, spilling hot sauce onto the baker boy. In his distress, the boy bangs his head, and breaks his plate, as a girl reaches for the scattered pieces of bread on the ground below. In the building above them an angry housewife throws the leg of lamb she's cooked for dinner out of the window and, on the other side of the street, down-at-the-mouth Huguenot elders walk out of the church behind a simpering, well-to-do couple with their fat child.

The lascivious, the deceitful, the quarrelsome, the prudish, the hypocritical, the self-interested, all these and more Hogarth found on Tottenham Court Road. His *March to Finchley*, set at the top of the road, shows a group of soldiers sprawled outside the Kings Head brothel, the worse for their 'entanglements with women, drink and crime'. At the bottom end of the road was St Giles, one of the most densely populated and poverty-stricken areas of 18th century London, where gin sellers did a roaring trade. Hogarth's *Gin Lane* dramatised the drunkenness and misery, and was part of a reform campaign that led to the passing of the 1751 Gin Act (said to have reduced the national gin consumption by 75%).

His pub sign for the inn, The Man with a Load of Mischief, 53 (*414*) Oxford Street, showed a man carrying a woman on his shoulder, and the woman holding a glass of gin, and a monkey. Hogarth lived in Covent Garden where he started an artists' academy in 1734. During a trip to France he was once falsely suspected of being a spy, and arrested, because he was drawing the fortifications at Calais.

RICHARD WILSON (1713-82), the father of English landscape painting and a major influence on Constable and Turner, was a founding member of the Royal Academy (1768), and later its librarian. He lived and had studios at 78, 76 (*36*), and 8 Charlotte Street, 85 Great Titchfield Street, 21 Bolsover (*Norton*) Street, Rathbone Place, and Tottenham (*Chapel*) Street east, where he died in poverty. He dressed in a dapper waistcoat, with a cocked hat and a cane, and was noted for his enormous red nose and his talent at skittles, which he played at the Green Man (*Farthing Pye House*) at the top of Bolsover Street.

His contemporary, ALLAN RAMSAY (1713-84), the son of a Scottish shepherd, had more success in his own lifetime, being appointed principal painter for George III. He lived in Berners Street, and was buried at the old St Marylebone Church.

It has been observed, that Hogarth's are exceedingly unlike any other representation of the same kind of subjects - that they form a class, and have a character, peculiar to themselves.

William Hazlitt

NINA HAMNETT

Hamnett's drawings and paintings were characterised by the strong modelling of their figures, giving them a sculptural quality.

JOSEPH NOLLEKENS by
Lemuel Francis Abbott
(1797)

*When Nollekens was sculpting
a bust of King George III he
breached courtly protocol by
pricking the King's nose with
his caliper and roaring like a
lion in his ear.*

A fashionable miniature painter, NATHANIEL HONE (1718-84), who lived at 30 and 44 Rathbone Place, had a propensity for vendettas with other artists. It was because of his painting *The Pictorial Conjuror, Displaying the Whole Art of Optical Deception*, which represented JOSHUA REYNOLDS (1723-92) as a plagiarist, that Hone was banned from the Royal Academy. Reynolds frequently called at Admiral Cotterel's in Eastcastle Street (probably *No.73*, opposite where Samuel Johnson lived at *No.6*) lured by his fascination for the admiral's daughters.

Sculptor JOSEPH WILTON (1722-1803), who designed George III's coronation coach, kept a model of the coach in his backyard on the corner of Langham Street (*Foley Place*) and Great Portland Street (27 *Queen Anne Street East*). After he inherited a fortune from his father, a plasterer, he lived sumptuously and dressed in style, adopting a bag-wig and carrying a gold-headed cane, until the money ran out. He also lived and had a studio in Langham (*Foley*) Place and Great Portland Street.

The engraver, WILLIAM WOOLLETT (1735-85), fired a cannon from his Tottenham Street studio every time he completed a new plate. As a result of the great success of his engraving of Benjamin West's *The Death of Wolfe*, he was appointed Historical Engraver to His Majesty.

When sculptor THOMAS BANKS (1735-1805), who lived at 5 Newman Street, wanted to make a sculpture of the Crucifixion, he acquired the body of the murderer, James Legge, who had been hanged. To construct his model, he made a cast of Legge's body, and affixed it to a cross.

When he was still establishing himself as a sculptor JOSEPH NOLLEKENS (1737-1823) kept solvent by using his plaster casts to smuggle contraband into the country. Born at nearby 28 Soho Square, Nollekens lived at 6 Mortimer (7 *Charles*) Street and, in 1771, moved to 44 (9) Mortimer Street. He lived there, careless of his surroundings, for the rest of his life – the place was infested with rats, tea-leaves were sprinkled on the carpets to soak up the dust, and valuable paintings by his friends, Gainsborough, Richard Wilson, Benjamin West and James Barry, lay jumbled.

Nollekens' 'deviations from the courtly norm' amused King George III but not the Prince of Wales, who was next in line to throne. Nollekens once asked the prince how his father was, and when the prince told him that George III was well, Nollekens replied tactlessly that he was relieved, because 'we shall never have another King like him'. 'Thank you', the prince said coldly.

Although Nollekens became a wealthy man, acquiring a fortune of £300,000, he was extremely parsimonious. One winter his butcher imprisoned him inside an igloo made with snow in Market Place (*Oxford Market*) to force Nollekens to pay his meat bill. Similarly drastic action was needed to make Nollekens pay the artist's model, Bet Malmanno, after she had modelled for him for eight hours, in the nude, during cold weather, and he had offered her nothing to eat or drink. When he tried to fob her off with just 2*s*., Malmanno's agent, Kit Lobb, called him a 'little grub' and Nollekens threw the insult back, calling Malmanno a 'yard bitch'. Lobb only persauded Nollekens to cough up another 5*s*. by threatening to have his dog, Cerberus, skinned and hung up in the Rat's Castle (St Giles rookery).

WILLIAM HOGARTH, self-portrait (*c.*1757)

Hogarth depicted the life of 18th century London through a moral lens and cast social attitudes into perspective.

By 1774 his friend, the painter BENJAMIN WEST (1738-1821), was earning enough from his portraits of King George III (64 portraits in all, for which he was paid nearly £35,000) to move into 14 Newman Street, and to have extensions built to the house, and employ five servants. He lived there for the rest of his life. When he wanted to set up a realistic model for a Crucifixion, West went one further than Banks, and arranged for a local anatomist to nail the body of an executed murderer to a cross. On a visit to Italy in 1760 the fact of his being an American was a novelty and the blind Cardinal Albani asked West whether he were a 'Red Indian.' West, who was a Quaker, turned down a knighthood on principle. Four mutes on horseback led his funeral cortege.

For most of his life JOHN BACON (1740-99), a tomb sculptor, lived at 17 Newman Street, just over the road from West, in premises that had been bought for him by a builder named Johnson (of Berners Street). He was described as 'piously and zealously attached to Methodism...yet knowing in the ways of the world', and was later able to repay the builder and also to lend him an additional £40,000. Bacon began his career making pottery models at George Yard, Oxford Street (near Soho Square). He was buried in Whitefield's Chapel at 79 Tottenham Court Road (now part of the American Church).

The painter JAMES BARRY (1741-1806), an uncompromising character, was the only artist to be expelled from the Royal Academy for 'outrageous misconduct': he lambasted the treasurer, Sir William Chambers, soon after the man's death. He was also considered rather too radical for the Academy, numbering among his friends Thomas Holcroft, John Horne Tooke, Franciso de Miranda, William Godwin and Mary Wollstonecraft.

Barry lived and had his studio at 36 Eastcastle Street (*Castle Street East*), where he moved in 1777. Formerly a carpenter's workshop, it was littered with cobwebs, had cracked window panes, a barn roof with no ceiling, and a huge grate in the fire place on which the carpenter had heated his glue pot. Barry grilled steaks on the grate for his friend, Edmund Burke.

Some locals thought Barry was a wizard who communicated with the dead and they vandalized the building repeatedly. By 1804 most of the windows were smashed, and the door and walls had been plastered with mud. Dog and cat skeletons, marrow bones and waste paper were tied to the outside of the house and, to avoid the missiles that were thrown in at him, Barry was forced to occupy an unfurnished back room. Almost penniless, he survived on bread and apples until he collapsed from under-nourishment.

In his final days, ill with pleuritic fever, his front door keyhole having been jammed with stones by his persecutors, lodgings were found for him in Mortimer Street, where he spent two feverish nights before he was thrown out because his nosebleed soiled the sheets. He died in the house of a friend, the architect Joseph Bonomi, at 76 Great Titchfield Street. The culmination of his life's work *Pandora*, a huge painting in the grand historical style, was sold to William Henderson of 33 Charlotte Street.

HENRY FUSELI (1741-1825), who once described himself as 'principal hob-goblin to the devil', lived at 37 and then at 40 Foley Street (72 and 75 *Queen Anne Street East*) from 1788 to 1792. From 1804 until he died, he lived at 13 Berners Street. A trainee priest in Switzerland in his youth, he was forced to flee the country after he had frightened a young woman by trying to produce an apparition of her deceased lover and published a pamphlet which exposed the dishonesty of a magistrate.

Initially he sold his drawings in order to make money to buy 'flame-coloured' clothes. Encouraged to paint by Sir Joshua Reynolds, whom he met in 1767, the painting that shot him to fame was *The Nightmare* (1781). It depicted a woman in the aftermath of a sexual dream, and Sigmund Freud famously described it as 'a horrid monster with a laugh or leer squatting upon a sleeping maiden's naked breast'. Fuseli supposedly ate raw meat to induce the dreams that were the subject of his paintings but, according to his pupil, Benjamin Haydon, Fuseli was inspired by the demonic, 'the engines in Fuseli's mind are blasphemy, lechery and blood'. Just as lurid was Haydon's description of why the Berners Street house was frightening at twilight, with its 'galvanised devils and malicious witches brewing their incantations'. Fuseli had a fetish for elongated necks, and he drew erotic pictures specifically for the amusement of George IV at Brighton.

After a fever left him with a shaking right hand, Fuseli trained himself to paint with the left. Mary Wollstonecraft was infatuated with Fuseli and wanted to live with him, but his wife objected.

GAINSBOROUGH DUPONT (1754-97), the nephew of Thomas Gainsborough, lived at 41 Fitzroy Square during the last four years of his life, where he completed some of his uncle's unfinished portraits.

A house at 28 Newman Street turned out to be tragically jinxed for THOMAS STOTHARD (1755-1834), painter, illustrator, collector of nosegays and butterflies, after he moved there in 1790. His silver plate was stolen by a thief, with the

He had a strong Swiss accent...all of a sudden, he would burst out with a quotation from Homer, Tasso, Dante, Ovid, Virgil, or perhaps the Niebelungen, and thunder round to me with 'Paint dat!'

R.B. Haydon on Henry Fuseli, when Fuseli was a professor at the Royal Academy (1799-1825)

help of his cook. His 13-year-old son was killed by a schoolmate in a shooting accident, following a premonition of death. When his wife was told the news, she saw the boy's ghost. In 1825 she died in the house, as did her mother, who died three years later. Stothard himself also died there, after he had been run over by a carriage.

One of the great sculptors of the age was JOHN FLAXMAN (1755-1826), who specialized in monuments. He had a humped shoulder and was the son of a maker of plaster figures. A Mrs Harriet Mathew of 27 Rathbone Place introduced him to Mr Knight of Portland Place, who gave him his first commission. Flaxman's work can be seen preserved in University College, Gower Street. He lived at 17 Rathbone Place, 12 Grafton Way (*Grafton Street*), and 7 Greenwell (*Buckingham*) Street, where he died, and where there is plaque to him (now covered in ivy).

America's early one-dollar bills carried a drawing of the goddess Athena done by GILBERT STUART (1755-1828), who lived at 7 Newman Street from 1782 to 1785. A very sociable man and keen on the theatre, he managed to spend more than his considerable earnings of £1,000 a year, and when he collapsed into debt, his house and its contents were seized and he fled to Dublin.

He had been Benjamin West's pupil in Newman Street, as was JOHN 'BRIDEWELL JACK' TRUMBULL (1756-1843), who was imprisoned and later deported for having fought in the rebel army during the American war of independence. In 1784 he returned to the Newman Street studio and became well known for his historical paintings of the war.

Mr Fuseli's...ideas are gnarled, hard and distorted like his features... His pictures are also like himself, with eye-balls of stone stuck in rims of tin, and muscles twisted together like ropes or wires.

William Hazlitt

The work of an uncouth illustrator named JOHN 'THE CORNISH WONDER'
OPIE (1761-1807) appeared in books on female flagellants. As a lad he lived in
Truro where he was regularly beaten by his father until a Dr Wolcott (who later
became a well-known satirist) helped him to escape by employing him to
clean knives and feed the dog. Opie also sketched locals for a few pence and
by the age of 15 he had saved enough to pay his fare to London, where he
found employment with the miniaturist OZIAS HUMPHREY (1742-1810) at 29
Rathbone Place. When Opie became successful he lived at 6 and at 8 Berners
Street.

GEORGE MORLAND (1763-1804), apprenticed aged 17 to his artist father
Henry Morland (1719-97), at 36 Windmill Street, was soon living it up in the
company of 'ostlers, potboys, horse jockeys, money-lenders, pawnbrokers,
punks, and pugilists'. He moved to Great Portland Street where he produced
obscene drawings to pay off debts and painted pub signs to pay for his beer.
Suspected of forging banknotes, his premises were raided. While on the run
from his creditors, he was accused of being a French spy and jailed for three
years. Although he was freed he was soon back behind bars for forging Dutch
landscapes, and he lost the use of his left hand and could no longer hold his
palette. For a while he lived at 3 Stephen Street (off Tottenham Court Road).
He died behind bars in a 'spunging house'. He had suggested that his epitaph
should read 'here lies a drunken dog', and he was buried in nearby St James
(Hampstead Road). His wife, whom he deserted, died three days later and she
was buried in the same grave.

The architect Sir William Chambers employed an apprentice by the name of JOSEPH MALLORD WILLIAM TURNER (1775-1851) at his 53 Berners Street practice until eventually he advised the young man that he was wasting his time studying architecture. Turner switched to art and became renowned for his magnificent landscapes of colour and light depicting the transcendent forces of nature. Turner was soon earning enough to move to fashionable 51 (64) Harley Street but he moved a short distance away, albeit a long way downmarket, to 75 Bolsover (Norton) Street, to live with his lover, Sarah Danby. He fathered three of her seven children. Later she faded out of his life and he cut the children out of his will. He moved back to Harley Street where he met visitors to his damp and chilly household surrounded by a swarm of tail-less cats and drifts of cobwebs.

On his deathbed Turner remarked, 'I am soon to become a nonentity.' His final words were, 'The Sun is God.'

By contrast JOHN CONSTABLE (1776-1837) strove to represent the natural world without sentiment or grandeur, 'Imagination alone', he said, 'can never produce works that are to stand by a comparison with realities.' In 1802 Constable lived in 50 Rathbone Place. In 1812 he moved to 85 (63) Charlotte Street, then in 1817 to 1 Keppel Street (where his family complained of feeling like 'bottled wasps'), and in 1822 to 63 (35) Charlotte Street, then finally to 76 Charlotte (35 Upper Charlotte) Street where he had a studio and a room* for the rest of his life, although it was, he said, full of noxious smells from the privy below and they 'played the devil with the oxygen in my colours'.

Constable kept so still while he was painting that a field mouse once crept into his back pocket, only to be crushed to death when the artist changed position. He painted to suit himself rather than for a market and did not sell a picture until he was 38 years old, and that was to a friend. Despite this he was dismissive of his more successful rivals at the time – such as William Etty (1787-1849) who, in Constable's words, painted nothing but 'women's bums' and the 'shaggy posteriors of satyrs', and WILLIAM COLLINS (1788-1847) one of whose landscapes he described as being 'like a cow turd'. Collins lived in Bolsover Street, Portland Place, 118 Great Portland Street and nearby 11 New Cavendish Street.

In 1821 Constable exhibited The Hay Wain to wide acclaim at the Royal Academy. Three years later a local tub maker from Tottenham Court Road, Mr Appleton, called on him, 'to know if I had a damaged picture which I could let him have cheap, as he is fitting up a room.' Later that year the French dealer, Arrowsmith, visited Charlotte Street and bought The Hay Wain and two other pictures for £250.

The day before he died, Constable was walking along Oxford Street with CHARLES ROBERT LESLIE (1794-1859), the American artist (whose local addresses were successively Charlotte, Great Titchfield, Cleveland and Warren Streets), and he gave a shilling and said some kind words to a little beggar girl who had hurt her knee. What hurt him most about unpaid debts, Constable told Leslie, was not the money but the betrayal of trust.

Constable's wife, Maria Bicknell, whom he married in defiance of her father's wishes in 1816, died of consumption in 1828. For the rest of his life Constable wore mourning clothes and he devoted himself to his painting and the care of his seven children. A death mask of Constable's face was made by the sculptor SAMUEL JOSEPH, of 11 Charlotte Street.

Another target of Constable's bile was JOHN VARLEY (1778-1842), 'the conjuror who is now a beggar, but a fat and sturdy one', who once tried to tell Constable 'how to do landscapes and was so kind as to point out all my defects.' A prominent water colourist, Varley was also a keen astrologer, who

Precisely as we are shallow in our knowledge, vulgar in our feeling, and contracted in our views of principles, will the works of this artist be stumbling-blocks to us: precisely in the degree to which we are familiar with nature, constant in our understanding of her, will they expand before our eyes into glory and beauty.

John Ruskin on J.M.W. Turner

* John Constable maintained two addresses for much of his life: one was the family home, the other was his painting studio, where he sometimes stayed overnight.

took delight when events matched his predictions, even when it was the destruction of his own house – 10 Great Titchfield Street, burned down in 1825, after which he moved to Foley Street, then Berners and Charlotte Streets. He foretold the date of William Collins' death, and that of his nephew, Paul Mulready, who was killed by a cricket ball. When he caught a chill while sketching some cedar trees, the doctors told him he would soon recover but on consulting his almanac, Varley told them that they were wrong, and he died soon afterwards (November 17).

Varley, who weighed 17 stone when he was alive, was once rescued from drowning by his pupil and brother-in-law, WILLIAM MULREADY (1786-1863), who pulled him from the Thames.

On another occasion Mulready strayed into the lions' den in Regent's Park zoo where, confronted by a fully grown lion on the prowl, he managed to keep the animal at bay 'by the power of his eye' for nearly an hour before a zoo keeper came to the rescue. Mulready, whose nude studies were described by the eminent critic John Ruskin as 'degraded and bestial', lived at 42 Newman Street, 11 Fitzroy Street, and Torrington Place (30 *Francis Street*) – where his wife divorced him after she found him in bed with fellow artist JOHN LINNELL (1792-1882) who shared the same house.

Linnell, born and bred in St Giles, become a dissenter, and befriended and promoted the work of William Blake. Linnell lived at 38 Rathbone Place, and 5 and 6 Holcroft Court, Great Titchfield Street (*5 and 6 Cirencester Place*). He left a fortune of £200,000.

The water colourist PETER DE WINT (1784-1849) was imprisoned as an apprentice engraver for loyally refusing to reveal the whereabouts of a runaway apprentice, WILLIAM HILTON (1786-1839). De Wint bought himself out of his apprenticeship and began to produce water colours. He lived at 40 Windmill Street, 19 Carburton Street, and 93 Bolsover (*Norton*) Street before moving to 10 Percy Street where he was joined by Hilton, who had married De Wint's sister Harriet, and who was also an artist. Subsequently they all moved to 113 Gower (*40 Upper Gower*) Street. De Wint and Hilton both illustrated the poetry of John Keats and John Clare, who visited them in Percy Street. When Clare was committed to a mental asylum (suffering from the delusion that he was Lord Byron), De Wint contributed to his expenses and visited him regularly. In return Clare wrote him a sonnet included in *The Rural Muse*.

Scottish painter DAVID WILKIE (1785-1841) played the bagpipes for his mother when they lived at 8 and 11 Bolsover (*Norton*) Street from 1805 to 1809. Later he moved to 84 Great Portland Street. His painting *The Chelsea Pensioners Reading the Gazette of The Battle of Waterloo* attracted so many spectators at the Royal Academy that it became the first exhibited picture to require a protective rail. Wilkie's death at sea was the subject of a painting by Turner.

Benjamin Robert Haydon (1786-1846), who led a tortured and uncompromising life, was taught by Fuseli at 13 Berners Street, and sold his first picture to Thomas Hope's gallery in Duchess Street. Haydon was deemed insensitive for having calmly made a sketch of the brother of CHARLES EASTLAKE (1793-1865) when the man was suffering from a severe attack of asthma. Eastlake became President of the Royal Academy and he lived at 39 Fitzroy Street, 7 Fitzroy Square, and 29 Devonshire Street.

Before becoming successful as an artist DAVID ROBERTS (1796-1864) painted houses and theatre scenery. He lived at 22 Howland and 38 (7) Fitzroy Streets. He died in Middlesex Hospital after being struck down with apoplexy while walking in Berners Street.

Painter of *The Stag at Bay* (reproduced in cards, posters and pictures), EDWIN LANDSEER (1802-73) was raised at 33 Foley Street (71 *Queen Anne Street*

I like de landscapes of Constable; he is always picturesque, of a fine colour, and de lights always in de right places; but he makes me call for my greatcoat and umbrella.

Henry Fuseli on John Constable

East). Encouraged by his father to play truant so that he could spend more time practising his drawing he became so proficient that he could sketch two subjects, using both hands, at one and the same time.

When he first exhibited at the Royal Academy at the age of 12, the title of his *Portrait of a Mule* was misprinted in the catalogue as *Portrait of a Mute*, and an admiring critic praised the young artist for his ability to 'convey in graphic terms the inability to speak.' By the time he was 18 years old he had a studio in Fitzroy Square. There he painted the portrait of the Duchess of Bedford (he also fathered the last two of her ten children). Society portraits had to satisfy those who commissioned them, and his portrait bills often listed additional touches such as 'taking out wrinkles in the cheek', 'altering mouth to a smile' or 'browning the grey hair'.

As a boy he brought home the carcass of a fox and other game (keeping them under his bed) in order to study their anatomy. Once when he was commissioned to paint a portait of a dog the animal was stolen before he started the work. Landseer described the animal to one of his criminal acquaintances, who informed him that the dog would be returned shortly, 'I sold it to a trump of an old lady in Portland Place for such an audacious good sum I feel it wouldn't be right not to let her enjoy it for at least a fortnight.' On another occasion Landseer went down on all fours to confront a

Everything that lives is holy.

William Blake

JOHN CONSTABLE, self-portrait (*c.*1804)

Constable thought that a reverential approach to the natural world was essential for any true representation.

notoriously savage dog, and snarled so convincingly that the animal broke its chain and ran off howling.

Landseer went hunting with Prince Albert. He had a riding accident in 1868 which led to symptoms of schizophrenia. Seeing one of his paintings in a dealer's window he inquired as to its cost and was told 2,000 guineas, 'I couldn't take a shilling less', the dealer said, 'he's gone, sir, you see. He's out of his mind. He'll never paint another.' Without revealing his identity Landseer pointed to another picture on display by his friend Clarkson Stanfield and, on being told that it was for sale at the same price, he exclaimed, 'My God, has Stanfield gone too?' Landseer's condition finally deteriorated and he turned to alcohol, suffered delusions and became seriously deranged.

Three years after he completed the statue of Sir Henry Havelock that stands in the south-eastern corner of Trafalgar Square, WILLIAM BEHNES (1795-1864), who lived at 27 Mortimer (*23 Charles*) and 31 Newman Streets, was found in the gutter with three pennies in his pocket outside Middlesex Hospital. Although he had been appointed Sculptor in Ordinary to Queen Victoria, he died 'in a state of the direst poverty, notwithstanding his many artistic successes'.

EDWARD HODGES BAILEY (1788-1867), who designed Nelson's column in Trafalgar Square, had a longer but more conventional life at 17 Newman and 8 Percy Streets.

DANIEL MACLISE (1806-70), 'very mad and Irish, but very affectionate', was the most successful history painter of his day. He illustrated the novels of Charles Dickens and he widened the then relatively unknown author's circle of acquaintances by introducing him to 'an assortment of Bohemians ranging from the romantically dissolute to the dandyesque'. Frequently depressed he also had an irrepressible appetite for fun. His affections extended to Lady Henrietta Sykes and there was a public scandal when he was discovered in her bed.

In 1827 Maclise lived in Newman Street, then Scala (*14 Pitt*) and 22 Mortimer (*14 Charles*) Streets before moving to 85 (*63*) Charlotte Street. When there was a fire at the latter premises, Constable, who lived opposite, rushed over to help, and salvaged the savings of Maclise's servant. Afterwards Maclise lived in Fitzroy Street (*14 Russell Place*), between Maple and Howland Streets.

The Pre-Raphaelite painter WILLIAM HOLMAN HUNT (1827-1910), so named because his gypsy mother's surname 'Hobman' was mistakenly written as 'Holman' on his birth certificate, was an agnostic and a Chartist supporter who became known for his religious paintings in which he went to great lengths to achieve realistic detail. For one of his major works, *Christ and the Two Maries*, he and a fellow student, James Key, obtained a 12-foot palm leaf from Kew Gardens, and as they took it home a dead bat dropped from it and fell down Keys' neck.

Unable to supply the requested donkey carcass, a knacker's yard gave Hunt the dismembered body of a horse to use as a model for *Triumph of the Innocents*. To extract the skeleton, Hunt boiled the pieces in his yard, but the stench was so appalling that the neighbours called the police. In the final work the image of the donkey is mainly hidden.

In 1848 Hunt took a studio at 46 (7) Cleveland Street, on the southern corner of Howland Street, next to what was then the Strand Union workhouse. FREDERICK GEORGE STEPHENS (1828-1907), the son of the workhouse master, shared the studio with him. He described it as damp, gloomy, and covered in dust. Once when a model failed to turn up, Hunt trapped some sparrows at the window, painted their heads green, and released them. At times he worked off his frustrations by galloping on horseback along Oxford Street. Often he had to pawn his possessions to pay the landlord, who eventually lost patience with the struggling artist, and threw Hunt out, seizing all his furniture, sketches and books.

Hunt caught malaria while travelling and sketching in Jerusalem and was to suffer bouts of it for the rest of his life. In Jerusalem he fended off bandits, then escaped from a fall into a slime pit, and he received a letter from Rossetti asking him to bring back an alligator for London zoo.

On his return to London, he married Fanny Waugh, who died within a year of giving birth to their son. Hunt then lived with her sister Edith, with whom he had two children. Barred from marrying in England they travelled to Switzerland, where to the outrage of English society, they were legally wed.

Hunt caught typhoid in Paris in 1878, but survived and lived for another 32 years.

His fellow Pre-Raphaelite DANTE GABRIEL ROSSETTI (1828-82) was born at 110 Hallam (*38 Charlotte*) Street. When Rossetti was eight years old the family moved a few doors away to 54 Devonshire (*50 Charlotte*) Street. He was sent to a small school in Foley Street and also to Mr Paul's school in Portland Place. Aged 20 he moved into Holman Hunt's studio in Cleveland Street before living at *12* Newman Street and sharing a studio with Madox Brown at 17 Newman Street. After a suicide attempt he spent time convalescing at Madox Brown's who was, by then, living at 37 Fitzroy Square. While there, Rossetti's legs went through the floor and the dinner table at which he was sitting crashed through into the cesspool below.

ELIZABETH SIDDAL (1834-62), a painter and poet who lived in Weymouth Street, off Great Portland Street, was one of the many women who found Rossetti irresistible. He spotted her working in a millinery shop and asked if she would pose for a painting because of her striking red hair, 'stately throat and fine carriage'. She frequently modelled for Rossetti and others in the group, and nearly died when posing in a bath for Millais as the drowning Ophelia. Refined and modest, she represented the exalted ideal of Victorian femininity and the Pre-Raphaelite allegorical Woman. Rossetti and Siddal married, and she gave birth to a stillborn baby. She suffered from

> The landscape painter must walk in the fields with a humble mind. No arrogant man was ever permitted to see nature in all her beauty.
>
> John Constable

> He gave me the courage to commit myself to imagination without shame.
>
> Edward Burne-Jones on Dante Gabriel Rossetti

consumption and died from a possibly suicidal overdose of laudanum in 1862, although the inquest declared her death accidental. Rossetti was distraught and buried a book of intimate poems he had written for Elizabeth in her coffin. Six years later Rosetti was persuaded to publish the poems. He dug up the coffin by torchlight and was moved to discover that Elizabeth's hair had continued to grow.

Rossetti surrounded himself with exotic pets: peacocks, a laughing jackass, a kangaroo, and a zebu (which attacked him). He suffered from insomnia and became pathologically reclusive. He would go for walks alone in Regent's Park in the middle of the night. Increasingly dependent on larger and larger doses of chloral hydrate and whiskey, he overdosed on laudanum in 1872. He survived this suicide attempt, but died ten years later, partially insane and crippled.

When he was a child JOHN EVERETT MILLAIS (1829-96) lived at 7 (57) and then 83 Gower Street. He was sent to the Henry Sass preliminary training school when he was eight years old, with his hair in long curls and dressed in velvet and lace (like some of the chocolate box pictures he produced in later years) which made him a target for some of the rougher pupils: they tossed him in the air, used him as a dumb-bell, and dragged him by the heels all over the British Museum. He was befriended by Holman Hunt, who helped him to ward off the school bullies. Ten years later Hunt visited Millais in Gower Street where they formed the Pre-Raphaelite Brotherhood (1848), which also met at Rossetti's in Hallam Street.

The Pre-Raphaelites challenged conventional cant and hypocrisy with their bohemian lifestyle and, rejecting the stiff Neo-Classicism of Royal Academy art, their work came to be characterised by its luminous colour, flat planes and attention to detail. They added PRB after their signatures and when they began to exhibit they were fiercely lambasted by the critics. Dickens said that Millais' *Christ in the House of his Parents* portrayed Christ as 'a hideous, wry-necked, blubbering, red-haired boy in a night-gown' and that his Mary 'would stand out from the rest of the company as a monster in the vilest cabaret in France or in the lowest gin-shop in England.' As a result of these attacks Millais did not sell many pictures for some time, and he accepted a suit of clothes as payment by three tailors who bought *Lorenzo and Isabella*.

When Millais and the other Pre-Raphaelites approached women in Tottenham Court Road asking them to model, the police warned them that they could be arrested for importuning.

John Ruskin, the painter and critic, was the first to defend their work. He wrote that Millais' sensual masterpiece *Mariana* laid 'the foundations of a school of art nobler than the world has seen for three hundred years.' However Millais fell in love with Ruskin's wife, Euphemia 'Effie' Gray. Ruskin had failed to consummate the marriage (his image of women was based on the marble statues he had admired and he was traumatised when he found that a real woman had pubic hair). Effie returned Millais' love and her marriage to Ruskin was annulled. She and Millais married and they moved into Langham Chambers, All Souls' Place. There Millais ditched his Pre-Raphaelite principles and supplied pictures such as *Cherry Ripe* and *Soap Bubbles* for advertisements and chocolate boxes, which not only made him extremely wealthy, but also earned him a baronetcy.

AUGUSTUS EGG (1816-63) and WILLIAM POWELL FRITH (1819-1909) shared digs with the painter Richard Dadd at 70 and 74 Charlotte Street. A drawing of Egg and Frith with their throats slashed was found in Dadd's studio after Dadd murdered his father.

They were friends with Charles Dickens. Frith, who had started off as an

itinerant portrait painter, and later moved to 11 Osnaburgh and then 31 Charlotte Streets, illustrated two of Dickens's novels, *Barnaby Rudge* and *Nicholas Nickleby*. After Egg joined Dickens' travelling theatre group, Dickens described him as 'one of the most popular of the party, always sweet tempered, humorous, conscientious, thoroughly good and thoroughly beloved.'

Frith asked Egg to accompany him to the racing track at Epsom to research his most famous picture, *Derby Day*, painted at Frith's studio in 15 Fitzroy Street. They visited a gambling tent, where Frith was drawn into a game of thimble rigging. As he was about to bet heavily on which thimble hid a pea, Egg warned him not to be rash, only to be sworn at by a card trickster dressed as a vicar.

To complete the painting Frith hired a pantomime artist and his son to model as the acrobats who entertained racing punters. The cockney lad mocked the accents of Frith's many children (he had 12 by his first wife Isabelle, and seven by his second wife Mary) and performed somersaults. 'Amusing enough,' commented Frith, 'but it did not advance my picture, and it was with much difficulty that I stopped him going head over heels into casts and draperies.' The finished painting drew such crowds when it was exhibited that it had to be protected by a rail and a watchful policeman, but Oscar Wilde was unimpressed, saying Frith 'has done so much to elevate painting to the dignity of photography.'

In 1849 ex-seafarer FORD MADOX BROWN (1821-93) had his first local studio in a former carpenter's shop, a 'rascally barn', at 20 'and a half' Clipstone Street. The place swarmed with rats and was so cold that his nude models went on strike. He put in a stove and a rat trap, both of which proved ineffective, and he moved to 17 Newman Street, where he stayed until 1852.

Madox Brown misinterpreted a fawning letter from Rossetti. Assuming it was written in mockery, he took a bludgeon to Rossetti's house in Hallam Street to teach the young whippersnapper a lesson. Fortunately Rossetti was

SIR EDWIN LANDSEER Sculpting His Lions by John Ballantyne (c.1865)

When Landseer was preparing to make his bronze lions for Trafalgar Square (they were to take him eight years to complete), London Zoo offered him a dying lion as a model. The ailing lion was delivered when Landseer was entertaining guests, and his manservant entered and asked, 'Did you order a lion, sir?'

able to convince him that he had written in earnest, and Madox Brown agreed to tutor him for two months at his Clipstone Street studio. Rossetti also stayed with Madox Brown and his future wife, Emma Hill, at Newman Street, although he was later asked to leave for making the place filthy and talking until four in the morning.

The stubborn and prickly Madox Brown opposed the artistic establishment and boycotted Royal Academy exhibitions. He also rejected formal membership of the Pre-Raphaelites although he was supportive of their work, pawning all his cutlery to finance their 1856 exhibition in Charlotte Street.

His most famous picture *Work* (1865), depicting the class antagonisms of the age, boosted his earnings enough to enable him to move into a large Georgian house at 37 Fitzroy Square, where he stayed until 1881. It became known as 'Thackeray House' because the novelist Thackeray used it as the address of the fictitious Colonel Newcome, describing the doorway, and its urn above, changing only its number to '120'. Madox Brown and Emma hosted fortnightly parties in the house at which they both sang around a piano decorated by William Morris. Among the many guests were Robert Browning, Lord Tennyson, Ivan Turgenev, Oscar Wilde, Mark Twain, Franz Liszt, and Karl Blind (who had fought in the Paris Commune). The Madox Browns gave Rossetti sanctuary at this house after his attempted suicide. Two years later, in 1874, Rossetti's brother, William, married Madox Brown's daughter, Lucy.

EDWARD BURNE-JONES (1833-98), who greatly admired Rossetti, sought him out at the Working Men's College in Bloomsbury, where he was directed to another address, most probably the West London School of Art, at 155 Great Titchfield Street, 'I was told that there was to be a monthly meeting that very evening, in a room in Great Titchfield Street and that, by paying threepence, anyone could get admittance, including tea. So without fail I was there, and sat at a table and had thick bread and butter, but knowing no one.' However, he was introduced to one of Rossetti's friends, and a meeting between the two artists was arranged a few nights later.

WILLIAM MORRIS (1834-96) also lectured at the Working Men's College. Designer, poet, industrialist, his romantic outlook was revolutionized by politics, and one of his fiery speeches on the evils of capitalism in Hyde Park got him thrown into the Serpentine. He was beaten by police truncheons at the Trafalgar Square demonstration that came to be known as 'Bloody Sunday' on November 13, 1887, and he described the Square as ideal for growing apricot trees in his utopian novel *News from Nowhere*.

An inspiration for the Arts and Crafts movement, Morris based his patterns for stained glass windows and wallpaper on the flowing shapes he found in nature. In 1877 he opened a showroom where Centre Point now stands (*449 Oxford Street*) to sell the products of his workshop, which included decorative mural work, carving, metal work, jewellery, furniture and embroidery.

His nickname was Topsy, and in his youth he had been known to throw plumb puddings at the housemaid, chomp on spoons and forks, to tear his hair and throw furniture in fits of rage. He kept an owl in his room and imitated an eagle by jumping off a chair with a heavy flop.

Morris went to revolutionary meetings in the anarchist club in Stephen Mews (off Gresse Street), the Working Men's Communist Club (basement of 49 Tottenham Street), and the Store Street Hall.

His most memorable painting is *Queen Guenevere* for which his model was Jane Burden, whom he married a year later. He loathed the painting and it was finished by Madox Brown and by Rossetti (who had an affair with Jane).

For one of his painter friends, JAMES McNEILL WHISTLER (1834-1903), Rossetti composed the ditty,

There is a young artist called Whistler
Who in every respect is a bristler,
A tube of white lead
Or a punch in the head
Come equally handy to Whistler.

Whistler was born in America and raised in Russia, where his father found work as a railway consultant, and Whistler entered art school. But Whistler nearly died of rheumatic fever and his family survived one epidemic of cholera only for his father to die during the next. They fled to London. Whistler then returned to America, but he moved back to London in 1859. He found rooms at 70 and then 72 Newman Street, where he was joined by art student and future novelist, George Du Maurier, who complained that the

[He] has tinged my whole inner being with the beauty of his own...If it were not for his boisterous mad outbursts and freaks, which break the romance he sheds around him...he would be a perfect hero

Edward Burne-Jones on William Morris

When she came into a room in her strangely beautiful garments, looking at least eight feet high, the effect was as if she had walked out of an Egyptian tomb at Luxor.

Bernard Shaw on Jane Morris, wife of William Morris

rooms were 'beastly uncomfortable' and that Whistler's 'amazing power of anecdote' wore a little thin when he kept it going late into the night.

Whistler's legendary repartee was more than a match for that of Oscar Wilde. When Wilde congratulated him on a witticism, 'I wish I had said that', Whistler drawled in response, 'You will, Oscar, you will.' Whistler resented the fact that Wilde had plagiarised his comment, 'The young artist who paints nothing but beautiful things misses one half of the world. In Gower Street at night you may see a letter box which is picturesque.'

When one of his students came out with the familiar cry, 'I can't paint what I see', Whistler replied, 'Your problems start when you see what you paint.'

Joanna 'Jo' Hiffernan, 'a handsome girl with red hair and altogether fine colour', who lived at 69 Newman Street, modelled for Whistler. They were friends and lovers, and she bore him a son. Although he sometimes found Jo's vulgarity and coarseness embarrassing, they stayed together for 17 years, and he admired her 'superlatively whorish air' which he tried to capture in his dockland picture *Wapping*. She posed more serenely for his controversial *The White Girl*.

The art critic Ruskin accused Whistler of being an impudent 'coxcomb' for pricing his painting *The Falling Rocket* at 200 guineas, which he claimed was 'flinging a pot of paint in the public's face'. A libel case followed, in which Whistler was asked how long it took him to paint the picture. 'Two days', Whistler replied. 'For the labour of two days you asked 200 guineas?' the barrister queried. 'No, it was for the knowledge gained through a lifetime', Whistler replied, which prompted loud applause from the public gallery, much to the judge's annoyance.

Whistler won the case but was awarded only a farthing in damages. Although bankrupted by the legal costs, Whistler was undaunted. He wore the farthing on his watch chain and was delighted when the picture subsequently sold for 800 guineas, 'four pots of paint' as he put it.

In later years he had a studio at 8 Fitzroy Street and he regularly dined in Pagani's restaurant at 48 Great Portland Street.

At the age of 16 ARTHUR BOYD HOUGHTON (1836-75), who had lost his right eye in India as a child when a playmate fired a 'toy' cannon at him charged with real gunpowder, went to study under the historical painter JAMES MATHEW LEIGH (1808-60) in his school at 79 Newman Street. Houghton specialised in painting scenes of low life in St Giles. His wife Susan died of blood poisoning just after giving birth to their third child, Cecily, in 1864. Houghton frequently visited Madox Brown in Fitzroy Square but turned to drink and died of cirrhosis of the liver, clutching a portrait he had painted of his wife.

A true Fitzrovian, WILLIAM FREND DE MORGAN (1839-1917), painter, novelist, and designer of stained glass, ceramic tiles and pottery, was born at 69 Gower Street, and later lived at 70 Newman and 17 Nassau Streets (next to Middlesex Hospital). He was evicted as a result of a fire while glazing pottery in his kiln at 40 Fitzroy Square, which he used as a model for the haunted house in his novel *Alice for Short*. He did not start writing until he was 64 years old but his first novel *Joseph Vance* was a best seller.

An exceptional young artist, SIMEON SOLOMON (1840-1905), exhibited at the Royal Academy when he was only 18 years old, but ended up destitute. He studied at the studio of his brother, ABRAHAM SOLOMON (1824-62), 18 Gower Street from the age of ten, and then at Leigh's Art School in Newman Street. In the mid-1860s Solomon lived at 26 Howland Street. Later in the decade he moved in with his sister Rebecca at 106 Gower Street. They then moved to 12 Fitzroy Street (1869-73), and 29 Mortimer (22 *Charles*) Street. Solomon worked

MORRIS reading poetry to Burne-Jones, caricature by Edward Burne-Jones (*c*.1865)

William Morris met Edward Burne-Jones at Oxford and they became life-long friends.

WILLIAM FREND DE
MORGAN by Evelyn de
Morgan (1909)

*De Morgan was enamoured
of the Middle East and the
mediaeval period. His
ceramics made use of a wide
range of exotic and historical
sources, and were especially
noted for their lustre glazes
and bright, strong colour.*

in Rossetti's studio, where he was befriended by Millais and Burne-Jones, and introduced to the dissolute poet and critic, Algernon Charles Swinburne. His painting was described by the art critic Sir William Richmond as 'pagan'.

At the age of 31, Solomon wrote *A Vision of Love Revealed In Sleep*, a mystical work adapted for the stage by Neil Bartlett in 1987, in which love is depicted as a figure with 'wings drooping, broken and torn' and 'a wound flowing with blood, but changing into roses of divinest odour as it fell.'

Two years later Solomon was imprisoned when he was caught having sex with a labourer, George Roberts, in an Oxford Street public urinal. Many blamed his downfall on his dissolute friend Swinburne, with whom he had enjoyed 'nude frolics'. On completing his sentence Solomon was placed by relatives in a mental institution. He was released and they rented a studio for him but then withdrew this facility when he used it as a place to sleep off drunken orgies. On the verge of starvation, he persuaded art dealers to commission work but then failed to produce it. He was affected by alcoholic shakes and his drawing degenerated.

In deepest poverty, he survived by selling matches and shoe laces in the street and chalking pictures on the pavement in return for pennies from passers-by, but he seemed to lack any sense of humiliation and would cheerfully accost anyone he recognised from his celebrated past and demand the price of a pint. W.B. Yeats met him at the home of the poet Lionel

Art itself has become an extraordinary thing - the activity of peculiar people - people who become more and more peculiar as their activity becomes more and more extraordinary.

Eric Gill

Johnson in Charlotte Street, and described him as 'a ragged figure' straight from 'some low public house'. He was often arrested for drunkenness or obscene behaviour and once for attempting to steal gold leaf from the studio of Burne-Jones after falling into the company of pick pockets and petty thieves.

Always ready to share his last penny with other down-and-outs, Solomon eventually grew too old to live rough and took refuge in St Giles' workhouse. By then he was bald, with a great, bushy, reddish-white beard. Challenged by fellow paupers to prove he had been a famous artist he roughed out a sketch in half an hour and sold it to a nearby dealer for a couple of sovereigns. It was drinks all round at the workhouse that night and he died shortly afterwards in the dining hall.

Born in Munich, of a Danish father and an Irish mother, the painter WALTER RICHARD SICKERT (1860-1942) was educated at University College School, 43 Gower Street. He mixed in social circles that ranged from Winston Churchill (to whom he gave painting lessons) to the local prostitutes who modelled at his studio in 8 Fitzroy Street. An inveterate dandy, he dressed in a variety of styles – sometimes as a vagrant, at other times in the formal, elegant suits of a prosperous man-about-town, or in vulgar 'very loud checks', as Nina Hamnett said, 'like something off a race course.'

SIMEON SOLOMON

The critic Swinburne praised Solomon's paintings for their 'supersexual beauty, in which the lineaments of woman and man seem blended.'

He was a travelling actor for four years before returning to Gower Street in 1881 to enrol at the Slade School of Fine Art. By 1889 he was an influence on the New Arts Club, already in reaction against the Pre-Raphaelites, and interested in painting that would show and celebrate the more workaday aspects of life. Sickert lived in and/or had studios at many addresses in Fitzrovia: 8, 15, 19, and 21 Fitzroy Street, 15 Cleveland Street, 76 Charlotte Street, 35 Maple Street, Warren Street, and nearby 13 Robert Street – at one of these places he installed a French floor-level lavatory and was gleefully amused by the discomfort this gave his British guests.

In 1905, at the 8 Fitzroy Street studio, Sickert suggested that he and the artists who came to see him to talk about their work, should formalise their gatherings. This evolved into the Fitzroy Street Group, held on Saturday afternoons at his studio. Later the gatherings took place in the two first-floor rooms of the studio at 19 Fitzroy Street, which became recognized as a centre for the avant-garde, and open to anyone who wanted to visit. Each person in the Group contributed an equal amount to the rent of the studio, where they exhibited their work informally and sold it at low prices. The original Fitzroy Street artists included Spencer Gore, Harold Gilman, Nan Hudson, and Ethel Sands. The two women were expected to act as hostesses, to serve the cake and pour the tea. The Fitzroy Street Group were noted for developing the style known as new English realism, which depicted the cluttered interiors and grimey backyards of the inner city in a style suggestive of both romance and squalor. Other women artists who subsequently became involved included Sylvia Gosse, Stanislawa de Karlowska, Therese Lessore and Enid Bagnold.

Sickert was also the driving force behind the celebrated Camden Town Group which grew out of the earlier Fitzroy Group and met in his studio at 21 Fitzroy Street on Sundays from 1911. An all-male assembly, it counted Gore, Gilman, Augustus John, Henry Lamb, Percy Wyndham Lewis, William Ratcliffe, Maxwell Gordon Lightfoot and Duncan Grant amongst its members, and was to evolve once more, at the end of 1913, into the London Group. Also meeting in Fitzroy Street, these artists included Gilman, Wyndham Lewis, Grant, Jacob Epstein, Eric Gill, Paul Nash, Vanessa Bell, and Chips Nevinson.

In his dotage, Sickert asked to be taken back to Fitzroy Street, believing that he was still teaching art there.

Associated with that original Fitzroy Street group, SPENCER GORE (1878-1914) was the son of the first champion of men's tennis at Wimbledon. He himself won the public schools' boxing championship and the Harrow one-mile race, before he went to the Slade in 1896. Ten years later he lived at 18 Fitzroy Street, from where he generously gave art lessons by post to a deaf stockbroker's clerk called JOHN DOMAN TURNER (c.1873-1938), who later joined the Camden Town Group. Gore died from pneumonia after painting in wet weather.

HAROLD GILMAN (1876-1919) started drawing aged 12 when he was bedridden with a broken leg. He studied at the Slade, then lived in various run-down areas, finally moving to 47 Maple Street, where he painted portraits of his landlady Mrs Mounter. When he was 42 years old he caught Spanish flu. Poor and undernourished he was unable to resist the infection and died in hospital.

NAN HUDSON (1869-1957), like Sickert cursed with irritable bowel syndrome, worked in a French hospital near Dieppe during the first world war. She was also in France when she was knocked over by a car in 1951. As a result of her injuries she had to wear a pelvic support corset for the rest of her life. She died of broncho-pneumonia in a nursing home just after her 88th birthday.

Her friend ETHEL SANDS (1873-1962) also worked as a nurse in the same

I didn't fall in love with him. Or hardly. We were all enslaved, enchanted. The day glittered because of him.

Enid Bagnold on Walter Sickert

hospital during the First War. She came from a wealthy family who lived at 40 Portland Place (1888-97), where the visitors included the Prince of Wales, the prime ministers Gladstone and Asquith, and the author Henry James, who formed a strong attachment to her.

AUGUSTUS JOHN (1878-1961), the most famous of the Camden Town Group of painters, also came to Fitzrovia via the Slade, where he formed the Three Musketeers with Ambrose McEvoy and Benjamin Evans. While there as a student (1894-98) he was thrown out of music halls for sketching the acts, but he was more sympatically treated when he did the same at anarchist meetings in Tottenham Court Road – where he heard Peter Kropotkin say that mutual aid was as important a factor in evolution as that of competititon. He cultivated a theatrical Bohemianism, with long hair, beard, gold earrings and a wide-brimmed hat, and first moved into Fitzrovia, the quarter with 'every form of low life abounding' in 1897 (76 Charlotte then 21 Fitzroy Streets). He made friends with high-spirited Iris Tree, and together they smoked hashish at her home at 4 Fitzroy Square. He later lived and had studios at 8, 18, 19, 20, and 21 Fitzroy Street.

He married the beautiful Ida Nettleship, also an art student at the Slade. They held their wedding reception in Charlotte Street, and lived in the top floor flat of 95 Fitzroy Street. They had five sons, but Ida died shortly after giving birth to the last. Augustus was too drunk to attend her cremation.

Augustus was a womaniser and notoriously promiscuous. Whenever he was in the Fitzroy Tavern, he patted any child he saw on the head in case it was one of his. Among his offspring were Casper, who was able to beat his father in a fight and who became an admiral, losing both legs in the second world war, and Edwin, who became the middleweight boxing champion of Wales.

His second wife, Dorelia 'Dodo' McNeil, a gypsy, introduced him to the Romany way of life, after which he sometimes signed his name in Romany, 'Gustavus Janik'. They had a son and two daughters and Augustus often took to the road in a caravan.

He was partially deaf as a result of being hit by a cricket ball, and it was said that his paintings improved after he banged his head diving into a rock pool – although the critics' view was that he never fulfilled the exceptional talent of his student days.

Like the Pre-Raphaelites before him, he found Tottenham Court Road a useful source for models. Late one night he approached a young women who had marvellous red hair. During the modelling session she fell asleep, and her hair slipped and was revealed as a wig.

Augustus' elder sister, very much a painter in her own right, GWEN JOHN (1876-1939), attended the Slade from 1895 to 1898. Augustus spoke of her 'lofty pride and implacable will' when they shared rooms in a first-floor flat at 21 Fitzroy Street, 'subsisting like monkeys on a diet of fruit and nuts'. As a student, Gwen also lived at 23 Euston Square and 76 Charlotte Street, and in a gloomy basement flat under a decorator's shop in Howland Street, which she described as her subterranean period (1899-1903). While there she had an affair with Ambrose McEvoy, who suddenly married another Slade student, Mary Spencer Edwards. Her self-consciousness was crippling, 'Shyness and timidity distort the meanings of my words in people's ears – that is one reason why I am such a waif.'

After leaving Howland Street she became homeless and stayed in an empty building at 122 Gower Street.

She befriended Dorelia, the second wife of Augustus, and travelled with her by foot through France, setting off in August, 1903.

Interior with Mrs
Mounter by Harold
Gilman (c.1916)

*Mrs Mounter was Gilman's
landlady, and the subject of
some of his most striking
portraits. This is a view of his
rooms at 47 Maple Street.*

Against stiff competition she won the Melvill Nettleship prize for figure composition at the Slade in 1898. She went to Paris where she posed for, and became the lover of, the sculptor Auguste Rodin (1840-1917) until, stressed and tormented, she left him and went to live in a nunnery run by Dominican Sisters – from where she wrote to Rodin of fearing that she was possessed by demons and of experiencing the heights of exultation. The final seven years of her life were spent in almost total isolation. She wrote in her diary, 'Leave everybody and let them leave you. Then only will you be without fear.'

She spent hours copying out passages from the lives of saints and from other spiritual books, her own prayers and meditations, and she neglected herself, becoming thin and wasted.

When Hitler invaded Poland she decided to return to England, but on leaving the train at Dieppe she collapsed in the street, and it was assumed she was a derelict. She died in hospital soon afterwards and the whereabouts of her grave is unknown.

Another member of the Camden Town Group, HENRY LAMB (1883-1960), had a studio at 8 Fitzroy Street. A medical student, he suffered from piles and depression, and he had a reputation as a practical joker. He looked down on the Bloomsbury set, saying that they spent most of their time 'drinking port and talking drivel.' He especially disliked Maynard Keynes and asked Lytton Strachey 'to fart for me under his [Keynes's] nose.' Lamb married Nina 'Euphemia' Forrest (and indulged in some partner-swapping with Augustus John and Dorelia). After Euphemia had a miscarriage, she and Lamb went their separate ways – Euphemia to satanist Aleister Crowley, and Henry to Lady Ottoline Morrell ('a haven from vagrancy and bohemianism'). His second wife was Lady Pansy Packenham. He served as a medical officer in Palestine in 1917 and was awarded the Military Cross.

Fellow member of the Camden Town Group, PERCY WYNDHAM LEWIS (1882-1957), trained at the Slade from 1898 to 1901. He began to write sonnets, until a sheaf of them was found among the belongings of William Sterling, another aspiring writer, whom he had met in Buzzard's coffee shop, 197-199 (350)

Oxford Street. Sterling had cut his own throat and his body was discovered chewed by rats. Wyndham Lewis switched to prose and did not write another sonnet for 30 years.

He took a studio in Charlotte Street, followed by a move to 4 Percy Street, where he planned the Rebel Art Centre. In 1914 he and and Ezra Pound celebrated the launch of their magazine *Blast* at the Restaurant de la Tour Eiffel, 1 Percy Street. *Blast* was the magazine of the Vorticist movement, which aimed to 'blast' away the old order, to stir up civil war, and provoke 'violent structures of adolescent clearness between two extremes.'

Wyndham Lewis fought in 1917. After the terrible battle of Passchendale, he said, 'A gunner does not fight. He merely shells and is shelled.'

He had a combative, vigorous brilliance but was prone to petty squabbles as well as serious disagreements. He left Roger Fry's Omega Workshop because he thought that the group's products should carry individual signatures rather than the Omega logo; it was also said that he broke away after Fry was commissioned to design a room for the Ideal Home Exhibition which Wyndham Lewis thought had been promised to him and Spencer Gore – at the time Wyndham Lewis imagined that Fry and Clive Bell were perched on his studio roof, spying on him.

The writer T.E. Hulme settled an argument with him about whether 'touch vitally assisted communication' by hanging him upside down over the railings in Fitzroy Square.

In the 1930s Wyndham Lewis lived in Fitzroy Street and 31 Percy Street, where he wrote poetry, novels, two autobiographies and a book in support of Hitler that he later retracted. After the second world war a pituitary tumour reduced his sight and eventually killed him.

A nomadic midget WILLIAM RATCLIFFE (1870-1955) enjoyed wandering the countryside with a rucksack and portable easel, and was on one of his *plein-air* expeditions when he met Harold Gilman, who persuaded him to enrol part-time at the Slade. Ratcliffe joined the Camden Town Group but could not afford oil or canvas and always painted with watercolours. Another member of the Camden Town Group MAXWELL GORDON LIGHTFOOT (1886-1911) was a man of nervous disposition. He became engaged to an artists' model and his parents expressed serious doubts about the match. The night before he was to take her to meet them, he destroyed all his paintings and committed suicide.

One of the world's best known sculptors, JACOB EPSTEIN (1880-1959), was a regular at the Fitzroy Tavern in Charlotte Street, as were two of his models, Dolores, who had long black hair and wore skimpy black dresses, and Betty May, who had blazing green eyes and dressed like a gypsy. Occasionally the two women came to blows in the bar. Epstein joined the Fitzroy Street Group, although Sickert initially vetoed his membership.

ERIC GILL (1882-1940), another sculptor in the group, who had sex with his sisters, daughters, and the dog, designed lettering and engraved tombstones. He created the *Gill Sans* typeface, which carries his name and is renowned for its elegant simplicity (making it easier to carve). In order to sculpture the figures of Prospero and Ariel on the facade of Broadcasting House, he stood on a scaffold – wearing a smock and no underclothes. When a crowd gathered below to watch him at work he shouted down, 'It's all balls, you know.' After the work was finished the BBC governors ordered that Ariel's genitals be reduced in size. Ironically, Gill himself refused to listen to the radio.

PAUL NASH (1889-1946), who lived and painted at 8 Fitzroy Street, was also in the London Group. Another official war artist, he wanted to convey the devastation of war, to rob it of 'the last shred of glory and the last shine of glamour'. To underline his intention, he gave his paintings ironic titles: a view

I don't pretend to know anybody well. People are like shadows to me and I am like a shadow.

Gwen John

If you haven't visited the Fitzroy, you haven't visited London.

Augustus John

Gwen John attended Whistler's academy in Paris. He taught her to consider the formal qualities of a painting and the tonal values of the palette. Later she added white to her work, which gave it an ashen look, to emphasise what she called 'the strangeness' of form.

of shell craters and dead trees was called *We Are Making A New World*.

After graduating at the Slade in 1898, WILLIAM ORPEN (1878-1931) set up his studio at 35 Maple Street. Augustus John reported that when Orpen was sketching animals at the zoo, an ape that he was studying gave the artist a hug, and that Orpen was 'touched by these overtures' and 'responded with a smile and a cordial handshake.' On subsequent visits, however, the caresses grew more passionate – 'he observed with some anxiety his model's attentions got more intimate' – and when the zoo swapped the beast for a duck-billed platypus, the final parting between Orpen and the ape was 'heart breaking and violent'.

Commissioned by the Imperial War Museum to produce three pictures of the peace conference at the end of the first world war, and unimpressed by the delegates (some of whom slept through the proceedings), Orpen had a crisis of conscience. In one painting he represented the delegates as faceless and insignificant, and dwarfed by the ornate hall, and for the group portrait he replaced their images with a coffin, and the museum refused to accept the painting.

By setting up the Omega Workshop at 33 Fitzroy Square in 1911 the writer, art historian, connoisseur, lecturer and painter, ROGER FRY (1866-1934), wanted to provide artists with an income from part-time work which would leave them free to pursue their own art the rest of the week. Omega's furniture, wall decoration, textiles and ceramics were designed to be in contradistinction to the glossy sameness of mass-production, and were in bold new shapes and vibrant, Italianate colours. Picasso visited the workshop and was intrigued by the methods used to paint pottery. Omega's informal discussion club also attracted writers such as W.B. Yeats, Arnold Bennett, and Lytton Strachey. In Omega's last year, 1919, Fry organised an exhibition at Heal's, 195 Tottenham Court Road, where drawings by Modigliani lay unceremoniously scattered in a basket, on sale for a shilling each.

Fry had studios and lived at 18 and 21 Fitzroy Street. He and his wife Helen had two children. It was after he realized that she suffered from an incurable mental illness that he had a passionate affair with Vanessa Bell and then, later, with Helen Anrep, the wife of the Russian mosaic artist, BORIS ANREP (1885-1969). In 1933 Fry was appointed professor at the Slade. The following year he died from heart failure after breaking his thigh in a fall.

Close friends and collaborators with Fry, VANESSA BELL (1879-1961) and DUNCAN GRANT (1885-1978), studied at the Slade and were co-directors of the Omega Workshop. Vanessa Bell initiated dressmaking at the Omega. Although Bell and Grant epitomised the saying that the Bloomsbury set lived in squares and loved in triangles, they became inseparable, personally and professionally. Vanessa maintained an air of dignified serenity, even while she delighted in the erotic scandal by which their group thought to shed private inhibition and challenge convention. She amused DAVID 'BUNNY' GARNETT (1892-1981), her one-time lover, by illustrating a dinner-party joke bawdily thrusting a rolled up napkin in and out of its ring. In 1911 she wrote to Roger Fry telling him that she and Duncan intended to do some Eric Gill style paintings, 'I suggest a series of copulations in strange attitudes and have offered to pose,' she wrote. 'Will you join? I mean in the painting.'

In 1914, a year after they became lovers, Duncan Grant moved in with Vanessa and her husband, Clive Bell, in Gordon Square. Grant had a studio at 22 Fitzroy Street. During the first world war he was a conscientious objector, and after the war Fry let him use his studio at 18 Fitzroy Street.

Vanessa Bell and Duncan Grant had a daughter, Angelica, 'a wistful, patient, contemplative little creature', born on a frosty, moonlit night,

PERCY WYNDHAM LEWIS (c.1914)

Novelist, artist and critic, Wyndham Lewis worked as a painter during the first world war, during which he said his purpose was to show war dispassionately, and to depict shell-fire 'as objectively as a vase of flowers'.

Christmas 1918. At the age of six Angelica was knocked over by a car that mounted the pavement in Tottentham Court Road, and was hospitalised at the Middlesex for three days.

In 1920 Grant rented the studio previously occupied by Whistler, Augustus John and Sickert, at 8 Fitzroy Street. With a high timber roof, and connected to the back of the house by a 'labyrinthine corrugated iron passage', it was also the venue for parties, meetings, and for showing work; it was where Virginia Woolf's play *Freshwater*, in which Angelica acted, was first performed and where Grant liked to entertain interesting 'characters from the criminal fringe around the Tottenham Court Road'. Later in the decade he moved there to

live and Bell rented the adjoining studio, but the studio was destroyed by an air raid in 1940.

In 1937 Grant and Bell, both staunchly pacificist and anti-fascist, went to Paris and saw Picasso while he was working on his anti-war masterpiece *Guernica*.

That year Vanessa Bell learned that her son Julian, a volunteer ambulance driver for the republicans in the Spanish civil war, had been killed. Told of his death over the telephone, the sound of her venting her grief, 'howling like a wild beast', stunned the neighbours.

In 1955 Grant and Vanessa took a flat on the top floor, 28 Percy Street. While giving a dinner party there Vanessa fell into a faint and had to be taken by ambulance to Middlesex Hospital. In the winter of 1960 she became ill with pneumonia and Grant was devastated when she died the following spring.

A bisexual, Duncan Grant had lived with Maynard Keynes at 21 Fitzroy Square, and he had been the lover of Vanessa's brother, Adrian Stephen, as well as his cousin Lytton Strachey. Grant also became the lover of the artist David Garnett – who was later to become his son-in-law, when Garnett married Angelica. As a child Angelica had been impressed by Garnett's explanation of the mating habits of worms. Garnett had a studio at 15 Charlotte Street.

After Vanessa Bell's death, Duncan Grant moved to 3 Park Square West, Portland Place, and renewed his contact with avant-garde art. He attended cocktail parties into his 90s and spent time with his daughter, Angelica, and his grandchildren. He made a visit to a Cezanne exhibition in Paris in 1978 but while there caught a cold that developed into pneumonia and died in a delirious state. Paying tribute to her father Angelica said he lacked petty egotism and pre-judged no one, 'He was profoundly convinced that every living creature, even a mouse or an insect, had a right to its own point of view.'

The artist and sculptor BENITA JAEGER, friend of Vanessa Bell, who had a seven-year relationship with Bell's husband, Clive, lived at 30 Charlotte Street, where she improvised a party dress with two scarves pinned to her necklace and nothing else.

CRISTOPHER 'CHIPS' NEVINSON (1889-1946) was the leader of a group of Slade students (1908-12) called the Coster Gang because they dressed in the garb of barrow fruit-sellers. They joined Wyndham Lewis' Rebel Art Centre and drove an ambulance for the Red Cross during the first world war. As an official war artist, Nevinson was shocked when his painting of dead English soldiers was censored by the government. To call attention to the fact he placed a 'censored' sticker over it, but he was then told by the war authorities that this sticker was itself 'censored'. Irritated, he called another of the war paintings *Tum-Tiddly-Um-Tum-Pom-Pom*. He became a regular at the Fitzroy Tavern in Charlotte Street, where he sketched both customers and the landlord, Pop Kleinfeld (1864-1947).

In his youth he befriended MARK GERTLER (1891-1939), a fellow Slade student, and DORA CARRINGTON (1893-1932). Long-haired, serious, intense, Gertler was a misfit at the Slade. He and Nevinson were rivals for Carrington, who said she felt an equal affection for both men, but was committed to neither. Carrington declined Gertler's proposal of marriage and, at a meeting in Percy Street in 1917, told him of her love for Lytton Strachey. Gertler said he never wanted to see her again but they continued to meet until the 1920s.

Carrington first met Strachey on a walk with Virginia Woolf, and he tried to kiss her. She liked to play practical jokes and retaliated by creeping into his room when he was asleep and cutting off his beard. He woke, their eyes locked, and she dedicated her life to him. Later Strachey fell in love with

OMEGA INVITATION CARD

designed by Duncan Grant with lettering by Roger Fry (December 1939)

Then we got softer clay and both of us turned out some quite nice little bowls and pots. It's fearfully exciting when you do get it centred and the stuff begins to come up between your fingers. V. never would make her penises long enough, which I thought very odd. Don't you?

Roger Fry to Duncan Grant

ROGER FRY and others at work in the Omega Workshops (c.1913)

The Omega showrooms and studios at 33 Fitzroy Square. Clientele was wide-ranging, from members of the public to 'ladies of fashion', and included George Bernard Shaw, W.B. Yeats, Arnold Bennett, Rupert Brooke, Gertrude Stein and Derain.

**Vanessa said no more, he
said nothing, and I
remained closeted in
dreams.**

Angelica Bell, after being
told, at the age of 17, that
Duncan Grant was her true
father, not Clive Bell.

Ralph Partridge, who had proposed to Carrington. She believed in 'abolishing private property' in relationships, and the three lived together. When Strachey was dying of stomach cancer, he whispered that he should have married Carrington. Six weeks after his death she tried to shoot herself, but her aim slipped. Her dying words were, 'I have bungled my life and my death.'

Carrington lived at 3 Gower Street. She was an 'autobiographical artist who painted the people and places she loved.' Although she bucked conventions of the day and was one of the first women to be a 'crophead' with her defiantly short hair, she was diffident about showing her work. Sir John Rothenstein, a director of the Tate Gallery, commented that she was the 'most neglected serious painter of her time' because she exhibited so rarely. She also painted pub signs, rococo tiles, tinselled glass pictures, decorations, woodcuts and illustrated letters.

STANLEY SPENCER (1891-1959) was a student at the Slade from 1908 to 1912. He later taught there, and he both studied and taught lithography at Regent Street Polytechnic. He married two ex-Slade students. The first was HILDA CARLINE (1889-1950), whom he married in 1925. They had two daughters, Sirin and Unity. In 1929 Spencer met the artist PATRICIA PREECE (1894-1971). A lesbian, Preece had a life-long relationship with DOROTHY HEPWORTH (1898-1978), with whom she shared a student studio in Gower Street.

Spencer was fascinated by Preece, and they started a long-term relationship. Spencer and Hilda Carline divorced, and Spencer married Preece. The relationship remained a platonic one and the marriage was never consummated. In 1942 Hilda had a mental breakdown and Spencer planned to remarry her. He applied for an annulment of his marriage with Preece, but he cancelled the application when Hilda died of cancer in 1950. Spencer and Preece formally separated in 1951.

Fitzrovia's unchallenged queen of Bohemia was painter and model NINA HAMNETT (1890-1956). Her father insisted she should study commerce in Regent Street Polytechnic, but she rebelled and left to study art at the Slade, taking a room in Charlotte Street at the age of 21, and then moving to Grafton Way – where she tried to get rid of the bugs by sprinkling petrol on the floor. Hamnett was one of the team of artists at the Omega Workshops, where she collaborated with Fry and others on several interior decoration schemes. She said that although she was 'never very good at decorative work', the £2 or £3 she received a week for painting Omega candle sticks and batik made her 'feel like a millionaire'. Fry, with whom she had an affair, painted and drew her several times.

Hamnett herself preferred to paint 'human beings than landscapes', and was known for her 'careful, often penetrating portraits, sturdy still lives and fluent line drawings'. The sharp, sensitive line of her drawing was influenced by Modigliani, whom she met during one of her many sojourns in Paris. She rented a room in Montparnasse and danced nude on the tables of the cafés Dôme and Rotonde. Seeking the same uninhibited Bohemian style in London, she adopted the Fitzroy Tavern, 'where drink was cheap and the people amusing'. In later years, broke and alcoholic, she sought out pub customers to buy her drinks, and regaled them with stories, 'Modigliani said I had the best breasts in Europe.'

In 1913 she had met the sculptor HENRY GAUDIER-BRZESKA (1891-1915) at the Omega. They attended local anarchist meetings, and modelled for each other since they could not afford to pay professionals. Using marble that she helped him to steal from a stonemason's yard, he carved her torso. After it was exhibited in the Victoria and Albert Museum, she often introduced herself saying, 'I'm in the V&A with my left tit knocked off.'

When she wanted to lose her virginity at the age of 22, she asked satanist, Alan Odle to oblige, which he did, at 35 Howland Street. During the 1930s she flaunted a sexual preference for sailors and boxers, declaring that she preferred sailors because they left in the morning.

One evening when she and a companion were drinking at the Windmill (run by music hall artists Daisy Dormer and Albert Gee in Windmill Street), she noticed a monkey at the bar and claimed that it had stolen their drinks. They were given another round, and she tried to repeat the ruse, but this time she was told that it was a stuffed monkey. She took to collecting money from

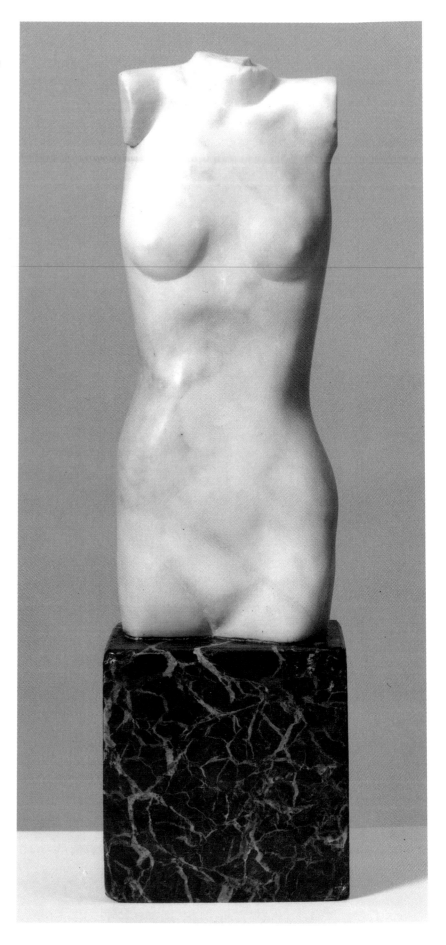

TORSO OF NINA by Henri Gaudier-Brzeska (1914)

Nina Hamnett let her own art drift on her return from Paris in 1926, but she never lost the commanding position she had in Fitzrovia's bohemia, nor what Anthony Powell, who was briefly her lover, said was her 'unshakeable confidence in her own myth'.

other drinkers in a tobacco tin. When she had sufficient coins, she changed them into a 10s. note, which she posted to herself, to finance the next day's drinks.

She moved from one rented room to another, 17 Fitzroy Street, 30 Charlotte Street, 35 Maple Street, 33 Percy Street and 31 Howland Street. In 1947 there was a fire in her block of flats, from which a girl tried to escape by leaping out of the window, only to be impaled on the railings below. When Nina next went to the Fitzroy Tavern she heard this story being told as if she were the one who had died this way.

She was made homeless by the fire. She refused a place in Marylebone workhouse and was re-housed in Paddington. Eight days before her own death she was upset by a radio play, *It's Long Past the Time*, which she felt caricatured her as a has-been. She died in a fall from a window, but contrary to myth, she was not impaled on the railings.

Surrealist painter and sculptor EILEEN AGAR (1899-1991) was inspired by driftwood and rock formations and experimented with many techniques in her art. She used materials as diverse as feathers, fur, beads, shells, scarves and embroidery, combining them all for her blindfolded *Angel of Anarchy*, which was modelled on her husband's head, and based on an earlier version that she had made in 1938, which alluded, among other things, to 'an uncertain future'.

She was shunned by her wealthy parents for having married 'beneath her' to fellow Slade student Robin Bartlett, her first lover. She soon tired of him and went to live with Hungarian writer, Joseph Bard, whom she married a decade later. In 1927 they moved into 29 Fitzroy Square, where they lived until 1930. She described their life there as happy and satisfying, despite the fact that 'urchins were inclined to piss into our letter box on the ground floor'. She did not take the intrusion personally, 'We felt that this was done for the hell of it rather than maliciously, so managed to forgive them so long as no important letters were damaged.' Evelyn Waugh was one of the many writers who visited. She rebuffed the pass he made at her. He used her as the model for one of his fictional characters (and met his future wife, also called Evelyn, at a party in Portland Place).

Eileen Agar described her close friend, JOHN BANTING (1902-72), as almost unique in 'riding the two spirited horses of surrealism and communism'. A painter and Communist Party member (until the crushing of the 1956 Hungarian uprising) he dyed his hair green and cut off the tops of his shoes to display his painted toenails. His house in Fitzroy Street was often rowdy with all-night dancing and jazz, and the party-goers were all and sundry: sailors, black singers, painters, journalists, prostitutes and casual passers-by. 'It's a pity he thinks about nothing but drinking and fucking,' wrote Clive Bell, 'because I believe he has a talent – not for painting pictures but for decorating.'

When his lover, Nancy Cunard, was certified insane in 1960, Banting comforted her with the news that he had been certified insane himself when very young, but had been 'decertified' with the greatest of ease.

With his friend Eileen Agar, Banting attended the surrealist meetings that were held on Wednesday evenings at 6 p.m. in the Horseshoe, 267 Tottenham Court Road during the 1930s and 1940s. The pub manager agreed to the suggestion put to him by the meetings' organiser, CONROY MADDOX (b.1912), that the saloon bar walls should be used to exhibit the surrealists' paintings, but when several of the artists brought their (now invaluable) works the publican was aghast, 'I'm not having that sort of work in my place!'

Others to attend these meetings were: the Slade trained sculptor and artist HENRY MOORE (1898-1986), GEORGE MELLY (who was regularly thrown out of

My ambition is to paint psychological portraits that shall represent accurately the spirit of the age.

Nina Hamnett

My dear, could you advance me a quid? There's the most beautiful GI passed out stone cold and naked as a duck in my kitchen.

Nina Hamnett

restaurants for drunkenly reciting poems to the others while dropping knives and forks over his head), Picasso's close friend ROLAND PENROSE (1900-84), the anarchist knight HERBERT READ (1893-1968), zoological broadcaster DESMOND MORRIS (b.1928), Slade-trained and Fitzrovia Street resident JOHN NASH (1893-1977), Nash's brother Paul, the automatic drawing producer EDITH RIMMINGTON (b.1902), and a nun called MARY WICKHAM (or Wickhome). They often traded friendly insults with a group of poets, led by J.M. Tambimuttu, who met in the same bar.

Just before the second world war a new generation of artists set up what became known as the Euston Road School, which had its start at 12 Fitzroy Street in October 1937, and moved to 314-316 Euston Road in February, 1938. The four were Claude Rogers, William Coldstream, Victor Pasmore, and Graham Bell.

CLAUDE ROGERS (1907-79), fat, clumsy, with an air of jollity, taught art for three years after graduating from the Slade, and set his pupils subjects with humorous titles, such as 'fly swatting man' and 'dog taking man for walk'. When he noticed that a pupil was coating his penis with bright blue paint in class, he drawled in the lad's ear, 'Put that away.' One of his tasks was to pay the funfair attendant in the street below the school some copper coins to play the models' favourite tunes on his hurdy-gurdy.

Before the war Rogers lived at 28 Charlotte Street. He had a studio in Goodge Street, and finally moved to 76 Charlotte Street.

When drafted during the war, he found the discipline as difficult to take as it had been to dispense as a teacher. On the orders of a psychiatrist he was detained in hospital, where he confined himself to self-portraits until he was released on the grounds that his personality was incompatible with the army. After the war he became a lecturer at Slade.

The eminent Slade professor, WILLIAM COLDSTREAM (1908-87), had also been a student at the Slade. He lived at Howland Street. When he met Victor Pasmore they moved into 76 Charlotte Street 1930. Later they lived at 9 Robert Street (corner of Howland and Fitzroy Streets) and at 8 and 12 Fitzroy Street.

In 1933, when Coldstream was mentally blocked over his painting, he went into film-making at the General Post Office Films Department (27-39 Oxford Street) where his first task was to provide a live bee, 'and be responsible for its buzzing'. He worked as an extra in *Night Mail* (directed by W.H. Auden) during which a railway guard dropped dead moments after being filmed.

A socialist and anti-fascist, Coldstream designed camouflage during the war. He was made a captain and became a war artist in the Middle East.

Following the early death of his father, VICTOR PASMORE (1910-98) could not go to art school full-time, so he worked for the London County Council and took evening classes. A lyrical landscape and abstract painter with left-wing political connections and sympathies, he moved to Howland Mews in 1936. In 1938 he left the LCC and moved to 8 Fitzroy Street. There he started painting *The Wave* in 1939 – it was still unfinished the following year after too many drams of whiskey and soda in the Blue Posts (Newman Street) and he only finished the picture at the end of 1944. He later lived at 10 Fitzroy Street.

GRAHAM 'SMILER' BELL (1910-43) arrived from his native South Africa in 1931. Although he was warned that she tended to prey on her male employees, he was apprenticed to the potter Phyllis Keyes, who had a kiln and workshop in Warren Street, and then a pottery in Clipstone Street, which was bombed during the war. In 1937 Bell painted *The Café* based on the Café Conte at 44 Goodge Street, where the Euston Road School group often met for breakfast. The picture shows Coldstream, Rogers, and Pasmore tucking in.

Bell had a studio on the corner of Howland Street and Fitzroy Street, and also lived in Charlotte Street. A militant leftist he persuaded the Euston Road School students to paint 'Arms For Spain' banners for a Popular Front march. During the London blitz, while staying with Kenneth Clark at 30 Portland Place, he signed up for the RAF. A rugby player, he also played football for his unit, but broke a leg during a game, after which his heel turned septic and he was prevented from walking for nine months. He was commissioned as a pilot officer, and was killed when his plane crashed as he waited for landing clearance during a training flight.

Pasmore and Coldstream were both members of the Artists International Association, which united communists, socialists and liberals against fascism. The Association (1933-71) opened a centre at 84 Charlotte Street in August 1943, proclaiming, 'We feel that the place of the artist is at the side of the working class. In this class struggle we use our abilities as an expression and as a weapon, making our first steps towards a new socialist art.' The centre was run by the marxist art critic, sociologist and historian FRANCIS KLINGENDER (1907-55).

One of the Association's active members was FELICIA BROWNE, a Slade student, who joined the Communist Party in 1933. She worked as a kitchen maid to raise funds for the Party, and set off idealistically to travel the world aiming to draw 'the real and rooted life of peasants and workers'. At the outbreak of the Spanish civil war, she joined the republicans in Barcelona, on August 2, 1936. Three weeks later, aged 32, she was the first British volunteer to be killed: riddled with bullets by a fascist patrol while rescuing a wounded colleague at Aragon.

ADRIAN HEATH (1920-92), an RAF pilot shot down and imprisoned in Bavaria, studied at the Slade when the war ended. In 1949 he moved to 22 Fitzroy Street, and supplemented his income by teaching art at Regent Street Polytechnic and Wormwood Scrubs. In 1957 he moved to 28 Charlotte Street,

THE INTERNATIONAL
SURREALIST EXHIBITION
(1936)

(back row, from left) *Rupert Lee, Ruthven Todd, Salvador Dali, Paul Eluard, Roland Penrose, Herbert Read, E.L.T. Mesens, George Reavey and Hugh Sykes-Davies.* (front row, from left) *Diana Lee, Nusch Eluard, Eileen Agar, Sheila Legge and friend.*

Eileen Agar took part in the first surrealist exhibition in London. Salvador Dali attended the opening dressed in a diver's suit, with two Irish wolfhounds on a leash. A young woman wearing a rose mask walked around holding, in one hand, a model of a leg filled with roses and, in the other, a raw pork chop

Between 1958 and 1962 Doris Lessing sometimes ate at a local restaurant where the patrons were supplied with pencils and paper. Nude 'models' were allowed under the law provided they remained perfectly still.

A naked girl was wheeled in and held a pose for 20 minutes and then she was removed while the eaters applauded, and showed each other their sketches, and another girl arrived, as often as not goose-pimpled from cold.

Doris Lessing

where he was often visited by his friends, Victor Pasmore and Francis Bacon.

Another of Heath's friends, the painter and mathematician, ANTHONY HILL (b.1930), never watched his father, Adrian Hill, present the early television programme *Sketch Club* for fear that he would put his father off. He lived at 28 and then until recently at 24 Charlotte Street. He used to live at Colville Place and remembers that the area in the 1950s was shabby, 'full of thieves' kitchens', without running water in the flats, and that they relied on sinks out on the stairway which were shared by the residents in common. A conscientious objector, he spent his national service teaching art therapy. He has taught art at Regent Street Polytechnic, and is an honorary research fellow in maths at University College, London. He signs some of his work, painted in the Dada style, with the pseudonym Red or Rem Doxford. His Japanese wife, Yuriko, works in ceramics.

MICHAEL AYRTON (1921-75), painter, sculptor, and broadcaster, went to Heatherley's art school, 79 Newman Street, and lived from the war years up to 1952 at 4 All Souls' Place, in the shadow of Broadcasting House. A regular on the Brains Trust, he first joined the radio programme after the producer, desperately looking for someone to replace an ill participant, met Ayrton in the George round the corner at 55 Great Portland Street, and he volunteered. His lodgers in All Souls' Place included, at various times, ballet dancer Margot Fonteyn, broadcaster John Arlott, and composer Constant Lambert, and they were often visited by Dylan Thomas, Aleister Crowley, and Henry Moore. Both he and Lambert died from diabetes.

In 1973 the first of the Fitzrovia street festivals, started by local residents to assert and celebrate their community presence in the face of increasing office development, was embellished by the work of pavement artist JOCK MCPHERSON of Warren Street. He had moved to London in the 1920s, and then chalked his way round the world, from America to Australia. The sculptor BILL PHILBY (1918-94) made the festival's giant model cat, Fitz, with the assistance of his nephew 'Leaping' Jack Marlow. Bill liked to tell risqué jokes over a pint in the One Tun in Goodge Street, which were made all the more amusing when he stammered over the cruder parts. Like the singer Alan Breeze, Bill's stutter vanished when he sang.

Another contributor was TIM HUNKIN (b.1950), a television presenter, who drew cartoons for the *Observer* and other national newspapers in the 1970s, when he lived at 28 Charlotte Street – his festival specialty was sawing people in half.

The famous *Evening Standard* cartoonist RAYMOND 'JAK' JACKSON (1927-97) was the son of a local (Clipstone Street) tailor and went to school at 115 New Cavendish (*56 Upper Marylebone*) Street. His first job was painting out the pubic hair on photographs of naked women for the naturist magazine *Health & Efficiency*. A black belt in judo, his motto was 'Never explain, never complain.'

A group of three contemporary cartoonists, DAVID AUSTIN (b.1935), KIPPER WILLIAMS (b.1952), and NICK NEWMAN (b.1958), took over a Windmill Street studio in 1980 that used to belong to an agency supplying ugly models – before that it was an anarchist club. Individually they produce topical, pocket cartoons for newspapers and magazines such as the *Guardian* and *Private Eye*, and claim to be inspired by the delicious aromas from the neighbouring Indian and French restaurants.

The flamboyant, bohemian water-colourist GLYNN BOYD HARTE (b.1948), who lives in Gower Street, was first introduced to Fitzrovia by his brother, who took him to dine at Bertorelli's and Schmidt's in Charlotte Street. His pictures of Pollock's toy museum, Beardmore's ironmongers, and other

MICHAEL AYRTON, at work
on *The Captive Seven*, at 4
All Souls' Place (1951)

Fitzrovian scenes have been exhibited in Curwen's art gallery at 4 Windmill Street.

REBECCA HOSSACK, an Australian who worked for the diplomatic services, opened her own art gallery at 35 Windmill Street in 1988. She planted a snow eucalyptus tree in a tub outside the gallery and named the tree Herb, after the native Australian novelist, Herb Wharton. Camden council announced that the tree was an infringement of a by-law and promptly removed it. Rebecca researched the by-laws and discovered that she could place a skip outside the gallery – so she hired a skip in which she planted another eucalyptus, to replace Herb, which died in the council's captivity.

The pavement and the outside of the gallery have been decorated by Jimmy Pike, an Australian Aborigine. Pike was raised among the Walmajarri, and did not start painting until 1980, after he had met Pat Lowe while he was in prison serving a sentence for murder. Lowe, a prison psychologist, encouraged him, and they later married. Pike's first job was at the Fitzroy Crossing, a cattle station in the Western Australian outback, where he remembers that a Fitzroy cocktail was made with methylated spirits, ginger beer and a teaspoonful of boot polish.

CHAPTER 7
The Literary Set

DANIEL DEFOE (1660-1731) drank at the Green Man tavern (*Farthing Pye House*), opposite today's Great Portland Street station. Prodigious writer of journalism, political pamphlets, travel books, commercial manuals, tales of adventure, as well as memoirs on behalf of criminals due to be hanged, he is best known today for his novels, *Robinson Crusoe* and *Moll Flanders*. Defoe was placed in a public pillory and twice imprisoned as a dissenter, and almost certainly took part in the Duke of Monmouth's rebellion against the Roman Catholic James II, at Sedgemoor, 1685, the last pitched battle fought on English soil. He escaped capture and death by slipping away in the thick fog.

Another of the writers to frequent the Green Man was the satirist ALEXANDER POPE (1688-1744), author of the invective *Epistle to Dr Arbuthnot* (1735). He mentions the tavern in his *Instructions to a Porter*. Pope, whose growth was stunted by a severe illness when he was 12 years old, also knew the area from his visits to his friend, Colonel Richard King, at 23 Rathbone Place; in his poem *The Dunciad* (1728) he describes the 'roaring' fair at Tottenham Court, 'Tot'nam Fields'.

But perhaps SAMUEL JOHNSON (1709-84), who took lodgings with a Mrs Crow at what is now Eastcastle and Great Castle (*6 Castle*) Streets, when he first arrived in London in 1737, was the most taken by the delights of the tavern, 'There is a general freedom from anxiety', he wrote, 'You are sure of a welcome; and the more noise you make, the more trouble you give, the more good things you call for, the welcomer you are…there is nothing which has yet been contrived by man, by which so much happiness is produced as by a good tavern or inn.' To compile his magisterial lexicon, *A Dictionary of the English Language*, 'by which the pronunciation of our language may be fixed', took him from 1746 to 1755, and landed him in debt. He was sent to Fleet Prison where a clergyman criticised his habit of gobbling his food 'so fast that the veins stood out on his forehead', perhaps a reason for his constant flatulence.

Shabby, uncouth, physically grotesque and pock-marked, Johnson liked to keep company with glamorous actresses and said that he resisted the temptation to have sex with prostitutes because he disapproved of pimps, 'whoremongers', who traded in women 'like a dealer in any other commodity'. He resorted to 'relieving himself by onanism', and observed ruefully that 'Marriage has many pains, but celibacy has no pleasures.'

His friend JAMES BOSWELL (1740-95), who distinguished himself by writing *The Life of Samuel Johnson* (1791), did not share his friend's qualms about prostitutes. On his arrival in London from Edinburgh in 1762, aged 22, he marvelled at the city's buildings, the crowd, the anonymity offered to the delighted observer, 'the liberty and whim that reigns there occasions a variety of perfect and curious characters.' A patron of the Percy Street Coffee House, which opened in the 1760s at 29 Rathbone Place, Boswell would have appreciated the debate over the virtues of drinking coffee. Surely it bolstered male sexual performance, one enthusiast argued, 'by drying up those crude flatulent humours, which otherwise would make us only flash in the pan.'

When a man writes from his own mind, he writes very rapidly. The greatest part of a writer's time is spent in reading, in order to write: a man will turn over half a library to make one book.

Samuel Johnson, quoted by James Boswell

JULIAN MACLAREN-ROSS AND THE LITERARY SET

Writers and small magazine publishers gathered in Fitzrovia's pubs during the 1940s. 'MacLaren-Ross…became a symbol of wartime London Bohemia. He had his regular post at the end of the bar in the Wheatsheaf,' wrote Anthony Burgess.

SAMUEL JOHNSON, engraving by James Heath after the portrait by Sir Joshua Reynolds (1756)

Frontispiece to the first edition of James Boswell's LIFE OF JOHNSON *(1791)*

This portrait smartened up Samuel Johnson, putting buttons on his waistcoat, and emphasising his reflective frown. He is portrayed as the new man of the era, thoughtful, learned, and bourgeois rather than aristocratic.

A promiscuous drunk with 'high aspirations and low inclinations', he spent the last five years of his life at 122 (47) Great Portland Street. By then he had outlived his wife, and the friends he described vividly in the pages of his *London Journal* (1762-73). If he could not find a prostitute for quick, standing sex, which he was wont to do in public, he was as likely to turn to the nearest tree. He used condoms made from a sheep's intestine, which were washed and re-used, but he died from gonorrhoea.

During his Fitzrovia years Boswell was mugged and left lying in the gutter in Great Titchfield Street, and in 1790 he was locked up in the Oxford Street Watch House for arguing with the night watchman.

GUISEPPE BARETTI (1719-89), author of books on Italian culture, who lived in All Souls' Place (*10 Edward Street*), was arrested for stabbing and killing a pimp who attacked him in the street in 1751. He was tried for murder, successfully pleaded self-defence, and was acquitted. He had a reputation as a sponger, which made him unpopular in some circles. He so annoyed the American heiress Lucy Paradise (who ended her days in a lunatic asylum) during a visit to her house at 13-17 Mortimer (*28 Charles*) Street, that she poured scalding tea over his head.

WILLIAM COWPER (1731-1800) was the author of the poem *John Gilpin*, and of 68 hymns that have given us such aphorisms as 'God moves in a mysterious way', and 'Variety's the very spice of life, That gives it all its flavour.' He often visited his friend, Samuel Rose, at 23 Percy Street. After he went to look at the inmates of the Bedlam asylum, which was open to any member of the public who wanted to visit, in 1764, he too was incarcerated in an asylum, where he tried to strangle himself with a garter. Charles Greville, a literary acquaintance, thought it was because he was hermaphrodite, but the writer Hazlitt said Cowper's effeminacy was the cause of his madness. Cowper was released from asylum, but was still subject to fits of depression, and on his last visit to see Samuel Rose, in 1792, he stayed completely silent.

Author of anti-royalist and anti-establishment satire, JOHN 'PETER PINDAR' WOLCOT (1738-1819), ex-clergyman and Physician-General of Jamaica, nearly died while trying to save the life of one of his maidservants when a fire broke out in his house at 39 Howland Street. He also lived at 1 Gildea (*Chapel*) Street.

The Shakespearean scholar EDMOND MALONE (1741-1812), laboured for seven years to edit the works of Shakespeare. The year after his *An attempt to ascertain the order in which the plays attributed to Shakespeare were written* (1778) was published, he moved to 40 Langham Street (*1 Foley Place*), where he lived until his death, and gave his friend, Boswell, scholarly editing assistance with the *Life of Dr Johnson*. 'Make a skeleton with reference to the materials in order of time', he advised Boswell at the start of the biography. Boswell saw him often, although there were days when he wrote, 'Malone was busy with his Shakespeare, so I could not get any of his time.'

During the American War of Independence, EDWARD BANCROFT (1750-1820), an inventor who published works on medicine and science, lived on the corner of Rathbone Place and Charlotte Street. He became friends with Benjamin Franklin, who asked him to act as an interpreter for the Americans during their arms negotiations with the French. Unbeknown to Franklin, Bancroft was already acting as a spy on the British side (for £1,000 a year and the promise of a professorship at Columbia University). When the British were defeated, Bancroft had to be content with a generous life pension.

The diarist and novelist FRANCES 'FANNY' BURNEY (1752-1840) had instant fame when it was revealed that she was the author of *Evelina or The History of a Young Lady's Entrance into the World* (1778). Her stepmother had burned the first draft, and she re-wrote it secretly at night. It was published, anonymously, when she was aged 25. Sir Joshua Reynolds said that he had not been able to go to bed without finishing *Evelina*, and offered £50 to anyone who would tell him the name of the author. If it were a woman, he said, he was sure he should make love to her.

Fanny Burney's world was the drawing room, the ball room, the public places of literary, musical and fashionable London, where the light of candles glittered on the satin coats of the beaux and the women in their richly embroidered, hooped skirts. She made fun of the fops, vapid dandies, the ennuyé, with their free use of jessamine and lavender drops, powder and pomade cloaking the scars of small pox, who tormented the unsophisticated Evelina. She amusingly described the young heroine's mortifying visit to the theatre with her relatives who, in their ignorance, wear full evening dress to sit in the two shilling gallery.

Fanny Burney went to the Pantheon in Oxford Street, where her father, Dr Charles Burney, a fashionable music teacher, was employed. She also went to the literary gatherings 'for men and women of intellect and wit' held by Harriet Mathew, at 27 Rathbone Place. A new kind of social space had begun to open up in which educated women held court. Boswell noted of these literary receptions that, 'the fair sex might participate in conversation with literary and ingenious men, animated by a desire to please.'

Dr. Johnson has more fun, and comical humour, and love of nonsense about him, than almost anybody I ever saw: I mean when those he likes; for otherwise, he can be as severe and as bitter as repost relates him.

Fanny Burney on Samuel Johnson

WILLIAM GODWIN outside his bookshop in Hanway Street

The writer William Godwin contended that people would be able to bring about a change of governance through the power of human reason, and his philosophy seeded the intellectual tradition in English politics.

I am dissatisfied with myself for not having done justice to the subject. – Do not suspect me of false modesty – I mean to say, that had I allowed myself more time I could have written a better book, in every sense of the word.

Mary Wollstonecraft on *A Vindication of the Rights of Women*

As a consequence of her success, Fanny Burney was appointed Second Keeper of the Robes to Queen Charlotte in 1786. She stayed at this post until 1786, recording the events in her diaries, although Thomas MacAulay considered these were wasted years for a novelist, 'thousands might have been found more expert in tying ribbands and filling snuff-boxes.'

She married the French refugee General Alexandre d'Arblay in 1793. He was a royalist poet and military man, who returned to France when the revolution ended in 1802. Fanny joined him the same year. Napoleon admired Fanny's novels and she and her husband enjoyed some security until 1805, when d'Arblay refused to serve against England in the war. He and Fanny were interned until 1812, when they returned to England. That year, Fanny Burney moved to 23 Chenies Street.

WILLIAM BLAKE (1757-1827), poet, painter and mystic, also read his poetry at the *conversaziones* held by Mrs Mathew. She was the wife of the Reverend Henry Mathew, vicar of Fitzrovia's Percy Chapel (15-17 Percy Street) 1766-1804. A patron of the arts, she championed Italian composers, and helped William Blake publish some of his early poems.

Blake frequently visited his brother James, at the northern end of Great Titchfield Street (*Cirencester Place*). He saw his close friend and patron, Thomas Butts, at 17 Grafton Way, and visited John Linnell, who was a disciple of his work, and John Varley, at *6 Cirencester Place* (now Holcroft Court).

Butts once came across William Blake and his wife Catherine enacting Adam and Eve, naked, in their garden reciting lines from Milton's *Paradise Lost*. Blake set out to change our perception of reality, to speak for the soul and the imagination, against the limitations of 'cold science'. He despised capitalism for rewarding those 'who can sell a good-for-nothing commodity for a great price', and created his own mythic and religious cosmology, 'I must create a system, or be enslaved by another man's.' He was charged with having used seditious words and assaulting a soldier, and he was once arrested as a French spy while he was sketching on the Medway. After he died Catherine lived where Collingwood House now stands in Hanson (*17 Charlton*) Street. In 1831 she died there from inflammation of the bowels.

One of Blake's revolutionary friends, WILLIAM GODWIN (1756-1836), dissenting minister, philosophical atheist, and author of *Enquiry Concerning Political Justice*, ran the radical bookshop at 9 Hanway Street (1805-07), and lived at 44 Gower Place (1826-33). In *Political Justice* (1793) he criticised the institution of marriage as 'the worst of all laws', but he was married twice – first to Mary Wollstonecraft in 1797, and, after she died, to a Mrs Clairmont. Godwin and Mrs Clairmont cared for three children: Jane 'Claire' Clairmont (Clairmont's daughter by her first husband), Mary (Godwin and Mary Wollstonecraft's daughter, who married Shelley), and Fanny (Mary's daughter by her previous lover Gilbert Imlay).

It was while she was living in Store Street (1792) that feminist MARY WOLLSTONECRAFT (1759-97) wrote *A Vindication of the Rights of Women* in six weeks as 'a plea for my sex – not for myself', disclaiming the subordination of women, and claiming for them 'the virtues of humanity'. In 1795 she lived at 26 Charlotte Street, with Gilbert Imlay and also at 26 Percy Street. When Imlay began a relationship with an actress, she nearly succeeded in poisoning herself, 'You may render me unhappy; but you cannot make me contemptible in my own eyes.'

Mary's own mother had been abused and forced into poverty by her violent, alcoholic husband. He had once hanged a dog in a drunken rage, and Mary had defended her mother from her father's blows.

She coined the term 'legalised prostitution' for the exploitative nature of

marriage and, on marrying Godwin, told him that she preferred not to live
with him; the fact of his being 'riveted in my heart' did not mean that she
wanted him 'always at my elbow'. Mary gave birth to her second daughter in
harrowing circumstances, and developed puerperal fever. Treated with opium,
she told Godwin she was in heaven. She died of septicaemia a month later.

Wollstonecraft's argument against 'the divine rights of husbands' aroused
the wrath of writers such as HORACE WALPOLE (1717-97), who called her a
'hyena in petticoats'. In 1743 Walpole lived at 5 Portland Place, from where he
often went to Whitefield's Chapel in Tottenham Court Road, or to call on the
artist Fuseli, in Foley Street. Godwin complained to Wollstonecraft that she
talked too much at a meeting, preventing Tom Paine from getting a word in
edgeways.

In 1814, the poet PERCY BYSSHE SHELLEY (1792-1822) was living at 56 Margaret
Street, when he met Mary Godwin, and they fell in love. He had been sent
down from Oxford University for writing *The Necessity of Atheism* (1811), and he
went to the radical meetings of the Spenceans in the Cock Inn (Grafton Way).
Shelley supported women's right to independence, 'can man be free if woman
be a slave?' and to free union, 'love withers under constraint'. After he met
Mary, he left his first wife, Harriet Westbrook, whom he had wed when he was
19 and she 16 years old, and with whom he had two children – Shelley suffered
anguish when he was later denied custody of them. Two years later Harriet
drowned herself in the Serpentine.

**[My] dreams were all my
own; I accounted for them
to nobody; they were my
refuge when annoyed – my
dearest pleasure when
free.**

Mary Shelley

MARY SHELLEY (1797-1851) started a new genre of fiction by writing the enduringly popular, *Frankenstein* (1818), at the age of 18, when on holiday in Switzerland. She and Shelley had two children, Clara (b.1816) and William (b.1817), who were baptised at St Giles church in 1818, but both children died within a year, of fever in Italy. Their third child, a son, survived. Shelley drowned in Italy, while sailing to visit his friend Lord Byron (whose daughter Allegra, was born in 1817, and baptised in the same service as the two Shelley children; she died aged five).

The corpse-like appearance of the poet SAMUEL ROGERS (1763-1855), of Hallam (*Charlotte*) Street, repulsed many. Byron spoke of his 'mummy-like carcass', and Sydney Smith suggested that Rogers should sit for his portrait in the act of praying, so that his hands would conceal his face. Fanny Kemble said he had the unkindest tongue and kindest heart of anyone she knew. No one wanted to be the first to leave his parties because of his habit of denigrating people after they left his company. Those were the 'two ugliest adulterers I have ever had in this house', he said of some departing guests. He offered to lend Wordsworth a pair of breeches when he was appointed Poet Laureate. They were so tight that Wordsworth had to be helped up after kneeling before Queen Victoria.

After the novelist FRANCOIS RENE CHATEAUBRAND (1768-1848), author of *Atala*, had fled France in 1793, he found lodgings at Tottenham Court Road, for which he paid 6s. a week. He later moved to live with another French novelist, HINGANT DE LA TIEMBLAIS, in Rathbone Place. Chateaubrand, who was wounded while fighting against the French revolution, had also been a cavalry officer in North America at the age of 18. Both writers were terribly poor, and Tiemblais, desperate with hunger, tried to kill himself with a penknife. He was taken to Middlesex Hospital, after which Chateaubrand could no longer afford to pay the rent. He moved to a nearby garret overlooking a cemetery frequented by bodysnatchers.

The poet SAMUEL TAYLOR COLERIDGE (1772-1834), who was sent down from Cambridge University because of his heavy drinking and revolutionary politics, lived at 71 Berners Street from 1812 to 1816, where he tried to shake off his addiction to laudanum and opium. He used to visit the inventor Samuel Morse every day. Morse was then an artist, living in a studio at 141 Cleveland Street (*8 Buckingham Place*). When Morse read Coleridge's *Ancient Mariner* he recognised some of the drug-induced dreams recounted to him by the poet. Coleridge was often on the verge of suicide while he was living at Berners Street, where he also wrote *Kubla Khan*.

Coleridge and ROBERT SOUTHEY (1774-1843) planned to set up a commune in England after the French revolution. Southey visited Tottenham Court Road in the 1790s to trace the 'Field of the Forty Footsteps', just 500 yards to the east. There, according to a local legend, two brothers killed each other in a duel in the 17th century, with sword and pistol, while the woman they both loved watched from a nearby bank. Afterwards the grass did not grow over the imprint of their footseps – Southey claimed to have seen 76 footprints, each about three inches deep. He was appointed poet laureate in 1813 but soon grew to dislike the role. He regularly visited painter James Barry in Eastcastle Street.

Poet and song writer, famous for his *Ye Mariners of England*, THOMAS CAMPBELL (1777-1844), was also one of the founders of London University (and University College School, 43 Gower Street). He lived at 30 Langham Street (*Foley Place*) from 1830, and in Alfred Place from 1837. Campbell was impressed by the the gusto shown by an 80-year-old captain Morris, who sang of wine and women, during a visit he made to see the painter James Lonsdale, 8 Berners Street.

WILLIAM HAZLITT (1778-1830), the essayist and champion of civil liberties, lived in Percy Street in 1787, and at 12 Rathbone Place from 1799 to 1803. Fired by the French revolution he wrote of the distress suffered by the poor, and his essays punctured many an inflated reputation, earning him several enemies. His first wife, Sarah Stoddard, found him quarrelsome and divorced him. His second wife, Isabella Bridgewater, also divorced him. He was socially ostracised after publishing *Liber Amoris*, an agonising account of his infatuation for Sarah Walker, the daughter of his landlady, which 'lacked nothing in frankness', and which prompted Robert Louis Stevenson to abandon his plan to write Hazlitt's biography. On his deathbed at 6 Frith

On one occasion I heard him improvise for half an hour in blank verse what he stated to be a strange dream which was full of those wonderful creations that glitter like diamonds.

Samuel Morse on Samuel Coleridge

Street in Soho, Hazlitt's last words were, 'Well, I have had a happy life.' His tombstone lies beneath the tower at St Anne's churchyard by the Wardour Street entrance.

Known as the 'Italian Lord Byron', the poet UGO FOSCOLO (1778-1827), had to flee his native country after he fought in the French army under Napoleon, believing that this would lead to the liberation of Italy. Foscolo was continually involved in romantic intrigues, and lived with his illegitimate daughter at 1 Wells Street and 11 Soho Square. His final years were embittered, and he died in poverty and neglect.

PETER MARK ROGET (1779-1869) did not start to compile his indispensable word reference, *Roget's Thesaurus*, until he was in his 70s. He had lived at 3 Great Titchfield Street and 27 Gower Street when he was a medical student.

The poet and literary journal editor JAMES LEIGH HUNT (1784-1859) was living at 35 Great Portland Street in 1813, when he was jailed for two years for having described the Prince Regent as 'a fat Adonis', and as a 'libertine in debt and disgrace, despiser of domestic ties, companion of gamblers and demireps.' Charles Dickens, inspired by his friend's sunny nature, based the character Skimpole in *Bleak House* on Hunt.

THOMAS DE QUINCEY (1785-1859), author of *Confessions of an English Opium-Eater*, bought his first opium at 173 Oxford Street in 1804. Four years later he took lodgings at 82 Great Titchfield Street. He had run away from school at the age of 17, and collapsed in Oxford Street by Soho Square. Ann, a 15-year-old prostitute, brought him (at her own expense) a glass of port wine and spices that 'acted upon my empty stomach (which at that time would have rejected all solid food) with an instantaneous power of restoration.' Thereafter he met Ann regularly at the bottom of Great Titchfield Street, until one evening she missed their six o'clock assignation. To his great grief, he never saw her again, and he dreamed about her for the rest of his life. By 1812 he was an opium addict. He was frequently arrested for debt, became a well-regarded eccentric, and died in poverty, outliving all his children. His writing on the meaning of dreams influenced Edgar Allan Poe.

The vaudeville shows at the Royal West London Theatre (known as 'the French theatre') in Tottenham Court Road were of a sufficiently lowbrow nature to attract the poet JOHN CLARE (1793-1864). A ploughman from the age of ten he had mixed with gypsies who taught him ballads and stories. He wrote rhymes in the dust on barn walls, but feared being jeered at and kept them secret until both he and his father were out of work. Desperate for money, and emboldened by 'a free application of ale in the fair', he offered his poems for sale. His four volumes of poetry about rural life (1820-35) were a huge success, but he continued with the only work available to him, digging the ditches and planting the hedges for the enclosures that he despised.

Often during 1819, Clare and JOHN KEATS (1795-1821) visited the artist Peter De Wint at 10 Percy Street, where De Wint was illustrating their poems. In 1824 Clare was walking along Oxford Street when he witnessed the funeral procession of Lord Byron (whom he greatly admired) and was deeply moved; later he became insane and thought he was Byron. He was placed in a lunatic asylum in 1837, but he escaped four years later and walked back to his native Northamptonshire, eating grass along the way.

Author ANNA JAMESON (1794-1860), who engraved the illustrations for her own books, lived at 7 Mortimer Street with her 'adopted nieces', Adelaide Procter, Barbara Bodichon and Emily Faithfull, whom she supported when they formed the Society for Promotion of Employment for Women at 19 Langham Place. Her marriage to Robert Jameson (a judge with whom she lived in Chenies Street, 1825-29) was unconsummated after he told her on their

Robert Browning, my poet, is here – and with a wife he has run off with – and who, think you, is this wife? – no other than Elizabeth Barrett, my poetess – a pretty pair to go thro this prosaic world together!

Anna Jameson on the Brownings, who eloped to her hotel in Paris, where she found them apartments.

wedding night that he had married her solely out of spite – because she rejected his first proposal. They separated, but he then failed to pay her the allowance he had promised, and drank himself to death. Anna turned to writing to support herself and her sisters. In her best known work, *Characteristics of Women*, she praised Shakespeare for his portrayal of women as complex and individualised. In her essay 'Women's Mission and Women's Position', she argued that it was unfair to expect women to be 'angels at home' when they also had to work outside to support their families. Aware that people thought her garrulous, she styled herself Lady Blarney – but was known as 'The Woman of Bright Foam' by native Americans in Canada because of the daring and courage she displayed on a canoeing expedition in the 1830s.

She was visited in Mortimer Street by the poets ELIZABETH BARRETT BROWNING (1806-61), author of *Aurora Leigh* (1857), and ROBERT BROWNING (1812-89), author of *The Ring and the Book* (1868-69). Robert Browning learned Greek at University College in Gower Street, and often called in to see the artist Ford Madox Brown, at 37 Fitzroy Square.

Further along, at 25 Mortimer (*24 Charles*) Street, lived SAMUEL LOVER (1797-1868), the Irish novelist, songwriter and painter best known for his ballad *Rory O'More*, about the tragic events that occurred in Dublin, when he was a child. During the British reprisals for the Irish uprising of 1803, against the Act of Union two years earlier, he saw his own mother attacked by a British soldier with a bayonet. After his eyesight failed he stopped writing songs and began to sing for a living.

The 15th century Persian poet, Omar Khayyam, was practically unknown in Britain until his work was translated into English by EDWARD FITZGERALD (1809-83), an eccentric poet who had a 'quirky but engaging' personality. Born Edward Purcell, his name was changed at the age of nine when his mother, Mary, inherited her father's fortune, and her husband took on her surname. His mother dined off gold plate and drove in a glittering yellow coach drawn by four black horses – a lifestyle hated by Edward, who chose to live alone in shabby lodging houses, existing on a diet of bread, fruit and tea. A homosexual, his two great loves were a young man he met on a steamship (William Browne) and a fisherman (Joseph 'Posh' Fletcher). But he married Lucy Barton, the daughter of his friend Bernard Barton, a poet who, just before he died, had asked him to take care of her. They separated within a year. In his childhood Fitzgerald lived at 39 Portland Place. Later he lived at several addresses in Fitzrovia: 19 (1841), and 18 (1843) Charlotte Street; 'a dirty room' at 60 Charlotte Street (1844-48); 39 Bolsover Street (1848-50); 31 (1855-57) and 88 Great Portland Street (from 1859). When he died a rosebush grown from a clipping of a bush on the tomb of Omar Khayyam was planted by his grave.

The novelist WILLIAM MAKEPEACE THACKERAY (1811-63) lived in Fitzroy Street after he left Cambridge University with gambling debts and without a degree. He also lived at 35 Maple Street, which was said to be haunted by a ghost connected to a cottage that was on the site in the 16th century. Thackeray often illustrated his own work, including some satirical sketches for *Punch* magazine. Despite becoming mentally unstable in 1840, he continued to write.

The novelist CHARLES DICKENS (1812-70), was also an accomplished conjuror: he would pour raw ingredients into a bowler hat and pull out a plum pudding, or turn bran into a guinea pig. He lived at 22 Cleveland (*10 Norfolk*) Street from the age of two to four. As a lad he then lived at 70 Margaret Street, where he was often forced to hide from his father's creditors. In 1823 the family moved to 4 North Gower (*41 Upper Gower*) Street. While there his father was

Writing can be done [only with] the utmost application, the greatest patience, and the steadiest energy of which the writer is capable.

Charles Dickens

imprisoned for bankruptcy. Aged 12 the young Dickens went to work in a blacking (shoe polish) factory, which he hated, apart from one daily consolation, he 'could not resist the stale pastry put out on half price trays at the confectioners' doors in Tottenham Court Road.' A solicitor, Edward Blackmore, who lodged with Dickens's aunt, Mrs Charlton, at 16 Berners Street, then gave him a job as a clerk. It was in Berners Street that Dickens first saw the original for his fictional Miss Haversham (*Great Expectations*) – an elderly woman still wearing the bridal dress for her cancelled wedding to a wealthy Quaker. She kept her face hidden behind her faded white bonnet, and had a cold and distant manner. Between 1829 and 1831 Dickens again lived at 22 Cleveland Street. Thereafter he lived also in Greenwell (*Buckingham*) Street, off Cleveland Street, and at 25 (*15*) Fitzroy Street (near his Aunt Janet, 7 Charlotte Street) until 1833. By 1844, when Dickens was finishing his novel *Martin Chuzzlewit* (based on Richard Dadd's patricide), he had joined the Little Portland Street Unitarian Church, because the rationalist views espoused by the local minister, Edward Tagart, appealed to him.

In 1858 Dickens left his wife for Ellen Ternan, an 18-year-old actress (the age of his eldest daughter). Ellen wore geraniums in her hair and lived at 31 Berners Street. Their relationship lasted for the rest of Dickens' life.

The first editor of *Punch* magazine, HENRY MAYHEW (1812-87), a novelist better known as the author of the massive, meticulous social document, *London Labour and the London Poor* (1850), lived with his 15 brothers and sisters at 16 Fitzroy Square. He wanted to see for himself the conditions of the poor, and made a point of experiencing everything he described, even the prisoners' treadmill.

GERALDINE JEWSBURY (1812-80), author of six melodramatic novels including *Zoe* (1845), lived in Charlotte Street in 1830. Reviewers were shocked by her lack of feminine delicacy; one wrote that she had a 'right daring and in some aspects a masculine spirit'. She was kind, humorous, and one of the first to be described as a 'new woman'. She dressed in enormous plumed hats, wore parrot-shaped earrings, and delighted guests at 'genteel' parties by loudly discussing 'diverse intimate matters'. She loved Jane Carlyle (married to writer Thomas Carlyle) with whom she had a stormy relationship for 25 years. She visited Paris during the 1848 uprising that led to the Second Republic, because she wanted to experience the excitement and upheaval of revolution.

WILKIE COLLINS (1824-89) pioneered the detective novel with *The Moonstone* (1868), described by T.S. Eliot as 'the first, the longest, and the best of modern English detective novels'. His first major success was *The Woman in White* (1860), based on his encounter with Caroline Graves, 'a young and very beautiful woman dressed in flowing white robes that shone in the moonlight'. Collins had been walking with the painter, John Millais, when they heard a scream from the garden of a villa near Regent's Park. Its iron gate crashed open and the terrified Caroline appeared, escaping from the house where she had been held captive. With her daughter Harriet, Caroline moved in with Collins, who had lodgings at Howland Street. Collins described their life there as tough and morose, 'dirty work, small wages, hard words, no holidays, no social status, no future.' In 1858 they moved away from the area but by the end of the decade they were living nearby, at 2a Cavendish Square, where Wilkie, afflicted by a boil between his legs, wrote *The Woman in White*.

Collins then began a second relationship. He met Martha Rudd in 1864, and he lived with her at 33 Bolsover Street, where the couple used the names of Mr and Mrs William Dawson for the benefit of Mrs Wells, their landlady. Wilkie and Martha had two daughters, Martha (b.1869) and Constance ('Hettie', b.1871), and a son William, born 1873, after they had moved to 55

HENRY MAYHEW, writer and founder of *Punch*. Engraving after a daguerreotype by Beard.

Mayhew's classic study London Labour and the London Poor *documented the voices and conditions of the people with vivid realism.*

CHARLES DICKENS

Charles Dickens lived in Fitzrovia at different times of his life.

In Barnaby Rudge *he drew a fictional portrait of northern Green Lanes (now Cleveland Street) when it was still rural, occupied by the poor in a crazy tangle of huts, with stagnant pools overgrown with grass and duckweed.*

Marylebone Road. Martha and Constance were educated at the Maria Grey College, Fitzroy Square, (probably No.10) and enjoyed the company of Collins' four grandchildren (born to his stepdaughter, Harriet).

He suffered what he diagnosed as rheumatic gout in his eyes, 'enormous bags of blood', while he was writing *The Moonstone*, for which he took opium and large amounts of laudanum. The male secretaries to whom he dictated his novels were so disturbed by his cries of pain that they all left. Collins then engaged the services of a young woman, (probably his stepdaughter Harriet); he commanded her to take no notice of his woes and concentrate on his dictation, 'utterly disregard my sufferings and attend solely to my words.'

Collins was always fond of children and had agreed to be godfather to Alice Ward, having been the best man at her parents' secret, under-age wedding in All Souls, Langham Place, in 1848. At the christening, he drank too much, and accused the baby of swaying drunkenly. He continued his relationships with both Caroline and with Martha. The women kept apart from each other, but he made them equal beneficiaries in his will. Caroline died five years after Wilkie, from a heart attack brought on by acute bronchitis, while she was lodging above a cabinet-maker's in Newman Street.

The writer CHRISTINA ROSSETTI (1830-94), and her brother Dante Gabriel were born at 110 Hallam (*38 Charlotte*) Street, and christened at All Souls, Langham Place. Christina was a spirited child, who later denied her own desires and prioritised the spiritual life and the virtues of self-sacrifice. She

They jerked, zigzagged, advanced, retreated, he and his shadow posturing in ungainly indissoluble harmony. He seemed exasperated, fascinated, desperately endeavouring and utterly hopeless.

Christina Rossetti on watching a spider and its shadow

CHRISTINA ROSSETTI AND
HER MOTHER, FRANCES
ROSSETTI, by Dante Gabriel
Rossetti (1877)

*A melancholy portrait,
showing the poet, Christina
Rossetti, after a life of self-
denial, and her mother,
Frances, in a mood of rueful
self-reflection. Frances, who
had undertaken the early
education of all the Rossetti
children, had a 'passion for
intellect', but at the age of 70
she wished there were 'a little
less intellect in the family, so
as to allow for a little more
common sense.'*

once slashed her arm with scissors on being rebuked by her mother. The
family moved to a larger house further down Hallam Street, where she wrote
her first couplet at the age of five. She tended to write her ideas down on the
backs of envelopes. Her long poem, the sinister and sensual *Goblin Market*
(1862), drew attention to the Pre-Raphaelite Movement. Walking in Regent's
Park at dawn one morning she had a vision of a wave of yellow light surging
from the trees and transforming into a flock of canaries that flew upwards and
arched across the sky, before scattering. In her mind the birds had escaped
from their cages, met together at daybreak, and were now returning. She wrote
hymns and religious poetry, as well as articles campaigning for women's
independence, and lived a life of simplicity, refusing to marry the man she
loved because of their differences in belief. Among her suitors were the painter
James Collinson and the linguist Charles Cayley.

After losing the sight of one eye, GEORGE DU MAURIER (1834-96)
abandoned painting and started to write fiction. His best selling novel, *Trilby*
(1894), gripped readers on both sides of the Atlantic with its story of Svengali
who hypnotises a young artist's model; she becomes a concert star, but sings
only when under his spell. The novel drew on the bohemian life of the artist
James Whistler, with whom du Maurier shared a studio at 72 Newman Street.
He also lived at 8 and 16 Berners Street, and at 70, 85, 90, and 91 Newman
Street.

Critic, poet and social reprobate, ALGERNON SWINBURNE (1837-1909) called
'Swine Born' by *Punch* magazine, lived at 12 Grafton Way, 77 Newman Street,

and in North Crescent, off Chenies Street. When he was a schoolboy at Eton he discovered a taste for flagellation, which he later indulged in a whipping brothel in Portland Place. His poems about sadism, masochism, *femme fatales*, and his rejection of Christianity led to a public outcry and were withdrawn by the publishers, but his passionate poetry readings could thrill his audience. He wrote a pornographic novel, *Lisbia Brandon*, and had a collection of erotic literature. Carlyle, full of scorn, described him as 'standing up to his neck in a cesspool, and adding to its contents.' The most depraved act of which he boasted, was that he had dressed up his pet monkey, had sex with it, grilled it and eaten it.

To put Swinburne's proclaimed homosexuality to the test, Rossetti bribed a popular entertainer, Adah Isaacs Menken, ten pounds to seduce him. Later she returned the money explaining that Swinburne would not stop biting her.

He often visited Ford Madox Brown at 37 Fitzroy Square, as well as Guiseppe Mazzini in Goodge Street, and his close friend, the scandalous novelist OUIDA, pseudonym of Marie Louise de la Ramée (1839-1908), who lived in a fifth-floor suite at the Langham Hotel from 1866 to 1871. When Swinburne collapsed, drunk, on a visit to the Langham, he was picked up from the floor by Oscar Wilde and dumped on a chaise longue.

Ouida shocked society by frequently entertaining guests in her hotel room, with its black velvet curtains. Among these were Millais, Browning and Lord Lytton and, it was rumoured, a whole regiment of soldiers. She wrote romantic novels in which the women characters, such as the original wild child, *Cigarett*, who never wore corsets, defied the morals of the age. Although Ouida's novels sold well, she ended her days destitute, surrounded by her many stray dogs, which she refused to house-train as she considered this to be a cruel practice.

In 1871 PAUL VERLAINE (1844-96) became besotted with ARTHUR RIMBAUD (1854-91), 'a beautiful insufferable hooligan', and they left France in 1872, when they were aged 28 and 18 respectively, and ran away to London. They lived at 35 Howland Street – a plaque to commemorate their stay was unveiled in 1922, but not replaced when the building was demolished in the 1930s.

There they felt lonely and depressed by the dreary English Sundays, until they settled into a life of reading, walking around London, and studying English. Verlaine said he was so happy that he wished this existence could continue forever, and he finished his collection of poems, *Romances sans Paroles* (1874). Their poetry, a *tour de force* of symbolism, has inspired future generations of writers, including Bob Dylan. But their relationship was tempestuous and violent. The bisexual Verlaine was temperamental in the extreme. He drank heavily, and had a taste for the fashionable green absinthe that gave him cirrhosis of the liver. When Rimbaud attacked Verlaine with a knife, accusing him of being too respectable, Verlaine left London and went to Brussels. Rimbaud followed. Verlaine wrote a drunken suicide note and aimed a gun at Rimbaud, wounding him in the wrist. Verlaine was jailed for two years for attempted murder. On his release he sought reconciliation with Rimbaud, who responded by knocking him out and abandoning him at a roadside – Verlaine had a syphilitic bad leg that later turned cancerous, and was amputated.

The author of *Treasure Island*, ROBERT LOUIS STEVENSON (1850-1894), stayed at 5 Fitzroy Square in 1886, before sailing to the south seas where he died from a brain haemorrhage after visiting a leper colony.

OSCAR WILDE (1854-1900), wit and playwright, married with two sons, was introduced to Lord Alfred Douglas, who later became his lover, by the Fitzrovian gay poet Lionel Johnson, of 20 Fitzroy Street. Wilde sued the Marquis of Queensbury (father of Douglas) for his famously mis-spelled note

Power is sweet and when you are a little clerk you love its sweetness quite as much as if you were an emperor, and maybe you love it a good deal more.

Ouida

Sometimes one would hear him mouthing some strange new word over and over on his tongue, shouting it in different tones, emitting it with sudden explosive energy as though to catch unaware its spirit, not resting until he had gained mastery of its vocal value.

Havelock Ellis on Paul Verlaine's fascination with learning new words in English

accusing Wilde of being a 'somdomite'. At the trial Douglas' barrister referred to two of Wilde's homosexual friends arrested in a club at 46 Fitzroy Street. They were Alfred Taylor, who had been playing the piano, and Charles Parker, who testified to having had sex with Wilde, and that there had been 'orgies of the most disgraceful kind' on the premises. Wilde later wrote 'like feasting with panthers; the danger was half the excitement'. Wilde was forced to withdraw his case. He was then arrested on April 5, 1895, and prosecuted under the 1885 Criminal Law Amendment Act for homosexual offences (the 'Blackmailer's Charter', it remained on the statute book until 1967). Among the young men brought into the dock to testify to sex with Wilde were Alfred Wood (in a room in Langham Street), and Fred Atkins (in a room at 25 Osnaburgh Street, where the landlady complained that after Wilde's visits, the sheets were 'stained in a peculiar way'). Wilde's public humiliation was aggravated by the withdrawal of both his plays, *An Ideal Husband* and *The Importance of Being Earnest*, which had opened earlier in the year.

Despite all the prurient detail of the testimonies, the jury failed to agree. While he was waiting a retrial Wilde was taken to a Great Portland Street restaurant (probably Pagani's) by author FRANK HARRIS (1856-1931). Harris later recounted that Wilde had said to him, 'Oh Frank, you talk with passion and conviction, as if I were innocent.' 'But you are innocent aren't you?' Harris had replied. 'No, Frank' Wilde had responded, 'I thought you knew that all along.' Wilde also consulted Mrs A. Robinson, a 'Sybil' (society fortune-teller), at 53 Mortimer Street, more than once in 1894 and 1895. She prophesised complete triumph in the trial for Oscar and 'a very brilliant life up to a certain point, then I see a wall.'

At the retrial the judge and chief prosecutor seemed especially affronted that Wilde had mingled with people of 'an inferior social class'. Wilde was sentenced to two years' hard labour. He served the full term under harsh conditions, losing 22 pounds in weight.

Wilde's novel *The Picture of Dorian Gray* (serialised in *Lippincott's Magazine*, July 1890) was commissioned by the publisher, Joseph Stoddart, over a meal at the Langham Hotel, Portland Place.

The feminist OLIVE SCHREINER (1855-1920) wrote *The Story of an African Farm* before she arrived in England in 1881, but the manuscript submitted under her own name was rejected by several publishers before it was finally accepted under the pseudonym of 'Ralph Iron'. Its enormous success brought her into contact with Gladstone, Herbert Spencer and Havelock Ellis (1859-1939), author of the *Psychology of Sex*. With Ellis she had a brief, unsuccessful affair that developed into a life-long friendship, 'a friendship with passion'.

At times resentful of her own feminity, she struggled to understand the psychology of male/female relations. She told Ellis that successful sex could make a woman feel that a man had 'put his finger into her brain, and stirred it round and round...her whole nature is affected.' She argued that feminism was more than an issue of women's rights, 'Man injures woman and woman injures man', she wrote, 'it is not a case for crying out against individuals or against sexes, but simply for changing a whole system.'

London's damp climate was not good for her asthma and she moved restlessly from one boarding house to another. In 1884 she lived at 32 Fitzroy Street, near her friend Eleanor Marx. In 1886 she moved to 9 Portland Place, and then to what Arthur Symonds described as bare, pleasant little rooms in the Ladies Chambers, Chenies Street. In 1889 she returned to South Africa, where she continued to write and to fight for the cause of women's emancipation.

GEORGE BERNARD SHAW (1856-1950) spent some of the toughest but most

creative years of his life in Fitzrovia. A discriminating vegetarian who avoided certain vegetables, especially asparagus, because it 'gave one's urine a disagreeable smell', he chose the area because it was handy for cheap vegetarian eating places, such as the Wheatsheaf, 25 Rathbone Place, and the Alpha, Oxford Street. He took an unfurnished apartment on the second floor of 37 Fitzroy Street in December 1880 and lived there in relative squalor for 16 months. While there he contracted smallpox, and to hide the scars he grew a beard. In April 1882 he moved to 36 Osnaburgh Street. Two years later he joined the newly formed Fabian Society, for which he wrote the manifesto: Britain was divided into two classes, 'with large appetites and no dinners at one extreme and large dinners and no appetites at the other'.

Friend and fellow playwright, WILLIAM ARCHER (1856-1924), who later moved into 27 Fitzroy Square, was shocked to see Shaw warming his cold porridge over a gas fire, and arranged for him to earn some money as a theatre critic. Shaw first began to make his name as a dramatist in 1892, with *Widowers' Houses*, which he wrote in collaboration with Archer. While at Osnaburgh Street, Shaw had an affair with EDITH NESBIT (1858-1924), author of *The Railway Children*, and they dined together in the Wheatsheaf. He also had an affair with ANNIE BESANT (1847-1933), who was prosecuted on a charge of obscenity for publishing a pamphlet about birth control. Shaw met Besant at a lecture on socialism that he gave to a meeting of the Dialectical Society by Oxford Circus in January 1885. He admired her impulsiveness and energy and they became intimate friends. In the winter of 1885, while having his portrait painted 'in a little hole off Euston Road' by Slade art student Nellie Heath, Shaw was given four weeks' notice to leave the rooms in Osnaburgh Street.

In March 1887, Shaw moved, with his mother, to the third and fourth floors at 29 Fitzroy Square, 'a most repulsive house'. It had a depressing hall and no bathroom, but this did not dampen his spirits. During the 11 years that he lived in Fitzroy Square, 'in grand disorder', Shaw wrote seven plays, his

A CORNER OF THE TABLE by Ignace H.J. Fantin-Latour (1872)

Paul Verlaine (left, seated) typically muffled in a scarf, next to Arthur Rimbaud, smartly suited, with other writers and politicians.

In 1872 Verlaine left his 18-year-old wife and baby in Paris, and travelled with Rimbaud to Belgium, then across to England.

Olive Schreiner, from a last passport photo, taken on a visit back to London in 1920

She grew up on the South African veldt, the setting for her first novel, The Story of an African Farm, *which featured (controversially) an unmarried mother, and was concerned with the passionate desire for growth and understanding, 'the deepest pulse of human beings'.*

finest theatre criticism, and was at his most politically active. One night on his way home from a ballet performance by Vincenti, the master of leaping pirouettes, he danced around the Square, and was joined by two policemen, a postman, and a milkman 'who unfortunately broke his leg.'

Actor-manager Richard Mansfield signed the contract for the first of Shaw's plays, *Arms and the Man*, in 1894 at a meeting in the Langham Hotel, Portland Place.

In 1898, suffering from a swollen foot, Shaw limped down Tottenham Court Road to seek help from Charlotte Payne-Townsend, his fellow-Fabian, a 'green-eyed Irish millionairess', whom he had met at the house of Sidney and Beatrice Webb in 1896. She visited him in Fitzroy Square and was appalled at the mess. They married later that year.

For many years Shaw was a member of the council for St Pancras. He pointed out that the area had a population of 200,000, with plenty of 'houses of ill fame', especially around the slums of Tottenham Court Road and Warren Street, but not a single bookshop. As a member of the health committee, he visited the local workhouse, saw the sweatshops and slums, and called for measures to prevent over-crowding and for the provision of basic amenities. After much opposition, he succeeded in having the first public lavatory for women built in the area.

Novelist and essayist VIOLET PAGET (1856-1935), a lesbian, wrote under the pen-name Vernon Lee. A brilliant conversationalist, she befriended Rossetti, Wilde and the historian Walter Pater (1839-1894) and then satirised them in her novels. She was against sexual inequality, vivisection, nationalism, and war. During 1881-82, she lived at 84 Gower Street with a friend, Mary Robinson. She had a nervous breakdown when Robinson left to be married. In her dotage she needed an ear trumpet, which she only used when she herself was speaking.

In his semi-autobiographical novel, *The Private Papers of Henry Ryecroft*, GEORGE GISSING (1857-1903) recalled his student days at University College London. He was once suspended for a month for stealing money from other students – he claimed that he had needed the cash in order to help Marion Harrison, a prostitute, become an honest seamstress. In 1878 he lived in a 'rather tatty' garret on the top floor, 22 Colville Place, but soon moved to the cellar to save sixpence a week rent which, 'in those days was a great consideration, why it meant a couple of meals.' In the novel *New Grub Street* he describes a writer's struggle to make his way in London, living in such conditions, 'From a certain point of Tottenham Court Road there is visible a certain garret window…' And after paying for the essentials, there might be a little left over for books, 'volumes which cost anything between twopence and two shillings; further than that he durst not go.' None of these 'mean apartments in back streets' had washing facilities, which meant that the cloakrooms of the nearby British Museum were useful, until the museum officials put up a warning notice, 'These basins are intended for casual ablutions only.' As well as Bozier's Court, 'Boozer's Court', the alley over the road from the Horse Shoe inn (264-267 Tottenham Court), where Gissing was a regular, Gissing's other local addresses were 31 Gower Place and 70 Huntley Street. His novels about failure were a success, but they never made him rich.

JEROME K. JEROME (1859-1927) was educated at Marylebone Grammar School and lived in Whitfield Street, where he began to write *On the Stage and Off, The Brief Career of a Would-Be Actor*, about his three years of touring. To save on lighting bills he wrote some of the manuscript under the street-lights in Portland Place. He moved to Newman Street, where he met the friend upon whom he based one of the characters in his most successful novel, *Three Men in a Boat* (1889).

International pacifist and humanist historian GOLDSWORTHY DICKINSON (1862-1932), who coined the term 'league of nations' for one of his peace pamphlets, lived at 1 All Souls Place as a child, where he developed a boot fetish (he asked his brothers and sisters to tread on him). His first love affair was with the artist Roger Fry.

When the poet and playwright W.B. YEATS (1865-1939) who lived in Euston Road in 1900, was initiated into the occult society, the Hermetic Order of the Golden Dawn, at 17 Fitzroy Street in 1890, he was given the magical name *Demon est Deus inversus* (the Devil is the inverse of God). The society met in a vault in Clipstone Street. Its ceremonies were conducted by the actress Florence Farr, who had an affair with Yeats. Previously Yeats had been to meetings of The Hermetic Students Society held in the studios of artists CHARLES RICKETTS (1866-1931) and CHARLES SHANNON (1863-1937) in Charlotte Street. Interested in the supernatural, Yeats once claimed to see fairies and a hawk on a rug at a party in Fitzroy Square. His interest in mysticism influenced his early poetry, which developed through automatic writing into visionary symbolism.

Do you keep a journal of your reading? It is very interesting to do so and make slight critical notes.

George Gissing in a letter to his brother. A devoted reader all his life, he based all his friendships on a shared interest in books.

[Don't] nail the hawk on the board. The hawk is one of my symbols and you might rather crudely upset the subconscious.

W.B. Yeats in a letter to Sturge Moore, who was designing a book-plate for him.

Wells did not strut; that would have been vulgar; and Wells is not vulgar. He did not stalk or prance for he is not tall enough for such paces. He did not merely walk; he is too important for that. Having eliminated all possible alternatives, I conclude that he trotted. If not, what did he do?

Bernard Shaw replying to H.G. Wells' criticism of his description of their trip to the Soviet Union in 1930.

Ricketts and Shannon were friends with the unconventional gay poet, LIONEL JOHNSON (1867-1902). Yeats often visited him, and he was also a friend of Oscar Wilde. Johnson supported the artist Simeon Solomon after his fall from grace, and lived with the poet SELWYN IMAGE in Charlotte Street, then 20 Fitzroy Street, where he never got out of bed before seven in the evening. Before alcoholism destroyed his life, he established himself as the 'greatest English authority upon Italian life in the 15th century'.

The father of science fiction, H.G. WELLS (1866-1946) first started writing for *Tit Bits* magazine to supplement his income when he was a student at London University (and living at 181 Euston Road). In his novel, *The Invisible Man* (1897), the protagonist Griffin makes himself disappear for the first time in a 'large unfurnished room in a big ill-managed house in a slum near Great Portland Street'; the invisible cat is heard 'down a grating in Great Titchfield Street', much to the consternation of the crowd who cannot understand where the miaowing is coming from.

During the 1920s Wells shared a flat with an actress in 11 Belmont House, 5-6 Candover Street, and was a frequent dinner guest at 90 Gower Street, home of the politician Alfred Duff Cooper. Bernard Shaw sponsored Wells for membership of the Fabian Society until they fell out, partly because Shaw was unappreciative of Wells's crude cockney humour. Wells had been aroused by seeing Greek statues as a boy and spent his life seeking their real life equivalent – his Venus Urania. He married his cousin Isabel Wells, and then one of his students, Amy Robins. He also had a ten-year affair with the novelist Rebecca West (1892-1983), who had a son by him, named Anthony. She finally lost patience with Wells when he tried to move his two ex-wives into her home.

Short story writer Hector Hugh Munro (1870-1916), who published under the pseudonym SAKI, suffered malaria while serving with the Burmese police. He returned to London in 1896, and in 1909 rented rooms at 97 Mortimer Street, his last address. He was homosexual and renowned for his sense of humour. He fought in the trenches during the first world war, commenting that it was 'Awful, my dear. The noise! And the people!' Seconds after shouting at a fellow soldier, 'Put that bloody cigarette out!' he was shot through the head.

EDGAR WALLACE (1875-1932), playwright and author of *The Four Just Men* and other novels, had been abandoned as an orphan in the street. He was found, and raised by a Billingsgate fish porter. Wallace worked as a newspaper vendor, a factory hand, a Grimsby trawler boy, a milk boy, a soldier, and a war correspondent. But by the time he moved into 31 Portland Place in 1928 he was earning £50,000 a year in royalties from his novels and plays, and could afford to install a soundproof glass cabinet, from where he dictated his thrillers at the rate of 4,000 words an hour to a secretary in another room.

When he was bedridden as the result of an accident in 1914, the Scottish novelist JOHN BUCHAN (1875-1940) wrote his classic thriller, *The Thirty-Nine Steps*, which begins with the 'Portland Place murder' in the first floor flat 'behind Langham Place'. Between 1912 and 1919 Buchan and his wife, Susan Grosvenor, lived in an 18th century house (now demolished) at 76 Portland Place. They regularly had dinner with notables such as THEODORE ROOSEVELT (1858-1919, US president 1901-09), professor J.B.S. HALDANE (1892-1964, author of books popularising science), LORD MILNER (1854-1925, secretary for war 1916-19), and F.E. SMITH (1872-1930, attorney general, later the first earl of Birkenhead and the writer of books on famous trials). In 1917 Buchan was diagnosed as having a duodenal ulcer and he elected to undergo the two-hour operation at home, after which he was ordered to have a long convalescence – he used his time between and during zeppelin raids to write more thrillers. Later he was

I had never before come in contact with any one family who economised so much on themselves and gave away money so unsparingly.

Susan Grosvenor on meeting John Buchan's family

GEORGE BERNARD SHAW

*Irish writer and dramatist.
On* Pygmalion *(re-made as*
My Fair Lady)*, he
commented, 'I have not
achieved success but I have
created an uproar and the
sensation was so agreeable
that I have done it again and
again.'*

appointed Governor-General of Canada.

Following the death of her brother Thoby, and the marriage of her sister, Vanessa, to Clive Bell in 1907, novelist, critic and essayist, VIRGINIA WOOLF (nee Stephen, 1882-1941) moved into Shaw's old address, 29 Fitzroy Square, with her brother Adrian, where they stayed until the lease expired in 1911. The dilapidated Square offered cheap accommodation, but it had a rough reputation and friends begged her 'not to take the house because of the neighbourhood'. To allay their fears, she praised its charm, 'All the lights in the Square are lighting, and it is turning silver gray, and there are beautiful young women still playing tennis on the grass', although before moving in she made inquiries with the local police about its safety. The house had electricity, but she had to have a bath put in, and double-windows – the noisy traffic of vans, carts and railway vans around the square always disturbed her. On the second floor, which she had all to herself, her sitting room soon had 'great pyramids of books, with trailing mists between them; partly dust, and partly cigarette-smoke.' She decorated the drawing room with bright green carpets and red brocade (later purple) curtains, and a pianola.

She had already started to earn a living as a writer. Her first (unsigned) review had appeared in the *Guardian*, and she had been writing for the *Times Literary Supplement* since 1905. At Fitzroy Square she started her first novel, *The Voyage Out* (1915), 'I wrote it originally in a dream like state...Giving the feel of

[Though] her head was often above the clouds, her feet were firmly enough planted on the earth.

Angelica Garnett on Virginia Woolf

running water…I want to bring out a stir of live men and women, against a background. I think I am quite right to attempt it, but it is immensely difficult to do', she wrote to Clive Bell, grateful for his support, 'Ah, how you encourage me! It makes all the difference.' She broke from the tradition of the linear, plot-driven, 19th century novel, and produced modernist literature in which the shifting, interior consciousness of the character speaks directly to the reader.

She and Adrian revived the 'Thursday evenings' that had been started by Thoby Stephen and interrupted by his death. At these literary gatherings her dog, Hans, was often sick on the carpet. At the end of 1907 they embarked on regular Friday evening readings of authors ranging from the Restoration dramatists to Shakespeare, and from Swinburne to Ibsen. One of her guests, Lytton Strachey (1880-1932), proposed to her in 1909. She accepted despite knowing that he was homosexual, but the next day Strachey withdrew the offer. In 1915 Virginia married another of her guests at these gatherings, Leonard Woolf (1880-1969), with whom she founded the Hogarth Press. She endured four mental breakdowns and bouts of insanity during which she had hallucinations. In 1941, she filled her pockets with stones and drowned herself in the River Ouse, Sussex. In the suicide note that she left for her husband she wrote, 'I don't think two people could have been happier than we have been.'

The American poet Ezra Pound (1885-1972) was labelled insane and confined to a mental institution in 1945, after he was found unfit to plead against the charge of treason for his pro-Mussolini wartime broadcasts in Italy. As a young man, he had a 'fox's muzzle' beard, wore a billowing cape and a single dangling earring, and lived in Great Titchfield Street and at 8 Duchess Street (on the corner of Hallam Street). In 1908 he moved to 48 Langham Street. While there the first volume of his poems *A Lume Spento*, was published, and he made an unsatisfactory attempt at writing fiction, 'burnt m/s of damn bad novel'. In 1909 he went to the Regent Street Polytechnic and when asked if he wanted to enrol, replied that he wanted to teach; he gave courses on the development of literature in Southern Europe, and mediaeval literature. He was the driving force behind the Poet's Club, which began to meet at the Tour Eiffel, the restaurant/hotel run in Percy Street, in 1909. It was he who coined the word 'Vorticism' for the avant-garde movement launched by his friend, Percy Wyndham Lewis, with whom he produced its magazine, *Blast*. He moved to Italy in 1925, and returned there after his release in 1958.

The unexpurgated *Lady Chatterley's Lover* was finally published in 1960, 32 years after D.H. Lawrence (1885-1930) wrote it. Lawrence was living at 73 Gower Street, in 1925, when he wrote *The Plumed Serpent*, and was informed that the tuberculosis, which he had contracted in 1911, was in an advanced state. He died of the disease five years later.

Rupert Brooke (1887-1915) had his first poetry published while he was living at 76 Charlotte Street in 1911. That year he also had rooms at 21 Fitzroy Square. During the summer he and Virginia Woolf went skinny-dipping at midnight in a pond that smelled of wild peppermint and mud, after which she gave him the sobriquet 'Neo-Pagan'. Katherine 'Ka' Cox, whom he met at Cambridge University when she was treasurer of the Fabian Society, found him alternative accommodation, a 'love-nest', later that year, at 76 Charlotte Street, where he made love to her, his first time with a woman. He suffered a mental breakdown in 1913. After a farewell party 'in a dive off Regent Street', he set off for America and Tahiti, but in 1914 he joined the Royal Naval Volunteer Reserve. He wrote his patriotic and idealistic *War Sonnets* before he died in Greece, of blood poisoning, as a result of his injuries.

His fellow war poet Wilfred Owen (1893-1918) was killed a week before the first world war ended, 'I am the enemy you killed, my friend…' He had been a medical student living at 21 Devonshire Street in 1915, where he witnessed some horrifying diseases.

In 1917 the novelist and author of exquisitely subtle short stories, KATHERINE MANSFIELD (1888-1923), lived at 3 Gower Street. By then she had already married, left her husband after a few days, become pregnant by somebody else, and given birth to a still-born child in Bavaria – experiences that formed the background of her first collection of short fiction, *In a German Pension* (1911).

As German bombs fell on London during the second world war, public morale was boosted by the broadcasts of novelist and playwright, J.B. PRIESTLEY (1894-1984). In September 1940 he was nearly hit when he left his room at the Langham Hotel and crossed the road to Broadcasting House to make an unscheduled programme. He returned shortly afterwards to find that the wing of the hotel with his room was destroyed. When he aired his opinion that anyone who fled the country at the start of the war should have his or her property confiscated, Conservative MPs objected, and his broadcasts were stopped.

Playwright, literary editor and BBC producer J.R. ACKERLEY (1896-1967), who had been a prisoner of war in Germany in 1917, lived at 76 Charlotte Street in 1925. He wrote candidly of his homosexual adventures but his interests changed utterly – 'my obsession with sex fell wholly away from me' – when he acquired an Alsatian bitch named Queenie, about whom he wrote two novels, *My Dog Tulip* (1956) and *We Think the World of You* (1960).

Novelist and short story writer V.S. PRITCHETT (1900-97) lived at various addresses in Charlotte and Fitzroy Streets in the 1920s, and at 60 Fitzroy Street in the 1930s. In his two volumes of autobiography, *A Cab At The Door* and *Midnight Oil*, he describes the seediness of his rooms – one 'stank of mice,

VIRGINIA WOOLF with her father, SIR LESLIE STEPHEN, in 1902.

Following the death of Sir Leslie Stephen, a major intellectual figure of the Victorian era, in 1904, Virginia and her sister and two brothers left the sepulchral gloom of their Hyde Park mansion. In 1907 Virginia took a 5-year lease for £120 a year on 29 Fitzroy Square, where she lived with her brother Adrian, and held parties at which their friends discussed the arts and freed-up their talk, throwing off the inhibitions of the previous generation.

Rhythm is a form cut into
TIME, as a design is
determined SPACE.

Ezra Pound

Blast No.2 (1915)

*Front cover by Wyndham
Lewis.*

Group portrait of the Vorticists meeting at the Restaurant de la Tour Eiffel, Percy Street, Spring, 1915. Painted from memory by William Roberts in 1961-62

At the table on far left is Ezra Pound. In the centre, wearing a hat, is Wyndham Lewis. Next to him is the restaurant's waiter, Joe, and on the right, the chef-patron Rudolph Stulik, with one of his specialities, Gâteau St Honoré.

which scampered out of a safe where stale food had been left' – and the rowdiness of the street, 'At night it was not uncommon to see a policeman struggling on the pavement with a man he was arresting while the small hostile London crowd stood by watching fair play.' During the day the air was full of the noise of lathes from local workshops, and alcoholics were not uncommon, 'There were several cases of DTs. I remember a man racing along demented, driving off imaginary rats from his throat.'

On arriving in London, the South African poet ROY CAMPBELL (1901-57) became friendly with Augustus John, whose 'careless buccaneer air' had attracted him. An art student, Mary Garman, took a liking to Campbell on a bus, and followed him to the Tour Eiffel restaurant in Percy Street, where she went up to him and introduced herself. In 1922 she and Campbell had a gypsy wedding, hosted by Augustus John. They went to Wales, where they lived in a cowshed, made love on the cliff tops, and went poaching at night. Their first daughter, Teresa, was born in 1923. That year they returned to Fitzrovia, and Campbell's *The Flaming Terrapin* was accepted for publication. They lived at 90 Charlotte Street, where Roy's cousin, Natalie, visited them, and was shocked at their poverty. Campbell liked to take baby Teresa, strapped African-style on his back, for long walks in London.

Mary had an affair with the poet Vita Sackville-West but when Campbell tried to unburden himself to one of the Bloomsbury group he was told, 'Fancy being cuckolded by a woman.' Campbell's animosity for the members of the Bloomsbury group deepened when he was ostracised for *The Flowering Rifle*, in which he expressed the pro-facist views that he formulated in 1936 as a result of seeing Spanish republicans shoot 17 monks and burn their library of books during the civil war. But he described himself as an anarchist at heart – he volunteered to fight fascism in the war and he fought apartheid in his native South Africa. In 1941 the family returned to London and took rooms at 8 Conway Street, where Dylan Thomas and his wife Caitlin were staying. Campbell volunteered for the army and trained for jungle warfare but was discharged after breaking his hip and contracting malaria.

At the end of the second world war Campbell became a producer for the Third Programme (precursor to Radio Three). He was often seen in the pub favoured by the BBC editors and producers, the George, wearing his riding chaps and a picador's hat. In the same pub he once punched the poet LOUIS MACNEICE (1907-63) in the mouth during an argument. But MacNeice, as Tony van den Bergh (1916-2000) recalled, did not lose his aplomb, 'MacNeice, with admirable self-control, staunched the blood with a white silk handkerchief, and quietly remarked, "There is no need to behave like that, Campbell". They then bought each other pints and always defended each other against criticism from others.'

Campbell's other drinking companions at the George included writers W.R. 'BERTIE' ROGERS (an ex-parson who was de-frocked for living up to his surname), and JULIAN MACLAREN-ROSS (1912-64). When MacLaren-Ross first arrived in London, he met J. Meary Tambimuttu, who persuaded him to visit the pubs of Fitzrovia, warning him that they could be too seductive, '"Only beware of Fitzrovia", Tambi said…with a flicker of his amazing fingers. "It's a dangerous place, you must be careful." "Fights with knives?" "No, a worse danger. You might get Sohoitis you know." "No I don't. What is it?" "If you get Sohoitis", Tambi said very seriously, "you will stay there always day and night and get no work done ever."'

In the 1940s MacLaren-Ross published short stories, two novels, three volumes of memoirs (the decade's definitive portrait of Fitzrovia), worked on film scripts and contributed to literary magazines. But by the 1950s he was a penniless and somewhat sinister figure amongst the black-clad Beat generation, with his shabby officer's overcoat and silver-knobbed cane. He sponged drinks and delivered drink-fuelled monologues barely enlivened by his fantastical character impressions. He had been court-martialled in the war, and he once saw a man kicked to death outside the Marquis of Granby at 2 Rathbone Street. The character called X.Trapnel, in Anthony Powell's series of novels, *A Dance to the Music of Time*, is based on him.

In 1953, when Roy Campbell was in America, he heard that DYLAN THOMAS (1914-53), who was touring America for the fourth time (where he was paid huge fees and an audience of a thousand would come to hear him read), had died, after four days in a coma. Campbell commented that whiskey, 'American hospitality' no doubt played a part. While the cause of Dylan Thomas' death has been argued over, his consumption of alcohol was legendary: his last words were, 'I've drunk 18 straight whiskies…I think that's the record.' At a boozing session Thomas and Campbell once munched daffodils on St David's Day in response to a bet, and at Dylan's funeral an inebriated Louis MacNeice 'threw his sandwiches on the coffin in the belief that they were a bunch of daffodils.'

Dylan's innovative poetry continues to have a popular resonance, but he was poor and unknown when he first moved to London in 1934 and found Fitzrovia's pubs. Nina Hamnett introduced him to Augustus John in the Fitzroy Tavern. John later remarked that Dylan became 'repetitive and tiresome' when drunk. Of course, John had another reason to be bitter, for it was Thomas who won their rivalry for Caitlin Macnamara, the beautiful, eccentric dancer and sometime model.

Caitlin Macnamara walked into the Wheatsheaf, Rathbone Place, with Augustus John in April 1936 – Dylan was later to crow that he and Caitlin had rushed off and spent five nights together in the hotel rooms of the Tour Eiffel. Caitlin once likened Augustus John to some unsatisfactory Pan, saying that he had 'leaped on her, ripped off her clothes and penetrated her like some mindless hairy goat.' Caitlin and Dylan Thomas married in 1937, but not before the ceremony had been postponed twice because they had spent the licence fee on drink.

Thomas felt pulled constantly between Wales and London. The city was stimulating, but at the cost of drunkenness – it was his 'capital punishment'. He was once thrown out of one of Fitzrovia's afternoon drinking dens, the Rathbone Arts Club (in the basement of 28 Rathbone Place), even though, by then, he was a media celebrity. Compulsively in debt, despite the earnings that fame brought him, his survival owed much to the generosity of his patron, Margaret Taylor. When she tried to track him down at the Stag's head, 102 New Cavendish Street, where he usually started his drinking day, he hid behind the bar, from where 'his hand would sneak round the flap, groping for another pint.'

While Dylan was living at 8 Conway Street in 1941 Ivan Moffat helped him to find work writing scripts for the ministry of information. In 1944 Dylan moved into the top floor flat at 12 Fitzroy Street – 'not without some disturbance to other tenants in the house', including composer Elizabeth Lutyens.

After the war he did readings at Broadcasting House, and would often stop for a glass of Frascati on the way with Michael Ayrton at 4 All Souls' Place. At the Wheatsheaf he might recite passages of *Under Milk Wood* (including parts later censored), which he finished writing the year he died.

Composer of orchestral works under the name of Joseph Kell, but better known as the author of *A Clockwork Orange*, ANTHONY BURGESS (1917-93), spent

[The] green light flickered and Dylan, short, bandy, prime, obese and famous among the bards screamed as I have never heard, but sometimes imagined a scream, and we were all appalled, our pencils silent, above the crossword puzzles, and invisible centuries-gone atavistic hair rose on our backs.

Actor Richard Burton on hearing Dylan Thomas scream 'Mam! Mam!' for a BBC radio play.

ALF KLEIN depicted on a beer mat.

time during his war leave in Fitzrovia. In his autobiography *Little Wilson and Big God*, he wrote that he and his first wife, Lynne, were having a drink in the Duke of York, between Charlotte Place and Rathbone Street, 'Jekyll and Hyde Alley', when Pirelli's mob, the infamous razor gang, swaggered in. The gang proceeded to order pints of bitter, and refused to pay for them. They poured the drink on the floor, threw the glasses at the wall, and threatened the customers with the 'jagged butts'. When Lynne said that it was a dreadful waste of good beer, the gang told her to drink up and ordered a succession of pints. She downed three with no trouble. The leader was impressed, 'You're a good kid, you are,' he said, 'If you're ever in trouble with those bastards of O'Flaherty's or the Maltese mob you just call on Pirelli.' He threw some fivers on the bar before stalking out.

Shortly afterwards the pub landlord Major Alf Klein, 'an irritable but sometimes generous man whose whisky intake was formidable', bought a giant bloodhound named Colonel as a guard dog. It later appeared in the film *Hound of the Baskervilles*. Major Klein ran the pub from 1938 until his death in 1964. He quirkily initiated all his new male customers by snipping off the ends of their ties and hanging them behind the bar – his final collection of tie-trophies numbered over 1,500.

Burgess went to the Wheatsheaf, 25 Rathbone Place, which became the haunt of the literary and arty crowd during the 1940s, escaping the tourists who flocked to the Fitzroy. A prostitute called Sister Ann, dressed in tweed suits, plied her trade between the Wheatsheaf and the Guinness Clock in Tottenham Court Road. At the Marquis of Granby, Rathbone Street, which operated under Westminster's licensing laws, and stayed open until 10.30 p.m. Paul, the bearded, homosexual pianist, who wore gold earrings, would chirp, 'My dear, this boogie-woogie makes me wet my knickers. I prefer something more raffine.' For more privacy, there was the Bricklayers Arms, 31 Gresse Street, also known as the Burglars Rest, because a robber once broke into the premises, and drank so much of the stock that he passed out, and was found on the floor the next morning.

At the Wheatsheaf Burgess often saw George Orwell (1903-50) who was working as overseas literary producer at the makeshift BBC studios on the corner of Oxford Circus (200 Oxford Street), during the second world war, from where he broadcast allied war propaganda to the Far East. Later Malcolm Muggeridge told him that the signal was so weak that no one would have heard a word. Orwell also worked at Broadcasting House – joining others who would go for a drink at the George – and at the ministry of information, Senate House, in nearby Malet Street. He used this war experience to write his novel *Nineteen-Eighty-Four*: the blitz-damaged city, the food and drink restrictions (margarine instead of butter, saccharine instead of sugar), the bureaucracy, and the disinformation of Newspeak. The Prole's pub in the novel is based on the Newman Arms. The original of the room where Julie and Winston conduct their dangerous affair is at 18 Percy Street (where his second wife, Sonia Brownell, lived during the 1940s). The novel was published in 1949. In September that year Orwell, who was suffering tuberculosis, was admitted to University College Hospital. In a bedside ceremony, he married Sonia, 'the Venus of Euston Road' (who was then living in a flat in Charlotte Street). He died in January, and the funeral was at Christ Church, Albany Street, just north of Great Portland Street.

In 1932 the poet and playwright W.H. Auden (1907-73) lived at 46 Fitzroy Street with Rupert Doone, who produced some of his plays. Three years later Auden married Erika Mann to provide her with a British passport, allowing her to escape from Nazi Germany, where she had been declared an enemy of

Good prose is like a window pane.

George Orwell

the Third Reich. In 1937 he volunteered for the republicans in the Spanish Civil War. He was an ambulance driver and stretcher-bearer. After he fled to the United States at the start of the second world war, one of his followers said to Stephen Spender, 'He told us that the duty of all was to fight Fascism, and then he went away.'

Author and playwright BRENDAN BEHAN (1923-64) first encountered Fitzrovia in Easter, 1939, when the Irish Republican Army (IRA) sent him as a courier to Goodge Street station. He was told to deliver an envelope to a man reading *Picture Post*, using the coded introduction, 'Can I have a look at your magazine?' On his arrival he saw only a woman reading *Picture Post*. Thinking that she must be his contact, he spoke the words, and she screeched that he

DYLAN THOMAS

The poet Dylan Thomas could lose whole days in Fitzrovia's pubs and illegal after-hours clubs. 'He needed London for talking and pubbing', said his wife Caitlin, 'but he could only write away from it.'

BEHAN TYPING (1952) *Irish dramatist Brendan Behan, a Dublin intellectual and ex-borstal boy, who acquired legendary fame by the age of 29, through his IRA exploits, and as a writer, singer and radio personality.*

was trying to pick her up. A hand gripped his shoulder and he braced himself against arrest, but it was his IRA contact, who had arrived late. Not long afterwards Behan was found in possession of explosives and he was sent to Borstal for three years. On his release in 1942 he shot at two detectives while resisting arrest for another offence, and was sentenced to 14 years. He was let out under an amnesty in 1946.

His best known plays during the 1950s were *The Hostage* and *The Quare Fellow*, both directed by Joan Littlewood. Because she had extensively re-written the latter, the joke in the Fitzroy, where he drank, was that, while Dylan Thomas wrote *Under Milk Wood*, Brendan Behan wrote 'under Joan Littlewood'.

Behan collapsed after a three-day drinking binge in 1960, and dried out at Middlesex Hospital, where he stayed for two months. He resisted the doctors' attempts to have him admitted to a psychiatric ward, believing that treatment would destroy the source of his creativity.

JAMES MEARY TAMBIMUTTU (1915-83), the poet and founder-editor of *Poetry London*, arrived in London from Sri Lanka in 1938. He showed his first secretary, Kitty, from Oxford, the pile of manuscripts accumulated in his room at 45 Howland Street, saying that perhaps 'the rats have eaten some', and asked her to write to their authors. He then 'borrowed' £5 from her, to have lunch with T.S. Eliot. Eliot had been impressed by him and helped him to start the review. When Tambimuttu moved to Whitfield Street, the manuscripts were flung, just as carelessly, into an empty chamber pot. To an author who threatened him over a delay in publication he replied blithely, 'I haven't a European conception of time.' His evening pub route took in the Wheatsheaf, the Bricklayers Arms, the Fitzroy Tavern, and ended at the Newman Arms (then known as the Beer House because it lacked a spirit licence). By the time the 1950s arrived, with its 'dry cold wind' of academia, the quarterly had ceased to publish, and Tambimuttu decided to return to Sri Lanka.

Julian Maclaren-Ross described their last meeting. After he bought Tambimuttu 'a hamburger and chips in some Charlotte Street café', Tambimutu said to him and his girlfriend, that, 'being a Prince in his own country, he would arrange for us a truly royal reception, should we ever decide to visit... "A feast", he said, "and the food will be served on plates of gold." His tongue flicked out to absorb a last morsel of hamburger clinging to the corner of his mouth. "Gold dust will be smeared upon the meat".'

In 1948 JAMES KIRKUP (b.1918), poet and travel writer, rented a room above a shoe shop at 77A Tottenham Court Road, for 30s. a week, where his landlady was Madame Sheba. A large and formidable black woman from South Africa, she was often raided by police, who were deeply suspicious of the fact that Africans and West Indians visited the premises at all hours of the day or night and played township jive.

Madame Sheba introduced Kirkup (known as 'Cock-up' by the other lodgers, mostly West Indian immigrants) to the area's drinking and music clubs, such as the Moonglow in Percy Street. In his autobiographies *I, Of All People* and *A Poet Could Not But Be Gay*, Kirkup wrote that he found it thrilling to mix with the *louche* clientele at the Fitzroy Tavern, 'London's most notorious bohemian pub, where the Union Jacks hung down from the grimy ceiling like unmade beds.' But even the Fitzroy refused him entry when he arrived with his room-mate Errol, a limbo-dancing West Indian who had peroxided his moustache, armpits and pubic hair.

He liked the Black Horse for its decadence – the upstairs billiard table made do as a bed for drunks or sex – and he went to the Duke of Wellington in Charlotte Street. After closing time, he hung out in the all-night drinking clubs, with the spivs and dodgy car dealers from Warren Street. He also sought out the dance halls of Tottenham Court Road, which 'thronged with vital, lissom figures of wildly carefree blacks dancing with a gay vigour and abandon unequalled anywhere else in the world.'

In 1977 the charge of blasphemous libel was resurrected, and used for the first time in 50 years, against *Gay News*, for publishing Kirkup's poem *The love that dares to speak its name*. The prosecution was upheld – the editor was fined and given a suspended prison sentence.

Novelist COLIN MACINNES (1914-76) lived at 29 Great Portland Street and 28 Tottenham Street. A member of the Moonglow, he featured the club in his *City of Spades*. Like his friend Kirkup he was bisexual. He described Fitzrovia's black and gay culture, the casual sex, the violence and racial tension, in his novels *City of Spades* and *Mr Love and Justice* (1957-60).

DORIS LESSING (b.1919) wrote her celebrated novel *The Golden Notebook* depicting a woman writer in the throes of a breakdown, in the tiny, fourth floor flat at Holbein Mansions, 25 Langham Street, where she lived from 1958 to 1962, with her son Peter. Lessing has described the novel as a warning against the way divisions such as race, gender or age, 'false dichotomies', can

Every man has poetry within him. Poetry is the awareness of the mind to the universe.

James Meary Tambimuttu

I later discovered that she judged people's character by the way they closed doors.

James Kirkup on his first visit to the flat owned by Madame Sheba, who rented him a room.

[What] elation, what
pleasure, and feelings of
achievement: we really did
feel that this was a step
forward for all humankind.

Doris Lessing on watching
for the Russian Sputnik
from the roof of the flats
in Langham Place

'make us look for what separates us rather than what we have in common.' Reviewers at first panned the book as shockingly feminist, 'They were so disturbed by the sex war aspects of the novel they did not see anything else.' The flat had been offered to her by the socialist, self-made millionaire publisher, Howard Samuels, at the low rent of £5 a week. She painted the bedroom white, with one dark plum wall to disguise the ugly fireplace, and sewed the curtains on an old Singer. She enjoyed its proximity to the theatre, from which she was never afraid of walking home alone late at night. Two prostitutes lived in the same building she used one as the model for 'Mrs Fortescue' in a short story. She liked to sunbathe on the roof, from where she could hear the shouts of the market stalls floating up from below, 'people came from the BBC to get vegetables'. She took visiting Americans to the local Jewish restaurant, which had good cheap food, but when Mordecai Richler tried to persuade her to enjoy stuffed chicken necks, she told him he was 'eating nostalgic memories of childhood.' Her most 'improbable' visitor was Henry Kissinger, who wanted to meet campaigners for nuclear disarmament.

In 1949 crime novelist P.D. JAMES (b.1920), now Baroness James, worked as a clerical assistant at the London Skin Hospital, 40 Fitzroy Square (founded 1891). It was run by Mrs McBain, 'an intimidating, woman, grey-haired, stocky and with the face of an angry Pekinese', who, because she feared that the new National Health Service would mean state bureaucracy, would pretend to forget the names of familiar patients, 'You're just a number to us now.' James herself welcomed the introduction of free health care, because she remembered the agonies suffered by her mother who had been unable to afford treatment for kidney stones. James, who first began to write detective stories in order to support her family, was awarded the crime writers' Diamond Dagger in 1987.

The unrepentantly alcoholic columnist, JEFFREY BERNARD (1932-97) was only 15 years old but pretending to be 18, and dressed in his nautical cadet uniform, when he met 19-year-old Anna Grice, in the Duke of York in Rathbone Street in 1947. They played a game of darts and at closing time he walked her to the tube station. They were to meet by chance three more times, and they married in 1951. In 1994 he had his foot amputated at the Middlesex, where he was also treated for diabetes until his death.

[He] closes his veins each
day with sixty cigarettes
and then opens them again
with a bottle of vodka.

Middlesex hospital
specialist on Jeffrey
Bernard

Playwright JOE ORTON (1933-67) lived in the basement at 31 Gower Street in 1951, after he had won a scholarship to RADA – where he first met Kenneth Halliwell, his lover (who hammered him to death and then committed suicide).

An innovative publishing house, Allison & Busby, was set up in the 1960s, at 11 Fitzroy Square, where its co-founder, MARGERET BUSBY, (born in Guyana in the 1940s, and educated in England) had her first publishing job with a literary publisher, Cresset Press. She and Clive Allison had met at a party during their last term at Oxford University and, not knowing what they would do after graduation, conceived the idea of founding a publishing company, 'We didn't know what we were doing', says Margaret, 'we just had ideals. I suppose I would describe myself as an internationalist. We were going to publish what no one else was'. They sublet an office from Merlin Press, who published Hoffman, the music cartoonist, and brought out cheap, 5s. paperback editions of poetry in their first year, 1967. Two years later they published their first fiction, and initiated the practice of publishing quality paperbacks, 'Alternative Editions'.

Literary agent DEBORAH ROGERS took the top floor office over a fish and chip shop at 29 Goodge Street in the 1960s, and had offices at 5 Mortimer

Street from 1978 to 1983. She was the agent for John Pearson, author of a biography of the Kray brothers, *Profession of Violence* (1972). The Krays contacted Pearson only a week after they had murdered Jack the Hat McVitie. Knowing that they were going to be caught, and, hungry for publicity, they wanted to promote their public reputation, 'What mattered to them was their legend.'

Attempts were made to suppress the biography when it was first published. The Goodge Street offices were burgled, and papers relating to Lord Boothby and the Krays were stolen. 'It was quite a colourful episode', Deborah Rogers remembers. In 1995, Pearson wrote, 'To this day I have no idea who raided my agent's office and my home to steal some letters I possessed from Lord Boothby to the Krays. At the same time lawyers acting for Boothby made it all too clear that I proceeded at my peril if I tried to publish all I knew.'

In 1972 JOHN BOOTH and WILLIAM MILLER started their publishing business, Quartet Books, in two rooms which they rented from Deborah Rogers, whose Goodge Street office had expanded to two floors below. Quartet announced that they would be the first to integrate the two divisions of publishing, hardback and paperback, under the same imprint. At the time readers were accustomed to waiting months or even years before a paperback edition of a traditional casebound book appeared, and Quartet had picked up on the idea

> **Surely the civil-rights and women's movement affected the choices of publishers: an audience can only respond to what is presented to them, and how.**
>
> Margaret Busby

DORIS LESSING (1962)

Ground-breaking writer Doris Lessing arrived from Africa in 1949, with her son and the manuscript of her first novel. When she moved into Langham Place in 1958, she noticed that war-damaged London was being transformed. 'For instance, a band called the Happy Wanderers played traditional jazz up and down Oxford Street, which made it a pleasure to go shopping. Window boxes and hanging baskets and decorous little trees in tubs were appearing in new-painted streets.'

of also publishing quality paperbacks ('Midway' editions). Quartet moved next door to 27 Goodge Street, where they partnered the first feminist publishing house, Virago, launched by its founder, CARMEN CALLIL (b.1938), in September 1973 (producing its first eight titles from September 1975, and going independent). In an early report for Quartet, Carmen listed all the Oxford dictionary definitions of 'virago' and quoted from Pope,

> *To arms! To arms! the fierce virago cries*
> *And swift as lightening to the combat flies.*

When NAIM ATALLAH (b.1931) bought Quartet Books in 1974, he already knew the area from his days as an impoverished student, 'I used to go to discos and jazz clubs in Soho and Tottenham Court Road, and really loved Charlotte Street, which has always been cosmopolitan and alive.' The son of a Barclays bank cashier, he was born in Haifa, a town then in Palestine. He showed an early interest in journalism, producing at the age of nine *The Palestine Gazette*, based on radio news items, which he sold to friends and relatives. But his parents considered journalism too dangerous an occupation in the Middle East, and in 1949 despatched him to London to study engineering. After 18 months, the Israeli government put a stop to money going abroad, including the fees for Naim's college. With only a student visa, he was told he would have to leave the country. He appealed, his case went to the House of Commons, and he was allowed to stay as an unskilled labourer. For five years he worked in a variety of manual jobs, including a stint as a porter at Elizabeth Garrett Anderson hospital. 'When I got married we lived in one room and could not even afford the bus to work, so had to walk,' he said. Eventually the home office restrictions were lifted, and he began work as a foreign exchange dealer for a French bank in the City. He founded his own company, Namara, and realised his dream of becoming a publisher by buying Quartet with the aid of a bank loan. To counter what he called the 'deadly prejudice of the literary ruling class', he gave 'bigger parties', and courted young, well-connected, female literary talent, 'establishing Quartet as a finishing school for talented society gels' (including Sophia Sackville-West, Daisy Waugh, Emma Soames and Nigella Lawson). In 1977 Attallah supported the foundation of another feminist imprint, the Women's Press. His other ventures have included magazines, the *Oldie* and the *Literary Review*, as well as films and plays. For his first, and best-known book of interviews, *Women* (1987), he questioned almost 300 women about sex, feminism and motherhood. When publicising *Dialogues*, (2000), an anthology of interviews, he said he intended to sell all his publishing interests and retire to France.

Playwright, author, and poet HEATHCOTE WILLIAMS (b.1941), lived with a striptease artist in Howland Street when he was 20 years old. 'She had a merkin – pubic wig', he remembered, 'because strippers were then forbidden to be entirely nude.' Years later he organised a squat in empty houses in Goodge Place, under the auspices of the Ruff Tuff Creem Puff Estate Agency, 'founded by Wat Tyler in 1321 – we will squat the building of your choice.'

Children's author MICHAEL ROSEN (b.1946), a medical student at Middlesex Hospital from 1964 to 1967, was blacklisted as a communist in 1972 and sacked from his job as a trainee at Broadcasting House, although he had revised his views and no longer thought 'that the Soviet Union was anything to do with socialism.' He was diplomatically informed that he would fare better as a freelance, which proved to be the case.

DENNIS POTTER (1935-94), the television playwright who continued writing regardless of the ravages of psoriasis and later the cancer that killed him, bought Flat 2, Collingwood House (on the north east corner of Great Titchfield Street and New Cavendish Street) in 1981. It was close to his favourite haunts, including the Needles wine bar (5 Clipstone Street), and the Regents Hotel bar, 25 Carburton Street, (where he and actress Kika Markham assumed the roles of his fictitious characters, and acted them out while meeting socially). He used the flat when in London, and while writing his last two television plays *Karaoke* and *Cold Lazarus*.

Of authors currently living in the area, ELISABETH BROOKE, a self-declared Aires witch, is one of the most prolific. Writer on goddesses, witches, and herbalism, she moved to 27 Langham Street in 1984 and now has a flat in Great Titchfield Street.

Time is a false alarm.

Heathcote Williams

On saying I am a witch, people often jokingly ask if I can do a spell for them; sometimes they are not joking. Spells are acts of will which can transform reality.

Elisabeth Brooke

CHAPTER 8
Worthy Persons

The evangelical preacher GEORGE WHITEFIELD (1714-70) had a tabernacle built in 1756 at 79 Tottenham Court Road, where he attracted huge congregations with the hell-fire fervour of his sermons and his melodramatic delivery, projecting his voice, stamping his feet and rolling his eyes heavenwards. Although the ecclesiastical authorities refused to consecrate the site Whitefield was not to be defeated, and arranged for a delivery of topsoil from another churchyard to give the grounds a sacramental layer, a 'surface' consecration. The front was extended in 1760, making it the largest nonconformist church in the world, capable of seating up to 8,000 people. It became known as the 'soul trap' and stood for a century, before it needed repair. (It was destroyed by enemy action in the second world war. The American Church now stands on the site.)

Whitefield enraged the aristocracy by denouncing the high and mighty as sinners – 'It is monstrous to be told that you have a heart as sinful as the common wretches that crawl on the earth', complained the Duchess of Buckingham. His admirers included Horace Walpole, David Garrick (who once said he would give a hundred guineas to deliver 'oh' with the same pathos as Whitefield) and William Hogarth (who drew Whitefield firing up from 'Blood Heat' to 'Bull Roar' in *Enthusiasm Delineated*). In 1761 Whitefield travelled to America (he made 17 visits in all) where his bombastic open-air preaching drew crowds of up to 30,000.

Preachers who succeeded him at the chapel included the hymnwriter and founder of Methodism, JOHN WESLEY (1703-91), and HENRY PECKWELL, whose last sermon, uttered with his dying breaths as a result of an infection he had caught officiating at the funeral of a putrid corpse, moved his congregation to tears.

In 1798 bodysnatchers were caught stealing eight corpses from the tabernacle's burial grounds. A contemporary of Whitefield's, the anatomist and surgeon WILLIAM HUNTER (1718-83), received many of these while practising at Middlesex Hospital, and its medical school, then at 8-10 Windmill Street. When over a hundred bodies were discovered, concealed in a Tottenham Court Road shed in 1776, it was suspected that they were destined for Hunter.

The philosopher JEREMY BENTHAM (1748-1832) was one of the founders of University College at 43 Gower Street. Established in 1826 as a non-sectarian college 'open to members of all religions or none', it was soon known as 'Godless Gower Street'. Prolific author and advocate of utilitarianism, 'the rightness of an action is to be judged by the contribution it makes to the increase of human happiness', Bentham was an early proponent of women's rights, sexual freedom, and the welfare state. Forced into a career in law he became one of the most outspoken critics of the British judicial system, saying that while justice was denied to the poorest 90 per cent of the population, it was sold 'at an unconscionable' price to the richest ten per cent. His campaigns for law and prison reform were acclaimed internationally and he was invited as a guest of honour to the French Courts of Justice in 1825.

God trusted man once, he set Adam up, gave him a blessed stock, placed him in a paradise of love, and he soon became a bankrupt, some think in twenty-four hours, however all agree it was in six or seven days.

George Whitefield

UNDERGROUND SHELTER

George Caffell forced open the gates to Goodge Street station, liberating the tube for use as an underground shelter against bombing raids during the second world war.

His skeleton, padded out, fully dressed, is in a display case in the north building of the South Cloisters of University College London (UCL), Gower Street. The head is a wax effigy since the students used the embalmed original once too often as a football. To discourage the practice of body snatching, Bentham chose to donate his corpse for medical research – the room was lit with flashes of lightning during a violent thunderstorm while it was dissected.

In life Bentham cut an extraordinary figure, with his long white hair, yellow straw hat and embroidered carpet slippers. He called himself 'the hermit', kept both a cat and a mouse, and gave pet names to familiar objects – his teapot was 'Dick' and his walking stick 'Dapple'. He invented a type of refrigerator, and coined words such as 'international' and 'codify'

The Jeremy Bentham pub, 31 University Street, carries his name, and his ghost is said to chase the staff around the corridors of University College, waving Dapple.

The first major operation in Europe using general anaesthetic was performed by the great Scottish surgeon ROBERT LISTON (1794-1847), at University College hospital (a plaque at 52 Gower Street honours his memory). On December 19, 1846, he amputated the leg of the patient, Frederick Churchill, who felt no pain, and the operation took less than thirty seconds. Once when Liston's knife slipped he cut off a patient's testicle.

As a boisterous medical student he took up boxing, where he made friends with Ben Crouch, leader of a body-snatching gang. He and Crouch dug up the body of someone who had died of a rare disease. They put it in a sack and concealed it under a nearby hedge, then repaired to a tavern for a drink. Liston flirted with a the barmaid, but her brother found the sack, which he assumed to be filled with thief's booty, and hauled it to the pub. When he opened it, he and his sister ran off in revulsion, while Liston and Crouch downed their ale before they took the body away. There is a statue of Crouch in the Ben Crouch Tavern at 77A Wells Street.

The Middlesex Hospital was funded by the charity subscriptions of a group of humanitarian, wealthy citizens, including Samuel Whitbread, whose endowment for a cancer ward introduced the specialist interest at the hospital that has continued to the present-day. The ghost of a nurse, wearing a grey uniform, was reported standing beside anyone about to die in the Nassau Street cancer ward during the 1920s, and last sighted in 1931.

The ghost of LIZZIE CHURCH who was a trainee nurse at the end of the 19th century, is said to keep watch over patients injected with morphine at the University College Hospital, Gower Street. Lizzie mistakenly killed her lover by giving him an overdose of morphine, and her ghost is said to hover to make sure that the mistake is not repeated.

Appointed Architect to the King in 1760, SIR WILLIAM CHAMBERS (1726-96), began designing, and partly financing, the building of town houses in Berners Street in 1764. These were Nos. 15, 19 and 55, and his own, at No.13, then at No.53, where he lived from 1769 to 1807. The house, which had fine stone doorways, terminated in a stable. He used an adjacent large room for a drawing office, which his assistants could enter via the mews behind the house. Chambers was greatly respected for his eclectic, if conservative, synthesis of classical styles, producing eminent, rather solemn buildings such as Somerset House, in the Strand. Yet he decorated the back of his Berners Street house with elegant, *papier-mâché* chinoiserie, and wrote a fanciful dissertation on oriental gardening, meant to inspire a more imaginative approach than the 'naturalistic' lawns styled by 'Capability Brown'. The book was derided by Horace Walpole, 'more extravagant than the worst Chinese paper', but when published in France, it had enormous influence over the

French style of gardening. He had an intense interest in painting and sculpture, 'architecture is indebted to sculpture for a great deal of its magnificence'. He also designed a house in Bolsover (*Norton*) Street, where he died.

GEORGE DANCE the Younger (1741-1825), the architect of Newgate prison, which replaced the old gatehouse jail, bizarrely decorated the entrance with a pair of iron shackles. He developed a geometric, Neo-classical, style, influenced by Giovanni Batttista Piranesi, whom he met in Rome. In the 1790s he designed the ensemble of North and South Crescent linked by Alfred Place. He lived and died at 91 (*Upper Gower*) Gower Street.

The architect THOMAS HARDWICK (1752-1829) undertook a major renovation of St Paul's in 1788, including re-facing the interior with stone. His work was destroyed by fire in September 1795, and the building had to be restored once more. He designed St Pancras workhouse, and lived at 53 and 55 Berners Street, and 64 Bolsover (*Upper Norton*) Street.

GEORGE WHITEFIELD, with a congregation of five, by John Wollaston (1742)

Lord Chesterfield was so overcome on hearing Whitefield preach in the Tottenham Court Road tabernacle that, when he heard him compare a sinner to a blind man who, losing both guide dog and cane, is about to step into a yawning chasm, he jumped to his feet exclaiming, 'Good God! He's gone! He's gone!'

SIR ROBERT SMIRKE (1781-1867), a successful architect who travelled in Italy and Greece, and was elected to the Royal Academy at the age of 30, lived at 81 Charlotte Street, 13 Berners Street, and the top end of Fitzroy (3 *Upper Fitzroy*) Street. He had a strong interest in the technical aspects of his designs but his preference for simplicity sometimes produced dull buildings. His best-known work, a homage to Greek architecture, is the British Museum, which was completed in 1847.

Two future American presidents visited another architect, JOHN PARADISE and his American wife LUCY LUDWELL, at 13-17 Mortimer (*28 Charles*) Street. The first was JOHN ADAMS (1735-1826, president 1797-1801), who was amused by the petulant Lucy's antics: she broke plates over the heads of servants if they annoyed her, and poured tea on guests she found displeasing. The second was THOMAS JEFFERSON (1743-1826, president 1801-09), who drafted the declaration of independence of the United States of America, inscribing the hallowed line, 'we hold these truths to be self-evident – that all men are created equal.'

Another future US president and temporary Fitzrovian resident, JAMES MONROE (1758-1831), president 1817-25, then a diplomat) lived in Portland Place in 1805. More recently, DWIGHT D. EISENHOWER (1890-1969, president 1953-61), occupied the deep-level war shelter under Goodge Street tube station when he took part in planning the 1944 invasion of France. The Eisenhower Centre for Security Archives is now across the road in Chenies Street. During the second world war, the Scala, in Tottenham Street, was turned into the United States Theatre Unit Base. RONALD REAGAN (b.1911) went to the Scala as the guest of Ben Lyons and Bebe Daniels to record the radio comedy *Hi Gang*. After he was elected US president (1981-89), Reagan made a visit to University College, London, in 1988. During the visit his body-guards nipped across to visit the strip clubs, the Capricorn and Jack's, in Goodge Street.

Leading anti-slavery campaigner and proponent of reform, WILLIAM WILBERFORCE (1759-1833), preached at the Percy Chapel, 15-17 Charlotte Street – unexpectedly, he was also a heavy gambler and an opium addict. The chapel was later taken over by a fiery poet, ROBERT 'SATAN' MONTGOMERY, who officiated from 1836 to 1838 and 1843 to 1855.

A craze for ballooning followed the first sensational balloon assents in France in 1783, using hot air and then hydrogen. The pioneering Italian balloonist, COUNT ZEMBECCARI, flew the first small hydrogen balloons over London. In 1785 he took off from Hall's Cheap Bread Warehouse, on Tottenham Court Road, opposite Whitefield's Tabernacle. He had planned to take with him a Miss Grist, but she had to be jettisoned with 'gentle force', at the last minute, because the balloon was carrying too much weight. His other passenger was Admiral Sir Edward Vernon. The balloon soared upwards, but was blown into a snowstorm. Three of its ropes were broken in the fierce weather and it was forced to land many miles away. On 13 May, 1785, VINCENZIO LUNARDI took off on his maiden flight, from the Honourable Artillery Company ground, and descended at the Adam and Eve Tea Gardens, at the top of Tottenham Court Road, within 20 minutes. 'He was immediately surrounded by great numbers of the populace and though he proposed re-ascending they were not to be dissuaded from bearing him in triumph on their shoulders.' Lunardi exhibited his balloon at the Oxford Street Pantheon, which earned him enough money to make a further attempt the following year. Later he took the first woman to fly in a balloon, Mrs Sage. Seventy years later French balloonist M GARDONIA also flew from the Adam and Eve, only to fall from his craft while drifting over St Giles's cemetery, injuring his head against a gravestone.

Using water from the pond pump in Rathbone Place, the natural

THE AUTO-ICON OF JEREMY BENTHAM

This dressed-up skeleton of Jeremy Bentham, one of the founders of the University College, is wheeled out once a year to preside over a dinner of distinguished medical doctors. 'He was a boy to the last' wrote John Stuart Mill, 'Self-consciousness...never was awakened in him.'

You can tell a lot about a fellow's character by his way of eating jelly beans.

Ronald Reagan

philosopher HENRY CAVENDISH (1731-1810) conducted his inductive experiments which showed that hydrogen would combine with oxygen to form water, so proving that this liquid was not, after all, one of the basic elements. A wealthy and morbidly shy man, he only communicated with his servants through notes, and lived at nearby 11 Bedford Square from 1796 until his death. He was also the first to describe the composition of nitric acid and to isolate the inert gas argon.

In 1817 the scientist ALEXANDER VON HUMBOLDT (1769-1859) left Prussia and moved into 17 Portland Place. He designed a safety lamp and rescue apparatus, started free evening classes for miners and promoted anti-slavery legislation. An intrepid explorer, he set a new mountaineering record by climbing the 20,000 feet of the Chimborazo in Venezuela. He met Simón Bolívar, who praised him as having 'done more good for America than all her conquerors', and he travelled through Venezuela, Columbia, Ecuador, Peru, Cuba and Mexico, where he collected 60,000 plant specimens (6,300 of which were unknown in Europe). Both a breed of penguin and an ocean current are named after him, along with over 1,000 other places or features.

The first practical steam locomotive built by George Stephenson in 1814 owed much to the pioneering work of the Cornish engineer RICHARD TREVITHICK (1771-1833), who invented the high pressure steam engine. He lived in Gower Street in 1808. He first came to London to secure a patent on his invention and raise funds in 1802, and he first demonstrated his steam engine in public at the northern end of Gower Street that year. Energetic Londoners could race a carriage driven by his chugging locomotive along Oxford Street in 1803, and he offered rides in his steam engine that ran on rails built in 1808 at the top of Gower Street. But he disagreed with the theories of JAMES WATT (1736-1819), whose methods had first converted the steam engine into a powerful and efficient workhorse. Watt lived for a time at Foley House, at the bottom of Portland Place. Later, George Stephenson forged ahead with his

View of the interior of the
Pantheon, Oxford Street,
showing Mr Lunardi's
Balloon. Engraving by
Valentine Green (1785)

*Vincenzio Lunardi displayed
his gorgeous red and white silk
hydrogen balloon in the
Pantheon to raise funds for his
second ascent.*

RICHARD TREVITHICK'S
RAILROAD by Thomas
Rowlandson (1809)

*Trevithick laid this circular
track at the top of Gower
Street to demonstrate his
'Catch me who can' steam
locomotive, which reached a
speed of ten miles per hour, in
1808. Delighted passengers did
not realise that it was more
than a fairground novelty.*

steam locomotive based on Watt's principles, while Trevithick spent ten wasted years attempting to employ steam pumps in American silver mines – a venture that left him penniless. A bust of Trevithick commemorating his achievements is at III Gower Street.

Navigator and explorer CAPTAIN MATTHEW FLINDERS (1774-1814) spent the last year of his adventurous life peacably at 56 Fitzroy (7 *Upper Fitzroy*) Street. In 1790 he had sailed with William Bligh to the West Indies – just a year after Bligh had been cast adrift by mutineers on HMS Bounty. As the first European to discover the narrow seaway of Bass Strait between Australia and Tasmania (1796), he was commissioned to circumnavigate the southern continent. 'Sea, I am thy servant', he wrote of the force that dominated his life. The charts he drew up of the Australian coast between 1802 and 1803 are still in use today, and the Flinders river (Queensland) and the Flinders Ranges (South Australia) were named after him. Unfortunately for Flinders he was shipwrecked on his journey home. He made his way to the Isle de France (Mauritius), but because England and France were at war, he was incarcerated there for seven years, writing to his wife Ann, 'I may truly say, that I have no pleasure in life: the nearest approximation to it is to forget my pain.'

SAMUEL MORSE (1791-1872) developed the telegraph, with its dot and dash alphabet known as the Morse code (in use until the end of the 20th century), which made communication over long distances possible, after Joseph Henry, an estranged colleague, had laid the foundation for the theory of electromagnetism in 1844. An accomplished artist before he turned to science,

OMNIBUS

ILLINGTON SOMERS TOWN | PADDINGTON to the BANK | DIORAMA REGENTS PARK

Morse came to London to improve his skills as a painter. He was quickly accepted into the Royal Academy, and lived in different houses in Great Titchfield Street from 1811 to 1813, before moving to 141 Cleveland Street (*8 Buckingham Place*) where he stayed until 1815. While there he observed that the British class system affected even the way people knocked on the door: from the servant's single, light tap, through the various tradesmen's rat-a-tats, to a loud assertive knock given by a member of the nobility. He was tutored by one of the most successful society painters, Benjamin West, an American from Pennsylvania. He expressed great regret when, not receiving an expected artistic commission, he decided to give up painting at the age of 46, 'the very name of *pictures* produces a sadness of the heart I cannot describe.'

In July 1829 GEORGE SHILLIBEER (1797-1866), a coach-builder born on Tottenham Court Road, introduced London's first omnibus service. His omnibus was drawn by three bay horses with seating for 20. Passengers could travel along the Marylebone and Euston (*New*) Roads for the price of a shilling each. In the ensuing competition for omnibus business, his company failed, and he was declared bankrupt in March 1831. He then turned to the undertaking trade, for which he designed a funeral coach.

The founder of modern evolutionary theory, the naturalist CHARLES DARWIN (1809-82) moved into 110 Gower (*12 Upper Gower*) Street in 1838, with his newly wedded wife and cousin, Emma Wedgwood. Appropriately, the building has since been incorporated into the biological science buildings of University College London. Their first two children were born in Gower Street – including Annie who died at the age of 11. While there Darwin made the observations of his children's behaviour, which led him to write *The Expression of the Emotions in Man and Animals* (1872), his attempt to explain how abstract thinking developed from instinctual behaviour. Darwin liked the locality, 'I am becoming a thorough-paced cockney', and admired the 'grandeur' of its 'smoky fogs', until the sight of government troops marching past his house in 1842, heading north to quell Chartist uprisings, alarmed him and he decided to move his family to safer environs.

The Liberal prime minister WILLIAM EWART GLADSTONE (1809-1898) would leave his home at fashionable 73 Harley Street to search for prostitutes in Fitzrovia, avowedly with reformist intentions, although the time he spent in their company made some question his motives. In his diary he wrote that he whipped himself in punishment after these trips. He was an avid reader of pornography, and regularly visited a bookshop in *Boziers Court*, an alley off Tottenham Court Road. He would visit the Salvation Mission for Prostitutes at 309 Regent Street (now part of the University of Westminster), and at the stately 40 Portland Place, he would call on Mary Sands, the wealthy American socialite to whom he was attracted.

Another Liberal, SERGEANT WILLIAM BALLANTINE (1812-87), the famous barrister with a ready wit immortalised as Mr Chaffanbrass in Anthony Trollope's novel *Orley Farm*, was born in Howland Street.

JOHN TOWNSEND, born in Middlesex Hospital, died in 1832 leaving a large, unexplained fortune of £20,000. He had been a Bow Street Runner, and dropped hints that the runners supplemented their low wages (a guinea a week) by doing deals with offenders to share the rewards offered for recovering stolen goods. He told a government committee of inquiry in 1816 that, because runners often shared the rewards made upon conviction, they did all they could to secure conviction, even if the evidence was doubtful. The investigation of the Bow Street Runners by a Select Committee in 1828 concluded that runners were often 'private speculators in crime rather than efficient officers for the ends of justice'. Following the committee's recommendations, the Metropolitan Police Force was established in 1829.

The distinguished surgeon and ear specialist JOSEPH TOYNBEE (1815-66) died when he accidentally inhaled chloroform while experimenting on himself to find a new treatment for ear inflammation. After studying anatomy at Windmill (*Little Windmill*) Street, he practised at University College Hospital, and lived a short walk away, in Little Argyll Street.

The nursing heroine, 'the lady of the lamp', FLORENCE NIGHTINGALE (1820-1910), was working at the Middlesex Hospital in Mortimer Street in 1854 during one of the four major epidemics of cholera that afflicted London in the 19th century. All through the night 'wretched shrieking creatures' were carried in and Florence was 'up day and night undressing them...putting on turpentike-stupes [flannel used as a surgical dressing] herself, to as many as she could manage.' Many of the patients were prostitutes, 'filthy and drunken, crazed with terror and pain.' Over 200 patients were admitted, and the mortality rate was very high. Florence Nightingale kept a pet owl called Athena, and had nursing connections with the Anglican Sisterhood of All Saints, 7 Margaret Street (where the Rossettis' sister, Maria, 1827-76, lived).

When JOSEPH ROGERS (1821-89), a star pupil at Middlesex Hospital, went on to become medical officer of the Strand Union Workhouse, 44 (6) Cleveland Street, he was appalled by the stench and overcrowding. There were nearly twice as many inmates as there were beds, and the death rate was over 50 per cent. The workhouse master, Catch, was forced to resign. He then committed suicide rather than end up there himself. Rogers, a persistent medical campaigner, was instrumental in the building of 20 new hospitals in London to provide for the insane and those with infectious diseases, who would otherwise have been consigned to the workhouse. Funded by the Poor Law levy, a public hospital system was established in 1867.

Even after the French chemist, Pasteur, published his germ theory of disease, in 1865, septic infection, which was known as 'hospital gangrene' and killed many hospital patients after surgery, was regarded as an untreatable hazard. JOSEPH LISTER (1827-1912) who studied and became a house surgeon at

It may seem a strange principle to enunciate as the very first requirement in a Hospital that it should do the sick no harm.

Florence Nightingale

I have seen a child standing at some distance from any one, clearly express its feelings by raising one shoulder, giving it a little backward movement, and then turning away its whole body.

Charles Darwin on the 'cold shoulder', for his study of the language of emotions

University College Hospital, realized that the illness might be caused by airborne bacteria. He experimented with various anti-septic treatments but the medical world remained unconvinced. In 1877 he moved into 12 Park Crescent, where he lived until 1908. In 1887 he finally proved that sterilization dramatically reduced the death rate, and his methods were adopted world-wide, as standard medical practice. In 1897 he became the first man to be awarded a peerage for his services to medicine.

Research by another great medical scientist, SIR JONATHAN HUTCHINSON (1828-1913), contributed greatly to the understanding of syphilis. He lived at 22 Chenies Street and claimed to have examined over a million cases, an average of 44 a day, during the course of his working life. The medical term 'Hutchinson's triad' describes an aspect of congenital syphilis.

DAVID HUGHES (1831-1900), a genial man with a social conscience, had already made a fortune from the teleprinter, which he invented and patented in the United States and Europe, when he moved to a flat at 94 Great Portland Street in 1877. There, in 1879 he demonstrated the world's first wireless transmission of sound. G. Marconi, aged five at the time, later acknowledged the importance of Hughes' work, and said that if he had persevered, he would have invented the radio. In 1880 Hughes beamed sound from his Great Portland Street flat out to Langham Place (coincidentally the future site of Broadcasting House). But the secretary of the Royal Society who came to observe the experiment would not accept that it was a transmission of sound waves (which Hughes called electrical conduction) and Hughes was discouraged, and went on to other projects. Already a rich man, and believing, that society should benefit freely from his work, he refused to patent his future inventions, which included the microphone (1878), and the metal detector (1879). He never lost his great sense of fun, and enjoyed dining and indulging in horseplay at the Horseshoe pub (267 Tottenham Court Road) with friends three times a week. When he died he left £470,000 to four London hospitals.

Radical social reformer EDITH SIMCOX (1844-1901) moved into Chenies Street in 1875, where she stayed until 1885. She supported women's suffrage through her involvement in the trade union movement – she represented the Society of Shirt and Collar Makers and was one the first two women delegates to attend the annual Trades Union Conference – and campaigned vigorously against low pay. She set up a shirt-making co-operative in Soho, which later moved to larger premises in Mortimer Street.

The age of electronic communication was brought closer when SIR JOHN AMBROSE FLEMING (1849-1945), educated at University College School, 43 Gower Street, and appointed professor of electrical engineering at University College London, invented the thermionic valve in 1904. Called a 'diode' by scientists because it has two electrodes, it could convert, 'rectify', an alternating to a direct current, making further electronic developments possible, including long distance radio.

At the age of 17, MILLICENT GARRETT (1847-1929) was at the same gathering as HENRY FAWCETT (1833-84) a radical Liberal member of parliament who had been blinded in a shooting incident in 1858 (which did not stop him learning to skate), when they heard of the assassination of the US president, Abraham Lincoln. On hearing Millicent exclaim, 'It is the greatest misfortune that could have befallen the world, greater than the loss of any of the crowned heads of Europe', Henry instantly asked the hostess to introduce him to 'the owner of that voice.' They married when Millicent was 20, and she became his reader and secretary. Henry Fawcett became a prominent economist and politician, and was appointed postmaster general. Millicent Fawcett was one of the founders of Newnham College, Cambridge. When a thief who had

snatched her purse was charged with having stolen goods 'belonging to Henry Fawcett', she began her campaign to change the Married Woman's Property Act, under which women's property automatically belonged to their husbands. Henry died from pneumonia, aged 51, and Millicent went to live permanently with her sister Agnes at 2 Gower Street. She wrote eight books, including *Political Economy for Beginners*. She was created a Dame of the British Empire in 1925, and lived to see all women gain the vote in 1928.

Her elder sister, ELIZABETH GARRETT ANDERSON (1836-1917), resolved to become a doctor on hearing a lecture given by the visiting American Dr Elizabeth Blackwell when she was 26, and still living at home with her family in Aldeburgh. Medicine was barred to women, and she fought to be allowed to observe medical practice, working as a nurse at the Middlesex Hospital. After six months a deputation of male students insisted that she leave, 'the presence of young females as passive spectators in the operating theatre is an

The day that Darwin moved into 12 Upper Gower Street, just before his marriage, he was so excited that he wrote to Emma, his fiancée, 'I can neither write nor think about anything, but the house...would you believe it, I find by the Compasses, we are as near, within a hundred yards of Regents Park.'

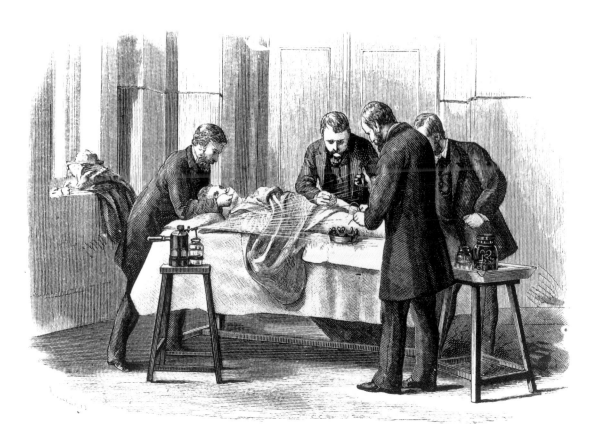

outrage on our natural instincts and feelings.' She was forced to study privately with professors, and finally gained a qualification through the Society of Apothecaries. In 1870 she was able to take her final medical exams in Paris. That year she also became the first woman to be elected to the new School Board. She married James Anderson a year later, and they had three children. She joined the feminist Society for Promoting the Employment of Women, which held its meetings at 19 Langham Place (the Langham Place circle), but later disagreed with them over the enforced testing of prostitutes for VD. In 1872 she opened the New Hospital for women, later renamed the Elizabeth Garrett Anderson, and in 1908 she was elected mayor of Aldeburgh.

OCTAVIA HILL (1838-1912), so-named because she was the eighth child of James Hill, the radical editor of *Commonweal*, was only 14 years old when she was put in charge of children who made toys, including dolls house furniture out of wire and chintz, at the Society for the Employment of Ladies, 8 Fitzroy Street (*4 Russell Place*). She was appalled to realize that the children lived in over-crowded slums that were dark, filthy, cold, and lacking water and privies. She undertook to give them an education, read to them, and gave them lunch to which they contributed a shilling of their wages, after which they tended a garden at the back. She went on to become a housing reformer, advocating dwellings of 'light and air', along with proper financial management. Her vigorous campaign to save recreational space that would be open to all, 'the healthy gift of air and joy of plants and flowers', led to the foundation of the National Trust in 1895.

Another philanthropic reformer, QUINTIN HOGG (1845-1903), a sugar merchant, pioneered the first true polytechnic at 309 Regent Street. It evolved from the Youths' Christian Institute that he opened there in 1882. Shocked at the lack of recreational and educational facilities for working class youth and determined to provide an opportunity for their 'athletic, intellectual, spiritual or social' development, he had first tackled the problem by running a Bible class for road sweepers – using an empty beer bottle as a candlestick. Seven thousand students joined the polytechnic (now part of the University of Westminster) in the first year, and the number had doubled by 1900. He lived at 5 Cavendish Square, and died suddenly at the polytechnic. His funeral was held at All Souls, Langham Place. A statue of Hogg by Sir George Frampton was erected at the bottom of Portland Place in 1906.

Without AGNES BERTHA MARSHALL (1855-1905) ice creams might never have found their cones. An ice-cream maker, she established a cookery school at 31 Mortimer Street in 1883, which she ran for the rest of her life. In 1888 she created the first cornet that was as deliciously edible as the scoop of ice-cream it was designed to hold, and in 1885 she invented an early form of refrigerator, a wooden box insulated with zinc which had to be restocked with ice every two days. The school was so successful that she expanded its premises on both sides (30 and 32 Mortimer Street) and added a kitchen shop. She wrote several cookery books but when she died after a riding accident, a rival publisher (whose list included the best-selling Mrs Beeton), bought the rights to Marshall's works in order to buy out the competition, and stopped their publication.

The founding father of brain surgery was SIR VICTOR HORSLEY (1857-1916), who lived at 101 Charlotte Street (1882-91). In 1882 he performed the first cerebral surgical operation, when he removed scar tissue from the brain of a young Scotsman who had been suffering almost continuous fits (200 a day) following a skull fracture in a boyhood road accident. After the operation, the fits stopped completely.

EDIBLE ICE-CREAM CONES invented by AGNES BERTHA MARSHALL (1885)

The ingredients for the cornets were 'half a pound of ground almonds, 4 oz caster sugar, 4 oz of fine flour, two whole eggs, a saltspoon full of vanilla essence and one tablespoon full of orange flower water.' She filled them with a combination of apple ice-cream and ginger sorbet.

MARGARET BONDFIELD (1873-1953) was about 18 years old, and working as a shop assistant, when she walked through Fitzroy Square in 1894 and spotted an advertisement for the newly formed National Union of Shop Assistants, Warehousemen, and Clerks, in the newspaper that wrapped her fish and chips. She joined the union and in 1896 she became assistant secretary. Three years later she became the first woman delegate to attend a trade union conference. In 1907 she gave evidence to a government inquiry about the 'living-in' system that was used by employers to fine shop assistants for such offences as 'addressing a customer as *miss* instead of *madam*' and 'not using paper or string with economy'. In 1923 she was elected a Labour MP. The following year she was appointed parliamentary secretary to the ministry of Labour, the first woman to hold a ministerial office, and in 1929 she was made minister of Labour, the first woman to hold a cabinet post. She was opposed to family allowances in the 1920s, and was widely criticized by her constituents for supporting cuts in public spending at a time of recession and unemployment after the Wall Street crash.

In 1902 she met MARY MACARTHUR (1880-1921), 'In the years between 1903 and 1921', wrote a Mrs Hamilton, 'the romance of her life – and a very real romance – was her association with Mary Macarthur'. In 1903 Margaret shared a flat with Mary Macarthur in Gower Street, and they worked together in the Women's Trade Union League, of which Mary became secretary the following year.

Mary was acutely aware of the predicament of women workers, 'While women are badly paid because of their unorganized condition they may be unorganized mainly because they are badly paid'. With Margaret, she established the National Federation of Women Workers in 1906, the first general union for women. She was its first president and later general secretary, and she campaigned against sweated labour and for equal pay. In one memorable case she argued that there should be equal pay for the women and men working as lift attendants in the same government office. The

DAVID HUGHES, radio pioneer.

He first transmitted sound from the basement to the attic of his house in 94 Great Portland Street, using a steel needle and sand in a jam jar.

Whenever you save five shillings you put a man out of work for a day.

John Maynard Keynes

I spent the greater part of Friday trying to persuade myself that those terms were good enough for me. I tried to swallow them – I did not want to do what I have done – but they stuck in my throat.

Duff Cooper on his resignation from Chamberlain's cabinet

authorities countered her claim by asserting that women did not repair the lifts. MacArthur forced them to concede that the men as well as the women were specifically forbidden from repairing the lifts, but they still did not grant the women equal pay. Macarthur then concluded that women trade unionists would need to deploy more than arguments based on pure reason if they were to achieve their rights.

The cause of women was also advanced by MARIE STOPES (1880-1958) who opened the first birth-control clinic in 1921, and challenged the ignorance surrounding sex education. In 1925 the clinic moved to 108 Whitfield Street, where it has been ever since – and where sightings of her ghost have been reported. Marie Stopes studied and lectured on botany at University College London. In 1918 she published *Married Love, A new contribution to the solution of sexual difficulties*, aimed at providing contraception information. It was immediately banned as obscene by the postal authorities, but it sold over half a million copies and prompted a vast volume of correspondence. One man wrote suggesting that, in order to prevent unwanted advances, women should wear pink bows to indicate that they were in the mood for sex. Marie Stopes replied that a more subtle reading of partners' inclinations was needed. Her own first husband (1911-16), Dr Reginald Gates, was impotent. She married her second husband Humphrey Roe (who later stayed at 23 Fitzroy Square) in 1918, and with him she had a son, Henry, when she was 43-years-old.

She wanted to free women from constant pregnancies, to help prevent the high incidence of infant mortality in poor families, and inhibit the spread of venereal disease, but in her later years the reactionary basis of her views became clear. She supported eugenics and called for the sterilisation of those deemed unsuitable to breed, the 'hopelessly rotten and racially diseased.'

The most influential economist of the 20th century, JOHN MAYNARD KEYNES (1883-1946), resigned from the Treasury in protest at the punitive terms imposed on Germany at the end of the first world war, expounding the likely results in *The Economic Consequences of the Peace* (1920). An admirer of the painter Duncan Grant, he lived with him at 21 Fitzroy Square 1909-11, provoking the jealousy of Lytton Strachey, who dismissed Keynes cattily as a 'safety bicycle with genitals'. Keynes also lived at 3 Gower Street in 1916. He travelled in Italy with Duncan Grant and Vanessa Bell to celebrate the publication of his first book and while there he was amused when some Italians confused the two men, addressing financial questions to Grant and showing Keynes works of art (Keynes was, in fact, an amateur artist of distinction). In *A General Theory of Employment, Interest, and Money* (1936), after examining why the market economy had no automatic capacity to generate full employment, he proposed that government take a more interventionist role in the economy and reduce unemployment by state policy. A bisexual, he married the Russian ballerina, Lydia Lopokova (1892-1981).

One of those to put Keynes' economic policies into practice in the aftermath of the second world war, SIR STAFFORD CRIPPS (1889-1952), chancellor of the exchequor (1947-50), had been a student at University College London. He was president of the student union, and later worked as a laboratory researcher. He was one of the first to make a party political broadcast on television, but the presenter Macdonald Hobley, who was under strict instructions to show absolute impartiality in his introductions, referred to him as 'Sir Stifford Crapps'.

Another prominent politician, ALFRED DUFF COOPER (1890-1954), lived at 90 Gower Street. As a student he had been banned from Oxford's Balliol College for drinking, gambling and dancing with actresses who wore skirts above the knee. He married LADY DIANA MANNERS (1892-1986), ex-Slade art

student and film actress, whom he met at a party attended by the prime minister, Herbert Asquith (1852-1928); he disliked Asquith for 'pawing' Diana's knee. The couple took up residence at Gower Street, where Cooper relied on his new bride's earnings as a film star for a couple of years. They fitted in easily with the literary set and among their frequent guests were Hilaire Belloc, H.G. Wells, Somerset Maugham, Arnold Bennett, J.M. Barrie, Maurice Baring, A.E.W. Mason, and E.V. Lucas.

In 1937 Neville Chamberlain appointed Cooper as the first lord of the admiralty. Cooper resigned in 1938 because he disagreed over the signing of the Munich agreement, on the grounds that it would encourage the German invasion of Czechoslovakia. Over the next month he was deluged at Gower Street by the arrival of four thousand letters from all over the world in support of his action. In 1940, after the start of the war, Winston Churchill appointed Cooper as minister of information, at Senate House, Malet Street. Later Cooper switched to diplomacy and writing, publishing a war novel *Operation Heartbreak* and his autobiography *Old Men Forget* in the 1950s.

Professor of genetics at University College London, J.B.S. HALDANE (1892-1964), was a regular participant on the radio discussion programme, the *Brains Trust*, where one of the few questions to stump him was 'Why can't people tickle themselves?' But he was tickled enough by some of the artists whom he met on his regular visits to the Fitzroy Tavern, including Augustus John, Chips Nevinson, Nina Hamnett and George Bissill, to compose the ditty:

For I have only got to whistle
To have my portrait done by Bissill
And if he does not do me justice
I take a sitting with Augustus.

His articles explaining science in layman's terms for the *Daily Worker* were minor masterpieces of popular journalism. He often made himself the object of his scientific experiments, once staying inside a small steel chamber for 14 hours to simulate conditions in a submarine.

He met his second wife HELEN SPURWAY (student and lecturer at UCL) at another Fitzrovian pub, the Marlborough Arms – where Spurway was once arrested for treading on the tail of a police dog.

As bombs fell during the blitz in September 1940, GEORGE CAFFELL, a communist transport worker who had fought in the International Brigade during the Spanish Civil War, went against the orders of the home secretary, Herbert Morrison. The government, fearing privately that the underground would provide a sanctuary for deserters, and saying publicly that it feared that 'children might fall on the line and be killed', had decreed that all gates to underground tube stations should be locked when air-raid sirens sounded. Caffell took up a crow bar and smashed open the gates of Goodge Street station, very close to where he lived, and shouted through a loud-hailer to announce that shelter was available. Caffell's action initiated a government policy reversal. Today pictures of people huddling in the underground, sheltering from the bombs, symbolise Londoners' wartime grit.

One of Caffell's comrades in the Spanish civil war, PATIENCE EDNEY (1911-96), was a trainee nurse at University College Hospital in the 1930s, where she observed the effect of poverty on health, 'Poor families could not afford the one and sixpence it cost to see a doctor. By the time we picked them up they knew that they were too far gone for us to help them, that they were going to die. It was terrible.' At the start of the Spanish civil war she joined a medical convoy organised by the left-wing *News Chronicle* newspaper and a group of communist doctors. She was one of seven nurses sent to the Aragon front attached to the Carlos Marx Communist division. Her unit deserted to join an uprising in Barcelona and she switched to the International Brigade. She helped to deal with an outbreak of typhoid before she transferred to a mobile hospital, which took shelter in a cave from Nazi bombs during the battle of Ebro. In 1952 she went to China where she met her husband, Eric Gordon, who had previously lived locally, in Fitzroy Street. There they stayed until they were forced to return to London by the cultural revolution. Patience Edney died in Madrid, after being awarded honorary Spanish citizenship for her service during the civil war.

VENGALI KRISHNAN KRISHNA MENON (1896-1974), who later became India's representative at the United Nations, was a student at University College from 1927 to 1930, where he gained an MA with honours in Educational Psychology, then worked as a laboratory researcher. He was elected as a Labour Party Camden Councillor in 1934, but in 1941 he resigned in protest against Labour's imperialist Indian foreign policy. When India gained independence in 1947, and Menon was appointed the first high commissioner of India in London, he continued to travel by bus to his grand office from his tiny, rented bed-sit in Camden. Later he returned to live in India, where he became minister of defence. Michael Foot unveiled a bronze bust of Menon on the south east corner of Fitzroy Square in 1977, but it was stolen a couple of years later.

DR DEBORAH DONIACH, a senior lecturer and later professor at the Middlesex Hospital medical school, advanced the understanding of a thyroid condition known as Hashimoto's disease. Hakaru Hashimoto (1881-1934) first identified this form of thyroiditis in 1912, but its precise pathology remained elusive until 1956, when Dr Doniach and her colleagues at the Middlesex demonstrated the presence of thyroid antibodies in their patients. As a result it became easier to diagnose the disease and obtain reliable results. Dr Doniach who had qualified in 1944, remained a professor at the medical school until retiring in the late 1990s.

KENNETH CLARK (1903-83) made the landmark television series on the history of western civilization and was chairman of the Independent Television Authority, yet he himself never owned a television set. He lived in Charlotte Street as a young man. Between 1934-39 he lived in a mansion at 30 Portland Place, where he gave refuge to struggling artists including Graham Sutherland and Henry Moore and, with his wife Jane, hosted parties, at which Winston Churchill, Neville Chamberlain, the Duke and Duchess of Kent,

The expression "positive neutrality" is a contradiction in terms. There can be no more positive neutrality than there can be a vegetarian tiger.

V.K. Krishna Mernon

Cover of the *Woman Worker*, 1907-8, edited by Mary Macarthur

'Knowledge is power,' wrote Mary Macarthur in a 1908 issue, 'Organization is power. Knowledge and organization mean the opening of the cage door.'

At Portland Place they were hidden away at the top of the house and brought down to be exhibited as *objets d'art* to our friends.

Kenneth Clark on his three children, when the family lived in Portland Place.

Sam Idrissu and Marge, the waitress, at the door of the Rambler café.

Sam Idrissu ran a café for night workers in Euston Road before moving to this address in Cleveland Street, where he lived and worked for 20 years. The café was then taken over by his brother Den.

George VI, Queen Elizabeth (now the Queen Mother) and Queen Mary were among the guests.

The Labour Party leader HUGH GAITSKELL (1906-63), then an economics lecturer at University College, London, was in the Fitzroy Tavern when he saw a young woman, Dora Frost, pour beer over the head of a man who had made an anti-Semitic remark. Admiring the woman's spirit, he introduced himself. She later accepted his proposal of marriage and they announced their engagement in the same pub. Gaitskell also enjoyed informal lunchtime debates at the Fitzroy with Aneurin Bevan, Barbara Castle, Michael Foot, and Tom Driberg.

In 1963 Gaitskell was in the Middlesex Hospital when David Frost read out the latest prediction made by the well-known columnist, the Beachcomber, on the satirical television programme *That Was The Week That Was*. The Beachcomber predicted that Gaitskell would soon recover, and as most of the Beachcomber's predictions proved inaccurate, Frost said, 'Sorry Hugh'. Gaitskell died suddenly a few days later.

The ephemera of everyday life fascinated MAURICE RICKARD (1919-1998), who thought that the throw-away material – printed matter intended to be useful for a single day – was the intrinsic stuff of history, 'fugitive evidence' that could be collected and studied. He ran a photography business in Soho, and took his staff out to fly kites at Regent's Park when work was slack. His posters for a 1955 road-safely campaign conveying the lives of people damaged in car accidents were so shockingly realistic that they were banned by local authorities. In 1975 he held the inaugural meeting of the Ephemera Society in his basement flat in Fitzroy Square, and the Society organised its first exhibition that year. Displaying items such as a first-class ticket for the maiden-voyage of the Titanic, a souvenir printed at the Thames Frost Fair in 1740 in honour of Hogarth's dog Trump, and a prostitute's calling card of 1860, the exhibition sparked world-wide interest, and spawned other similar societies internationally. Rickard gave up his business and devoted himself full-time to writing about the subject, working from his basement flat crowded with ephemera and his 'huge collection of books'. He had 'little in the way of creature comforts', and slept on six chairs arranged facing each other, so that he would not fall on the floor. He set up the Foundation for Ephemera, and succeeded in seeing the subject established as an academic discipline, with the formation of the Centre for Ephemera Studies at Reading University in 1993.

The huge Trust House Forte chain of hotels (following a merger in 1970), started with the milk bar that CHARLES FORTE (b.1908) opened at Marcol House, Regent Street, next door to the polytechnic, in 1934. By the end of the decade he was living in Hallam Street, and had taken over a large warehouse in Percy Street to supply soups, sandwiches, cakes and ice cream for his growing empire of milk bars, decorated with their signature red and white stripes, including one at 141 Oxford Street. Yet at the start of the second world war, Forte was interned as an Italian national, and shipped off to the Isle of Man.

GEORGE SWITLIK, a Polish chess master, ran the Tower coffee bar at 80 Cleveland Street in the 1970s, where the tables were always set with chess boards. On one memorable occasion he played 17 chess games simultaneously, against opponents such as local butchers and lorry drivers, while continuing to cook meals for the customers.

One of the most popular and community-minded café owners in the area was MALLAM 'SAM' IDRISSU (1920-94) who ran the Rambler, 145 Cleveland Street, 1972-91. A cook from Ghana, he worked at the café 17 hours a day, 365 days of the year. He was renowned for his generosity, and gave local squatters

Then one day, in Upper Regent Street, where the polytechnic is, next door to Boosey & Hawkes, the music publishers, I found an empty shop...I counted the numbers in the queues at the nearby bus stop; I counted the students and teachers coming in and out of the polytechnic; and became increasingly convinced that this was the site for me.

Charles Forte on choosing the site for his first milk bar

**Mama's philosophy was
always that if you can't do
anyone a good turn don't do
them a bad one.**

Elena Salvoni

free meals during the 1980s, including the then-unknown pop stars Boy George and Marilyn. Customers sometimes took advantage of his good nature – a homeless man whom he fed and sheltered one Christmas, stole the week's takings – but Sam kept on smiling and helping people down on their luck.

Elena Salvoni (b.1920) is now one of the most acclaimed restaurateurs in Fitzrovia, yet if it had not been for wartime rationing she might have stayed in the ragtrade. On leaving school at the age of 14 she became an apprentice tailor for Mr Arnaldi of Dorville Models on the third floor, 40 Mortimer Street. Five years later, when the firm's supply of cloth was reduced by the outbreak of the second world war, a friend who worked in a local café suggested that Elena join her, 'The boss thought I was a natural, and I stayed there until it burned down four years later', and she followed him to another restaurant. During the food shortages immediately after the second world war, 'Our customers would peer suspiciously at the occasional meat dish and ask, a bit querulously, whether it was horse-flesh. I used to say I didn't know.' She was not repelled by horse-meat, having tasted it in Italy, on a visit to her aunt,

English birth control pioneer, DR MARIE STOPES (1953)

Marie Stopes's radical approach to sex education combined technical explanations of the body with mystical descriptions justifying sexual pleasure, 'The half swooning sense of flux which overtakes the spirit in that eternal moment at the apex of rupture sweeps into its flaming tides the whole essence of the man and woman...'

'I suppose she was what you would describe as a peasant and peasants have never been choosy when it comes to survival.'

Elena worked at Bianchi's and L'Escargot, and took over L'Etoile, 30 Charlotte Street, in 1996 – a century after it had been first opened by the Italian Rossi family. 'At first I was concerned about whether my customers would follow me to Charlotte Street', she said, 'but most of them have come with me, and some new ones as well.' On the walls are signed pictures of some of the famous who have dined at her restaurant including John Mills, Richard Attenborough, Ruth Rendell, Judy Dench, David Jason, Barry Humphries and the television chat show host, Michael Parkinson, who has written on his photograph, 'Where you go, I follow.'

CHAPTER 9
Mavericks and Misfits

WILLIAM HUNTINGTON (1743-1813), known as the 'Coalheaver Preacher' after his previous job as a coalman, took to the pulpit in order to avoid responsibility for maintenance payments when he was on the run from his first wife. He made his fortune from the pew rents he charged at his private chapel in Great Titchfield Street. There the worshippers paid handsomely for the privilege of hearing him routinely denounce them as 'snoring sinners', 'noisy numbskulls' and 'drunken dogs', and his sermons featured the imagery of mammon: god was the 'divine Banker' and heaven, the 'inexhaustible Bank'. He acquired all the trappings of wealth, including a farm and a country house. He had 13 illegitimate children with his second partner, Mary Short, then deserted her, and she died of 'gin and grief' in 1803. His chapel burned down in 1810.

The farmer's daughter turned prophetess, JOANNA SOUTHCOTT (1749-1814), who promised land and personal salvation to her followers, sold 144,000 'seals' guaranteeing access to heaven to the gullible. In the second frenzied wave of her cult, she convinced her disciples that she was going to be the mother of the second Christ – for which she prepared herself by eating 160 heads of asparagus. Two months after the due date, she died. Her body was carried to an undertaker's in Oxford Street, and was buried by Regent's Park. An explosion shattered her tomb in 1874, and her followers thought she was being resurrected, but inside they found only a pistol and a box of dice.

An eccentric doctor and author, WILLIAM KITCHINER (1775-1827), who lived at 43 Warren Street from 1817 onwards, would not allow any guest who arrived a minute late to enter. For those who were on time, he played the piano and drums. In his *Traveller's Oracle* he said that the two essential items for anyone setting out on a journey were a sword and a set of portable door bolts.

In 1809 the wit and author THEODORE HOOK (1788-1841) made a wager that has gone down in history as the Berners Street Hoax. While walking down Berners Street with a friend he pointed to a house and bet his companion a guinea that by the following week it would be the most famous address in London. Over the next few days he ordered thousands of goods and services to be delivered, on the same day and at the same time, to 54 Berners Street, home of an unsuspecting widow named Mrs Tottingham. Even the Archbishop of Canterbury was duped into visiting, expecting to hear the unfortunate woman's 'deathbed' confession. On the appointed day Hook watched gleefully from a lodging house opposite as the lanes around the house jammed solid. The chaos and commotion attracted great crowds and a dray of beer was plundered by the mob. Despite a 'fervent hue and cry' to catch the perpetrator, Hook managed to escape detection.

In his youth Hook had been in trouble for playing truant from a school in Soho Square, just southwest of his birthplace, 23 Bloomsbury (3 *Charlotte*) Street, and he had been expelled from Harrow. In 1819, when he was accountant general and treasurer of Mauritius, a young clerk accused him of embezzlement. He was arrested but the young clerk later shot himself, and it was rumoured that Hook had tricked the clerk into agreeing to a joint-suicide pact. Hook was shipped back to London (meeting Napoleon at St Helena en

O England...I warn you of dangers that now stand before you, for the time is at hand for the fulfillment of all things.

Joanna Southcott

NANCY CUNARD and HENRY CROWDER

On learning that Nancy was staying at the Eiffel Tower hotel with Henry, Lady Cunard, Nancy's mother, was outraged and threatened the proprietor, Stulik, that if he did not make them leave she would see that he 'got the works'.

route) on the charge of emblezzement. A five-year investigation followed, after which he was imprisoned for non-payment of debts. He ridiculed himself in jail with a song,

Let him hang with a curse – this atrocious, pernicious
Scoundrel that emptied the till at Mauritius!

And he wrote a successful novel, which earned him enough to be released, although he always managed to avoid paying the Mauritius debt. His health suffered in prison and he was put on a diet of rum, milk and bottled porter for a diseased liver, from which he died.

In the 19th century, fortune-telling was an offence punishable by up to three months' imprisonment, but this did not prevent ROBERT SMITH (1795-1832) from achieving fame as the astrologer 'Raphael', and compiling horoscopes. He was dubbed 'England's Junior Merlin', and he lived at 5 and 75 Eastcastle (*Castle Street East*) Street from 1820 until his death. He wrote books about witchcraft, 'invoking spirits, curious secrets, anecdotes of the dead, and terrific legends.' After the death of King George IV, he claimed that the king had visited him, incognito, for a consultation, at which he had accurately predicted the date of the regent's death. Just as he had begun to earn enough to support his wife, Sarah, and their six children, he died of tuberculosis.

NCANEN

A friend of his, FRANCIS BARRETT, was the central figure in the magical order of the Rosy Cross, a secret occult group that met at his house, 99 Bolsover (*Norton*) Street.

When women were still barred from the study of medicine, Miranda Stuart swapped her skirts for breeches, and enrolled in December 1809 at Edinburgh University as 'James Barry, literary and medical student'. She was precocious, fascinated by the books in the library of General Francisco de Miranda, who was a friend of her uncle, the irascible, impoverished Fitzrovian painter, James Barry. He named her Miranda, after his friend, and the men connived in the deception that would enable her to study. She qualified as Dr James Barry (1795-1865) and maintained her male disguise all her life.

Dr Barry joined the army as a hospital assistant and was posted to Cape Town in 1813. While there she performed the second successful Caesarean section in medical history, saving lives of both the mother and child. But she was demoted for protesting against the filthy conditions and the daily flogging endured by lepers and prisoners on Robben Island, and she returned to England. There she gained promotion again, after which she went back to Cape Town. Following further disputes, she was sent to the West Indies, where she contracted yellow fever. Her next post was Canada where her pay was docked for trying to reform hospital conditions.

In order to appear a convincing man, she flirted with women at parties. She had a reputation as a passionate termagent full of reforming zeal, who badgered the authorities over her campaigns, and as a patient doctor, who was generous to her patients.

When Dr Barry retired and returned to England, she lived at 14 Margaret Street, with her black servant, John, who had been with her since the West Indies, and her dog, Psyche. In 1865, bad drains and a particularly hot summer produced an epidemic of diarrhoea during which 300 people died a week. Marylebone residents were particularly badly affected, and one of those who succumbed was Dr James Barry. After she died her charwoman, Sophia Bishop, was greatly surprised to discover that the doctor had been 'a perfect female', and that there were stretch marks on her stomach, 'marks on her of having a child when young.' Soon after her death a mysterious footman dressed in livery arrived at the house, collected the dog, Psyche, and some papers that the doctor had always kept guarded in a box, paid off the servant, and left.

Prince Jung Bahadoor of Nepal went to buy a black mourning band at William Jay's Mourning House, 247-249 Regent Street, by Oxford Circus, in 1850, where he took a shine to the shop assistant, Laura Bell. He subsequently paid £250,000 for her favours, which led to a furore back in Nepal. To avoid an international incident, the British government was forced to reimburse the money to the Nepalese government. Laura had spent her fortune on a luxury flat, and in marrying a Captain Thistlewaite, who was in the habit of summoning the servants by firing his pistol. When he was later found with a bullet through his head, no one knew if it was a freak ricochet or suicide.

After her husband's death, Laura opened her flat as a prayer house to women 'of her previous position'. So many prostitutes attended to pray for their salvation that she moved their meeting place to Regent Street polytechnic, a stone's throw from where she had first encountered the prince.

In 1874 the madcap Polish inventor and jeweller, Gustave Bernard Gennovich, who lived in Store Street, was so frustrated when the war office ignored his letters about his new mobile cannon, that he decided that the cannon should speak for itself. Aiming for 'a louder correspondence' and hoping to provoke royal intervention on his behalf, he prepared his cannon for firing near the residence of Prince Edward of Saxe-Weimar (1823-1902), nephew of King William iv and childhood playmate of Queen Victoria, at 16 Portland Place. After the demonstration he knocked on the door, only to be confronted by the alarmed butler. The prince, who had just left, heard the explosion from down the street. When the inventor returned a few days later the butler called the police and Gennovich was arrested. At his trial it emerged that he had also tried to demonstrate his invention to the prime minister, Disraeli, and to Queen Victoria's daughter, princess of Prussia, by firing the cannon outside Buckingham Palace. He offered to show how the cannon

I well remember how in a harsh and peevish voice she ordered me out of the cabin – blow high, blow low – while she dressed in the morning. "Now then youngster, clear out of my cabin while I dress" she would say.

Colonel Roberts on sharing a ship's cabin with Dr James Barry

Dr James Barry

James Miranda Barry, who lived her adult life as a man, was promoted from army hospital assistant to Inspector General of the Army Medical Corp. An army captain later commented that it was generally believed that the doctor was 'hermaphrodite'.

worked in court, but the magistrates declined, and ordered that he be remanded for a mental health report.

Between 1890 and 1900 the Isis-Urania Temple of the Hermetic Order of the Golden Dawn held their magical rituals, which were conducted by three priestesses, in a vault in Clipstone Street. MINA 'MOINA' BERGSON (1865-1928), a student at the Slade art school between 1883 and 1886, co-founded the order, which held its first ceremonies at her studio at 17 Fitzroy Street. By 1892 the membership had grown, and the order moved to Clipstone Street, where Moina was one of the priestesses who consecrated the vault. In 1900 Moina's husband, MacGregor L. Mathers, was exposed as a fraudulent magician, and the couple were expelled from the order. They moved into cheap lodgings in Percy Street.

When Moina's friend, ANNIE 'TABBIE' HORNIMAN (1860-1937), also a Slade student, was initiated into the order at the Fitzroy Street studio, she was sworn to secrecy or she would be 'slain by the lightning flash'. In 1896 she was expelled for insubordination, after which she pursued her interest in drama. She opened two theatres and promoted repertory theatre.

The third priestess, FLORENCE FARR (1860-1917), actress, writer, and co-founder of the group, who took part in the rites in the vault, had love affairs with two other members of the group, the writers W.B. Yeats and Bernard Shaw. Her understanding of sex was that it was a source of power so long as it was kept light: sex could give 'every happiness we know on the condition that we never give way to it in our serious relations.' She said that she preferred not to give her whole life to a man, not because she would be bored by him, but because she would be bored by herself if she were to do so.

> The idea of the priestess is at the root of all ancient beliefs...What do we find in the modern development of religion to replace the feminine idea, and consequently the Priestess?
>
> Moina Bergson

Journeys of a more earthbound kind were revealed in the memoirs of a determined pauper, W.H. DAVIES (1871-1940). The success of his *Autobiography of a Super Tramp* (1916) describing his travels through most of America and Canada as a hobo, enabled him to settle down in rooms on the corner of Tottenham Court Road and Great Russell Street (opposite the YMCA headquarters). There he refused to make a complaint about his nights being disturbed by 'a piano thumping Belgian prostitute' in the room above because he distrusted and hated the police, having been punished with 12 lashes of the cat-o-nine-tails for shoplifting in his youth.

While Davies was trying to catch an illegal ride near Ottawa, another drifter, 'Three Fingered Jack', got in his way just as he was making his jump for the train. Davies managed to grab the handlebar, but his feet failed to reach the step. He was dragged along the line and his right foot was severed at the ankle, as he discovered when he had difficulty standing up. Davies was taken to hospital where he smoked his pipe with a nonchalant air while the doctors amputated his leg at the knee. Supplied with an artificial limb back in England, he traded it in for a traditional wooden peg leg, because it was better for his business as a street peddler.

> To hell with Christianity, Rationalism, Buddhism, all the lumber of the centuries...I want blasphemy, murder, rape, revolution, anything, bad or good, but strong.
>
> Aleister Crowley

Striking out on another limb, was a young police constable, GEORGE PRATT, based at the Police Station, 55-59 Tottenham Court Road. When he met sergeant Jack Hayes, the general secretary of the National Union of Police and Prison Officers, at an evening economics class at St Pancras Working Men's College, Pratt decided to join the union. He then participated in the successful 1918 national strike, during which the police force demanded union recognition and a pay increase in line with inflation. But in 1919 the government reneged on its promise to recognise the union, and the members decided to take action. Hayes suggested that they should refuse to make arrests for petty offences, but he was out-voted and the members decided on an all-out strike. During the strike Pratt worked as an unpaid assistant at the police

We went through it into bright light, leaving much of our grosser astral bodies behind. As we rose it was as if we were passing through a crevice in impenetrable solid light...My heart beat violently (a most unusual thing) and the light became almost unbearable...

Annie Horniman on contacting 'spritual realms' through visual 'skrying' in a ceremony of the occult Order of the Golden Dawn.

union's office. The strike was defeated, and all members were sacked. Pratt found work with the All Russia Co-operative Society in Holborn, which sought to build trade with the Soviet Union. During the anti-Soviet hysteria of 1927, which followed the general strike of 1926, the police raided the Society's offices and Pratt found himself unemployed once more.

Adding to Fitzrovia's notoriety in the 1930s was the presence of the mountain climber and self-styled 'Great Beast', ALEISTER CROWLEY (1875-1947). Branded by the press as the 'King of Depravity', Crowley cultivated and revelled in his devilish reputation. After studying moral sciences at Cambridge, he reacted against the fanatical strictures of his Plymouth Brethren background and turned to satanism and black magic, declaring that his aim was to produce a monster baby after the ultimate orgasm. He was admitted to the occult Silver Star society as Brother Perdurabo in 1898, and he delighted in the outrageous stories that began to circulate about him. One of his party tricks was to defecate on the carpets at parties held by his adoring hostesses, and he sold pills made from his own semen, marketing them as Elixir of Life. A more palatable cocktail was the one he invented, Kubla Khan No.2 (a mixture of gin, vermouth, and laudanum), which he drank at the Wheatsheaf and the Fitzroy. Another of his drinks was purported to have been blood from the neck of Nancy Cunard, which he drew with his specially-filed fangs' teeth, a 'serpent's kiss', giving her blood poisoning.

BETTY MAY, drawn by Nina Hamnett (undated)

In 1930 he lived at 2 All Souls' Place – but was evicted when the landlords read that he planned to exhibit the erotic paintings of D.H. Lawrence. Crowley lived at the Tour Eiffel for a while then stayed in 'the stinking slum of Charlotte Street' in 1932 (when he dined often at Pagani's). In 1943 he revisited All Souls' Place for a séance with Michael Ayrton, at No.4.

In his autobiographies, *The Diary of a Drug Fiend* and *Magical Record of the Beast 666*, Crowley boasted of acts of lewdness to satisfy 'the quenchless fires of lust and the eternal torment of love.' He wrote that he persuaded one of his 'Scarlet Women' to have sex with a goat, then cut the hapless animal's throat, because it demonstrated 'an insulting lack of enthusiasm for the operation.' Despite this self-publicity, he accused his friend, the artist Nina Hamnett, of libel, for having described his ritual magic in her autobiography. At the subsequent trial evidence was given that he had performed animal sacrifices: a toad was baptised Jesus, accused of sedition, and crucified. Hamnett's star witness was the artist's model, Betty May. May told the court that she had visited the temple and watched Crowley slaughter a cat. Crowley had forced her husband, Raoul Loveday, to drink the cat's blood, and her husband died shortly afterwards, 'of fever'. Unsurprisingly, Crowley lost his case.

Crowley's request to be buried in Westminster Abbey was not granted by the ecclesiastical authorities. He was cremated with a heretical requiem in Brighton, after which the Brighton Corporation resolved never again to permit such 'pagan or blasphemous ceremony'.

A Crowley disciple when she was younger, BETTY MAY (1901-58), was known as Tiger Woman following a knife fight with a rival while living in Paris. A petite, graceful artist's model with fierce green eyes, she had many lovers including Jack Lindsay. Like her friend Nina Hamnett, she held a central place at the Fitzroy Tavern, where, if the whim took her, she would squat down on all fours and lap her drink from a saucer. At Wally's, a basement club in Fitzroy Street, she performed her other party piece: taking off her skirt and weaving it about in front of her as she sang 'The Raggle-taggle Gypsies'.

Wearing tribal robes with feathers in his hair and shouting, 'I've got an 'orse', racing tipster and showman RAS PRINCE MONOLULU (1881-1965) was well-known on England's racetracks over many decades. He sold envelopes that were supposed to contain the name of a winning horse, sealed to hide the fact that each envelope held the name of a different horse for the same race. Most punters were aware of the ruse but superstitiously bought an envelope anyway – after all, one had to have the name of the winner.

At an early age Prince Monolulu, like his fellow Ethiopian, the ex-slave Olaudah Equiano, was press-ganged onto a ship sailing for America. After he gained his freedom he travelled to Germany, but he was taken prisoner at the outbreak of the first world war. Following his escape to London, he lived at 55 Howland Street, where he met and married Margaret Carley. Their son, Peter, was born in 1924. During the second world war, Peter ('Macky') was awarded the title of jitterbug champion of the British empire for jive-dancing to the Glen Miller Band playing at Oxford Street's Swing Club.

In 1927 Monolulu and Margaret divorced. Three years later Monolulu married Nelly Atkins. The couple had two sons, Ronald (b.1932) and Raymond (b.1935). The marriage did not last, and Nelly left Howland Street and moved to Great Titchfield Street.

At the end of the second world war, Monolulu changed his name to Peter McKay. He moved to 83-85 Cleveland Street, where he was visited by the great Afro-American singer, Paul Robeson, who was a friend.

Monolulu often went to Danny's Bar in Tottenham Street. Dave Hagi, a Gresse Street resident, remembers that the neighbouring children, of whom

I am a true coster in my flamboyance and my love of colour, in my violence of feeling and its immediate response in speech and action.

Betty May, granddaughter of a London coster woman

God made the bees, the bees make the honey, the public backed the favourites, the bookies take the money.

Ras Prince Monolulu

RAS PRINCE MONOLULU
calling card.

The darker a colored man was the more she liked him. She often told me she wished that I was darker.

Henry Crowder on Nancy Cunard

* There are differing accounts of the whereabouts of Nancy Cunard and Iris Tree's studio. Peter Gibson refers to 109 Fitzroy Street in *The Capital Companion*, while Ann Chisholm refers to Fitzroy Place, at the top of Charlotte Street, in *Nancy Cunard*. Several authors have since repeated the latter address. A 1913 map shows a Fitzroy Place just north of Euston Road, opposite the top of today's Fitzroy Street. It is possible that there were studios at each of these addresses, and that Nancy and Iris used both, at different times.

Hagi was one, would gather around to receive the threepenny bit that Monolulu always gave them, along with his predictions, 'He told small lads they would be jockeys, strong ones boxers, and others runners.'

Jeffrey Bernard, then a journalist on *Sporting Life*, visited Monolulu when he was near the end of his life, in Middlesex hospital, taking with him a gift of a box of chololates. 'Just because I'm a better tipster than you there's no need to kill me off', Monolulu joked on being given the chocolates.

In 1991 the Yorkshire Grey, 28 Maple Street, was renamed the Prince Monolulu in his honour. The sign with his portrait has since been replaced by one bearing his name only, and the outside of the pub now carries the title 'PMBar'.

The society heiress turned penniless scrounger, SYLVIA GOUGH (1894-*c*.1967), the daughter of a millionaire diamond king, George Cawston, lived over Schmidt's, the restaurant at 33-37 Charlotte Street. In the 1920s she was a stage and screen actress, and a Ziegfeld Follies dancer in New York. She turned to modelling, and sat for Augustus John. She became his lover and he was cited in her second divorce. By 1936 she was living with another of her lovers, the 21-year-old writer, Douglas Bose, who beat her up, and who was then murdered by a jealous rival. Her third husband was killed in action during the second world war, and she received a generous pension, most of which she spent on booze and young men. When her Charlotte Street flat was bombed in the London blitz, she took her time about leaving, and a friend shouted out to her to hurry because the building was on fire. 'I know', she called back, 'but I can't find my pearls.' In her later years she sat by the fire in the Fitzroy Tavern looking frail and skeletal but still genteel, and would always spend her last sixpence on a bath.

Aristocratic individualist, NANCY CUNARD (1896-1965), whose great grandfather was the founder of the famous shipping line, wasted no time in escaping from her father's Victorian country estate. Like her mother (Lady Maud 'Emerald' Cunard, who was passionately in love with Thomas Beecham and had moved to London in 1911 to be closer to him), as soon as Nancy came out as a debutante in 1914, she left home and went her own way. She rented a studio in Fitzroy Street*, which she shared with Iris Tree. She became friends with one of her mother's ex-lovers, the novelist George Moore, who was rumoured to be her real father; he encouraged her to write poetry and praised the beauty of her naked back, 'as long as a weasel's'.

While at Fitzroy Street she became close to Alvara Guevera, an upper class South American, and student at the Slade. He was a boxer as well as a poet and painter and the two might have married, had Nancy not met and married a wounded soldier, Sydney Fairbairn, in 1916, although they separated soon after.

She met two of her other lovers at the 'Eiffel Tower Restaurant', as she liked to called the Restaurant de la Tour Eiffel, in Percy Street, the meeting place of the artistic and the literary avant-garde where she had a favourite corner table. Both men were writers who created fictional characters based on Nancy. The Armenian novelist MICHAEL ARLEN (1895-1956) used Nancy as the original for the convention-flouting Iris March in his novel *The Green Hat* (1924) and for Virginia Tarlyon in *Piracy*, and Aldous Huxley used her as the model for Lucy Tantamount in *Point Counterpoint* (1928) and as Myra Viveash in *Antic Hay* (1923), 'Her elbows propped on the mantlepiece, her chin resting on her clasped hands, she was looking fixedly at her own image in the glass. Pale eyes looked unwaveringly into pale eyes. The red mouth and its reflection exchanged their smiles of pain.' Cunard commented that Huxley repelled her, sex with him was like 'being crawled over by slugs'. Once Cunard and Huxley

were sunbathing together, and a dead dog dropped out of the sky and landed on them (it had fallen from a plane).

She travelled through France and Italy and began a relationship with Louis Aragon, the French Dada artist and Communist Party member. In Paris in the 1920s she mixed in bohemian and artistic avant-garde circles and shared their enthusiasm for Black culture. By 1926, she wrote to a colleague that was leaving for Southampton, 'to look for African and Oceanic things – because that is the most recent and now very large interest in my life, ivory, gods, masks, fetishes.' And by 1927 she had found her vocation as a publisher. With an old printing press in a Normandy farmhouse, she set up the Hours Press, through which she was to publish poetry by Ezra Pound, Robert Graves, Harold Acton and Samuel Becket. She was assisted at the Press by Henry Crowder, a black jazz pianist, whom she had met in Venice. With him she had the longest relationship of her life, lasting from 1928 to 1935 (he was also the cause of her disinheritence and estrangement from the Cunard family).

Whenever she visited London, Nancy stayed at Eiffel Tower's hotel, upstairs from the restaurant and reached by a separate door, 'The comfort was nil, the room cheap, the convenience considerable...Food, drink and hours perfect.' But twice when she reserved rooms for herself and Henry at the hotel, he was turned away because he was Black. Nancy was committed to the cause of Black rights and worked tirelessly, with the assistance of Henry, on compiling an anthology of Black culture. Finally published in 1934, *Negro* was 800 pages long, and banned as seditious in several countries. The only contribution she rejected was one that described African bracelets, like the ones that jangled on her own arms, as giving off a semen-like scent when heated by the wearer's body. While preparing the anthology she made friends with a left-wing poet, EDGELL RICKWORD (1898-1982). She shared an attic flat with him in Percy Street from 1933 to 1934.

I'VE GOTTA HORSE (1954)
Horse racing tipster, Prince Monolulu, with fashion models at Epsom race course

Monolulu backed Irish horses, saying that they were 'better fed'. But if a horse had already won three times that season, he would not tip it as a winner, 'Only exceptional horses can stand up to continuous training to keep them at the peak of condition to win more than three races in a couple of months or so.'

Musical Tableau (1914)
(from left to right) *Felicity Tree* (sister of Iris Tree), *Nancy Cunard, Lady Violet Chateris and Lady Diana Manners in a musical tableau* La Damoiselle Elue.

Nancy Cunard called her friends the 'Corrupt Coterie'. The group's bohemian lifestyle was envied by Lady Diana Manners, until she went to one of Nancy's parties at 8 Fitzroy Street, and saw the 'champagne bottles broken at the neck to save the trouble of drawing the cork, pools of blood and vomit, frowsty unmade beds, a black velvet divan thick with dust.'

Back in London, she was arrested several times for her pro-communist views, and she began to suffer from paranoia. As she grew older, she became more fanatical, her drinking increased and her behaviour became more sexually predatory. She stayed in several cheap Fitzrovian guesthouses in the 1950s. One night in 1960 she set fire to her clothes, and was arrested for being drunk and soliciting. She was certified insane and confined to a mental hospital for several months. Her friends rallied to her support and she recovered and returned to France, but signs of her mental disturbance reoccurred: she ate a railway ticket rather than show it to the collector, spent several nights sleeping in a wheelbarrow, and set fire to a hotel room. She died a few days after her 69th birthday. She was widely admired for her commitment to anti-discrimination, whether on grounds of gender, race or class. A school in Nigeria was named the Cunardia, one of the many tributes to her memory.

In her early days Nancy befriended two other Slade students, Iris Tree (1897-1968) and Lady Diana Manners (later Lady Diana Cooper, 1892-1986), and the trio became known as the 'Coterie', notorious for their hell-raising antics. Free-minded, stylish, making the most of their independent means, they dared to go out at night without a chaperone, to wear make-up, dress in trousers or unusual costumes, and to drink and smoke in public. Iris was the daughter of actor-manager Sir Herbert Beerbohm-Tree, and she took a room with Diana Manners near Fitzroy Square, which they hung with whips to signify that they were 'unashamed of decadence'. Iris also had a room at 4 Fitzroy Square, where Augustus John would visit her, share sardines, wine and hashish, and collapse with 'uncontrollablle laughter about nothing at all'. Iris did some acting with Diana, on a tour of America, and the pair went to a party in a Turkish bath where they gazed down through a transparent floor at a 'love nest' of black satin mattresses beside a tank of albino goldfish.

Iris Tree wrote poetry and joined the Fitzroy Street Group of artists and the Omega Workshop in Fitzroy Square. She married the art dealer, Curtis Moffat, and lived with him at 4 Fitzroy Square.

While she was at the Slade, Diana Manners was taken by a lecturer, Ambrose McEvoy, to what she later described as orgies, where she once injected morphine with Katherine Asquith, daughter-in-law of the prime minister. She married Alfred Duff Cooper against her parents' wishes. They lived at 90 Gower Street and had an open marriage. However, she managed to resist the advances of one of their visitors, the bulky foreign secretary, Ernest Bevin. In 1922 she agreed to star in two films, so providing the money to support her husband's decision to go into politics. She continued with her lucrative acting career and toured American in the role of Madonna, in Max Reinhardt's play, *The Miracle*.

A communist who was also, surprisingly, a fox hunter could once be spotted in Fitzrovia in the person of CHARLIE ONION (1900-96). A gas fitter and ardent trade unionist, Onion was born at 9 Scala (*Pitt*) Street and raised at 5 Warren Street. He swam every day, even after one of his legs was amputated. In 1949 he formed the London Amateur Boxing Association, and at the age of 93 he set three world swimming records for the over-70s.

The larger-than-life character, MADAME SHEBA (*c*.1903-68), a landlady from South Africa, rented out rooms over Goodge Street station, at 77A Tottenham Court Road, in the 1940s. She weighed 20 stone and described her colour as light, 'café au lait'. Madame Sheba was harrassed by frequent police raids of her premises, although this did not discourage her West Indian and African visitors from dropping in vivaciously at all hours of the night. She said that she was an orphan, who had been adopted by missionary nuns and brought up as a 'very high class' Roman Catholic. She entertained her guests with revivalist hymns and witchdoctors' 'juju', boiling up various concoctions in a pot and taking pinches of snuff which helped her to communicate with the spirits of the departed. After stamping tribal dances and township jive, she would shake all over and go into trances. One of her tenants was the poet James Kirkup, to whom she let a room on two conditions, that he play the piano for her every day, and promise never to touch her bottom. She was rather protective of her ample posterior and even slept on a high bed to stop any rats from biting it. She always wore voluminous silk turbans that she sometimes modelled, for a little extra income.

With his dyed hair, lipstick, mascara, and flamboyant dress, QUENTIN CRISP (1908-99) never made any attempt to hide his homosexuality, although he knew that he was likely to be beaten up and brought before the courts, since he was well into middle-age before homosexuality between consenting adults was legalised. After boarding school he took a journalism course and then drawing classes at Regent Street Polytechnic. He began to frequent the cafés and pubs of Charlotte Street, to which he had been introduced at the age of 18 by a friend of his mother's, an ex-artists' model, the 40-year-old Mrs Longhurst. She had a xenophile's love of anything foreign, and covered the walls of her room in Charlotte Street with a collection of African knives. Her attitude to his homosexuality was one of humorous tolerance, 'mocking curiosity but never savage'.

When Crisp took part in a ballet performance at the Scala Theatre, Tottenham Street, the roars of laughter from the audience at his entrance looking like 'an insufficiently basted chicken', turned deafening as he clung to the ballerina, smearing 'her unattainable whiteness with my orange make-up'.

During the second world war he rediscovered Fitzrovia, 'I began a whirlwind courtship of an entire district' he wrote in his autobiography *The*

Never in the history of sex was so much offered to so many by so few. At the first gesture of acceptance from a stranger, words of love began to ooze from their lips, sexuality from their bodies and pound notes from their pockets like juice from a peeled peach.

Quentin Crisp on American soldiers in Fitzrovia during the second world war

...back-slapping, laughter, excitement that seemed to tinkle thrillingly along the very glasses on the shelves.

Philip Lindsay on the Fitzroy Tavern in the 1920s

Naked Civil Servant, 'as soon as the bombs started to fall, London became like a paved double-bed'. Enamoured of American GIs, liberated by being among people to whom his homosexuality was of no consequence, he felt he had found a 'new self', especially in Charlotte Street, where 'there prevailed an effortless acceptance of the other person's identity'. He found company in the pubs, 'Drink and the world drinks with you; eat and you eat alone'. He was offered loans to buy black market goods and given café meals on credit. At his favourite cafés, Toni's and the Scala, 'The helpings were large, even discounting the portions of drowned cockroaches which were served, at no extra cost, with every dish'. Although the service was slow, 'The staff were friendly and unhurried to the verge of immobility', everyone was welcome, 'Customers were never barred permanently, even if they had been thrown out for fighting.' His favourite pubs were the Wheatsheaf and the Fitzroy Tavern, where the crowd was noisy, 'some drinkers erroneously imagined that they had become wiser and wittier, and consequently spoke louder than usual.' But the police put pressure on the pubs to exclude him. Even the Wheatsheaf, where the landlord tolerated most eccentricities, was intimidated. Crisp said the pub ban might be good for his health, but he regretted 'relinquishing half my audience.' Afterwards he only visited the district to see his friend Gillie Burke, a lecturer, at 31 Goodge Street, who was one of the founders of the Fitzrovia Neighbourhood Association in the early 1970s.

The appeal of the Fitzroy Tavern had always been the broad range of its clientele, including gay customers, who were disbarred from other pubs. This open-minded tradition was continued by the governor, Charlie Allchild (1907-88), when he took over the Tavern following his marriage in 1934 to Annie, the daughter of Judah 'Pop' Kleinfield (1864-1947), the incumbent publican. Annie had won prizes when she attended the Westminster Jews Free School, in Hanway Street, and although she at first had other plans for her career, she became as enthusiastic about the Fitzroy as her parents. During the second world war, when beer was short, and some Americans ordered the best vintage brandy, asking Annie to top up their drinks with orange squash, she said, 'That's sacrilege', and refused to serve them. The guest list for Annie and Charlie's wedding numbered 600 and was all-inclusive. Bernard Levin attended, and 'a cabinet minister and a road sweeper'.

But in 1955 the police clamped down, and prosecuted Allchild for running a 'disorderly house', and a 'den of vice'. The police testified that the number of prostitutes and homosexuals in the pub was between 50 and 80: people who 'paraded themselves unashamedly', with 'rouged' cheeks and 'blatantly dyed' hair. In his evidence Constable Pyle said that a prostitute had gone up to him with a winsome smile, and asked, 'Are you looking for a naughty girl or a naughty boy?'

Several customers testified on behalf of Allchild, including the broadcaster Wynford Vaughan-Thomas and barrister Geoffrey Bing, but Allchild was convicted on nine counts, and the brewery that owned the Fitzroy, Charringtons, suspended Allchild. Although the convictions were overturned on appeal, and Charlie was vindicated, he resigned in disgust at the lack of support shown by the brewers. He moved to Ridgmount Gardens where he lived for the rest of his life.

Two of the regulars at the Fitzroy Tavern during the war, Tom Salter and Professor Lustig, former chess champions, would stagger back, drunk, after closing time to their top floor flat in Charlotte Street. The lure of drink was to cost Salter his chance at the British chess championship title in 1941. On being told that his opponent could not stand the smell of alcohol, he set about imbibing everything he could, including methylated spirits. He finally

turned up for the match two days late, and his opponent claimed a walkover.

Scientology made its founder, L. RON HUBBARD (1911-86), a rich man. By the end of his life he had acquired both an apartment in Hollywood and a sea-cruiser. In his youth he had been closely associated with a Crowley-inspired sect, the Agape Lodge of the Church of Thelema. He ran off with the wife of its leader, Jack Parsons, a rocket engineer, who later blew himself up in a fuel experiment. Hubbard had arrived in Fitzrovia in 1952 when he was a science fiction writer. He lived in a £5-a-week bed-and-breakfast guesthouse at 102-104 Whitfield Street, where he played cards with Prince Monolulu and other locals. In the early 1950s, he established the London Church of Scientology, defined in his words as 'the study and handling of the spirit in

CHARLIE ALLCHILD (*second from right*) at the bar of the Fitzroy Tavern with DETECTIVE ROBERT FABIAN (*far right*) and others

In 1948 Ingrid Bergman took a blue handkerchief out of her handbag and gave it to Charlie with 30s. in coins, to make one of his famous, money-collecting darts that were stuck to the ceiling. Each year the money was used to give local children a party or a trip to the country.

relationship to itself, universes and other life', at 37 Fitzroy Street. In 1968 the scientology headquarters moved to its current address at 68 Tottenham Court Road.

In the 1960s, while he was still living in England, Hubbard was a member of the Atomic Gardeners Society, where horticultural researchers concluded that plants had feelings, and a new orchid hybrid was named after him. In his later years he took to the sea in his cruiser to escape the hostile attention of various governments; they suspected that scientology took unfair advantage of naive believers, who were then persuaded to pay for expensive courses. He died in California, a paranoid recluse with long hair and long fingernails.

A provocative orator, ROBERT MATTHEWS, of the Coloured Workers' Welfare Association and the Black People's Liberation League, had been born in Kenya, where his fingers had been cut off in his youth, as punishment for a minor misdemeanour. During the 1950s and 1960s he would walk most Sundays from his home address in Foley Street to Speakers' Corner in Hyde Park. There, wearing his cracked bowler hat and with his briefcase tied to his waist and hanging round his knees, he would climb onto his soap box, knock on a board with his finger stumps to get the attention of the crowd, and challenge any 'white trash' to disagree with him. 'He gave racists a taste of their own medicine by calling them white monkeys, but he never really descended to using the race card,' wrote Heathcote Williams in *The Speakers* (1982), 'He was very defiant, but had great dignity. It also took great courage for a black man to stand up and confront colonialism in those days.' A fellow speaker, Tom Durkin, remembers that Matthews was aggressive and progressive in his arguments for colonial freedom, 'He took people on and argued with them about how civilisation had existed among the African people when the British were savages running around in woad.'

When Matthews was heckled by a student from Galway named John Lennon, he invited him up to join him. Their subsequent double-act attracted quite a crowd, 'He would make outrageous statements', Lennon remembers, 'and I would act as his foil, modifying and analysing his comments.' They collected (illegally) a small fortune in donations, 'One Sunday the collection came to £24', says John. 'That was when I was getting paid £8 a week as a porter at Paddington station. There would be about two thousand people listening to us winding each other up.' Afterwards Matthews and Lennon would go to pubs such as Tottenham Street's Hope, and Goodge Street's Northumberland Arms, to swap their coins for notes and beer. Matthews's widow, a Portuguese woman, lived over Baloney's, a delicatessen in Charlotte Street.

One of the bluntest boozers to grace local pubs was ANNIE BAKER (1918-90), who was known as 'Sherry Annie' (within her hearing) and 'Fat Annie' (out of earshot). Annie herself had no such inhibitions about whether the targets of her occasionally barbed comments heard her or not. Well past retirement age, she would hold court over her young followers, her bulky frame perched precariously on the bar stools of the One Tun or the Cambridge in Goodge Street.

She had been left as a baby on the doorsteps of Liverpool's Anglican cathedral and brought up in Preston, where one of her lovers was Bill Shankley (then a football player with Preston and later manager of Liverpool). While working in Fitzrovia before the second world war Annie counted among her clients Dr Hastings Banda (then a medical student and later head of Malawi).

She lived firstly at 24 Charlotte Street (Anthony Armstrong-Jones, later Lord Snowdon, often visited the artist Anthony Hill in the same block) and, secondly, at 10 Charlotte Place over Fred's Café (Dennison's) where she worked as a waitress serving cheap, solid food early every morning.

An old friend of Annie's, DR PAT AHERN, lived and had his practice at 62a Goodge Street from 1934 to 1979. He was once a member of the IRA (for which he was paid an Irish government pension), and he liked a dram. In the summer he often conducted his surgery sitting outside on a bench belonging to the next door pub, the One Tun. After one such surgery, the drunken doctor had to be carried upstairs to his flat by a patient, who unfortunately stumbled and broke a rib.

The birth of the maverick MP ALAN CLARK (1926-99) at 30 Portland Place, was so traumatic and painful for his mother, Jane, that she never forgave him for being so big-headed: it led to a posterior sinus condition, for which she was treated with a cocaine spray. Young Alan and his large head grew up to become a military historian and minister of defence. He made his name with *The Donkeys*, an account of the incompetency of British generalship in the first world war, which inspired Joan Littlewood's *Oh, What a Lovely War*. As a

A true gaffe is accidental. Mine never are. I like to shock, and I do it (although not as often as I could) deliberately.

Alan Clark

Conservative MP he was famous for his unconformist views and his wildly indiscreet diaries revealing his extravagant sex life. He supported animal rights and when he died wanted it to be known that he was joining 'Tom and the other dogs', Tom being his favourite Jack Russell.

JOE SZABO (b.1934), 'Hungarian Joe', the chef at the Cambridge, Newman Street, in the 1970s and 80s, was known to the locals as a rock of craggy cheerfulness except for one fateful day. He planned a surprise visit to his girlfriend on the Isle of Wight, and spent half his week's wages on buying a return ticket but when he arrived she was not there, and he had lost the return half of his ticket. He paid another half-week's wages to travel home, only to be told, as he walked back into the Cambridge, 'You've just missed your girlfriend. She paid you a surprise visit.'

FELIX DENNIS (b.1948) found space for a new office up a rickety staircase at 39 Goodge Street in 1973, 'The building was 250 years old and looked every inch of it.' This was after he had endured the longest conspiracy trial in history, along with Richard Neville and Jim Anderson, his co-editors of *OZ*, the flagship magazine of the 1960s 'underground' counterculture. The three were charged at the Old Bailey with 'conspiring to debauch and deprave the morals of the young of the Realm' for No.28, School Kids Issue, put together by teenagers. At times the trial proceedings reached the heights of farce. The defendants appeared dressed in school uniforms. The comedian Marty Feldman referred to the judge as an 'old fart', and the London University psychologist, Michael Schofield, solemnly declared that the main point of the cartoon of Rupert Bear having it away with his grandmother was the element of surprise, 'Rupert Bear is behaving in a way one would not expect a little bear to behave.' During the trial Dennis showed the rumbustious, unabashed spirit that would later help to make him one of the 100 richest men in Britain, when, after two hours in the witness box, he had only conceded one minor point to the crown prosecutor, Brian Leary. By the time he was finally dismissed from the stand, he had the jury on his side. In the words of trial commentator, Tony Palmer, it was a turning point, 'Astonishingly, Dennis had kept to his word. As near as was conceivable, he had "got" Mr Leary. Things began to look a little better.' Nevertheless, the three editors were found guilty. But they were released from jail and their sentences were suspended on appeal. Subsequently, the 'dirty squad' officers who had raided OZ magazine were found to have been on the payroll of Soho porn merchants. Two senior detectives from the obscene publications squad were among 18 Scotland Yard officers, who were sent down for a total of 84 years for crimes ranging from corruption to conspiracy to defraud.

As a teenager, Dennis discovered the blues, learned to play the drums, and wanted to be a musician, but after moving into magazine-territory at *OZ*, he never looked back. When he and Dick Pountain, ex-*OZ* Production Manager, set up at Goodge Street, with less than £50 in the bank, Dennis started a fledgling company, called Bunch Books (H. Bunch Associates Ltd) after the hippy icon, Honeybunch Kaminski, created by the American cartoonist, Robert Crumb. He began to publish Cosmic Comics but the venture was not a resounding success. With no money coming in, Dennis walked past a queue of teenagers waiting to see a Bruce Lee film, and realised that this was the current hit. The next publication coming out of Goodge Street was *Kung-Fu Monthly*, which took the form of a fold-out Bruce Lee poster because they could not afford to staple magazine pages together. It ran for 13 years and was published in 17 countries.

In 1974 he formed Dennis Publishing, which also had offices at 14 Rathbone Place. Dennis' second breakthrough came in 1975 when he bought

'Fucking in the streets' does not mean copulating in the highways and byeways of the metropolis. It...has its roots in politics, in the freedom of sexuality if you like. It's a political slogan which has emerged from groups such as Women's Liberation and Gay Liberation. It's just a battle cry.

Felix Dennis to the crown prosecutor, Leary, at the Old Bailey

Personal Computer World, which he sold in 1982 for £3 million. Now with offices at 19 Bolsover Street and 30 Cleveland Street, with a staff of 400, Dennis publishes four of the six top-selling computer magazines in Britain. The Dennis Group consists of several companies in the UK and the USA, including a vast computer warehouse, an internet agency, and the men's lifestyle magazine, *Maxim*. He finally sold 39 Goodge Street in 1999. He owns six homes around the world because, he says, he hates packing when travelling, and he would not care if he lost it all tomorrow, 'It seems inconceivable that I can go on and continue to win most of the throws.' He has nearly died twice, once of Legionnaire's Disease, and says that he considers the rest of life as a bonus, 'I've built a lot of guest houses in the expectation that in the end I'll throw one time too many, lose the vast majority of my wealth, and end up quite happily smelling the roses in one of them.'

While Dennis has travelled from scourge of the establishment to successful businessman, the life of PETER WRIGHT (1916-95) went in the other direction. In his book *Spycatcher* (1987), which was prosecuted and banned in Britain under the Official Secrets Act, but was widely published abroad, Wright describes the 20 years he spent working for the British secret service. He wrote about his early days, 'I was a glue, sticks, and rubber-band improviser from the war', between the 1950s and 1990s, when the MI5 headquarters were in an anonymous looking office block with an unmarked entrance at 140 Gower Street. He spent his last night in the building in January 1976, sleeping in its top floor flat. He revealed that MI5 had tried to unseat the prime minister, Harold Wilson, in 1974, by leaking documents to the press that purported to show that Wilson was a security risk.

This was not the only secret government organisation in the area. In *A Spy's London* (1994), Roy Berkely described the Special Operations Executive, a 'wartime sabotage and subversion organisation', based at 35 Portland Place. There they developed extraordinary sabotage devices. One looked like a dead rat: the corpse was fitted with explosives and could be dropped into enemy territory

After she trained as a police officer, ALISON HALFORD (b.1940) joined the police station, 55-59 Tottenham Court Road, in 1975. She stayed for three years, as chief inspector. She involved herself in the local community and took part in the planning discussions for the annual Fitzrovia Festival. One of the festival organisers, Ron Gauld, said she enjoyed socialising, 'She liked a drink and said that what was good enough for her male colleagues was good enough for her.'

When she was assistant chief constable in Merseyside in 1983, she realised that further promotion was blocked, and took the difficult decision to file proceedings under the Sex Discrimination Act. The police reacted by suspending her on the charge of serious misconduct. She was accused of having sex with a male police sergeant in a jacuzzi, as well as having a lesbian affair with a woman police employee. 'One minute I'm as queer as a nine bob note and the next I'm bonking furiously in a jacuzzi with a man', she commented. 'You've got to laugh, haven't you?' She began to doubt the integrity of an organisation that would go to such lengths to discredit her, 'I began to believe that they would stop at nothing to blacken my name. We are talking about people who are employed to uphold the law. If they could do that to me, what could they do to anybody else?'

The case dragged on until 1992, when both sides dropped proceedings. Alison, who had started her working life as a waitress, retired early with a lump sum of £142,000 and a pension of £35,000 a year.

> Your problem, Peter, is that you know too many secrets.
>
> Victor Rothschild to Peter Wright

OZ APPEAL (1971)

The three editors of OZ, the 'underground' magazine of the 1960s, on their way to the Old Bailey for their appeal against a conviction for obscenity: Jim Anderson (left), *Richard Neville* (centre), *and Felix Dennis* (right).

MARC KARLIN (1943-1999), a radical, independent film maker, who was involved in the start of Chanel 4 Television, to provide for those 'who had no means of expression on the other channels', spent his latter years with Lusia Films, 20 Goodge Place, from where he also published the film magazine *Vertigo*.

Of Russian origin, he was born in Switzerland and raised in Paris, where he became fascinated by the cinema when he was a child, the 'Palais du Parc used to have acrobats and jugglers and singers in the intervals between the short film and the feature film, and the whole thing was an extraordinary event.' In the mid-1960s he was studying theatre direction in London at the

Central School of Speech and Drama. When the staff were sacked, he and the rest of his class resigned in solidarity, despite a threat from Laurence Olivier that none of them would ever be able to work in the theatre as a result. They formed their own drama school in a church hall.

Karlin soon switched from theatre to the cinema. He made a film about an American deserter from the Vietnam war. At the time the prime minister, Harold Wilson, said in parliament that there were no deserters in England, and when the film was shown, 'all hell broke loose'. While Karlin was filming a follow-up, with the same deserter, in Paris, he was caught up in the events of May 1968, where he was assigned the role of producing 'newsreels for the revolution'. He filmed a railway driver who had to clasp and unclasp the wheel every 15 seconds or his train would stop. Designed as a safety measure, to show that the driver was alert, it led to repetitive strain injury.

In the mid-1970s, Karlin helped to launch the Independent Film Makers' Association, and made experimental and innovative films, including *The Night Cleaners*, about the women, many of them immigrants, who worked in the City at night as contract cleaners. During this period he was a founder member of The Other Cinema, in Tottenham Street, until the site became part of the studios of Channel 4. A socialist and libertarian, his later avant-garde documentaries were on such subjects as the revolution in Nicaragua. John Wyver described him as 'the most significant unknown film-maker working in Britain during the past three decades.'

In the 1960s, a man known as the MAD MAJOR, who lived in Maple Street, became the first person to fly a plane under all the bridges of the River Thames. 'I knew his friend Hughie well – we all went often to listen to the West Indian steel bands in the Albany pub, Great Portland Street [now the Fitz & Firkin],' said Les Nelson of Hanson Street. Otherwise little is known about the Mad Major, and it would be no surprise if he was not unlike the final character in this book.

JOHN McCRIRICK, television's famous turf tic-tac man, who is known for his eccentric garb and excitable patter, 'Burlington Bertie, 100 to 30', delights some viewers and infuriates others. When he was struggling to pay off gambling debts, he worked as a weekend security guard at the student hostel, 20-28 Bolsover Street, attached to the Polytechnic of Central London (now the plush Fitzrovia Hotel). He lived at the hostel with his wife, Jenny, who was bursar at the polytech from 1973 until it was turned into a private hotel in 1990, and was often to be seen pedalling his tricycle or taking his giant pedigree poodles for a walk around Fitzrovia. Very extrovert when in the public eye, he was modest with locals. In fact, like so many Fitzrovian characters, he could be described as a regular curate's egg.

Seeing these groups of women at night was really awesome. It was as if these people owned London, in a very strange way, owned the offices.

Marc Karlin on filming night cleaners in the early 1970s

The women were lined up alongside each other and paraded in front of a mixed panel of very senior police officers who instructed us to remove all our upper clothing – bras as well. Then we were given a looking over and expected, in this highly vulnerable state of undress, to answer a series of questions put by a po-faced panel of experienced police officers.

Alison Halford on the selection procedure for women joining the police force in 1962

Author Acknowledgements

I would like to thank the public libraries of the boroughs of Westminster and Camden (which cover Fitzrovia's original parishes of Marylebone, St Pancras, and Holborn), as well as the British Library, and British Telecom archives for their reseach assistance.

Many thanks for supplying personal recollections and material to the following: Richard Adams, Ken Ames, Eve Barker, Eddie Barrett, Francis Beckett, Gordon Bennett, John Bermiston, Sue Blundell, Richard Bowden, Elisabeth Brooke, Peter Brooke, Harold Brookstone, Dolorata Buttiglione, Pal Carter, Dave Cash, Jim Charman, Jim Clayson, Costi Costas, Tony Cox, Keith Crook, Jim Currie, Patrick Curry, Karl Dallas, Jan Davis, Peter Davis, Tony Davis, Paul Day, Felix Dennis, Diz Disley, Tom Durkin, Jean Fergusson, John Fisher, Michael Foot, Louis Freidman, Peter Fryer, Janet Gauld, Ron Gauld, Angela Goldacre, Ann Goodburn, Billy Grainger, Benny Green, Fiona Green, Martin Green, Ernie Greenwood, Pete 'DJ' Grinderdale, Christabel Gurney, Dave Hagi, Nick Hagi-Savvr, Peter Halle, Stephanie Hamilton, Tony Hart, Pete Harvey, Paul Ioannou, George Johannes, Margaret Jollie, David H. Jones, Brian Keats, Jerry Kirker, Peter Kirker, James Kirkup, Joan Komlosy, Norman Lawrence, John Lennon, Barry Levene, Peter McKay, Conroy Maddox, John Malone, 'Leaping' Jack Marlow, Les Nelson, Paddy O'Donnell, Joss Parsons, Valerie Peart, Tony Peters, 'Uncle' Bill Philby, Phil Piratin, Steve Race, Richard Rawles, Frankie Rickford, Felix Rooney, Marsha Rowe, P.T. Saunders, Jeff Sawtell, Pete Smith, M.F. Sturridge, Christine Sveinsson, Kieron Tyler, Tony van den Bergh, Kathleen Vick, Jane Walmsley, Frank Warner, Harold Warren, Heathcote Williams, and Joebear Webb.

Finally, thanks to Linus Rees and David Turner for providing computer assistance, and Peter Arkell for taking photographs.

Mike Pentelow

My thanks to co-author Mike Pentelow, whose initial, rollicking draft of the manuscript had us all reading until late into the night, and opened up the possibilities for a book focusing for the first time on the people of an area, as individual characters, with all their foibles. His good cheer and willingness to collaborate were vital. My special thanks to Felix Dennis, for his faith that we would, together with Richard Adams, produce a book that would do justice to Fitzrovia, and for investing in the project. And special thanks to Richard Adams also, for walking me around the area, pointing out the architectural detail, for his expert art direction that pulled all the elements of this project into a unity, and for his unfailing enthusiasm – also to his assistant, Sam Adams. Thanks to Clifford Harper for his drawings that introduce each chapter with a definitive flourish and to Juliet Brightmore who showed perception and persistence in her search for the right images.

Felix, Richard, Cliff and Juliet, all plied me with invaluable books and suggestions. I am grateful to Felix Dennis, Alison Samuel and Mike Pentelow, for editorial comments that improved my introduction, and to Sheila Rowbotham, for her scholarly and generous suggestions on how to condense several of its passages. Judith Thomas spent an afternoon talking to me about Fitzrovia in the 1970s and provided essential copies of the community newspaper. Thanks to everyone else who gave suggestions or material, and to the British Library and British Telecom archives. Thanks too, to David Fryer for the artistry of the maps, to John Barker, for assembling the index in record time, and to all the staff at Felix Dennis office, for their help. Lastly, thanks to Alison Samuel at Chatto & Windus, for her warm encouragement and for skilfully steering this book through to completion.

Marsha Rowe

Notes to Introduction

1 The Fitzrovia Trust was established in 1985. A registered charity, its contact address is Melbourne House, 1 South Parade, London W4 1JU.

2 Quoted in Francis Sheppard, *London, A History.*

3 Thomas Pennant, *Some Account of London*, 5th edition, J. Faulden and others, 1813.

4 Quoted in Robert Hughes, *The Fatal Shore*, Pan Books Ltd, 1988.

5 Quoted in Nick Bailey, *Fitzrovia.*

6 Quoted in Paul Langford, *Englishness Identified: Manners and Character 1650-1850*, Oxford University Press, 2000.

7 F. Barker and P. Jackson, *The History of London in Maps*, Barrie & Jenkins, 1990.

8 Petition to the Privy Council (1632) quoted in Stephen Inwood, *A History of London.*

9 John Farman, *The Very Bloody History of London.*

10 'An eminent doctor' (1665), quoted in Peter Thorold, *The London Rich.*

11 Daniel Defoe, *A Tour Thro' the Whole Island of Great Britain*, vol.II.

12 C.H. Collins Baker, 'The Life and Circumstances of James Brydges, First Duke of Chandos', quoted in Keith Thomas, *Man and the Natural World*, Penguin Books, 1984.

13 J.T.Smith, *Nollekens and his Times.*

14 Quoted in 'Euston Road', Ben Weinreb and Christopher Hibbert (eds.), *The London Encyclopaedia.*

15 William Hogarth quoted in Jenny Uglow, *Hogarth, A Life and a World.*

16 Fanny Burney, *Evelina or a Young Lady's Entrance into the World 1778*, Clarendon Press, 1930.

17 Samuel Pepys, quoted in Weinreb and Hibbert (eds.), *The London Encyclopaedia.*

18 I am grateful for this information on Mrs Stewart and the 1778 quote, supplied by Mike Pentelow from a 1991 lecture given by Peter Davis at Westminster Adult Education Service on the history of Marylebone.

19 'The London Journal of Alessandro Magno 1562', quoted in Inwood, *A History of London.*

20 'A German Traveller's Guide, A Picture of England, 1789', quoted by Dan Cruikshank in his programme, *One Foot in the Past*, BBC 2, April 22, 2000.

21 Quote supplied by Mike Pentelow, with reference to the description of the Middlesex as a 'hospital for sick and lying-in women' from F. Peter Woodford, *Streets of Bloomsbury and Fitzrovia.*

22 'Sophie in London 1786' (trans. C. Williams 1933), quoted in Thorold, *The London Rich.*

23 John Nash quoted in John Summerson, *Georgian London.*

24 H. Traine, 'Notes on England' (1873), quoted in Inwood, *A History of London.*

25 *Charles Booth's Descriptive Map of London Poverty 1889*, London Topographical Society (1997)

26 Oscar Wilde quoted in Charlotte Grere with Lesley Hoskins, *The House Beautiful, Oscar Wilde and the Aesthetic Interior*, Lund Humphries/Geffrye Museum, 2000.

27 William Morris quoted in Edward Thompson, *William Morris, Romantic to Revolutionary.*

28 Vanessa Bell quoted in Fiona MacCarthy, 'A Radical Regained', *Guardian Weekend* , October 23, 1999.

29 Alexis Soyer quoted in Edwinda Ehrman, Hazel Forsyth, Lucy Peltz, Cathy Ross, *London Eats Out.*

30 Charles Kingsley quoted in Inwood, *A History of London.*

31 A century later Oxford Street has been affected by the ubiquitous spread of car ownership and the development of the shopping mall. In an assessment of 'turnover and profitability per square mile', Oxford Street came 11th and the top three retails sites were all malls, reported Gary Younge, 'The Big Picture', *Guardian*, 26 July, 2000.

32 Patrick Ensor, 'Sausage Shop', *Tower* (community newspaper now *Fitzrovia News*) No.25, February 1975.

33 'Fears as Schmidt's shop closes', *Tower* No.29, July 1975.

34 Nancy Cunard, 'To the Eiffel Tower Restaurant', quoted by Hugh David, *The Fitzrovians.*

35 Charles Jennings, 'Almost Fitz', *Guardian*, May 27, 1999.

36 Doris Lessing, *Walking in the Shade.*

37 Judith Thomas, personal interview.

38 Paul Cohen-Portheim, *The Spirit of London*, Batsford, 1935.

39 Arthur Tietjan, *Soho: London's Vicious Circle* (1956), quoted in Marek Kohn, *Dope Girls.*

40 Henry James, *The Art of Fiction and Other Essays*, Oxford University Press, New York, USA, 1948.

41 'The Needle Exchange', Fitzrovia Neighbourhood Association Annual Report, 1996. I am grateful to Dave Ferris, who found and forwarded to me the relevant excerpts on this subject from several years' worth of FNA Annual Reports.

42 John Vidal, Vikram Dodd, Rebecca Allison, Tania Branigan Jeevan Vasagar, Linus Gregoriadis and Stuart Millar, 'A day of skirmishes then stalemate', *Guardian*, May 2, 2001.

43 John Ruskin quoted in John McIlwain (ed.), 'Historical Notes', *All Saints*, Pitkin Pictorials, Andover, 1990.

44 *Karaoke* scene background information supplied by Mike Pentelow.

Picture Acknowledgements

Every reasonable effort has been made to contact copyright holders, but should there be any errors or omissions, the publisher will be pleased to insert the appropriate acknowledgement in any subsequent printing of this publication.

©The Artist's Estate/Bridgeman Art Library:70. ©Estate of Michael Ayrton, by permission (photo ©Copyright Reserved):167. Ashmolean Museum, Oxford/photo Bridgeman Art Library:154. ©Bethlem Royal Hospital Archives and Museum:78. The British Council (photographer unknown):199. The British Museum:138. J.C. Cannell *In Town To-night*, London 1935:130. *The Choice Humorous Works of Theodore Hook*,1902:226. City of Westminster Archive Centre, London/photo Bridgeman Art Library:210. The Coram Foundation, London/photo Bridgeman Art Library:94-95. Mary Evans Picture Library:17, 24-25, 27, 47, 69, 76, 82, 112, 119, 170, 184, 209, 213, 218 right(Fawcett Library), 222. ©1978 Estate of Duncan Grant, courtesy Henrietta Garnett:161 photo ©2001 Christie's Images Ltd. Fotomas Index:214. ©Guildhall Library, Corporation of London:x, 10, 43, 208. ©Estate of Nina Hamnett, courtesy Edward Booth-Clibborn:230. Hulton Archive:28, 55, 74, 102, 104-5, 116, 117, 122, 127, 128, 156, 165, 187, 189, 195, 196, 200, 223, 233, 234, 237, 242. *Illustrated Police News* 1892:81. Collection David Jaques:229. ©Gwen John/2001 All Rights Reserved DACS:157. Laing Art Gallery, Newcastle-upon-Tyne (Tyne and Wear Museums) © Estate of Malcolm Drummond:153. ©Estate of Osbert Lancaster, courtesy John Murray (Publishers) Ltd:31. *Londina Illustrata* vol.II, 1819:111. Courtesy Maas Gallery, London:150. Henry Mayhew, *London Labour and the London Poor*,1851:12,178. ©MSI Mirror Syndication International:85. ©Inge Morath/Magnum Photos, London: 238. Musée d'Orsay, Paris/photo Bridgeman Art Library:183. Musum of London:20-21 ©Mrs F. Bonifaccio Meschini, by permission, 38. The National Portrait Gallery, London:37, 61, 62, 65, 70, 134, 137, 141, 145, 146, 149, 173, 174, 179, 180, 205. The National Trust Photographic Library/John Hammond:115. Nick Oakes:56. ©Ordo Templi Orientis, 1918,2001:229. Mike Pentelow:221. Planet News:90. Popperfoto:218 left. The Royal Academy of Arts Photographic Archives:44. The Royal Society (photo by Maull & Fox, London):217. Tallis's *London Street Views*,1838:19. ©Tate, London 2001:157, 162, 190-191. ©The Treasury Solicitor (Estate of William Roberts):190-191. University College Museum, London/photo Bridgeman Art Library:206. V&A Picture Library, London:148. ©Kipper Williams:166. Estate of Mrs G.A. Wyndham Lewis, by permission:191 right. Private Collections:5, 7, 18, 32, 36, 40, 41, 44, 49, 52, 53, 66, 86, 89, 96, 97, 98, 108, 135, 142, 158, 172, 215, 227.

Select Bibliography and Sources

This book started out as the product of Mike Pentelow's reading which, as he said, pursued his personal interest in 'crime, art, entertainment, politics and the macabre'. This skewed the book along a certain direction, one that meshed coincidentally with the character of Fitzrovia. The range of books we eventually consulted, however, was eclectic and extensive. A full list would be twice as long as that given below. It would include further biographies about, or autobiographies by, the characters or those associated with them, as well as books of essays and of their letters, and more of the fascinating literature on the history of London. There would be bibliographical and literary dictionaries, and other guides to the city.

We have limited the books below to the 'most' essential that we consulted and to sources for the many, brief quotes scattered throughout. Where a source for a quote was other than a book, then it is also included alphabetically below. (M.R.)

Agar, Eileen, *A Look at My Life*, Methuen, 1988.

Alexander, Peter, *Roy Campbell, A Critical Biography*, Oxford University Press, 1982.

Amor, Ann Clark, *William Holman Hunt, The True Pre-Raphaelite*, Constable, 1989.

Anglo, Michael, *Nostalgia, Spotlight on the Forties*, Jupiter, 1977

Arlen, Michael, *The Green Hat*, Robin Clark, 1991.

Arlott, John, *Basingstoke Boy, An Autobiography*, Fontana, 1992.

Arlott, John, *The Essential Arlott on Cricket*, ed. David Rayvern Allen, Fontana, 1989.

Arlott, Timothy, *John Arlott, A Memoir*, Andre Deutsch, 1994.

Aronson, Theo, *Prince Eddy and the Homosexual Underworld*, John Murray, 1994.

Arora, K.C., *V.K. Krishna Menon, A Biography*, Sanchar Publishing House, New Delhi, India, 1998.

Bagnold, Enid, *Autobiography*, Heinemann, 1969.

Bailey, Nick, *Fitzrovia*, Historical Publications, 1981.

Baker, Richard Anthony, *Marie Lloyd, Queen of the Music Halls*, Robert Hale, 1990.

Bakewell, Michael, *Fitzrovia: London's Bohemia*, National Portrait Gallery, 1999.

Barker, Felix and Denise Sylvester-Carr, *The Black Plaque Guide to London*, Constable, 1987.

Baron, Wendy, *The Camden Town Group*, Scolar Press, 1979. *Miss Ethel Sands and Her Circle*, Peter Owen, 1977.

Beckett, Francis, *The Rebel Who Lost His Cause*, London House, 1999.

Bellas, Ralph A., *Christina Rossetti*, Twayne Publisher, Boston, USA, 1977.

Benson, Capt. L. (ed.), *Remarkable Trials and Notorious Characters 1700-1840*, John Camden Hotten, 1872.

Berkeley, Roy, *A Spy's London*, Leo Cooper, 1994.

Besterman, Theodore, *The Druce-Portland Case*, Duckworth, 1935.

Bleakley, Horace (ed.), *The Trial of Henry Fauntleroy and other Famous Trials for Forgery*, William Hodge, 1924.

Bloom, Edward A., and Lillian D. Bloom (eds.), *The Journals and Letters of Fanny Burney (Madame d'Arblay)* vol.VII 1812-1814, Oxford University Press, 1978.

Bolívar, Simón, *The Hope of the Universe*, Unesco, 1983.

Boswell, James, *The Life of Samuel Johnson*, 3 vols., privately printed for the Navarre Society, 1924.

Boswell, James, *The Journals of James Boswell 1762-1795*, selected and introduced by John Wain, William Heinemann, 1991.

Boy George, and Spencer Bright, *Take It Like A Man, The Autobiography of Boy George*, Sidgwick & Jackson, 1995.

Bragg, Melvyn, *Laurence Olivier*, Sceptre, 1984.

Brennand, Tom, *Eamonn Andrews*, Weidenfeld and Nicolson, 1989.

Briggs, Asa, *Marx in London*, BBC, 1982.

Brooke, Elisabeth, *A Woman's Book of Shadows*, Women's Press, 1993.

Brooks, J.A., *Ghosts of London*, Jarrold, 1982.

Brown, Tony, *Jimi Hendrix Concert Files*, Omnibus Press, 1999.

Browne, Douglas and F. V. Tullett, *Bernard Spilsbury, His Life and Cases*, George G. Harrap, 1951.

Bryant, Julius, *Robert Adam, Architect of Genius*, English Heritage, 1992.

Burford, E.J., *Wits, Wenchers and Wantons, London's Low Life*, Robert Hale, 1986.

Burford, E.J. and Joy Wotton, *Private Vices – Public Virtues*, Robert Hale, 1995.

Burgess, Anthony, *Little Wilson and Big God*, Penguin, 1988.

Burney, Fanny, *Dr Johnson & Fanny Burney, Being the Johnsonian Passages from the Works of Mme. D'Arblay*, introd. Chauncy Brewster Tinker, Andrew Melrose, 1912.

Burman, Rickie (ed.), *From Prodigy to Outcast, Simeon Solomon*, The Jewish Museum, 2001.

Busby, Margaret (ed), *Daughters of Africa*, Jonathan Cape, 1992.

Bushell, Peter, *London's Secret History*, Constable, 1983.

Butler, Ivan, *Murderers' London*, Robert Hale, 1994.

Bygot, David, *Black and British*, Oxford University Press, 1992.

Bynum, W.F. and Roy Porter (eds.), *William Hunter and the Eighteenth Century Medical World*, Cambridge University Press, 1985.

Cannell, J.C., *In Town Tonight*, George G. Harrap, 1935.

Carpenter, Humphrey, *Dennis Potter, The Authorised Biography*, Faber & Faber, 1998.

Caws, Mary Ann, *Women of Bloomsbury*, Routledge, 1990

Chadwick, Whitney, *Women Artists and the Surrealist Movement*, Thames & Hudson, 1991.

Chalfont, Fran C., *Ben Johnson's London*, The University of Georgia Press, Athens, USA, 1978.

Chancellor, E. Beresford, *London's Old Latin Quarter, being an account of Tottenham Court Road and its immediate surroundings*, Jonathan Cape, 1930.

Charmley, Julin, *Duff Cooper, The Authorised Biography*, Weidenfeld & Nicolson, 1986.

Chester, Lewis, David Leitch, and Colin Simpson, *The Cleveland Street Affair*, Weidenfeld and Nicolson, 1976.

Chisholm, Anne, *Nancy Cunard*, Sidgwick &Jackson, 1979.

Chitty, Susan, *Gwen John, 1876-1939*, Hodder & Stoughton, 1981.

Clark, Alan, *Diaries*, Weidenfeld and Nicolson, 1993.

Clark, Kenneth, *Another Part of the Wood: A Self-Portrait*, Coronet Books, 1976.

Clarke, William M., *The Secret Life of Wilkie Collins*, W.H. Allen, 1988.

Clements, Keith, *Henry Lamb, The artist and his friends*, Redcliffe, 1985.

Clinch, George, *Bloomsbury and St Giles's, Past and Present*, Truslove & Shirley, 1890.
Marylebone & St Pancras, Truslove & Shirley, 1890.

Cohen, M.J. (ed.), *The Penguin Thesaurus of Quotations*, Penguin, 1998.

Cohen-Portheim, Paul, *The Spirit of London*, Batsford, 1937.

Collie, Michael, *George Gissing, A Biography*, Folkestone Dawson, 1977.

Collins, Judith, *The Omega Workshops*, Secker & Warburg, 1983.

Cone, John Frederick, *Adelina Patti, Queen of Heaven*, Scolar Press, 1994.

Connett, Maureen, *Walter Sickert and the Camden Town Group*, David & Charles, 1992.

Constable, John, *Memoirs of the life of John Constable, composed chiefly of his letters*, Charles Robert Leslie, Phaidon, 1980

Cooper, Diana, *Diana Cooper*, Michael Joseph, 1979.

Cox-Johnson, Ann, *Handlist of Painters, Sculptors and Architects associated with St Marylebone 1760-1960*, Borough of St Marylebone, 1963.

Crisp, Quentin, *The Naked Civil Servant*, Flamingo, 1985.
Manners from Heaven, Hutchinson, 1984.

Crowder, Henry, with Hugo Speck, *As Wonderful As All That? Henry Crowder's Memoir of His Affair with Nancy Cunard 1928-1935*, Wild Trees Press, California, USA, 1987.

Cullen, Tom, *Crippen, The Mild Murderer*, Bodley Head, 1977.

Curry, Patrick, *A Confusion of Prophets*, Juliet Gardiner, 1992.

Dakers, Caroline, *The Blue Plaque Guide to London*, Macmillan, 1981.

Dallimore, Arnold A., *George Whitefield*, The Wakeman Trust, 1990.

Darley, Gillian, *Octavia Hill*, Constable, 1990.

Darwin, Charles, *The Expression of Emotion in Man and Animals*, Julian Friedmann Publishers, 1979

The Correspondence of Charles Darwin, vol.II. 1837-43, ed. Frederick Burkhardt and Sydney Smith, Cambridge University Press, 1986,

David, Hugh, *The Fitzrovians, A Portrait of Bohemian Society*, Joseph, 1988.

Davies, Andrew, *Literary London*, Macmillan, 1988.

Davies, W.H., *The Autobiography of a Super-Tramp*, Jonathan Cape, 1977.

Davis, Michael, *William Blake A new kind of man*, Paul Elek, 1977.

Deacon, Richard, *A History of the Russian Secret Service*, Frederick Muller, 1972.

Defoe, Daniel, *A Tour thro' the Whole Island of Great Britain, divided into circuits or journeys. Giving a particular and diverting account of whatever is curious and worth observation. By a gentleman (i.e. D. Defoe). The fourth edition.* 4 vols. S.Birt [and others], 1748. [Daniel Defoe's spelling is occasionally modified for clarity.]

Dennis, Felix, *Britain's Richest People*, ITV programme, broadcast April 23, 1998.

De Quincey, Thomas, *Confessions of an Opium Eater*, Oxford University Press, 1990.

Driberg, Tom, *Ruling Passions*, Quartet Books, 1978.

Dunn, Bill Newton, *The Man Who was John Bull, The biography of Theodore Edward Hook 1778-1841*, Allendale Publishing, 1996.

Ehrman, Edwina, Hazel Forsyth, Lucy Peltz, Cathy Ross, *London Eats Out*, Museum of London/Philip Wilson Publishers, 1999.

Elliman, Michael and Frederick Roll, *The Pink Plaque Guide to London*, GMP, 1986.

Euiano, Olaudah, *The Interesting Narrative of the Life of Olaudah Equiano*, Self published, 1789.

Fabian, Robert, *Fabian of the Yard*, Naldrett Press, 1950.

Fairclough, Melvyn, *The Ripper and the Royals*, Duckworth, 1991.

Falk, Bernard, *Five Years Dead*, Hutchinson, 1937.
The Royal Fitz Roys, Hutchinson, 1950.

Farman, John, *The Very Bloody History of London*, Arrow, 1999.

Farr, Evelyn, *The World of Fanny Burney*, Peter Owen, 1993.

Fergusson, Jean, *She Knows You Know! The Story of Hylda Baker*, Breedon, 1997.

Fiber, Sally, *The Fitzroy, The autobiography of a London Tavern*, Temple House Books, 1995.

Fido, Martin, *Murder Guide to London*, Grafton Books, 1989.
Bodysnatchers, A History of the Resurrectionists, Weidenfeld and Nicolson, 1988.

First, Ruth & Ann Scott, *Olive Schreiner*, The Women's Press, 1989.

Fisher, John, *Burgess and Maclean*, Robert Hale, 1977.

Fleming, G.H., *James Abbott McNeill Whistler, A Life*, Windrush, 1991.

Foot, Paul, *Who Killed Hanratty?* Penguin, 1988.

Forte, Charles, *Forte, The Autobiography of Charles Forte*, Sidgwick & Jackson, 1987.

Foster, D., *Inns, Taverns, Alehouses and Coffee Houses in and Around London. c.1900* (hand written in Westminster Archive Library).

Fraxi, Pisanus (H.S. Ashbee), *The Encyclopedia of Erotic Literature*, Documentary Books, New York, 1962.

Freedland, Michael, *Kenneth Williams, A Biography*, Weidenfeld & Nocolson, 1990.

Fryer, Peter, *Aspects of British Black History*, Index Book, 1993.
Staying Power, The History of Black People in Britain, Pluto Press, 1989.

Furneaux, Robert, *The Medical Murderer*. Elek, 1957.

Garnett, Angelica, *Deceived with kindness, A Bloomsbury Childhood*, Oxford University Press, 1985.

Geoffrey, G. and C. Ingleton, *Matthew Flinders, Navigator and Chartmaker*, Genesis Publications Ltd, Australia, 1986.

Gerzina, Gretcham, *Carrington*, John Murray, 1989.

Gibson, Peter, *The Capital Companion*, Webb & Bower, 1985.

Gilbert, Michael, *Fraudsters, Six against the Law*, Constable, 1986.

Gimarc, George, *Punk Diary, 1970-1979*, Vintage, 1994.

Goddard, Henry, *Memoirs of a Bow Street Runner*, Museum Press, 1956.

Goodman, Jonathan (ed.), *The Oscar Wilde File*, Allison & Busby, 1995.

Green, Benny, *The Streets of London*, Pavilion Books, 1983.

Green, Dominic, *Benny Green, Words and Music*, London House, 2000.

Greer, Mary K., *Women of the Golden Dawn, Rebels and Pristesses*, Park Street Press (USA), 1995.

Greysmith, David, *Richard Dadd, The Rock and Castle of Seclusion*, Studio Vista, 1973.

Halford, Alison, *No Way Up the Greasy Pole*, Constable, 1993.

Hall, J.W. (ed.), *Trial of William Joyce*, Butterworths, 1946.

Hall, Ruth, *Marie Stopes*, Virago, 1978.

Hallam, Jack, *Ghosts of London*, Wolfe Publishing, 1975.

Hamnett, Nina, *Laughing Torso*, Virago Press, 1984.
Is She a Lady? Allan Wingate, 1955.

Harding, James, *George Robey & The Music Hall*, Hodder & Stoughton, 1990.

Harman, Claire, *Fanny Burney, A Biography*, Harper Collins, 2000.

Harris, John, and Michael Snodin, (eds.), *Sir William Chambers*, Yale University Press, USA, 1996.

Harte, Negley, *The University of London 1836-1986*, Athlone Press, 1986.

Harte, Negley and John North, *The World of U.C.L., 1828-1990*. U.C.L., 1991.

Harvey, Robert, *Liberators, Latin America's struggle for independence, 1810-1830*, John Murray, 2000.

Hazlitt, William, *The round table 1817, William Hazlitt and Leigh Hunt*, Woodstock, 1991.

The plain speaker, the key essays, William Hazlitt, introd. Tom Paulin, ed. Duncan Wu, Blackwell Publishers, 1998.

Headington, Christopher, *Peter Pears, A Biography*, Faber and Faber, 1993.

Henderson, David, *The life of Jimi Hendrix, 'Scuse me while I kiss the sky*, Omnibus Press, 1990.

Hewison, Robert, *Under Siege, Literary Life in London 1939-1945*, Quartet, 1979.

Heylin, Clinton, *Dylan:Behind the Shades*, Viking, 1991.

Hibbert, Christopher, *London: The Biography of a City*, Penguin, 1980.

Hickman Robertson, Patrick, 'Maurice Rickards 1919-1998', *The Ephemerist*, No.100, March 1998.

Hinds, Alfred, *Contempt of Court*. Panther, 1971.

Hitler, Bridget, *The Memoirs of Bridget Hitler*, Duckworth, 1979.

Hodge, Harry & James (eds.), *Famous Trials*, Viking, 1984.

Holden, Anthony, *Olivier*, Weidenfeld & Nicolson, 1988.

Holroyd, Michael, *Bernard Shaw, vol.1, 1856-1898*, Penguin, 1990.

Honeycombe, Gordon, *The Murders of the Black Museum*, Hutchinson, 1992.
More Murders of the Black Museum, Hutchinson, 1993.

Hook, Theodore, *The Choice Humorous Works, Ludicrous Adventures, Bon Mots and Hoaxes of Theodore Hook*, John Camden Hotten, 1873.

Hooker, Denise, *Nina Hamnett, Queen of Bohemia*, Constable, 1986.

Hopkins, Chris, *John Clare: A Natural Poet?*, Sheffield City Polytechnic, 1991.

Hopkins, Justine, *Michael Ayrton, A Biography*, Andre Deutsch, 1994.

Hubbard, L. Ron, *What is Scientology?* Bridge Publications, 1998.

Hudd, Roy, *Roy Hudd's Book of Music-hall, Variety and Showbiz Anecdotes*, Robson Books, 1993.

Hudson, Roger, *The London Guides, Bloomsbury, Fitzrovia & Soho*, Haggerston Press, 1996.

Humphreys, Anne, *Travels into the Poor Man's Country, The Work of Henry Mayhew*, University of Georgia Press, USA, 1977.

Hutchinson, Roger, *Aleister Crowley, The Beast Demystified*, Mainstream, 1998.

Huxley, Elspeth, *Florence Nightingale*, Weidenfeld and Nicolson, 1975.

Hyde, H. Montgomery, *The Cleveland Street Scandal*, W.H. Allen, 1976.
George Blake, Constable, 1987.
Sex Scandals in British Politics and Society, Constable, 1986.
A Tangled Web, Futura, 1986.

Ingleby, Richard, Jonathan Black, David Cohen, Gordon Cooke, *C.R.W. Nevinson, The Twentieth Century*, Merrell Holbeton/Imperial War Museum, 1999.

Inwood, Stephen, *A History of London*, Macmillan, 1998.

Ivry, Benjamin, *Arthur Rimbaud*, Absolute Press, 1998.

Jacob, Naomi, *Our Marie*, Hutchinson, 1936.

Jacobs, Arthur, *Henry J. Wood, Maker of the Proms*, Methuen, 1994.

Jaffa, Max, *A Life on the Fiddle*, Hodder & Stoughton, 1991.

James, P.D., *Time to be in Earnest*, Faber & Faber, 1999.

John, Augustus, *Autobiography*, Cape, 1975.

Johnson, David, *Regency Revolutions*, Compton Russell, 1974.

Johnson, Josephine, *Florence Farr*, Colin Smythe, 1975.

Johnston, Brian, *Its been a lot of fun*, W. H. Allen, 1979.

Johnston, Judith, *Anna Jameson, Victorian Feminist, Woman of Letters*, Scolar Press, 1997.

Jones, Nigel, *Rupert Brooke: Life, Death & Myth*, Richard Cohen, 1999.

Jones, Stanley, *Hazlitt: A Life*, Oxford University Press, 1989.

Jones, Steve, *In Darkest London, Anti-Social Behaviour 1900-1939*, Wicked Publications, 1994.

Kaplan, Fred, *Dickens, A Biography*, Sceptre, 1990.

Kapp, Yvonne, *Eleanor Marx – vol.1, Family Life, 1855-1883*, Lawrence & Wishart, 1972.
   Eleanor Marx – vol.2, The Crowded Years, 1884-1898, Lawrence & Wishart, 1976.

Karlin, Marc, from an interview by Sheila Rowbotham, published as 'Making Images Explode', *Looking at Class*, eds. Sheila Rowbotham and Huw Beynon, Rivers Oram Press, 2001.

Keane, John, *Tom Paine, A Political Life*, Bloomsbury, 1996.

Kelly, Linda, *The Kemble Era*, The Bodley Head, 1980.

Kelly, Richard, *The Art of George du Maurier*, Scolar Press, 1996.

Kendall, Alan, *David Garrick, a biography*, Harrap, 1985.

Kent, William, *London Worthies*, Heath Cranton, 1939.

Keyishian, Harry, *Michael Arlen*, Twayne Publishers, Boston, USA, 1975.

Kirkup, James, *I, Of All People*, Weidenfeld & Nicolson, 1988.
   A Poet could not but be gay, Peter Owen, 1991.

Kitchen, Paddy, *Poets' London*, Longman, 1980.

Knight, Stephen, *Jack the Ripper, The Final Solution*, Grafton, 1977.

Knowles, Elizabeth (ed.), *The Oxford Dictionary of Twentieth Century Quotations*, Oxford University Press, 1998.

Kohn, Marek, *Dope Girls*, Lawrence & Wishart, 1992.

Kray, Charlie and Colin Fry, *Doing The Business*, Smith Gryphon, 1994.

Kray, Reg, *Born Fighter*, Random Century, 1990.

Lambert, Frank, *Pedlar in Divinity*, Princeton University Press, USA 1994.

Lamont-Brown, Raymond, *A Book of British Eccentrics*, David & Charles, 1984.

Lane, Brian, *Murder Guide to London*, Magpie, 1992.

Lane, Eric, *A Guide to Literary London*, Dedalus, *c.*1988.

Langdale, Cecily and David Fraser Jenkins, *Gwen John, An Interior Life*, Phaidon Press, 1985.

Laughton, Bruce, *The Euston Road School*, Scolar Press, 1986.

Lawrence, D.H., *Selected Essays*, Penguin, 1976.
   Selected Letters, Penguin, 1976.

Lebrecht, Norman, *Music in London*, Aurum Press, 1992.

Lee, Hermione, *Virginia Woolf*, Vintage, 1997.

Lee, Jennie, *My Life with Nye*, Jonathan Cape, 1980.

Leeson, Benjamin, *Lost London, The Memoirs of an East End detective*, Stanley Paul, 1934.

Legget, Jane, *Local Heroines*, Pandora, 1994.

Lehmann, Rosamond, *The Weather in the Streets*, Collins, 1936.

Lehmann, John, *Rupert Brooke, His Life and His Legend*, Weidenfeld & Nicolson, 1980.

Lessing, Doris, *Walking In The Shade*, Flamingo, 1998.

Levey, Michael, *From Giotto to Cezanne*, Thames and Hudson, 1985.

Lewis, Percy Wyndham, *Rude Assignment*, Hutchinson, 1950.

Lennie, Campbell, *Landseer, The Victorian Paragon*, Hamish Hamilton, 1976.

Liebknecht, Wilhelm, *Karl Marx Biographical Memoirs*, Kerr, Chicago, 1901.

Lillywhite, Bryant, *London Signs*, Allen and Unwin, 1972.

Lindsay, Jack, *William Morris*, Constable, 1975.

Lloyd, Georgina, *For Love of Money, Sixteen Murders For Gain*, Robert Hale, 1991.

Lock, Joan, *Scotland Yard Casebook*, Robert Hale, 1993.

Lockwood, Annie, *Grace Colman, MP for Tynemouth Constituency 1945-51, Rt Hon Margaret Bondfield, MP for Wallsend Constituency, a celebration of pioneering women*, North Tyneside Fabians, *c.*1995.

Mabbett, Miles & Andy, *Pink Floyd, The Visual Documentary*, Omnibus Press, 1994.

MacCarthy, Fiona, *Eric Gill*, Faber and Faber, 1989.

Mackenzie, Gordon, *Marylebone, Great City North of Oxford Street*, Macmillan, 1972.

Maclaren-Ross, Julian, *Memoirs of the Forties*, Penguin 1984.

Macqueen-Pope, Walter, *Queen of the Music Halls*, Oldbourne, 1957.

Maggio, Rosalie (ed.), *The New Beacon Book of Quotations by Women*, Beacon Press, Boston, USA, 1996.

Mander, Raymond and Joe Mitchenson, *The Lost Theatres of London*, Rupert Hart-Davis, 1968 and New English Library, 1976.

Manton, Jo, *Elizabeth Garrett Anderson*, Methuen, 1961.

Marjoribanks, Edward, *Famous Trials of Marshall Hall*, Penguin, 1989.

Marks, Lawrence and Tony Van den Bergh, *Ruth Ellis, A Case of Diminished Responsibility*, Macdonald & Janes, 1977.

Marsh, Jan, *Pre-Raphaelite Sisterhood*, Quartet Books, 1985.
   Dante Gabriel Rossetti, Weidenfeld, 1998.

Marshall, Dorothy, *Dr Johnson's London*, Wiley, 1968.

Martin, Peter, *Edmond Malone, Shakespearean scholar*, Cambridge University Press, 1995.

Marx, Karl, *Capital*, vol.1, Lawrence & Wishart, 1970.
   The Revolutions of 1848, Penguin, 1973.
   – and Frederick Engels, *The German Ideology*, Lawrence & Wishart, 1970.

Mason, Eric, *The Inside Story*, Pan, 1994.

Masters, Brian, *The Mistresses of Charles II*, Blond & Briggs, 1979
   Killing for Company, The Case of Dennis Nilsen, Coronet, 1992.

Maxwell, John, *The Greatest Billy Cotton Band Show*, Jupiter, 1976.

May, Betty, *Tiger-Woman: My Story*, Cedric Chivers, 1972.

Mbeki, Thabo, *Africa, the time has come*, Tafelberg.Mafube, Cape Town, South Africa, 1998.

McAleer, Dave, *Hit Parade Heroes, British Beat before the Beatles*, Hamlyn, 1993.

McCormick, Donald, *The Hell-Fire Club*, Jarrolds, 1958.

McDermott, John and Eddie Kramer, *Hendrix, Setting the Record Straight*, Warner Books, 1994.

McDevitt, Chas, *Skiffle, The Definitive Inside Story*, Robson Books, 1997.

McLaren, Angus, *A Prescription for Murder, The Victorian Serial Killings of Dr Thomas Neill Cream*, University of Chicago Press, USA, 1993.

Merry, Smerdon, *Trevithick, The Cornish Engineer, 1771-1833*, Lodenek Press, 1975.

Middlemass, John Hunt, M.B., *Three British Aurists, An Appreciation of Wilde, Toynbee and Hinton*, Laryngological & Otological Association, 1898, Liverpool, 1899.

Mill, J.S., *Mill on Bentham and Coleridge*, Cambridge University Press, 1980.

Miller, A. L., *The Middlesex, 1745-1995*, Middlesex Hospital,

1995.

Miller, Frederick, *St Pancras, Past and Present*, Abel
Heywood, 1874.

Modin, Yuri, with Jean-Charles Deniau and Aguieska
Ziarek, tr. Anthony Roberts, introd. David Leitch, *My
Five Cambridge Friends*, Headline, 1994.

Monkhouse, Bob, *Crying With Laughter, An Autobiography*,
Century, 1993.

Moore, Lucy (ed.), *Con Men and Cutpurses: Scenes from the
Hogarthian Underworld*, Allen Lane, 2000.

Morris, Lynda and Robert Radford, *The Story of the A.I.A.
Artists International Association*, Museum of Modern Art,
1983.

Morton, Brian N., *Americans in London*, Macdonald Queen
Anne Press, 1988.

Motion, Andrew, *The Lamberts, George, Constant and Kit*,
The Hogarth Press, 1987.

Muravyova, L., and I. Sivolap-Kaftanova, *Lenin in London*,
Progress Publishers, Moscow, 1983.

Murphy, Robert, *Smash and Grab, Gangsters in the London
Underworld*, Faber and Faber, 1993.

Newman, Teresa and Ray Watkinson, *Ford Madox Brown
and the Pre-Raphaelite Circle*, Chatto & Windus, 1991.

Nicholls, David, *The Lost Prime Minister, A Life of Sir Charles
Dilke*, Hambledon Press, 1995.

Nichols, Roger, *Mendelssohn Remembered*, Faber & Faber,
1997.

Noakes, Aubrey, *William Powell Frith, Extraordinary Victorian
Painter*, Jupiter, 1978.

Nujoma, Dr Sam, *Our armed struggle in shaking the foundations of colonialism in Namibia*, statement by Sam
Nujoma, President of SWAPO, on Namibia, August 23,
1983.

O'Connor, Ulick, *Brendan Behan*, Abacus, 1993.

Olivier, Laurence, *Confessions of an Actor*, Weidenfeld and
Nicolson, 1982.

Page, Bruce, David Leitch, and Philip Knightley, *Philby, The
Spy who Betrayed a Generation*, Sphere Books, 1977.

Palacious, Julian, *Lost in the Woods, Syd Barrett and the Pink
Floyd*, Boxtree, 1998.

Palmer, Alan and Veronica, *A Dictionary of Historical
Quotations*, Harvester Press, 1976.

Palmer, Tony, *The Trials of Oz*, Blond & Briggs, 1971.

Parker, Robert, *Rough Justice, The Extraordinary Truth about
Charles Richardson*, Fontana, 1981.

Partnow, Elaine (ed.), *The New Quotable Woman*, Headline,
New York, USA, 1993.

Payne, Leslie, *The Brotherhood*, Michael Joseph, 1973.

Peacock, Carlos, *John Constable, The Man and his Work*, John
Baker, 1971.

Pears, Peter, *Armenian Holiday*, self-published, 1965.

Pearsall, Ronald, *A Worm in the Bud*, Weidenfeld &
Nicolson, 1969.

Pearson, John, *The Profession of Violence*, Harper Collins,
1995.

Phillips, Hugh, *Mid-Georgian London, a topographical and
social survey of central and western London about 1750*,
Collins, 1964.

Piper, David, *Artists' London*, Weidenfeld & Nicolson, 1982.

Piratin, Phil, *Our Flag Stays Red*, Lawrence & Wishart, 1980.

Poologasingham, Kalakeerthi Professor P., *Poet Tambimuttu –*

A profile, P. Tambimuttu, Colombo, Sri Lanka, 1993.

Pople, Kenneth, *Stanley Spencer, A Biography*, Collins, 1991.

Powell, Nicolas, *Fuseli, The Nightmare*, Allen Lane, 1973.

Pressly, William L., *The Life and Art of James Barry*, Yale
University Press, 1981.

Pritchett, V.S., *A Cab At The Door. An Autobiography: Early
Years*, Chatto & Windus, 1968.
Midnight Oil, Chatto & Windus, 1971.

Quail, John, *The Slow Burning Fuse, The Lost History of
British Anarchism*, Paladin, 1978.

Race, Steve, *Musician at Large*, Eyre Methuen, 1979.

Radford, Robert, *Art for a purpose, The Artists' International
Association*, Winchester Press, 1987.

Rae, Isobel, *The Strange Story of Dr James Barry*, Longmans,
Green, 1958.

Raine, Kathleen, *Yeats, the Tarot and the Golden Dawn*, The
Doleman Press, Dublin, Ireland, 1976.

Raven, Susan, and Alison Weir, *Women in History*,
Weidenfeld & Nicolson, 1981.

Reid, Colin, *Action Stations, A History of Broadcasting House*,
Robson, 1987.

Rennison, Nick, *The London Blue Plaque Guide*, Sutton
Publishing, 1999.

Retter, Catherine, and Shirley Sinclair, *Letters to Ann, The
love story of Matthew Flinders*, Angus & Robertson,
Australia, 1999.

Reynolds, Gerald and Anthony Judge, *The Night the Police
went on Strike*, Weidenfeld & Nicolson, 1968.

Richardson, Dorothy, *Pilgrimage*, vol.1, Virago, 1979.

Richardson, John, *A History of Camden*, Historical
Publications, 1999.

Rickards, Maurice, *Where they lived in London*, David &
Charles, 1971.

Rimbaud, A., *Rimbaud*, selected verse with prose transla-
tions, ed. Oliver Bernard, Penguin, 1962.

Robinson, Eric (ed.), *John Clare's Autobiographical Writings*,
Oxford University Press, 1986.

Rooksby, Rikky, *A.C. Swinburne, A Poet's Life*, Scolar Press,
1997.

Rose, June, *The Perfect Gentleman, The remarkable life of Dr
James Miranda Barry*, Hutchinson, 1977.
Marie Stopes and the Sexual Revolution, Faber & Faber,
1982.

Rothenstein, John, *Stanley Spencer, The Man*, Paul Elek, 1979.

Rothstein, Andrew, *Lenin in Britain*, Communist Party
Pamphlet, 1970.

Rowbotham, Sheila, *A Century of Women*, Penguin, 1999.
Women, Resistance & Revolution, Pantheon Books, New
York, 1972.

Rumbelow, Donald, *The Houndsditch Murders and the Siege of
Sidney Street*, W.H. Allen, 1988.

Ruskin, John, *Modern Painters*, ed. David Barrie, Deutsch,
1987.

Sagar, Keith, *D.H. Lawrence, Life Into Art*, Viking, 1985.

Salvoni, Elena, *Elena, A Life in Soho*, Quartet Books, 1990.

Sandford, Christopher, *Clapton, Edge of Darkness*, Victor
Gollancz, 1994.

Saunders, H. St George, *The Middlesex Hospital, 1745-1948*,
Parrish, 1949.

Saussure, César de, *A Foreign View of England in the Reigns of
George I and George II*, tr. and ed. Madame von Muydon,

John Murray, 1902.

Schreiner, Olive, *The Story of an African Farm*, Penguin, 1979.
    Women and Labour, pref. Jane Graves, Virago, 1978.

Secrest, Meryle, *Kenneth Clark, A Biography*, Weidenfeld and Nicolson, 1984.

Seymour, Miranda, *Ottoline Morrell, Life on the Grand Scale*, Hodder & Stoughton, 1992.

Sheppard, Francis, *London, A History*, Oxford University Press, 1998.

Sherrin, Ned, *Sherrin's Year*, Virgin, 1996.

Shipley, Stan, *Club Life & Socialism in Mid-Victorian London*, History Workshop, 1972.

Shone, Richard, *Bloomsbury Portraits*, Phaidon, 1993.
    The Art of Bloomsbury, Roger Fry, Vanessa Bell and Duncan Grant, with essays by James Beechey and Richard Morphet, Tate Gallery Publishing, 1999.

Shore, W. Teignmouth, *Trial of Browne and Kennedy*, William Hodge, 1930.

Sickert, Walter Richard, *Advice to Young Artists*, Norwich School of Art Gallery, 1986.

Simmons, Samuel Foart, and John Hunter, *William Hunter, A Memoir 1718-1788*, ed. C.H. Brock, University of Glasgow, 1983.

Simpson, Colin, *Emma, The Life of Lady Hamilton*, Bodley Head, 1983.

Sinclair, Andrew, *War Like a Wasp, The Lost Decade of the Forties*, Hamish Hamilton, 1989.

Sisman, Adam, *Boswell's Presumptious Task*, Hamish Hamilton, 2000.

Slater, John, *A short history of the Berners Estate*, Unwin Brothers, 1918.

Slater, Michael, *Dickens and Women*, J.M. Dent, 1983.

Slovo, Joe, *Slovo: the unfinished autobiography*, introd. Helena Dolny, Ravan Press, South Africa, 1995.

Smith, Denis Mack, *Mazzini*, Yale University Press, 1994.

Smith, Hammond, *Peter De Wint*, 1784-1849, F. Lewis, 1982.

Smith, Janet Adam, *John Buchan, A Biography*, Rupert Hart Davis, 1965.

Smith, John Thomas, *Nollekens and his times, vols.1 and 2*, Henry Colburn, 1828.

Spalding, Frances, *British Art since 1900*, Thames and Hudson, 1986.
    Vanessa Bell, Phoenix, 1994.

Sperber, A.M., *Murrow, His Life and Times*, Michael Joseph, 1986.

Stanhope, John, *The Cato Street Conspiracy*, Cape, 1962.

Stanley, Autumn, *Mothers and Daughters of Invention*, Rutgers, USA, 1995.

Stockdale, Tom, *They died too young, Sid Vicious*, Parragon, 1995.

Stopes, Marie, *Married Love*, 18th edition, G.P. Putnam's Sons, 1927.

Strachey, Lytton, *Florence Nightingale*, Penguin Books, 1996.

Sturtevant, Katherine, *Our Sisters' London*, The Women's Press, 1991.

Summers, Judith, *Soho, A History of London's Most Colourful Neighbourhood*, Bloomsbury, 1989.

Summerson, John, *Georgian London*, Barrie & Jenkins, 1988.

Symonds, John, *The Beast 666*, Pindar Press, 1997.

Tames, Richard, *William Morris 1834-1896*, Shire

Publications, 1990.
    Bloomsbury Past, Historical Publications, 1993.

Taylor, Anne, *Annie Besant, A Biography*, Oxford University Press, 1992.

Thomas, Frances, *Christina Rossetti, A Biography*, Virago, 1994.

Thomas, Kay, *Article in Marx Memorial Library Quarterly, No. 56*, 1970.

Thompson, E.P., *The Making of the English Working Class*, Penguin, 1980.
    William Morris, Romantic to Revolutionary, Merlin Press, 1977.

Thomson, H. Campbell, *The Story of the Middlesex Hospital Medical School*, John Murray, 1935.

Thorold, Peter, *The London Rich*, Viking, 1999.

Thurston, Gavin, *The Clerkenwell Riot*, Allen & Unwin, 1967.

Todd, Janet, *Mary Wollstonecraft, a revolutionary life*, Weidenfeld & Nicolson, 2000.

Tomalin, Claire, *The Life and Death of Mary Wollstonecraft*, Penguin, 1992.

Tremlett, George, *Dylan Thomas, In the mercy of his means*, Constable, 1991.

Trory, Ernie, *Truth Against the World, The Life and Times of Thomas Hughes*, Crabtree Press, 1993.

Tullett, Tom, *Strictly Murder*, Bodley Head, 1979.

Uglow, Jenny, *Hogarth, A Life and a World*, Faber, 1997.

Van den Bergh, Tony, *Who killed Freddie Mills?* Constable, 1991.

Vansittart, Peter, *London, A Literary Companion*, John Murray, 1992.

Wallace, Irving, Amy, and Sylvia, and David Wallechinsky, *The Secret Sex Lives of Famous People*, Chancellor Press, 1993.

Waugh, Evelyn, *Rossetti*, Duckworth, 1975.

Weightman, Gavin, *Bright Lights, Big City, London Entertained 1830-1950*, Collins & Brown, 1992.

Weightman, Gavin and Steve Humphries, *The Making of Modern London*, Sidgwick & Jackson, 1983.

Weinreb, Ben and Christopher Hibbert, *The London Encyclopaedia*, Book Club Associates/Macmillan London, 1987.

Weintraub, Stanley, *Four Rossettis, A Victorian Biography*, W. H. Allen, 1978.

Weir, Robin, Peter Brears, John Deith, and Peter Barham, *Mrs Marshall, The Greatest Victorian Ice Cream Maker*, Smith Settle, 1998.

Wells, H.G., *H.G.Wells, Interviews and Recollections*, ed. J.R. Hammond, Macmillan, 1980.
    The Invisible Man, Fontana, 1959.

White, Sidney H., *I Gotta Horse, the authorised biography of Ras Prince Monolulu*, Hurst & Blackett [undated].

Wilde, Oscar, *The Complete Letters of Oscar Wilde*, ed. Merlin Holland and Rupert Hart-Davies, Fourth Estate, 2000.

Wilkinson, George T., *An Authentic History of the Cato Street Conspiracy*, Thomas Kelly, 1820.

Williams, Heathcote, *The Speakers*, Robin Clark, 1982.

Williams, John, *Hume: Portrait of a Double Murderer*, Panther, 1961.

Williams, Kenneth, *The Kenneth Williams diaries*, ed. Russell Davies, Harper Collins, 1993.

Wilson, Colin and Pat Pitman, *Encyclopaedia of Murder*,

Pan, 1961.

Wilson, Colin and Donald Seaman, *Encyclopaedia of Modern Murder 1962-83*, Pan, 1986.

Wilson, Erasmus, *The History of the Middlesex Hospital*, John Churchill, 1845.

Winter, Gordon, *Inside B.O.S.S.*, Allen Lane, 1981.

Woodford, Peter F. (ed.), *Streets of Bloomsbury & Fitzrovia*, Camden History Society, 1997.

Woodham-Smith, Cecil, *Florence Nightingale, 1820-1910*, Constable, 1976.

Woof, Robert, Stephen Hebron, *Romantic Icons*, The Wordsworth Trust, 1999.

Woolf, Virginia, *The Essays of Virginia Woolf*, vol.III, Hogarth Press, 1986.
  Women & Writing, introd. Michèle Barrett, Women's Press, 1979.

Wright, Peter, *Spycatcher*, Heinemann, 1987.

Wyver, John, 'Marc Karlin', *Independent*, January 28, 1999.

Yeats, W.B., *Interviews and Recollections*, vol.II, E.H. Mikhail (ed.), Macmillan Press, 1977.

Young, Winifred, *Obsessive Poisoner, The Strange Story of Graham Young*, Robert Hale, 1973.

Index to Characters and Streets

Index to Maps

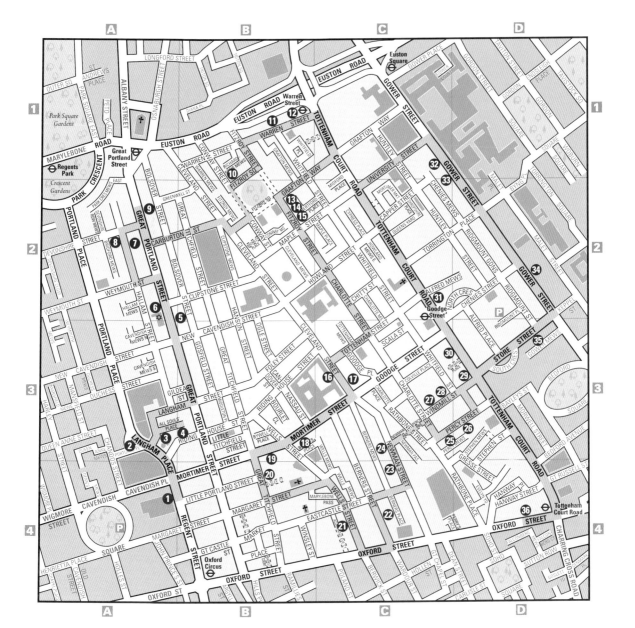

Infamous Characters

1   307-311 Regent St Laura Bell 1850 p227
2   1 Portland Pl Ouida (Marie Louise de la Ramée) 1866 author p181
3   2 All Souls' Pl Aleister Crowley 1930 satanist p230
4   5 All Souls' Pl George Blake 1956 Russian spy p103
5   144 Great Portland St Donald Hume 1949 murderer of Stanley Setty crook p87
6   143 Great Portland St Ron and Reg Kray 1962 gangsters pp90, 103
7   84-94 Hallam St Theresa Berkley 1828 brothel owner p97
8   54-57 Devonshire St (20 Goodwood Court) Ruth Ellis 1955 murderer p88
9   216 Great Portland St Frederick Guy Browne 1920s murderer p83
10 19 Fitzroy Sq Louise Michel 1890s anarchist p50
11 65 Warren St Sir Charles Dilke 1885 liberal MP p67
12 73 Warren St Emanuel Barthelemy 1855 double murderer p76
13 51 Grafton Way Marie Hermann 1894 manslaughterer p79
14 20 Fitzroy St Lionel Johnson 1890s gay poet p186
15 8 Fitzroy St Nina Hamnett 1915 queen of Bohemia p160
16 19 Cleveland St Lord Arthur Somerset, Earl of Euston, Prince Albert Victor Eddy 1889 gay brothel visitors p68
17 6 Cleveland St Mary Kelly 1884 victim of Jack the Ripper p77
18 29 Mortimer St Simeon Solomon 1862 artist p148
19 53 Mortimer St Oscar Wilde 1895 playwright, Mrs A. Robinson palmist p181
20 18 Great Titchfield St Martin Bourdin 1894 anarchist p50

21 77 Wells St Ben Crouch 1809 body-snatcher p204
22 6 Berners St Henry Fauntleroy 1824 bank fraudster p96
23 77 Newman St Algernon Swinburne 1862 poet p180
24 71 Newman St Richard Dadd 1843 murderer p75
25 1 Percy St Nancy Cunard 1930s seditious publisher p232
26 4 Percy St Alois Hitler (half-brother of Adolf) and wife Bridget 1910 p53
27 16 Charlotte St (Fitzroy Tavern) Brendan Behan 1950s terrorist p195
28 36 Windmill St George Morland 1780 espionage, fraud, obscenity p138
29 27 Windmill St Charlie Richardson, Mad Frank Fraser 1960s gangsters p103
30 55-59 Tottenham Court Rd Alison Halford 1975 suspended police officer p241
31 196 Tottenham Court Rd, 9 Tottenham St Sid Vicious and Johnny Rotten, punk group Sex Pistols 1973 p128
32 107 Gower St May Churchill 1907 blackmailer p98
33 99 Gower St Edith 'Swami', Frank Jackson 1901 religious racketeers p98
34 52 Gower St Robert Liston 1846 surgeon/body-snatcher p204
35 34 & 37 Store St Dr Crippen 1897 murderer p80
36 8-10 Oxford St Dennis Nilsen 1983 mass murderer p91

Unfamous Characters